The Psychological and Social Impact
of Physical Disability

Robert P. Marinelli, Ed.D., is a professor in the Department of Counseling Psychology and Rehabilitation at the College of Human Resources and Education, West Virginia University, Morgantown, West Virginia, where he was recently named an Outstanding Teacher. He received his master's and doctoral degrees in rehabilitation counseling from Pennsylvania State University in 1971. He is a past secretary of the American Rehabilitation Counseling Association and serves as a member of the editorial board of the *Journal of Rehabilitation* and as a consulting editor for *Rehabilitation Counseling Bulletin.* His scholarly pursuits focus primarily on the psychological and vocational impact of disability. Significant publications in the last few years include coauthoring a textbook, *Career Development: Resources and Strategies,* and authoring chapters in the *Encyclopedia of Clinical Assessment* and the *Encyclopedia of Educational Research.*

Arthur E. Dell Orto, Ph.D., C.R.C., is a professor and chairperson of the Department of Rehabilitation Counseling at Sargent College of Allied Health Professions, Boston University. He received his M.A. in rehabilitation counseling from Seton Hall University, and his Ph.D. from Michigan State University in 1970. Professionally, Dr. Dell Orto has worked in a variety of settings, both as a rehabilitation consultant and as a licensed psychologist. He is the coauthor of three books: *The Psychological and Social Impact of Physical Disability,* with Robert P. Marinelli (Springer, 1977); *Group Counseling and Physical Disability,* with Robert Lasky (Duxbury Press, 1979); and *Role of the Family in the Rehabilitation of the Physically Disabled,* with Paul Power (University Park Press, 1980).

The Psychological and Social Impact of Physical Disability
Second Edition

Robert P. Marinelli, Ed.D.
Arthur E. Dell Orto, Ph.D.
Editors

Foreword by Irving Kenneth Zola, Ph.D.

SPRINGER PUBLISHING COMPANY, New York

We dedicate this book to Gunnar Dybwad, J.D., a brilliant scholar and outstanding person, who has dedicated his life's work to helping all people reach their full potential.

Springer Publishing Company, Inc.
536 Broadway
New York, N.Y. 10012

87 88 / 10 9 8 7 6 5 4 3

Library of Congress Cataloging in Publication Data

Main entry under title:
The Psychological and social impact of physical disability.
   Includes bibliographies and index.
   1. Physically handicapped—Psychology.   2. Physically handicapped—Rehabilitation.
3. Physically handicapped—Family relationships.   4. Physically handicapped—Sexual
behavior.   5. Physically handicapped—Public opinion.   I. Marinelli, Robert P.,
1942–   . II. Dell Orto, Arthur E., 1943–   . [DNLM: 1. Handicapped—United
States.   2. Rehabilitation—United States.   HV 1553 P974]
RD798.P79 1984   155.9'16   83-20386
ISBN 0-8261-2211-6

Printed in the United States of America

CONTENTS

v

FOREWORD

In his Foreword to the first edition, my good friend and colleague Gunnar Dybwad introduced his remarks by noting that the Eleventh World Congress of Rehabilitation International declared the period 1970–1980 to be the Decade of Rehabilitation. Recently, the United Nations declared 1983–1993 to be the International Decade of the Disabled. These two pronouncements tell us something. Not only does the campaign that began well over a decade ago still need to be continued, but the change in name shows also a difference in emphasis. In my more optimistic moments I like to think of the latter as a coming of age—an indication that the needs of people with disability go beyond technical services (*i.e.*, rehabilitation) to something deeper.

That "something" is reflected in this book. Although the articles are written primarily by professionals for professionals, I suspect there will be a wider audience for this second edition—what Gunnar earlier referred to as "the interested citizen and above all the evermore alert consumers." I do not know whether many of the latter read the first edition but I know many will attend to the second edition.

There has been a change, alluded to and described by many writers in this volume, especially by DeJong. Those of us who are part of it speak of the Independent Living Movement, and we represent more than just a group of highly articulate consumers. We are not merely interested in being intelligent buyers of services; rather, we seek to change those services and even to participate in them. Therefore, in our efforts to work with, participate in, and change the professional world of rehabilitation we now read, comment, and criticize what the authors have to say. What this book says, it says well. It singles out for attention many of the most difficult issues facing individuals with a disability—the perspective of the world around them, be it professional or lay; the problems they have to deal with personally, interpersonally, and familially; and the help they need to lead full and independent lives.

By the time a next edition of this book comes out we shall see how the Independent Living Movement has fared. I am sure we shall need another decade of dedicated effort, although I do not know what it will be called. Perhaps it will reflect a lesson learned by those already in the movement that the line between able-bodied and disabled is a thin and often temporary one. In fact, if high technology medicine and our standard of living continue to improve, by 1990 that line may disappear. I do not mean that all of us will be healthy but, on the contrary, that as our population ages and medical supports and interventions continue, the majority of us will have a disability. In this sense, the reader may appreciate why those of us in the movement often refer to the rest of the world as TABs—temporarily able-bodied. I hope, however, that with this empirical reality comes some self-knowledge, and that future generations will no longer believe in what Réné Dubos called the Mirage of Health. For then as we age and change, both in body and mind, we shall not see this time as one of impending doom and decline but rather as a time when we will grow and manage our resources differently. We are a long way from such an understanding, I fear, but this book is a good beginning.

Irving Kenneth Zola, Ph.D.
Department of Sociology, Brandeis University;
The Boston Self Help Center

PREFACE TO THE SECOND EDITION

THE CHALLENGE OF PHYSICAL DISABILITY

Physical disability is a personal as well as a physical challenge. It challenges a person's resources, creates opportunities, and often presents a harsh reality. However, life's journey with a physical disability does not necessarily have to be better or worse than without one. Often this journey is made more difficult by those systems and persons who are supposed to make the process of rehabilitation more bearable. While ignorance, prejudice, negativism, and insensitivity still exist, progress has been made. The major intent of this edition is to present that progress.

The exploration and understanding of physical disability in light of its psychological and social impact continues as the main focus of this edition. The dramatic changes in rehabilitation since 1977 have resulted in two-thirds of this edition's being totally new material. Many factors account for these changes. New concepts of disability and how it affects functioning, and an expansion of legal rights and services to persons who are handicapped, are two important factors. Novel and apparently more effective models of helping persons who are disabled to cope with their disabilities and environments are highlighted in Part VIII of the book. However, helping is emphasized throughout.

The assumption that guided the first edition—that disability affects different facets of a person's life—continues in this edition. The presentation of readings organized around the topics of disability's impact on the child and family, its personal meaning and interpersonal impact, sexuality and disability, and disabled persons as consumers reflects this guiding notion. Practicality and utility for service providers have been used as benchmarks for selecting readings.

Others are the primary contributors to this edition, as they were to the first. We thank the authors and their publishers for permission to reprint their work. We would like also to acknowledge our colleagues in the Department of Counseling Psychology and Rehabilitation at West Virginia University and the Department of Rehabilitation Counseling at Boston University for their encouragement and support. Most especially, our thanks go to Bill Anthony, Dick Goldberg, Bob Lasky, Don Shrey, and Shari Thurer for their contribution of major articles. Our wives, Irene Marinelli and Barbara Dell Orto, continue to provide valuable counsel and support; they, and our children, are also thanked for their tolerance. We would further like to thank our staff—Rosemary Hess, Madelo Lambert, Margaret Riney, Doreen Correia, and Karin Loudis—for their clerical help, as well as Ken Paruti for his organizational skills and support during the project. A special acknowledgment is made to June Holt, Chief Librarian at the Massachusetts Rehabilitation Library, without whose assistance this project would have been most difficult. We also gratefully acknowledge Dr. Ursula Springer, Barbara Watkins, Nina George, and all others at Springer Publishing Company who contributed their invaluable expertise and assistance.

CONTRIBUTORS

Dan L. Adler, Ph.D.
American Association of University
Professors
Washington, D.C.

William A. Anthony, Ph.D.
Boston University
Boston, Massachusetts

Constance U. Battle, M.D.
The George Washington University
School of Medicine
Washington, D.C.

Betty E. Cogswell, Ph.D.
University of North Carolina
Chapel Hill, North Carolina

Theodore M. Cole, M.D.
University of Minnesota Medical School
Minneapolis, Minnesota

Arnold B. Coven, Ph.D.
Wayne State University
Detroit, Michigan

Victor Cummings, M.D.
Albert Einstein College of Medicine
Bronx, New York

Gerben DeJong, Ph.D.
Tufts-New England Medical Center
Boston, Massachusetts

Tamara Dembo, Ph.D.
Clark University
Worcester, Massachusetts

Milton Diamond, Ph.D.
University of Hawaii School of Medicine
Honolulu, Hawaii

Violette C. Eash, Ph.D.
Marshall University
Huntington, West Virginia

Richard T. Goldberg, Ed.D.
Massachusetts Rehabilitation
Commission
Boston, Massachusetts

Lloyd R. Goodwin, Jr., Ph.D.
Assumption College
Worcester, Massachusetts

Ernest Griffith, M.D.
University of Cincinnati School of
Medicine
Cincinnati, Ohio

John Guidubaldi, Ph.D.
Kent State University
Kent, Ohio

Thomas H. Hohenshil, Ph.D.
Virginia Polytechnic Institute & State
University
Blacksburg, Virginia

George W. Hohmann, Ph.D.
University of Arizona College of
Medicine
Tucson, Arizona

Fergus Hughes, Ph.D.
University of Wisconsin
Green Bay, Wisconsin

Charles W. Humes II, Ed.D.
Greenwich Public Schools
Greenwich, Connecticut

Marceline E. Jaques, Ph.D.
State University of New York at Buffalo
Buffalo, New York

Richard G. Johnson, Ph.D.
Michigan State University
East Lansing, Michigan

Thomas J. Kehle, Ph.D.
Kent State University
Kent, Ohio

Judith Sterling Kiefer, M.S.
Rehabilitation Consultant
San Francisco, California

Bernard Kutner, Ph.D. (Deceased)
Boston University
Boston, Massachusetts

Gloria Ladieu-Leviton, Ph.D.
(Deceased)
Schwab Rehabilitation Hospital
Chicago, Illinois

Robert G. Lasky, Ph.D.
Boston University
Boston, Massachusetts

Roger H. Livingston, Ph.D.
University of Cincinnati
Cincinnati, Ohio

Hanoch Livneh, Ph.D.
Rhode Island College
Providence, Rhode Island

William A. McDowell, Ph.D.
Marshall University
Huntington, West Virginia

Joseph N. Murray, Ph.D.
Kent State University
Kent, Ohio

Kathleen M. Patterson, Ph.D.
Erie Community College
Buffalo, New York

Franklin C. Shontz, Ph.D.
University of Kansas
Lawrence, Kansas

Donald E. Shrey, Ph.D.
Boston University
Boston, Massachusetts

Carol K. Sigelman, Ph.D.
Texas Tech University
Lubbock, Texas

Cynthia L. Spanhel, Ph.D.
Indiana University
Bloomington, Indiana

Shari L. Thurer, Sc.D.
Boston University
Boston, Massachusetts

Jerome S. Tobis, M.D.
University of California School of
Medicine
Irvine, California

Roberta B. Trieschmann, Ph.D.
University of Cincinnati School of
Medicine
Cincinnati, Ohio

Jean Vanier
l'Arche Movement
Oise, France

Linda P. Vengroff, Ph.D.
Texas Tech University
Lubbock, Texas

Hilda P. Versluys, M.Ed., O.T.R.
Boston University
Boston, Massachusetts

Beatrice A. Wright, Ph.D.
University of Kansas
Lawrence, Kansas

Irving Kenneth Zola, Ph.D.
Brandeis University
Waltham, Massachusetts

Part I

Perspective on Disability

The consequences of disability can have an impact at many levels. At the personal level, various life functions are frequently affected. At the interpersonal level, relationships with other individuals often change. Responses to disability at the social and cultural levels often result in legislative change and improved services and rights. The effects of disability—personal, interpersonal, and cultural—therefore have significant implications for disabled persons, rehabilitation workers, and the rehabilitation system. The purpose of Part I is to sensitize the reader to these general issues.

In Chapter 1, "Disability and the Concept of Life Functions," by Sigelman, Vengroff, and Spanhel, a model of disability that distinguishes between impairing conditions and limitations in human functioning with respect to five dimensions (health, social-attitudinal, mobility, cognitive-intellectual, and communications) is presented. Fourteen impairing conditions are categorized with respect to the model, and limitations in multiple areas of functioning are found for each of the conditions. The reader's understanding of the diverse impact of disability and of functional classification systems as applied in rehabilitation should improve as a result of this chapter.

Hohenshil and Humes focus in Chapter 2 on the broadened legal rights of handicapped persons in education, employment, health care, and welfare and social services. Their suggestions to counselors in assisting handicapped persons to achieve these rights are appropriate for all rehabilitation workers.

Bridging the gap between psychiatric rehabilitation and physical rehabilitation is Anthony's major focus in Chapter 3. He skillfully identifies the major constructs of physical rehabilitation and makes a direct application between these constructs and the evolving field of psychiatric rehabilitation.

In the final chapter in Part I, DeJong contrasts the independent living (IL) paradigm with the rehabilitation paradigm that has dominated disability policy, research, and practice. DeJong proposes and describes a future shift from the rehabilitation to the IL paradigm that will have a significant effect on rehabilitation clients, workers, researchers, and policy makers. To increase the reader's appreciation of the paradigm, DeJong provides a historical overview of independent living as a social movement.

1

Disability and the Concept of Life Functions

Carol K. Sigelman
Linda P. Vengroff
Cynthia L. Spanhel

As problems of the handicapped become increasingly visible in society, it becomes increasingly, often painfully, apparent that the rehabilitation community has only a loose grasp on the nature of the problems that handicapped citizens face—indeed, on the nature of handicap itself. Conceptualization of a problem has a great deal to do with how, and how effectively, the problem is solved. In that spirit, this article presents a conceptualization of the nature of handicap and, based on the literature for 14 different disabilities, explores the use and implications of that conceptualization.

IMPAIRMENT, DISABILITY, AND HANDICAP

For many years, rehabilitators have attempted to distinguish between impairing conditions and their implications for functioning. In the early attempt, Hamilton (1950) described a disability as a "condition of impairment," distinguishing it from a handicap, or "the cumulative result of the obstacles which disability interposes between the individual and his maximum functional level" (p. 17). Others have distinguished among three terms—impair-

From *Rehabilitation Counseling Bulletin*, December 1979, pp. 103–113. Copyright©1979 by the American Personnel and Guidance Association. Reprinted with permission. This study was conducted at Texas Tech University as part of a larger project, entitled "Technology Assessment: Human Rehabilitation Techniques," which was partially supported by National Science Foundation (NSF) grants ERP-10594 and ERP 75-10594 A01, monitored by the Directorate for Research Applications. The authors wish to thank Cathie Mannion, Melanie Schockett, Jodie Dixon, Jerry Morris, and Andrew Martin for their contributions to the data base, and Richard Dudek, Mohammed Ayoub, and Gerard Bensberg, the project's principal investigators. The findings, conclusions, and recommendations expressed do not necessarily reflect the views of NSF.

ment, disability, and handicap. Sussman (1969) defined impairment in terms of defective faculties; disability as limitations in activities experienced by impaired persons; and handicap as the largely socially created disadvantages imposed on an individual's "pattern of psychological, physical, vocational, and community activities" (p. 383) by an impairment or disability. Similarly, in its comprehensive needs study, the Urban Institute (1975) conceptualized impairment as the residual effects of defect, disease, or injury; disability as an inability to perform human tasks or functions; and handicap as the disadvantage associated with personal and environmental factors.

Refining these concepts still further, Nagi (1965, 1976) delineated four separate concepts related to disability: pathology (in medical terminology, organismic response to disease or injury); impairment (symptoms, abnormalities, or losses); limitations in the functioning of the organism (defined in terms of cognitive, emotional, and physical performance); and disability (limitations in the performance of major social roles, such as work and independent living).

Despite their many differences in terminology, these and similar conceptualizations have several features in common: (a) a recognition of the imperfect relationship between a diagnosed impairing condition and the extent of functional limitation; (b) a distinction between discrete human capabilities (e.g., hearing) and broad human adjustment phenomena (e.g., vocational success); and (c) an understanding that not only functional limitations but also environmental factors affect adaptation in major social roles, such as work. A consensus of sorts is emerging at the general level of conceptualization. What is still needed is explication of these concepts and of the relationships among them.

Toward this end, a policy-oriented study of the problems associated with disability in the U.S. and technological solutions to these problems was recently completed (Dudek & Associates, 1977). The study, titled "Technology Assessment: Human Rehabilitation Techniques," elaborated a conceptual model that is compatible with but also builds on those previously described.

A MODEL OF DISABILITY AND REHABILITATION

To analyze the implications of rehabilitation programs and technologies for the handicapped and the nonhandicapped, it was necessary to conceptualize the problems addressed by rehabilitation. Based on a preliminary search of the literature on disability and group work by rehabilitation experts, a distinction was drawn between major impairing conditions and limitations in human functioning, and a set of five life functions was proposed to describe the domains of human functioning and performance. The set was piloted in an application to problems of the mentally retarded and was sufficiently comprehensive to classify all functional difficulties. More specifically, limitations in the five life functions were defined as follows:

1. *Health functions.* If limited, the person lacks the physical well-being called good health; is characterized by functional impairments in one or more of the body's systems; must devote a large part of his or her energies to staying alive or coping with pain; and/or must avoid activities that would risk life or well-being.

2. *Social-attitudinal functions.* The person has difficulty accepting himself or herself and his or her abilities, has difficulty relating socially to other people, and/or lacks motivations to improve himself or herself as a person or social being.

3. *Mobility functions.* Limitation in the area of mobility involves difficulty using manual skills to manipulate objects or devices, difficulty moving in the home or work place, difficulty moving from place to place in the community, and/or difficulty participating in other physical activities.

4. *Cognitive-intellectual functions.* The person has difficulty intellectually manipulating symbols and objects, acquiring or storing in memory new cognitions and behavior patterns, and/or transferring learning to new situations.

5. *Communication functions.* If limited, the person has difficulty sending and receiving messages, and exchanging information and ideas with other persons.

Within this framework, it is possible to describe any disabled person — indeed, any person — in terms of capacities and limitations across the range of human functioning. Moreover, it is useful to regard limitations in one or more life functions as contributors, along with environmental factors, to an individual's life outcomes. Life outcomes are broadly conceived to correspond to the goals of rehabilitation: membership in the community (or adaptation and integration within residential, social, and community units), and membership in the labor force (or participation in productive activity, inside or outside the official labor force). The life-outcomes level of analysis parallels Sussman's (1969) concept of handicap and Nagi's (1965) concept of disability. It reflects the ideas that major outcomes in life are dependent on many behavioral capacities, and yet functional limitations may or may not constitute an adaptive disadvantage, depending on characteristics and influences of the physical, social, and economic environments.

Moreover, because membership in the community and participation in work are the two major goals of rehabilitation, rehabilitation technologies and practices can be considered a component of the environment expected to have an impact on life outcomes. In the technology assessment project, rehabilitation technologies were grouped into four major categories: physical intervention (e.g., surgery, prosthetics), training and counseling (e.g., psychotherapy, special education), environmental change (e.g., architectural barrier removal, adapted transportation systems), and service delivery (e.g., individual rehabilitation plans, follow-up services).

Figure 1 summarizes the major features of this broad model. An example of a young woman with cerebral palsy can serve to illustrate the model. She has an impairing condition, the severity and extent of which have some influence on her life functioning, not just in one area but in several, as they interact with one another. For instance, communication problems associated with cerebral palsy may result in learning difficulties in school and in lowered self-esteem, which might exacerbate communication problems. Environmental factors can augment or attenuate performance in the life function areas (e.g., physical therapy can improve gait, and rejecting parents can reduce self-esteem). Moreover, environmental factors can affect the implications that a given set of functional limitations have for life outcomes. For instance, architectural barriers and social stigmatization may reduce the chances of a capable person obtaining a job. By contrast, rehabilitation techniques may enhance life outcomes by directly improving life functioning and by altering the environment to decrease the number or strength of negative consequences linked to existing functional limitations.

ANALYSIS OF LIMITATIONS IN LIFE FUNCTIONING

In the technology assessment project, the aforementioned model was used as the conceptual framework for a review of the literature on 14 major impairing conditions. Given the breadth and financial constraints of the study, literature review seemed to be the most feasible way of collecting data on the range of disabilities as background for policy and program analysis. The specific impairments were selected because they are prevalent, are often associated with severe functional limitations, are chronic rather than acute, often result in a need for rehabilitation services, and affect a wide age range. Moreover, the impairments were chosen to represent, collectively, the body systems that can be impaired. The 14 conditions chosen were spinal cord injury, stroke, cerebral palsy, epilepsy, mental retardation, schizophrenia, rheumatoid arthritis, coronary heart disease, emphysema, colon-rectum cancer, kidney diseases, diabetes mellitus, hearing impairment, and visual impairment.

Through literature reviews we collected all statements indicating limitations in functioning associated with each major impairing condition. Recent

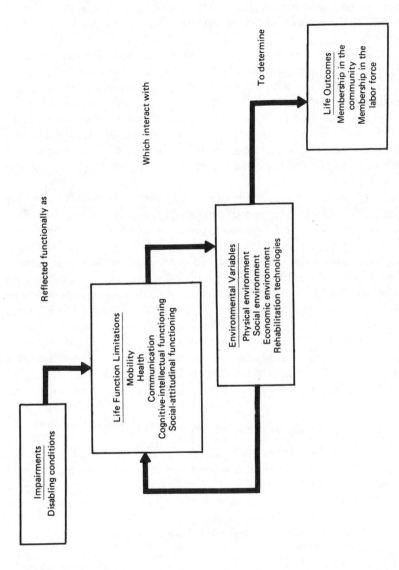

Figure 1. Disability model.

7

volumes of *Index Medicus* and *Psychological Abstracts* and card catalogs were used in initial identification of the relevant professional and research literature. We reviewed cited books and articles until we judged that we were uncovering no new information. Priority was placed on the empirical literature, but clinical observations were recorded when they were deemed to be consensual.

Each discrete statement of a limitation in functioning was tabulated individually, whether it came from only one source or had been documented by several. Statements of limitations were readily classified by life function. After all 14 literature reviews were completed, all statements of limitation in each of the five life functions were examined for likenesses and categorized to form a hierarchical classification tree or taxonomy. Each taxonomy was then thoroughly checked and revised by a second classifier until consensus was reached and the taxonomies seemed to have face validity and internal logic.

Given the state of the literature, the data obtained were less complete than we hoped. It proved impossible to collect comprehensive information on the proportions of each impairment group experiencing any given limitation, or to distinguish between temporary limitations and enduring limitations. The classification trees contained both relatively trivial or specific difficulties and substantial or broad problems, with many ramifications for adjustment. Finally, although the literature on some impairing conditions was voluminous, the literature on other conditions was relatively sparse and uninformative, or sometimes rich in detail about disease processes and complications, but unindicative of problems in life activities. As a consequence, the information presented here is an extremely limited but suggestive comparison of the nature and variety — but not the severity and prevalence — of limitations in life functioning associated with 14 impairing conditions.

RESULTS OF THE LIFE-FUNCTION ANALYSIS

Table 1 presents the percentages of statements of functional limitation that fell into each of the five life-function areas in the literature on each impairing condition. Of the 1,222 statements of limitation recorded, 32% pertained to health, 26% to social-attitudinal functioning, 18% to mobility, 12% to cognitive-intellectual functioning, and 12% to communication. Of considerably greater interest is a comparison of the life-function profiles of the various impairment groups.

Perhaps the most striking pattern in Table 1 is that for no impairment group are limitations restricted to only one life function. Most major impairments are associated with limitations in all five life functions. Because a primary impairment is, for instance, sensory, does not mean that functional difficulties are restricted to the communication life function, any more than

Table 1. Percentage of Statements (n = 1,222) of Limitation for Each Life Function by Impairment Group

| | Impairment Group | | | | | | | | | | | | | | | Total | |
| | Motor | | | Behavioral | | | Chronic Disease | | | | | | Senses | | | | |
Life Function	Spinal Cord Injury	Stroke	Cerebral Palsy	Mental Retardation	Epilepsy	Schizophrenia	Rheumatoid Arthritis	Heart Disease	Emphysema	Colon-Rectum Cancer	Kidney Disease	Diabetes Mellitus	Hearing Impairment	Visual Impairment		%	n
Health	28	24	14	14	26	11	47	33	80	69	58	52	7	7		32	386
Social-attitudinal	39	22	6	21	31	24	25	50	10	28	27	25	38	15		26	316
Mobility	33	35	44	16	8	8	24	17	3	0	8	6	13	17		18	221
Cognitive-intellectual	0	8	6	31	29	35	0	0	7	3	2	10	13	10		12	147
Communication	0	11	30	18	6	22	4	0	0	0	4	6	28	52		12	152

Note. Each column totals 100%.

paralysis of the limbs is associated only with limitations in mobility. Disability, whatever its cause, is a phenomenon with complex and multiple effects on human functioning.

At the same time, the analysis suggested that certain major impairments could be grouped by gross similarities in life-function profiles. The "motor" impairments grouped in Table 1 (spinal cord injury, stroke, and cerebral palsy) are characterized by a variety of problems in the mobility and health functions and by relatively few difficulties in cognitive-intellectual functioning. By contrast, the "behavioral" impairments (mental retardation, epilepsy, and schizophrenia) are associated with a variety of limitations in social-attitudinal and cognitive-intellectual functioning, but are associated with relatively few problems in mobility. The six conditions involving chronic disease all involve a variety of health limitations and diverse social-attitudinal problems, but very few problems in cognitive-intellectual or communicative functions. Finally, the sensory disorders (hearing and visual impairments) are, predictably, associated with multiple communication problems. The profiles of the two groups are not alike in all respects, however.

More detailed analysis of patterns of limitation in each life function uncovered further areas of similarity and difference across impairment groups. Needs in the health function predominated among those affected by chronic diseases, but were also significant for those with motor and behavioral impairments. Health limitations included generalized disruptions of bodily processes, such as those associated with pain and lowered resistance to disease. They also included a variety of secondary complications or correlates of the primary impairment (e.g., decubitus ulcers and kidney disease among persons with spinal cord injury). Judging from the literature, "secondary" complications are a significant part of the difficulties encountered by many handicapped persons. The specific nature of health problems, however, varies across impairment groups.

Limitations in social-attitudinal functioning were evident for all 14 impairment groups. Of all the statements of social-attitudinal limitations gathered from the literature, 58% pertained to problems in individual functioning or personality dynamics. Within this category, negative reactions to disability and treatment, such as denial and depression, were particularly evident, similarly affecting all 14 groups and accounting for 34% of all the instances of social-attitudinal limitations. Problems in relating to other people accounted for the remaining 42% of all limitations, with withdrawal or social isolation, social incompetence, and antisocial behaviors most widespread.

Mobility limitations were not restricted to those with physical impairments. Many of the limitations in this area involved deficiencies in basic motor functions (e.g., loss of muscle tone, uncontrolled movements, and loss of coordination). Others reflected problems in carrying out activities of daily life that require basic motor functions or physical exertion.

Limitations in cognitive-intellectual functioning were categorized as problems in general intellectual functioning, perceptual information processing, memory, learning, and reasoning or thought processes. All impairment groups considered to be behavioral had limitations in each of these five subareas. Moreover, hearing impairment was associated with limitations in all five subareas, visual impairment with limitations in three out of five subareas. Few cognitive-intellectual problems were associated with motor impairments or chronic diseases, however.

Similarly, communicative limitations were extremely rare among those groups affected by chronic diseases. Such problems were predictably varied among persons with sensory impairment, but they were also diverse among persons with behavioral impairments and cerebral palsy. Receptive communication problems, particularly those involving the sense of sight, were more frequently cited than expressive communication problems (61% vs. 39% of total statements).

CONCLUSIONS AND IMPLICATIONS

The model elaborated here was a useful starting point in comparing and contrasting the kinds of functional problems associated in the literature with diverse disabling conditions. Although the life-function classification scheme has not been formally validated, and it was applied to data considerably less reliable than assessments of client populations, it yielded several suggestive insights.

Commonalities among groups often considered and treated as distinct were evident. Every impairment studied was characterized by diverse limitations in multiple areas of functioning. At the same time, it was possible to distinguish among impairment groups based on their life-function profiles. The specific ways in which broad limitations in life functioning were manifested were even more diverse. Analysis of differences within major impairment groups would have revealed even greater diversity in the disabled population. The value of applying the life-function model – or any similar model that categorizes the range of human functions – is that one can detect both commonalities and differences. That is, one can apply the same analytical framework to assess the needs of any disabled individual or group. Moreover, because each life function can be considered a continuum ranging from optimal to severely deficient functioning, the framework can be used to compare the "disabled" and the "nondisabled."

A universally applicable system for analyzing functional limitations might foster new kinds of thinking about rehabilitation and the organization of rehabilitation services. It is generally agreed that diagnostic labels are woefully inadequate bases for assessing client needs. The labels do not reflect the diversity among persons with the same impairing conditions. By comparison, assessment of functional limitations may result in a recognition that two particular clients with different impairing conditions require more of the same services than do two other clients who happen to have the same impairing condition. The system would provide a way to define severe disability independent of diagnosed condition (see Koshel & Granger, 1978) and could aid in identifying service needs that take the same form in large segments of the disabled population. For example, the present analysis points to the feasibility and cost-effectiveness of developing social-attitudinal counseling and training techniques that could help virtually any disabled person adjust to being disabled. More generally, extensive analysis of functional limitations would permit judgment on the validity of any target population definition, program, or reorganization in the rehabilitation field designed around common needs for service.

The present model may serve as a heuristic device for those developing concrete methods of assessing functional limitations. Because it seems appropriate to assume that any impairing condition is associated with interrelated difficulties across the range of human functioning, the need is for comprehensive scales of human functional limitation applicable to the entire disabled population. The scales can be supplemented by more specialized assessment tools to be applied after prominent areas of limitation in the various domains of functioning have been identified. Several instrument-development efforts are underway. (See Indices, 1979, for a state-of-the-art review.) Their underlying conceptual frameworks are often unclear or divergent, however, and some scales are intended only for restricted uses with subsets of the disabled population. The model presented here may serve as a broad guide in future efforts or as the specific basis for operationalizing, measuring, and comparing functional limitations in diverse populations.

Finally, new tools for assessing functional limitations should incorporate or be complemented by tools for measuring environmental characteristics and forces. For example, Nagi (1976) recently reported that gross measures of pathology and functional limitation were significantly, but not substantially, related to work disability and limitations in the ability to live independently. Nagi's analysis further identified some environmental factors (e.g., whether or not any modifications in a person's work setting had been carried out) that accounted for the fact that persons with very similar physical and emotional limitations often had very different outcomes, or extents of work disability. It is important, then, for environmental factors to be taken into account along with functional limitations. Through more sophisticated conceptualizations and measurement of the problems associated with disability, rehabilitators can hope to achieve more effective solutions to those problems.

REFERENCES

Dudek, R. A., & Associates. *Technology assessment: Human rehabilitation techniques* (Vol. 1, Parts A and B, Final Report). Lubbock: Texas Tech University, 1977. (NTIS Nos. PB 277 276, PB 277 277)

Hamilton, K. W. *Counseling the handicapped in the rehabilitation process.* New York: Ronald, 1950.

Indices, Inc. *Functional limitations: A state of the art review.* Falls Church, Va.: Author, 1979.

Koshel, J. J., & Granger, C. V. Rehabilitation terminology: Who is severely disabled? *Rehabilitation Literature,* 1978, 39, 102–106.

Nagi, S. Z. Some conceptual issues in disability and rehabilitation. In M. B. Sussman (Ed.), *Sociology and rehabilitation.* Washington, D.C.: American Sociological Association, 1965.

Nagi, S. Z. An epidemiology of disability among adults in the United States. *Milbank Memorial Fund Quarterly: Health and Society,* 1976, 54, 439–467.

Sussman, M. B. Dependent disabled and dependent poor: Similarity of conceptual issues and research needs. *Social Service Review,* 1969, 43, 383–395.

Urban Institute. *Report of the Comprehensive Service Needs Study.* Washington, D.C.: Author, 1975. (HEW Contract No. 100-74-0309)

2

Roles of Counseling in Ensuring the Rights of the Handicapped

Thomas H. Hohenshil
Charles W. Humes II

Throughout the course of recorded human history, those persons who were different have often been destroyed, tortured, exorcised, sterilized, ignored, exiled, exploited, and even considered divine. Their problems have been crudely explained in terms of superstition and varying levels of scientific understanding. In the earliest primitive societies, physical abnormalities were not common beyond infancy because many tribes permitted the killing of such newborn children. In cases where primitive individuals were physically normal, but became deranged and behaved differently from members of their communities, they were frequently feared and considered to possess supernatural powers. The early writings of the Greeks, Chinese, and Egyptians reflect the belief that mental disorders were brought on by demons. Among the ancient Hebrews, such disorders were thought to represent the wrath of God. The primary treatment consisted of exorcism—an attempt to drive the spirits from the possessed through prayer, noisemaking, purgatives, flogging, or starving. In more recent societies the handicapped have been pitied and cared for, and finally, they have been gradually accepted, educated, and often employed, with the same rights as those who are not handicapped (Buscaglia, 1975; Hewett & Forness, 1976).

It is quite evident from even a cursory review of United States history that the handicapped were systematically discriminated against and denied many of the basic human rights that we know today. The right to a free and appropriate education; the right to competitive employment; the right to full participation in the political, social, and economic spheres; and the right

From *Personnel and Guidance Journal*, December 1979, pp. 221–227.Copyright © 1979 by the American Personnel and Guidance Association. Reprinted with permission.

to health and various social services have, in one manner or another, been denied or made less available to handicapped persons (U.S. Department of Health, Education and Welfare, 1977a).

Education, probably the most fundamental right in a democratic society, is an excellent example of a right denied to the handicapped. Generally, the nation's public schools have been highly ingenious and successful in denying equal educational opportunities to the handicapped. Their success has been described by indicating how many children were excluded: As reported in Section 602 (b) of PL 94-142 (Education for All Handicapped Children Act of 1975), Congress found that approximately 50% of the nation's eight million handicapped children were not receiving an appropriate education, and about one million received no education at all (Gilhool, 1976; National Advisory Committee on the Handicapped, 1976; Turnbull & Turnbull, 1978).

There are several ways in which education has been denied to handicapped youth and adults. Public and private schools have excluded school-aged handicapped persons individually and as a class. They have inadequately funded tuition-subsidy programs that would have enabled families to purchase appropriate education from alternative sources when appropriate education was not available in the schools. When appropriate programs were not available, the schools often placed handicapped students in special education programs that were not designed to meet their special learning needs. In addition, the schools created different admissions policies for the handicapped, who were frequently placed in situations in which practically no program of instruction was available. Schools excluded retarded children on the grounds that they created behavioral and disciplinary problems. And finally, the schools limited the number of students that could be enrolled in special education programs by using incidence projections that had little relation to the actual number of the handicapped in a specific school district. Special supportive services for the handicapped, including counseling, have also been generally inadequate (Foster, Szoke, Kapisovsky, & Kriger, 1977; Humes, 1978b; McBain, 1978; Turnbull & Turnbull, 1978).

Many readers may object to these generalized characterizations, even though similar examples could easily be drawn from practices of employment (or nonemployment) of the handicapped, and from other basic rights. However, the generalizations have been true more often than not, and the practices have been more the rule than the exception. Some of the better studies of school practices substantiate the generalizations; court decisions have set forth facts that support the generalizations; Congress has filed broad-based indictments of many of our basic educational and social institutions, and of business and industry (Abeson, Bolick, & Hass, 1976).

THE ROLE OF THE FEDERAL GOVERNMENT

The federal government's concern for the handicapped spans more than 150 years. Its earliest role, creating special schools for the mentally ill, deaf, and blind between the 1820s and 1870s, paralleled a similar movement at state levels, in which state schools for the handicapped were established as early as 1823. Little significant federal activity regarding the handicapped occurred until World Wars I and II, which moved the government into vocational rehabilitation programs for handicapped veterans and other handicapped persons. Such public assistance programs were clear evidence of increasing federal concern for the handicapped. The application of the Social Security Act to the disabled, blind, aged, and dependent; the grant of benefits under Medicare and Medicaid programs; the payment of Supplementary Security Income; and a number of programs under Title XX of the Social Security Act provide testimony to the federal government's concerns.

The parent movement was typified by the formation of the National Association for Retarded Citizens in the 1950s, and its power on the federal and state scene in the 1960s was increased when President Kennedy and Vice President Humphrey used their influence to advance the interests of the mentally retarded with the establishment of the President's Committee on Mental Retardation.

The 1970s have brought an increasing number of federal laws, at least parts of which include provisions for handicapped youth and adults. Several of the most important are the Rehabilitation Act of 1973 (PL 93-112), the Education for All Handicapped Children Act of 1975 (PL 94-142), the Education Amendments of 1976, the Career Education Implementation Incentive Act of 1977, and the 1978 Comprehensive Education and Training Act Amendments. By small steps, and then by ever-increasing strides, the federal government has become deeply involved with the rights of handicapped persons (La Vor, 1976; Moore & Engleman, 1977; National Advisory Committee on the Handicapped, 1976; Turnbull & Turnbull, 1978).

RIGHTS OF THE HANDICAPPED

What are the current rights of the handicapped? Basically, they are the same as those of nonhandicapped persons, especially in the public sector. Although more than 200 federal laws have been passed since 1827 to assist the handicapped, two current pieces of legislation are considered landmarks in the field. Taken together, they virtually guarantee that the handicapped have basically the same rights that are granted to any other citizen of this country. These two monumental federal laws are the Education for All Handicapped Children Act of 1975 (PL 94-142), and the Rehabilitation Act of 1973 (PL 93-112), especially Sections 501, 502, 503, and 504.

Education

PL 94-142 assures that all handicapped children, aged 3–21, have a free and appropriate public education in the least restrictive environment possible. The cornerstone of this legislation is the fact that a written Individual Education Program (IEP) must be developed for each handicapped child and be reviewed annually. Another major ingredient of this law guarantees various due process procedures for students and their parents. These due process procedures cover the procedural safeguards that govern both evaluation and programming. In terms of educational and psychological evaluations, the parents must be fully informed in their native language and must understand that the granting of consent is voluntary. Further, the parents of a handicapped child are afforded the opportunity to examine all educational records with regard to evaluation and programming. In addition, they have the right to obtain an independent educational evaluation by a qualified outside examiner at public expense, if it can be demonstrated that the public agency (school) evaluation was inappropriate. In essence, PL 94-142 tries to provide handicapped persons with the special additional services that will make them as educationally competitive with nonhandicapped students as possible (U.S. Department of Health, Education and Welfare, 1977b, 1978b; Hohenshil, 1979c; Humes, 1978a).

Section 504 of PL 93-112 not only assures an appropriate elementary and secondary education for handicapped children, it also assures that the handicapped have basically the same rights as anyone else to go to college, or to enroll in a job training or adult basic education program. However, a recent Supreme Court ruling (*Southeastern Community College v. Francis B. Davis*) may have significant implications for the education and training of handicapped persons. In that case the Supreme Court, by unanimous decision, upheld Southeastern Community College's right to refuse to admit a deaf student to a nursing program. Justice Powell (1979) wrote that

> Section 504 by its terms does not compel educational institutions to disregard the disabilities of handicapped individuals or to make substantial modifications in their programs to allow disabled persons to participate. Instead, it requires only that an "otherwise qualified handicapped individual" not be excluded from participation in a federally funded program "solely by reason of his handicap," indicating only that mere possession of a handicap is not a permissible ground for assuming an inability to function in a particular context. (p. 15)

The key here is the definition of "otherwise qualified handicapped persons." The Supreme Court ruled that an "otherwise qualified handicapped person" is one who is able to meet all of a program's requirements in spite of the handicap. In other words, handicapped persons still cannot be refused admission to a postsecondary or vocational program if they can meet the requirements of the program in spite of their handicaps, and without the necessity for "substantial" program modifications.

Although it is early to assess the full impact of this ruling by the Supreme Court, it still appears that under Section 504, a college or training program may not

1. limit the number of qualified handicapped students admitted; or
2. ask handicapped persons to take a preadmission test that inadequately measures academic level because no special provisions were made for the person who was deaf, blind, or otherwise handicapped.

Colleges are also not required to lower academic standards or significantly alter degree requirements for the handicapped, but depending on the handicap, they may have to

1. extend the time allowed to earn a degree or substitute one elective course for another.
2. modify teaching methods or examinations so the individual can fully participate in a degree program.
3. provide braille books or other aids for the individual if they are not available from other sources.

These Section 504 protections apply to all public and private institutions receiving federal assistance (Biehl, 1978; Powell, 1979; U.S. Department of Health, Education and Welfare, 1977a, 1978a; Von Hipple, Foster, & Lonberg, 1978).

Employment

Employers who are recipients of financial assistance from the Department of Health and Human Services, or who receive federal procurement contracts in excess of $2,500, are governed by the regulations of PL 93-112. Section 504 assures that the handicapped have the same employment rights and benefits as nonhandicapped applicants and employees. Employers may not refuse to hire or promote persons solely because they are handicapped. Preemployment physical examinations cannot be required, and preemployment inquiry cannot be made about a person's handicapping conditions, although employers may ask about an applicant's ability to perform job-related functions. Employers may make an offer of employment conditional on a medical examination as long as the examination is required of all employees, and no one is disqualified on the basis of a physical condition that is not job-related.

Reasonable accommodation may have to be made to the person's handicap, if necessary. Examples of reasonable accommodation might include a cassette recorder for a blind employee, changes in the physical location of the task to be performed, or similar actions. Under certain circumstances, an employer might find it necessary to make more extensive changes, such as job-restructuring. The size and type of employing agency and the cost involved are considered when determining the degree of accommodation required by an employer. Failure to employ or promote an employee who is unqualified, or who cannot be helped by reasonable accommodation, is not considered discrimination.

In addition to the rights discussed above, Title V of the Rehabilitation Act and the Developmental Disability Act provide the handicapped with other equal opportunity employment protections. They have the right to be considered for federal employment. Section 501 requires that federal agencies take affirmative action to hire and promote handicapped persons. All executive branch agencies must make an annual report to the Civil Service Commission on their progress in hiring and promoting the handicapped. The Civil Service Commission in turn reports to Congress. Handicapped persons have the right of access to federal and federally financed buildings. Section 502 sets up a federal compliance board to make sure the handicapped have access to all buildings owned, occupied, or financed by the U.S. government. Handicapped persons have the right to be considered for employment or service by federal contractors. Section 503 states that firms doing business with the U.S. government must take affirmative action to hire and promote the handicapped (U.S. Department of Health, Education and Welfare, 1977a, 1978a).

Health Care

The provisions for accessibility and reasonable accommodation that apply to other programs also apply to programs of health services. Hospitals are the largest group of health care providers affected by Section 504. A handicapped person is entitled to all medical services and medically related instruction available to the public. Hospitals receiving federal assistance (including Medicare payments) must take steps to accommodate those with handicaps. Among other things, hospitals must

1. provide an emergency room interpreter or make other effective provisions for deaf patients;
2. treat the physical injury of a person under the influence of alcohol or other drugs; and
3. admit handicapped persons to natural childbirth, antismoking, and other public service programs of instruction.

If a handicapped child is in a long-term health care facility, the facility and the local public school district are jointly responsible for providing a free and appropriate education for the child. If a handicapped person is a Medicaid patient, the private physician must have a physically accessible office, provide treatment in a hospital or private home, or if neither is possible, consult with the handicapped person and refer him or her to another physician whose office is accessible.

Further, health providers must ensure that persons with impaired sensory or speaking skills are provided effective notice concerning the provision of benefits, waivers of rights, and consent to treatment. Health services for handicapped people must be equal in quality to those in the institution's overall program, and equitable standards of eligibility are required (U.S. Department of Health, Education and Welfare, 1977a, 1978a).

Welfare and Social Services

As with health and other services, the provisions for accessibility and reasonable accommodation also apply to welfare and social service institutions. Handicapped persons have the right to participate, on an equal basis with nonhandicapped persons, in vocational rehabilitation, senior citizen activities, day care (for handicapped children), or any other social service program receiving federal assistance. For example, handicapped persons may not be denied admission because they use wheelchairs and need access to classrooms, recreation areas, or buses. They also may not be excluded from vocational training because they are blind, mentally retarded, or paralyzed, and may need more training for paid employment than students with other handicaps (U.S. Department of Health, Education and Welfare, 1977a, 1978a).

THE ROLES OF COUNSELING

The roles of counseling in ensuring the rights of the handicapped must be related to definitions in the legislation. As noted by Fagan and Wallace (1979), the handicapped are defined in both PL 94-142 and PL 93-112. In the former the handicapped are the hearing impaired, mentally retarded, multihandicapped, orthopedically impaired, other health impaired, seriously emotionally disturbed, speech impaired, visually handicapped, and those with specific learning disabilities. However, children are not considered handicapped unless they need special education services. Under the latter legislation (PL 93-112), a similar set of categories is stated. However, the physical or mental impairment must substantially limit one or more of the major life activities.

Most handicaps exist on a continuum; a condition that requires no educational or life-activity adaptations will not meet the legal requirements to be classified as handicapped. Counseling, which is a related or supportive service, is required only if the individual is handicapped as defined by law. This does not mean that counseling should not be available to the less handicapped, but it is not mandated. This distinction is subtle but important. Philosophically and legislatively, it means that counselors must provide services if an individual needs them to adjust or adapt to normal life situations. This is why individual assessments and individual programming are so important and receive great emphasis in state and federal legislation.

The roles of counselors and the counseling profession in ensuring the rights of the handicapped are many and varied. Until recently, with the obvious exception of rehabilitation counseling, counselors in agency and school settings have not devoted a significant portion of their resources to the provision of comprehensive services for the handicapped. Many of the major counseling professional organizations have shown a minimal amount of interest and involvement in serving handicapped youth and adults. In fact, it wasn't until after PL 94-142 was passed that the American Personnel and Guidance Association began to focus sustained attention on the law's implications for agency and school counseling.

For many counselors, providing effective services for the handicapped will require reorientation as well as retraining. The developmental model so prevalent in the 1960s and 1970s emphasized the provision of counseling services for "normal" persons experiencing "developmental" problems. As noted by Barclay (1979) and Humes (1978b), the traditional developmental approach may fall by the wayside as more and more of the counselor's time in the future is related to crisis intervention and treatment for handicapped individuals.

It is not our position that the traditional guidance and counseling services of assessment, information, placement, individual and group counseling, and consultation be abandoned. Rather, it is our contention that counselors will need to place more emphasis upon crisis intervention and treatment, rather than concentrate exclusively on a developmental approach. For many, this will require a comprehensive continuing professional development program. Most counselor education programs have not required significant coursework in the area of handicapping conditions. To assume that developmental counseling skills can be applied easily to handicapped populations glosses over serious questions about professional competence and responsibility. Counselors need to acquire additional knowledge about handicapping conditions and their implications for multifactored assessment, specialized information services, consultation skills, and individual and group counseling techniques (Hohenshil, 1979a; Humes, 1978c). . . . The following components of this article present five critical roles that counselors must assume if they are to be effective in ensuring that the handicapped have opportunities to fully develop their potential.

Information

Federal legislation for the handicapped requires that information be disseminated to inform them, in writing and orally, about their basic legal rights. Counselors in agencies and schools play a key role in this process either through assignment or by choice. PL 94-142 mandates that parents be provided information on child development and be helped to understand their children's special needs. Although this section of the law is rather vague, it appears to require information rather than therapy for parents. Parents should be informed of their basic rights of participation and due process under this legislation. Rehabilitation legislation also requires that clients be informed about the nature of the rehabilitation process, their right to appeal any decisions, confidentiality of records, and contingencies that might affect the written individualized rehabilitation program. In all cases, a heavy responsibility is placed on counselors to disseminate such information. It may well be that clients and parents can communicate better with counseling personnel than with psychologists and social workers because the former may be perceived as less threatening.

Advocacy

Federal legislation for the handicapped contains due process guarantees, although the safeguards governing the provision of services are probably most enforceable with school-age populations. With this population one is dealing with compulsory school attendance as well as the provision of special services. In many ways, due process is the most significant part of any of the statutes because it ensures compliance. The various pieces of legislation would be virtually meaningless without the opportunity for plaintiffs to seek redress.

While the need for due process is self-evident in terms of ensuring rights for the handicapped, it causes much institutional concern. Although most institutions and businesses probably mean well in their desire to provide full opportunities for the handicapped, many fall short because of what they perceive as a lack of human and financial resources. When challenged by someone aggrieved, administrators and employers often become upset by the "presumptuous behavior" of persons seeking their legal rights. At this point, or preferably before, the counselor enters the picture.

Above all else, counselors must be advocates of the rights of their clients. Their professional orientation can place them in no other position. Paradoxically, they are employed by institutions that expect loyalty and support for their administrative decisions. Counselors, while maintaining an advocacy position, must be objective and fact-oriented. This being the case, they must have access to comprehensive records and documentation. Hearing procedures often use counselors as witnesses, sometimes for both sides. In such situations the counselor must know the legislation, the capabilities of the individual, and the specific rights that may have been violated. Such rights may involve availability of regular and special education programs, educational program modifications, architectural barriers, or employment. In these procedures, a counselor must present accurate data and appropriate professional opinions about the handicapped person's case, while recognizing the rights and limits of the institution that employs the counselor.

The advocacy role should also be evident in a number of other, preventive ways. Counselors should be in the forefront of those recommending the elimination of architectural barriers that constrict educational and employment opportunities for the handicapped. They should be activists in recommending modifications in educational, training, and employment programs to assure that needless application, entrance, and instructional barriers are identified and eliminated. Counselors should also encourage appropriate continuing professional development programs for teachers and administrators, as well as for themselves, to assure quality services for handicapped persons.

Parent/Family Counseling and Consultation

As noted elsewhere (Prescott & Hulnick, 1979; Yura, Zuckerman, Betz, & Newman, 1979), parent and family counseling/consultation are important aspects of comprehensive services for the handicapped. The extent of this service depends to a large degree upon the needs of a particular family and the skills of the counselor. It may range on a continuum from merely providing information about legal rights and available services to in-depth, continuing individual and group counseling with the total family. As Kennedy and Bush (1979) vividly point out, the children of handicapped parents should not be overlooked in the rehabilitation process. Evidence is mounting that these children frequently need counseling to help them cope with the consequences of their parents' handicaps. The family is particularly affected by the onset of traumatic, sudden handicapping conditions, which lead to dramatically altered roles and responsibilities. Family counseling/consultation can be the key to overcoming a variety of obstacles in the reorganization of family roles. This, of course, is another area in which continuing professional development is necessary for many counselors.

Individual Educational Programs (IEPs)

Written individual program requirements are required by recent educational and rehabilitation legislation. All specify active participation by the handicapped person or the parents. Such plans must indicate what services will be provided and who will be responsible for implementation. Further, the plans must specify long-term goals and intermediate objectives, as well as objective criteria and evaluative procedures. Counselors, of course, are involved in these processes. In both education and rehabilitation, the individual program is the basis for services. It is a management tool, if not a contract, that becomes a blueprint for action. The counselor's involvement is likely to be in the three categories of participation, development, and monitoring (Humes, 1978b; Randolph, 1975).

For example, the school counselor can be involved in any of the three categories, perhaps at the same time. Frequently, school counselors serve as representatives to the corps of teachers. Although the development of the IEP is most often the responsibility of the instructional staff, an overlooked option is its development by the counselor. This can happen when the handicapped student is functioning entirely within regular education, but is able to do so only with regular, in-depth counseling. Such a case becomes even more important in those districts that have limited access to psychiatrists, psychologists, and psychiatric social workers.

The monitoring of progress under the IEP is the most common role assigned to school counselors. It involves, among other things, the interpretation of goals to administrators and teachers, the coordination of resources, and an assessment of the degree of accomplishment of objectives. This is a logical assignment, for counselors have long sought identification as individualizers of programs, and as catalysts and links among students and teachers. However, there must be recognition that it is not only the counselor who fulfills this obligation; it is the duty of the individual who is most knowledgeable about the student and who is in a position to initiate necessary changes in program direction.

The notion of least restriction is a familiar theme, running throughout the laws and regulations. Reasonable accommodations must be made to known physical and mental handicaps in terms of education and employment practices. Another consideration is for program accessibility, whether in education, business, or health, welfare, and social services. Counselors are required to counsel handicapped persons toward least restrictive options commensurate with their interests and abilities. The least restrictive notion, when applied to integration within regular settings, is designed not only to reduce bias and stereotyping but also to force schools and employers to modify academic and work environments to the maximum appropriate degree. When an individual is so severely handicapped that a regular environment is impossible, implications of the resulting restrictions imposed on that person are enormous. Clearly, the determination is an individual matter and must be based on unique needs.

This least restrictive aspect is often the most troublesome to educational institutions. Through apprehension and misinformation, teachers still believe that grossly handicapped students will be placed wholesale in their classrooms. The truth of the matter is that so-called mainstreaming has clearly occurred in most school systems quite successfully. Few severely handicapped students have been placed in regular class settings, and this will continue to be the case. Many parents and students do not prefer the alternative of regular class placement. In the choice of the least restrictive environment, the counselor is expected to make recommendations. A close reading of the regulations of PL 94-142 reveals that the key to the least restrictive environment is the existence of a continuum of alternative placements. They may range from regular class placement with supplemental tutoring or counseling, to a special education class, or even to a residential setting. The student's well-being must be the prime determinant in any such recommendation.

Career Development Programs

Career development for the handicapped is a specialized activity but, as with the nonhandicapped, the process must promote healthy emotional adjustment as well as social, educational, and occupational fulfillment. The individual's self-concept and perceived ability to perform an occupation are critical. The handicapped must feel that they can influence their lives and choice of careers, and not simply be fitted into a niche that seems suitable for someone with their impairment. The career counseling process should not be limited to individual sessions, but should also encompass vocational assessment, group activities, exploration, and trial work-related experiences. The goal is to use the full potential of an individual in an occupation that offers independence and economic security. The counselee must actively search for answers that relate to work accessibility, work performance, and work rewards (Bozarth & Rubin, 1972). These factors must be related to the coping levels of the handicapped person, levels that the person must understand when considering employment and training possibilities. Frequently, handicapped persons are so accustomed to having things done for them that it is difficult for them to realize that they may have some control over their vocational destiny.

Vocational education, as a subsystem of special and career education, is a relatively untapped resource (Broiling & Alonzo, 1979). A number of congressional committees have been highly critical of both public school vocational education and adult occupational training programs for not enrolling more handicapped youth and adults (Hohenshil, 1979b). Frequently, there appear to be built-in biases against the handicapped in occupational training, usually in regard to safety, accessibility, and supervision. Counselors should play a major role by ensuring that appropriate occupational training follows or coincides with academic education. If a person is under age 21, a suitable individual education program must be designed that includes short-term and long-term objectives for career counseling, skill training, personal development, and job placement. The gains in such an arrangement should accrue to handicapped persons and institutions both. Handicapped individuals have long had the potential for productive work, but lacked the avenues for action. There must be documented action steps to ensure selection and financial support for occupational training opportunities, including apprenticeships.

In terms of job placement, counselors, students, and prospective employers must be aware of federal legislation and regulations requiring equal employment opportunities for handicapped persons. As noted previously, the regulations for Sections 503 and 504 of PL 93-112 have a major and positive impact on the employment of the handicapped. These are important regulations, for as young people emerge from the schools after many years of assistance, they will not accept less as they seek to enter and advance in employment.

Employers, fearing higher accident rates, poor attendance, lower productivity, and increased insurance costs, may have biases against handicapped persons. They may also feel that unions may oppose hiring the handicapped. The foregoing reasons, while disproved, apply particularly to the hard-to-place exceptionalities—the severely physically handicapped, mentally retarded, and emotionally handicapped. To offset these prevalent points of view, the counselor must maintain close contact with the employment community so that opportunities can be opened and kept open. Counselors must be alert to point out the jobs that initially may seem inappropriate but can be job-adapted to meet the limitations of the handicapped person without sacrificing performance and productivity. In many ways this phase of the life-long corrective process is more important than the education and training components. Certainly, in terms of lifespan it will encompass two or three times as many years. Although the recent legislation and regulations will facilitate the process, success may be limited, for in large measure the vagaries of counselee motivation are involved. The counselor must actively seek out potential clients, engage them in meaningful counseling experiences, and facilitate their career aspirations. The opening-up of job opportunities may not be as critical as the realization of the handicapped that they can achieve satisfaction, success, and monetary rewards from employment of their choice.

DISCUSSION

The several related pieces of federal legislation are dramatic statutes that provide education, training, social services, and employment opportunities for the handicapped and, concurrently, have a heavy influence on the way counselors function. These are evolutionary pieces of legislation, to be sure, and the full effects will not be known for many years. During the intervening period, counselors will be called upon to fulfill the roles presented in this article. This will force a change in job role, more for some than for others. Many counselors are, and will continue to be, resistant. According to them, helping the handicapped should be left to those who have been traditionally trained and employed for this purpose. Nevertheless, changes in job role are often forced on professional groups by unexpected exigencies. The nation's counselors, whether school or agency, are being forced to assume expanded roles. None of this will happen without in-service opportunities. It is heartening to see that many counselors are welcoming the new opportunities, for they realize that only through changes can a professional discipline remain dynamic and strong. As a professional group, counselors should embrace the challenge, grasp leadership where necessary, and make sure that the best interests of the handicapped and counselors both are being served. Counselors must ensure that the rights of the handicapped are being met as directed by the applicable legislation and regulations.

REFERENCES

Abeson, A., Bolick, N., & Hass, J. Due process of law: Background and intent. In F. J. Weintraub, A. Abeson, J. Ballard, & M. L. La Vor (Eds.), *Public policy and the education of exceptional children*, pp. 22–32. Reston, Va.: Council for Exceptional Children, 1976.

Barclay, J. R. Editorial. *Personnel and Guidance Journal*, 1979, 57, 435.

Biehl, G. R. *Guide to Section 504 self-evaluation for colleges and universities.* Washington, D.C.: National Association of College and University Business Officers, 1978.

Bozarth, J., & Rubin, S. *Facilitative management in rehabilitation counseling: A case book.* Champaign, Ill.: Stripes Publishing, 1972.

Broiling, E. E., & Alonzo, B. Critical issues in career education for handicapped students. *Exceptional Children*, 1979, 45, 246–253.

Buscaglia, L. *The disabled and their parents: A counseling challenge.* Thorofare, N.J.: Charles B. Slack, 1975.

Fagan, T., & Wallace, A. Who are the handicapped? *Personnel and Guidance Journal*, 1979, 58, 215–220.

Foster, J. C., Szoke, C. O., Kapisovsky, P. M., & Kriger, L. S. *Guidance, counseling, and support services for high school students with physical disabilities.* Cambridge, Mass.: Technical Education Research Centers, 1977.

Gilhool, T. K., Education: An inalienable right. In F. J. Weintraub, A. Abeson, J. Ballard, & M. L. La Vor (Eds.), *Public policy and the education of exceptional children*, pp. 14–21. Reston, Va.: Council for Exceptional Children, 1976.

Hewett, F. M., & Forness, S. R. *Education of exceptional learners.* Boston: Allyn & Bacon, 1976.

Hohenshil, T. H. Renewal in career guidance and counseling: Rationale and programs. *Counselor Education and Supervision*, 1979, 18, 199–208. (a)

Hohenshil, T. H. Adulthood: New frontier for vocational school psychology. *School Psychology Digest*, 1979, 8, 193–198. (b)

Hohenshil, T. H. Introduction to pupil personnel services. In T. H. Hohenshil & J. H. Miles (Eds.), *School guidance services: A career development approach*, pp. 1–12. Dubuque, Iowa: Kendall/Hunt, 1979. (c)

Humes, C. W. School counselors and PL 94-142. *School Counselor*, 1978, 25, 192–196. (a)

Humes, C. W. Counselors' roles in PL 94-142. *Guidepost*, 1978, 21, 5–8. (b)

Humes, C. W. Implications of PL 94-142 for training and supervision. *Counselor Education and Supervision*, 1978, 18, 126–129. (c)

Kennedy, K. M., & Bush, D. F. Counseling the children of handicapped parents. *Personnel and Guidance Journal*, 1979, 58, 267–270.

La Vor, M. L. Federal legislation for exceptional persons: A history. In J. J. Weintraub, A. Abeson, J. Ballard, & M. L. La Vor (Eds.), *Public policy and the education of exceptional children*, pp. 96–112. Reston, Va: Council for Exceptional Children, 1976.

McBain, S. *Enhancing understanding of students with physical disabilities.* Palo Alto, Calif.: American Institutes for Research, 1978.

Moore, J. J., & Engleman, V. S. *Programming for handicapped students at the secondary level: Responding to the laws.* Salt Lake City: Southwest Regional Resources Center, 1977.

National Advisory Committee on the Handicapped. *The unfinished resolution: Education for the handicapped.* Washington, D.C.: U.S. Government Printing Office, 1976.

Powell, L. F. Text of high court's ruling on admitting the handicapped. *Chronicle of Higher Education*, 1979, 18, 1,15–16.

Randolph, A. H. The Rehabilitation Act of 1973: Implementation and implications. *Rehabilitation Counseling Bulletin*, 1975, 18, 200–204.

Prescott, M. R., & Hulnick, H. R. Counseling parents of handicapped children: An empathic approach. *Personnel and Guidance Journal*, 1979, 58, 263–266.

Turnbull, H. R., & Turnbull, A. *Free appropriate public education: Law and implementation.* Denver: Love Publishing, 1978.

U.S. Department of Health, Education and Welfare. Nondiscrimination on basis of handicap (rules and regulations for Section 504 of PL 93-112). *Federal Register*, 42(86). Washington, D.C.: U.S. Government Printing Office, 1977. (a)

U.S. Department of Health, Education and Welfare. Education of handicapped children (rules and regulations for implementation of Part B of PL 94-142). *Federal Register*, 42(163). Washington, D.C.: U.S. Government Printing Office, 1977. (b)

U.S. Department of Health, Education and Welfare. *Your rights as a disabled person.* Washington, D.C.: U.S. Government Printing Office, 1978. (a)

U.S. Department of Health, Education and Welfare. *Your responsibilities to disabled persons as a school or college administrator.* Washington, D.C.: U.S. Government Printing Office, 1978. (b)

Von Hipple, C., Foster, J., & Lonberg, J. *Civil rights, handicapped persons, and education: Section 504 self-evaluation guide for preschool, elementary, secondary, and adult education.* Washington, D.C.: U.S. Department of Health, Education and Welfare, 1978.

Yura, M. T., Zuckerman, L., Betz, M. J., & Newman, S. S. Parent involvement project. *Personnel and Guidance Journal,* 1979, *58,* 290–292.

3

Explaining "Psychiatric Rehabilitation" by an Analogy to "Physical Rehabilitation"

William A. Anthony

The problems of rehabilitating the severely psychiatrically disabled client are well known, by the treatment professional, the client, and the public (Pardes and Pincus, 1980). In many people's minds the nightmare of institutionalization has now been replaced by the horrors of deinstitutionalization. However, regardless of whether the treatment setting is in the community or the hospital, the treatment professional's goal remains the same — to provide the severely disabled person with effective care based on a humane and responsive treatment philosophy.

Out of the pursuit of this elusive goal has evolved the practice of psychiatric rehabilitation. Unfortunately, many mental health professionals do not understand what is involved in the principles and practices of psychiatric rehabilitation, because it is a new concept for them. Many think of rehabilitation as only vocationally oriented; others think of rehabilitation as something that is done to old houses or as something that was done in the prison system that never seemed to work. Thus it behooves psychiatric rehabilitation practitioners to be able to explain the rehabilitation approach to uninitiated mental health practitioners in a way they can appreciate and understand.

I have found that the concept of psychiatric rehabilitation can be meaningfully explained by drawing an analogy between the psychiatric rehabilita-

From *Psychosocial Rehabilitation Journal*, 5(1) (1982), 61–65. Reprinted by permission.

This paper is based in part on a presentation made at a conference entitled "Assessing Treatment Efficacy and Outcome of Schizophrenics and the Chronically Mentally Ill," sponsored by the National Institute of Mental Health, October 8–10, 1980, Portsmouth, New Hampshire.

tion approach and the approach used in physical medicine and rehabilitation. Severely physically disabled clients are less stigmatized than psychiatrically disabled clients, their disabilities seem more understandable, and the treatment processes seem more legitimate. Demonstrating parallels in both philosophy and practice between psychiatric and physical rehabilitation can help clarify the concept of psychiatric rehabilitation.

THE FIELD OF PHYSICAL MEDICINE AND REHABILITATION

While the strong emphasis on rehabilitating the psychiatrically disabled is a relatively new focus within the mental health field (Anthony, 1977), practitioners of physical medicine and rehabilitation have for many years been attempting to rehabilitate a severely disabled population, out of a long-standing concern for the medical, psychological, and vocational implications of chronic physical disability (Dembo et al., 1956; Kessler, 1935; Rusk and Taylor, 1949; Wright, 1980). Out of the traditions of physical medicine and rehabilitation has emerged a treatment philosophy that can serve as a model for the practice of rehabilitating the severely or chronically disabled psychiatric patient.

The practitioners of physical medicine have a successful history of wanting to serve and of serving the more severely disabled, such as those afflicted with blindness, deafness, hemiplegia, quadriplegia, and other severe conditions. In so doing practitioners in the field have developed a philosophy and expertise in helping persons whose residual disabilities impair role performance, who need a range of services, and who often need long-term and frequent care. Their successes in this regard have been notable: As an example, the Rehabilitation Services Administration reports that between 1973 and 1977 the number of spinal-cord-injured persons vocationally rehabilitated increased nearly 400%. Such success has not been the case in the mental health field. During the same time period there was a 3% decrease in the number of persons with the primary disability of mental illness who were successfully rehabilitated (Skelley, 1980).

Such comparisons may remind us of the obvious differences between persons with severe psychiatric disabilities and those with severe physical disabilities, but they can also point out the meaningful similarity between the two disability groups. Both groups of patients require a wide range of services, they exhibit impairment of role performance, and they may be involved for a long time in the care-giving system. As a reflection of this similarity in patient needs, the array and duration of services provided to the psychiatrically disabled by mental health practitioners are becoming more rehabilitation oriented.

THE GOALS AND TREATMENT APPROACHES
OF REHABILITATION

All the definitions of physical rehabilitation essentially converge around the idea that the client should achieve the best life adjustment possible in his or her environment, be it social, vocational, recreational, or educational (Wright, 1980). It is of course quite possible to adapt this goal of physical rehabilitation to arrive at a useful definition of the goal of psychiatric rehabilitation: to help assure that the psychiatrically disabled person possesses the physical, intellectual, and emotional abilities needed to live, learn, and/or work in his or her particular community (Anthony, 1977).

Flowing from this rehabilitation goal are the two primary treatment approaches of physical medicine and rehabilitation that can also be applied to psychiatric rehabilitation: (1) developing the client's skills and (2) modifying the environment in order to maximize the client's present skill level. For example, the techniques of physical therapy do not attempt to probe for or remove the cause of hemiplegia; rather, the physical therapist focuses on rebuilding the patient's damaged skills, on teaching the patient new skills, or on adapting the environment to better accommodate the patient's skill level (Anthony, 1980). Similarly, the interventions needed to achieve psychiatric rehabilitation involve teaching clients the skills they need to function in the community and/or modifying the community to accommodate or strengthen the clients' present level of functioning. The psychiatric rehabilitation treatment approach is directly analogous to the treatment approach used in physical medicine and rehabilitation.

REHABILITATION OUTCOME
IS ENVIRONMENTALLY SPECIFIC

The field of physical rehabilitation teaches us that measures of client outcome must be specific to the environment. Rehabilitation treatment focuses on the client's ability to perform certain tasks within certain environments, and the physical rehabilitation specialist needs to know the type of environment for which the person is being rehabilitated. For example, treatment outcome for a blind person is not just the learning of mobility skills; it is also the application of these mobility skills in certain environments of need (home, work, and so on). Thus the outcome is tied into an environment. Likewise, the psychiatric rehabilitation specialist must not just work toward improving, say, conversational skills, but must do so with respect to the conversational demands of the specific environment in which the client is presently or will be functioning.

SKILL TRAINING MUST ENSURE SKILL GENERALIZATION

One of the main treatment approaches of psychiatric rehabilitation is skill training, although practitioners who attempt to teach their clients the skills they need to function in specific environments have often failed to help the clients transfer those skills to the environment of need (Hersen and Bellack, 1976). Newly learned skill behaviors are usually situation specific: Occupational skills learned in a hospital setting, for example, are not readily used in the community (Anthony, 1979).

Practitioners of physical rehabilitation have understood this principle of situation specificity. They know that the ability to learn to transfer from a wheelchair to a hospital bed does not guarantee a successful wheelchair-to-bed transfer in one's own home. The practitioner must teach directly toward that application goal and understand the specific skill demands of the home environment, including the possibility of conducting training in the home environment.

In order to ensure skill generalization, psychiatric rehabilitation training programs must become less contrived and simulated. Efforts need to be made to arrange for training in the environment of need, or at least in more natural environments than a hospital or clinic. Psychiatric rehabilitation must operate, as physical rehabilitation does, on the principle that generalization does not just occur, it must be programmed.

THE NECESSITY OF AN INDIVIDUALIZED REHABILITATION DIAGNOSIS

A rehabilitation diagnosis ensures that the actual skills being taught to the clients are the skills they will most need in their environment. There seems to be a tendency in mental health settings to teach all clients the same skills because those are the skills practitioners teach best, rather than teaching clients the skills they most need. Thus, for example, all schizophrenics in a day treatment center are taught assertiveness skills, seemingly independent of whether assertiveness is their most critical skill need. A similar practice in physical rehabilitation might be to teach all physically disabled clients, including the spinal-cord-injured, the deaf, and the blind, how to use a guide dog!

The important rehabilitation principle is that skill needs must be diagnosed and skill training must be tailored to those diagnosed skill needs. Without such an individual diagnosis, any outcome benefits of skill training are problematic at best.

UNDERSTANDING THE CONCEPT
OF LEAST RESTRICTIVE ENVIRONMENT

The treatment of the psychiatrically disabled person seems to be based on a concept of least restrictive environment that is totally different from the intent of this concept in rehabilitation practice. Bachrach has correctly pointed out the error in the present application of this concept (Bachrach, 1980), arguing that the restrictiveness of an environment is not just a function of the environment but a function of the unique needs of the patient within that environment. An environment that is unduly restrictive for one patient may be ideal for another patient. The quality of restrictiveness does not reside totally outside the patient and exclusively in the environment.

Bachrach's argument accurately reflects the philosophy of physical medicine and rehabilitation with respect to the concept of least restrictive environment. Physical medicine and rehabilitation practitioners realize that environments cannot be graded in terms of their restrictiveness without taking into account the needs and abilities of the client who functions in that environment. For example, a quadriplegic might find his or her premorbid home setting (theoretically the least restrictive) much more limiting than an architecturally modified center for independent living. Similarly, a blind person who has not yet learned mobility skills will find a busy street corner much more restrictive than the hospital corridor.

An effective rehabilitation philosophy replaces the concept of least restrictive environment with the principle of *most facilitative environment*, in which no unnecessary restrictions are placed on the client's functioning but in which the client's present abilities are accommodated. And, yes, this means that for some clients at certain points in time a humane and responsively run inpatient setting may be the most facilitative environment.

THE IMPORTANCE OF THE CLIENT-PRACTITIONER
RELATIONSHIP

In the practice of physical medicine and rehabilitation the value of an understanding and respectful relationship between client and practitioner is rarely underestimated. As a matter of fact, it is routinely viewed as a source of treatment effect. A rehabilitation program is not done *to* a client, it is done *with* a client. The success of a rehabilitation practitioner in helping clients learn new skills or function in new environments is affected in part by the relationship that exists between the client and the practitioner. It is the potency of this human relationship that may account for similar therapeutic outcomes of seemingly disparate rehabilitation practices. For example, the treatment of some injuries with ice now accomplishes what in the past appeared to be helped by the administration of heat. Perhaps it is doing something apparently helpful with somebody that is the common source of treatment effect.

Several research studies have reaffirmed the importance of the relationship between rehabilitation outcome and the relationship or interpersonal skills of the practitioner. Bozarth and Rubin (1975) found a significant relationship between the rehabilitation counselor's interpersonal skills and the client's vocational gain. In an inpatient setting for alcoholics, Valle (1982) found that the level of interpersonal skills of the alcoholism counselors related to client relapse rate at follow-up periods of 6, 12, 18, and 24 months.

The critical rehabilitation principle is that the human element is always a part of the rehabilitation equation. Not only do the relationship skills of the practitioner correlate with rehabilitation outcome, these skills also ensure a more decent, humane rehabilitation process for the client (Anthony, 1979).

THE SOMETIMES EQUIVOCAL RELATIONSHIP BETWEEN TREATMENT PROCESS AND TREATMENT OUTCOME

It is appealing to our scientific values to be able to identify the exact process that achieved a particular outcome. Unfortunately, from a scientific standpoint, client rehabilitation outcome can seemingly be achieved without an awareness of the specific elements that account for the outcome. For example, a physically disabled client may obtain a job even though the client never accurately applied his or her newly learned job-interviewing skills as they were taught by the rehabilitation practitioner. Or in a slightly different vein, a client may benefit from the rehabilitation process without actually succeeding in achieving the immediate goal of the process, as in the case of a client who fails in her attempts to learn to walk, yet still profits from the attempt by developing a willingness to return to school, even though she is now confined to a wheelchair.

What then can account for this apparent independence of successful process from successful outcome? One explanation may be that the very process of an intense skill-training experience, in the context of a supportive human relationship, may change the client's values, expectations, or attitude toward the meaning of his or her life, even though it doesn't achieve the desired skill change. Physical rehabilitation practitioners have long recognized the importance of these changes in personal values and meanings that accompany a rehabilitation intervention (Wright, 1960). Phrases such as "enlarging the scope of one's values," "minimizing the spread of disability," and "coping with disability rather than succumbing" are used to describe those personal changes so often experienced by the rehabilitation client.

Psychiatric rehabilitation practitioners are also aware that clients can still reap benefits from a rehabilitation intervention even though the targeted skills were neither completely acquired nor accurately applied. The very process of rehabilitation appears to have an unexplained impact on outcome, an impact that is perhaps mediated by value changes that are stimulated and encouraged by involvement in the rehabilitation process. Because the potential of the rehabilitation process cannot be accurately predicted even as the process is occurring, every severely disabled client should be allowed to participate in rehabilitation programs. The process itself may trigger certain changes that bring about benefits the professional could neither predict nor scientifically explain.

DEPENDENCY AS A REHABILITATION VALUE

It seems that in some mental health treatment programs client independence has become so valued that client dependence has become devalued. Yet, from a rehabilitation perspective, "dependency" is not a dirty word. Rehabilitation interventions with the physically disabled often encourage dependency on persons or things in one environment so the client can function more effectively in another environment. Dependency in one area of functioning can set a client free in another area. For example, a quadriplegic's dependence on a personal-care attendant for help in dressing for work may allow him or her to hold a full-time job. Dependency in a physical rehabilitation client is a matter of degree, varying naturally between and within environments.

Psychiatric rehabilitation interventions also recognize the value of dependency. The technology of rehabilitation is limited in its ability to achieve maximal client independence. Furthermore, dependence on people or things is a normal state of affairs. Interventions that allow for a certain degree of dependency at certain times, such as through the use of "enablers" or aides, may in fact maximize the client's functioning in other environments at other times (Weinman and Kleiner, 1978).

CLIENT BENEFITS AS THE ULTIMATE CRITERIA FOR REHABILITATION OUTCOME

There are a number of ways in which treatment success can be calculated. Measures of cost, family burden, or other indices of societal effort or impact are often suggested. Yet, from a rehabilitation perspective, the crucial impact variables are assessments of client gain in specific environments of need (Anthony and Farkas, 1982). The old saw "The operation was a success but the patient died" has no quarter in the practice of rehabilitation. If the client's functioning in a particular environment has not improved, then no rehabilitation benefits have accrued.

Physically disabled clients must ask of the physical rehabilitation
cess: Will the process improve my chances of walking, talking, or work
Why should I go through the pain, put forth the effort, and take the ti...c
to be involved in a rehabilitation program?

Severely disabled psychiatric patients rarely ask this benefit question
so strongly or directly. If asked to participate in a rehabilitation program they
either submit to treatment or drop out (Freeman et al., 1980; Stickney et
al., 1980). However, other people are beginning to ask the benefit question
in the clients' stead. Clients' families, taxpayers, politicians, and ex-patient
groups are beginning to ask the question more vociferously. Just as physical
medicine and rehabilitation has had to do, the field of psychiatric rehabilitation has to provide answers to clients asking what is in it for them. As in
the case of the physically disabled client, psychiatrically disabled clients
should be able to expect answers in terms lay people can understand and
appreciate.

SUMMARY

The analogy between physical rehabilitation and psychiatric rehabilitation
is by no means perfect, but this article has presented many parallels between
the two fields for the purpose of more clearly explaining the practices of
psychiatric rehabilitation. An additional benefit of such an analogy is that
it can help legitimize the need for a rehabilitation approach to the psychiatrically disabled.

REFERENCES

Anthony, W. A. Psychological rehabilitation: A concept in need of a method.
    American Psychologist, 1977, 32, 658–662.
_____. *Principles of psychiatric rehabilitation*. Baltimore: University Park Press, 1979.
_____. A rehabilitation model for rehabilitating the psychiatrically disabled. *Reha-
    bilitation Counseling Bulletin*, 1980, 24, 6–21.
Anthony, W. A., & Farkas, M. A client outcome planning model for assessing psy-
    chiatric rehabilitation intervention. *Schizophrenia Bulletin*, March, 1982.
Bachrach, L. L. Is the least restrictive environment always the best? Sociological and
    semantic implications. *Hospital and Community Psychiatry*, 1980, 31, 97–103.
Bozarth, J. D., & Rubin, S. E. Empirical observation of rehabilitation counselor per-
    formance and outcome: Some implications. *Rehabilitation Counseling
    Bulletin*, 1975, 19, 294–298.
Dembo, T., Leviton, G. L., & Wright, B. A. Adjustment to misfortune—a problem
    of social psychological rehabilitation. *Artificial Limbs*, 1956, 3, 4–62.
Freeman, S. J., Fischer, L., & Sheldon, A. An agency model for developing and co-
    ordinating psychiatric aftercare. *Hospital and Community Psychiatry*, 1980,
    31, 768–771.

Hersen, M., & Bellack, A. Social skills training for chronic psychiatric patients: Rationale, research findings and future directions. *Comprehensive Psychiatry*, 1976, *17*, 559–580.

Kessler, H. H. *The crippled and the disabled: Rehabilitation of the physically handicapped in the United States*. New York: Columbia University Press, 1935.

Pardes, H., & Pincus, H. A. Treatment in the seventies: A decade of refinement. *Hospital and Community Psychiatry*, 1980, *31*, 535–542.

Rusk, H. A. & Taylor, E. J. *New hope for the handicapped: The rehabilitation of the disabled from bed to job*. New York: Harper, 1949.

Skelley, T. National developments in rehabilitation: A rehabilitation services administration perspective. *Rehabilitation Counseling Bulletin*, 1980, *24*, 22–23.

Stern, R., & Mindoff, K. Paradoxes in programming for chronic patients in a community clinic. *Hospital and Community Psychiatry*, 1979, *30*, 613–617.

Stickney, S. K., Hall, R. C., & Gardner, E. R. The effect of referral procedures on aftercare compliance. *Hospital and Community Psychiatry*, 1980, *31*, 567–569.

Valle, S. Alcoholism counselor interpersonal functioning and patient outcome. *Journal of Alcohol Studies*, 1982.

Weinman, B., & Kleiner, R. J. The impact of community living and community member intervention on the adjustment of the chronic psychotic patient. In *Alternatives to mental hospital treatment*, ed. L. Stein and M. Test. New York: Plenum Press, 1978, 139–150.

Wright, B. A. *Physical disability: A psychological approach*. New York: Harper, 1960.

Wright, G. *Total Rehabilitation*. Boston: Little, Brown, 1980.

4

Independent Living: From Social Movement to Analytic Paradigm

Gerben DeJong

> A significant social movement becomes possible when there is a revision in the manner in which a substantial group of people, looking at some misfortune, see it no longer as a misfortune warranting charitable consideration but as an injustice which is intolerable in society.[1]

Future historians of American social policy will look back to 1973 as a year which separates 1 epoch of disability policy from another. That year Congress passed a new Rehabilitation Act, which set into motion a whole set of new initiatives affecting the nation's disabled population, particularly its most severely disabled citizens.

The most visible feature of the 1973 Rehabilitation Act is Section 504, a 1-sentence statement prohibiting discrimination against "otherwise qualified handicapped" individuals "under any program or activity receiving Federal financial assistance." Because of this section's far-reaching implications, the 1973 Rehabilitation Act has sometimes been dubbed "the Civil Rights Act of the Handicapped."

The 1973 Act cannot be fully understood apart from an emerging social movement: the independent living (IL) movement. Sparked with a high de-

From *Archives of Physical Medicine and Rehabilitation*, 60 (1979), 435–446. Reprinted by permission.

This study was supported in part by Medical Research & Training Center 7 of Tufts-New England Medical Center with funds from the Rehabilitation Services Administration, Office of Human Development, U.S. Department of HEW, Washington, DC (grant 16-P-57856/1-04). Updated and condensed from a paper presented at the 55th Annual Session of the American Congress of Rehabilitation Medicine, New Orleans, November 17, 1978, and disseminated by the University Centers for International Rehabilitation, Michigan State University, East Lansing, MI.

gree of indigenous leadership from among the disabled population, the movement seeks a better quality of life for disabled persons.

The IL movement is more than a grass-roots effort on the part of the disabled to acquire new rights and entitlements; it is also reshaping the thinking of disability professionals and researchers, has spawned new service-delivery models, and has encouraged new research directions.

This article evaluates independent living as a social movement and as an "analytic paradigm" that is redirecting the course of disability policy, practice, and research. As a paradigm, independent living is redefining the problem of disability and is encouraging new interventions that are in marked contrast to the definitions and interventions provided by its predecessor — the rehabilitation paradigm. But to gain an appreciation of the IL paradigm, it is necessary to understand independent living as a social movement with a distinct constituency and history. Moreover, the movement is heavily indebted to a variety of other contemporary social movements such as civil rights, consumerism, self-help, demedicalization/self-care, and deinstitutionalization. The significance of independent living for the future of disability practice and research cannot be understood apart from the contributions of these other movements.

THE CONSTITUENCY OF THE IL MOVEMENT

The IL movement has always counted the "severely disabled" as its primary target group or constituency. But who are the severely disabled? How many are there? One common method used to define and measure severe disability is the inability to work or to carry on one's major activity. Based on results from its 1974 Health Interview Survey, the National Center for Health Statistics[2] estimates that 3.3% (6.8 million) of the nation's population—about 0.2% of all children, 2.6% of all working-age adults, and 17.1% of all the elderly—are unable to carry on their major activity.

Core Constituency

However, the movement's core constituency is more limited than that suggested by these national data. The movement has concentrated its energies on a relatively few major disability groups: those with spinal cord injury, muscular dystrophy, cerebral palsy, multiple sclerosis, and postpolio disablement. Moreover, the IL movement has concentrated its energies on a selected age group: the older adolescent and younger working-age adult. The emphasis on this narrow age range is, in part, a function of the disabling conditions mentioned above. For example, spinal cord injury is most common among males during their late teens and early 20s when they are most likely to participate in disability-prone activities. Multiple sclerosis generally becomes evident during one's 20s. Cerebral palsy and muscular dystrophy are developmental disabilities and thus are already evident during childhood. Those with a postpolio disablement are the senior members of the movement.

The emphasis on the younger adult is also a function of the communities where the movement has taken root. The IL movement has been most active in large academic communities containing critical masses of university-age persons. Free from some of the more demanding familial and economic responsibilities, this age group is often better able to organize around major social issues.

Notably absent from the movement's constituency are older persons with severe physical impairments resulting from stroke or other degenerative conditions. While the movement's philosophy may have direct relevance to older disabled persons, the movement has focused its concern elsewhere. The movement's present age bias is one that cannot last indefinitely. Medical science is not only enabling severely disabled persons to survive initial trauma but is also enabling severely disabled persons to live longer. Thus, as the movement's initial adherents grow older, we can expect the movement to enlarge its present age focus.

Also absent from the movement's constituency and leadership are racial minorities. This is noteworthy, since disability statistics indicate that blacks have a higher prevalence of disability than do their white counterparts. The absence of racial minorities deserves special analysis. Given the similarities among the civil rights movement, the black movement, and the IL movement, one would expect the IL movement to attract disabled persons from racial minorities.

Disability Professionals and Special Interest Organizations

There is another part of the movement's constituency that deserves mention: disability professionals and special interest organizations. The disability professionals include physicians in physical medicine and rehabilitation, physical therapists, occupational therapists, nurses, rehabilitation counselors, and disability researchers. The commitment of these professionals to the movement varies widely, and generalizations cannot be made except that the movement is increasing its number of adherents. The special interest groups include organizations such as the National Spinal Cord Injury Foundation, the Easter Seal Society, and various professional associations. Again, the commitment of these organizations varies widely from chapter to chapter.

In defining the movement's constituency one should not overlook the overlap between disabled "consumers" and disability professionals. Many disabled persons are themselves disability professionals. The participation of able-bodied professionals in the movement can to some degree be explained by the influence and the consciousness-raising impact of their disabled professional peers.

The movement's strength comes, in part, from linking the interests of its primary disability groups with the interests of other disability groups on issues of common concern. The issue of architectural barriers, for example, is one that unites other mobility-impaired groups, even though its greatest effect is on the core disability groups represented in the IL movement. Coalition building through organizations such as the American Coalition of Citizens with Disabilities (ACCD) has enabled the movement to enlarge its constituency around specific issues.

Thus it can be seen that the movement's constituency is difficult to define. National survey data enable us to identify that portion of the population most likely to come within the scope of the movement's concern. We can identify a core constituency, but there are many other interested parties—professionals and special interest groups—who have come to recognize the movement and have joined forces to one degree or another (see Figure 2). Moreover, common interests with other disability groups enable the movement to extend its influence beyond the boundaries of the core disability groups.

The movement's constituency is defined not only by *who* participates but also by *what* it advocates. The constituency, in some respects, extends to others who do not actively participate but who nonetheless come under its consciousness-raising spell and thus become informal advocates of its philosophy and ideology.

ORIGINS AND LEGISLATIVE BACKGROUND

It is difficult to point to an exact time when or place where the IL movement began. The movement has sprung from 2 main sources: (1) the efforts of disabled persons to seek a more fulfilling life in an able-bodied world, and (2) the efforts of rehabilitation professionals to reach disabled persons for whom a vocational goal was, until recently, unthinkable. While the efforts of both groups often converge on specific legislation, their interests and origins are sufficiently different to warrant separate consideration.

Indigenous Origins

The disabled students program at the University of Illinois at Champaign-Urbana was among the first to facilitate community living for persons with

Figure 2. Constituency of the movement for independent living.

severe physical disabilities. In 1962, 4 severely disabled students were trans-
ferred from a campus-isolated nursing home to a modified home closer to
campus. The disabled students program has since emerged as a significant
self-help effort and has helped to make the University one of the most architecturally accessible institutions of its kind.

It was not until the early 1970s that the movement gained greater visibility and momentum with the creation of the Center for Independent Living (CIL) in Berkeley, California. The Berkeley CIL incorporated itself in
1972 as a self-help group, to be managed primarily by persons who were
themselves disabled. The Center provides a wide range of related services,
such as peer counseling, advocacy services, van transportation, training in
independent living skills, attendant care referral, health maintenance, housing referral, wheelchair repair, and others.[3,4] Unlike other centers that have
since emerged, the Berkeley CIL has no residential program and serves persons with a greater variety of disabling conditions than do many other existing centers.

On the East Coast, the Boston Center for Independent Living (BCIL)
began its activities in 1974. BCIL emphasizes transitional housing and attendant care services.[5] Similar centers and organizations have sprung up in
Houston, Columbus, Ann Arbor, and elsewhere. Each center offers its own
unique blend of advocacy and consumer services; together the various

centers have given the IL movement both an organizational focus and a vehicle for realizing some of the movement's more important goals.

The movement's organizational efforts have not been limited to centers for independent living. Allied organizations such as the ACCD, mentioned earlier, have been instrumental in monitoring federal legislation affecting disabled persons. The ACCD also helped to organize the coast-to-coast demonstrations that goaded the US Department of Health, Education and Welfare (HEW) to promulgate regulations implementing Section 504 of the 1973 Rehabilitation Act.

Professional Origins

Developing concurrently with the organizational initiatives of disabled persons were the efforts of rehabilitation professionals in the formulation of national legislation. In 1959, HR 361 was introduced, containing language that would extend IL services to individuals for whom employment was not an obtainable objective.[6,7] That attempt failed and in 1961 a new bill, written largely by the National Rehabilitation Association, was introduced. The new bill contained a separate title on IL services. That bill also failed.

If adopted, the 1961 bill would have authorized $15 million in the 1st year and $25 million in the 2nd year for IL rehabilitation services. The new title was to be administered by state vocational rehabilitation agencies. The reasons for Administration opposition to the bill are unclear but anecdotal evidence has it that HEW was unable to determine which of its component agencies should administer the new title.

The 1973 Rehabilitation Act

In 1972, Congress passed HR 8395, amending the Vocational Rehabilitation Act to provide IL services to those individuals "for whom a vocational goal is not possible or feasible." The bill was twice vetoed by the President on the grounds that it "would divert the [vocational rehabilitation] program from its basic vocational objectives" toward more ill-defined medical and welfare goals.[6] Eventually, the President did sign what became known as the 1973 Rehabilitation Act, albeit with the IL provisions deleted.

The 1973 Rehabilitation Act contained other breakthroughs important to the IL movement. First, it mandated that those who were most severely handicapped were to receive 1st priority for services under the Act. Second, Title V extended new statutory rights to handicapped persons. Sections 501 and 503 mandated affirmative action programs for the employment of disabled persons within the federal government and by organizations contracting with the federal government. Section 502 created the Architectural and Transportation Compliance Board. And Section 504 banned discrimination on the basis of handicap in any program or activity receiving or benefiting from federal financial assistance.

The 1978 Amendments

A statutory authorization for IL services finally came into being when President Carter signed PL 95-602 in 1978. This law created a new Title VII—"Comprehensive Services for Independent Living," which establishes a 4-part program: (1) an IL services program to be administered by the state vocational rehabilitation agencies; (2) a grant program for IL centers; (3) an IL program for older blind persons; and (4) a protection and advocacy program to guard the rights of severely disabled persons. Title VII authorizes $80 million for fiscal year 1979; $150 million for 1980; $200 million for 1981; and "such sums" in 1982. Given the Administration's current efforts to hold down federal spending, it is very unlikely that the amounts appropriated by Congress will approach authorized spending levels.

Differing Views of Independent Living

Two things need to be said about the concept of IL services as advocated by vocational rehabilitation professionals.

First, the concept of IL rehabilitation has changed since it was originally introduced to Congress almost 2 decades ago. Since then, medical and rehabilitation technology has advanced significantly. Those who would have been targeted for IL rehabilitation services 15 years ago are now routinely prepared for gainful employment by state vocational rehabilitation agencies.

Second, vocational rehabilitation professionals, as reflected in the legislation reviewed here, have a different conception of independent living than do their consumer counterparts in the IL movement. For many vocational rehabilitation professionals, IL services are for those for whom a vocational goal is thought to be impossible. Independent living is seen as an alternative to the vocational goal—thus, the term "independent living rehabilitation" as distinct from "vocational rehabilitation." IL rehabilitation refers to those medical and social services that enable a disabled person to live in the community short of being gainfully employed. From this perspective, independent living and rehabilitation are seen as competing policy goals. Throughout the history of the legislative debate on independent living, there has been the fear that independent living would dilute the specificity of the vocational outcome. Some professionals feared the IL services would result in the same charges of nonaccountability often levied against more ill-defined social services such as those administered under Title XX of the Social Security Act.

Others in the IL movement, whose involvement does not originate in the vocational rehabilitation tradition, reject the conception of independent living and employment as competing policy goals. To them, such a conception is potentially sinister in that it implicitly places an undesirable arbitrary upper limit to the goals a disabled person might set for himself; the vocational objectives should be seen as an integral part of the IL goal, not as a competing goal.

RELATION TO OTHER SOCIAL MOVEMENTS

The IL movement has flourished at a time when several other complementary social movements have also developed; these include:

- Civil rights
- Consumerism
- Self-help
- Demedicalization/self-care
- Deinstitutionalization/normalization/mainstreaming

While these movements share common values and assumptions, each arises from a somewhat different source in response to different social problems. Each has influenced the IL movement in its own unique way. The origins and ideology of the IL movement cannot be fully appreciated without also noting the contributions of other social movements.

Civil Rights

The civil rights movement of the 1960s has had an impact far beyond the racial minorities it sought to benefit. The movement made other disadvantaged groups aware of their rights and of how their rights were being denied. During the initial stages, the movement was mainly concerned with *civil* rights as opposed to *benefit* rights. Civil rights include the right to vote, to hold elective office, to be tried by a jury of one's peers, and so forth. Benefit rights include the entitlement to income and medical assistance benefits, educational benefits, and other entitlements. The benefit rights issue was taken up later in the civil rights movement by the Poor People's Campaign and by spin-offs such as the National Welfare Rights Organization.

The concern for both civil rights and benefit rights has spilled over to other vulnerable groups. In the area of mental health, patients have, in some instances, acquired the right to refuse treatment and to expect quality care. In the area of child welfare, children have acquired new procedural rights that are slowly replacing the best-interest-of-the-child rule as the legal standard for adjudicating abuse and delinquency cases. Moreover, children are receiving rights to treatment and education under special education statutes.

The IL movement has been similarly concerned with both civil and benefit rights. The movement's interest in civil rights is reflected in Title V of the 1973 Rehabilitation Act prohibiting various forms of discrimination, particularly in the area of employment. However, the concern for civil rights has not stopped there. Persons with severe mobility impairments are insisting that architectural barriers in effect deprive them of their civil rights when these barriers prevent them from participating in the political life of the community. In like fashion, disabled persons have become aware that their benefit rights are prerequisites for living in a community setting. Without income assistance benefits or attendant care benefits, many disabled persons would be involuntarily confined to a long-term care facility.

The civil rights movement has not only had an effect on the securing of certain rights, but also on the *manner* in which those rights have been secured. When traditional legal channels have been exhausted, disabled persons have learned to employ other techniques of social protest, such as demonstrations and sit-ins.

The black movement that eventually grew out of the civil rights movement has had its own effect on the IL movement. According to the critique offered by the civil rights movement, racial discrimination was an American anomaly that could largely be removed through the enactment of new legal protections. The black movement saw the issue as one of the racism that was central to the definition of white America and beyond the scope of simple legal remedies. The IL movement has come to recognize that prejudice against disability is rooted in our culture's attitudes about youth and beauty, and in the able-bodied person's fear of vulnerability to physical disability. The black movement has inspired the IL movement to search more deeply for the sources of attitudes and behavior toward persons with disabilities.

Consumerism

The parameters of the consumer movement are hard to define. It is a movement that affects nearly all social classes and groups. It is most personified by Ralph Nader, but also includes public interest lawyers representing various disadvantaged groups, and embraces both the person who devotedly reads *Consumer Reports* and the person who campaigns for new consumer protection legislation.

A more profitable venture here would be to briefly evaluate the movement in terms of its ideology and in terms of its expression in disability policy. Basic to consumerism is a distrust of seller or service provider. It is up to the consumer to become informed about product reliability or service adequacy. Consumer sovereignty has always been the hallmark of free market economic theory. In practice, however, it is often the professional who has been sovereign.

With the rise of consumer sovereignty, professional dominance in disability policy and rehabilitation is being challenged. In vocational rehabilitation, for example, the professional counselor does not necessarily have the final word in case planning as he/she once did. Instead, the Rehabilitation Act of 1973 provides for an "individualized written rehabilitation plan" (IWRP) to be drawn up jointly by client and counselor. Outside vocational rehabilitation, the IL movement has spawned new advocacy centers to advise disabled persons of their legal rights and benefits. With the awareness generated by the IL movement, the disabled person with several years of disability experience is often better informed about governmental benefits and regulations than his/her professional counterpart in the human services system.

The doctrine of consumer sovereignty, sometimes referred to as "consumer involvement," is now very much a fixture within the IL movement. The doctrine asserts that because disabled persons are the best judges of their own interests, they should have the larger voice in determining what services are provided in the disability services market.

Self-Help

The self-help movement embraces a large variety of groups, from the Female Improvement Society to Alcoholics Anonymous.[8] There now appears to be a self-help group for almost every conceivable human condition or problem—drugs, gambling, death, homosexuality, child abuse, women's health, old age, sex, neighborhood crime, cigarette smoking, childbirth, and of prime interest here, physical disability.[8-12] Such organizations view themselves as mutual aid groups that serve as adjuncts or as valid alternatives to established human service agencies.[8,13-16] They usually address problems and needs not dealt with by other institutions in society.

Among disabled persons, IL centers have become the primary self-help unit; they seek to serve both as an adjunct to the present human service system and as an alternative service provider. As an adjunct to the system, the centers at times serve as conduits for funding human services such as attendant care. As an alternative to the system, the centers may provide peer counseling and advocacy services not provided by mainline human service organizations.

The self-help movement is fueled by the same distrust of professionally dominated services as exists in consumerism. Self-help organizations are intended to give people the opportunity to exercise control over their own lives and services they use. They are the knowledge-giving, awareness-providing organizations that help to confer sovereignty on the consumer.

Demedicalization/Self-Care

"Demedicalization" is a trend that is challenging the dominance of medical professionals in selected spheres of human life. The trend is exemplified by well-known critics such as Ivan Illich,[17] who have expressed the concern that too many social problems and life conditions are being unnecessarily "medicalized."

Over the last several decades, an increasing number of behaviors considered sinful or criminal have come to be considered illnesses.[18-25] Alcoholism and mental disorders, for example, have been removed from the categories of sin or crime and are now labeled illnesses. Some have begun to call child abuse a "disease." Similarly, life events such as birth and death now almost always entail a considerable degree of medical intervention.

Many have begun to react to the excesses of medicalization and have urged that certain conditions and life events be demedicalized. One example is pregnancy and childbirth. Some urge that pregnancy be removed from the category of illness and that childbirth be supervised by a midwife rather than a physician. Another example is death.[26-29] "Death with dignity" is the phrase being used for allowing the terminally ill to die at home rather than in a hospital, wired to the latest array of monitoring devices.

Implicit in the argument for demedicalization is the assumption that individuals can and should take greater responsibility for their own health and medical care. In many ways, demedicalization is an extension of the self-help movement to the fields of health and medical care, and is so referred to in some quarters. The movement goes beyond the keep-fit, watch-your-weight, stop-smoking, and drink-less campaigns of the recent past. The self-care movement encourages people to administer their own treatment for minor health problems and to avert potential complications arising from chronic health conditions.

The IL movement is very much a partisan in the demedicalization/self-care debate. At issue for the IL movement is the extent to which the management of disability should remain under the aegis of the medical care system once medical stability has been substantially obtained. Today, most public policy with respect to disability requires some type of professional medical presence, whether in the acute stages of disability, in the determination of eligibility for income maintenance benefits, or in long-term institutional care. The IL movement asserts that much of this medical presence is both unnecessary and counterproductive.

Central to the goals of the IL movement is the belief that the management of medically stabilized disabilities is primarily a personal matter and only secondarily a medical matter. A constant medical presence in the lives of disabled persons is said to entail behavior on the part of both medical practitioners and patients that induces dependency and thus is in conflict with rehabilitation and IL goals.

The Medical Model

To understand how such behavior arises, it is helpful to turn to the concept of the "medical model," a loosely used concept that often varies with the context in which it is discussed. As used here, the medical model consists of the following assumptions and role expectations in the provision of medical care:

- The physician is the technically competent expert.
- Medical care should be administered through a chain of authority wherein the physician is the principal decision maker; accountability for the care of the patient is centered on the attending physician.
- The "patient" is expected to assume the "sick role" that requires him/her to cooperate with the attending medical practitioners.
- The main purpose of medicine is the provision of acute/restorative care.
- Illness is muted primarily through the use of clinical procedures such as surgery, drug therapy, and the "laying on of hands."
- Illness can be diagnosed, certified, and treated only by trained practitioners.

Like most models, this version of the medical model is a rather rigid construction of what is supposed to exist and happen in the provision of medical care. The model does not attempt to be exhaustive; it focuses primarily on those elements that can also help us understand what the demedicalization of disability is all about.

Before evaluating the role expectations of the medical model, it is worth noting some of the model's other features that have been unpalatable to the IL movement. One important reason for demedicalizing disability, the movement implicitly argues, is that many of the assumptions of the medical model do not fit or apply to the needs of disabled persons. For example, the model's emphasis on acute/restorative care is not in keeping with the needs of long-term disabled persons well beyond the acute phase. Likewise, once beyond the acute phase, and living independently, many disabled persons are not in need of surgery, drugs, or the laying on of hands that characterize clinical medicine. Moreover, experienced disabled persons often do not need the diagnostic, certification, or treatment services of medical professionals, since they have developed sufficient familiarity with the idiosyncrasies of their own condition to be able to do much of their own medical monitoring and treatment.

The Sick Role

The IL movement has been particularly critical of the behavioral expectations of the medical model as defined in the sick role, which, in this context, has a very specific meaning. This concept, originally formulated by Talcot Parsons,[30] is considered the single most important concept in medical sociology. By understanding its requirements we can gain a better insight into the position advocated by the IL movement.

The sick role consists of 2 interrelated sets of exemptions and obligations:

- A sick person is exempted from "normal" social activities and responsibilities, depending on the nature and severity of the illness.
- A sick person is exempted from any responsibility for his/her illness. He/she is not morally accountable for his/her condition and is not expected to become better by sheer will.

These exemptions are granted conditionally. In exchange,

- A sick person is obligated to define the state of being sick as aberrant and undesirable, and to do everything possible to facilitate his/her recovery.
- A sick person is obligated to seek technically competent help and to cooperate with the physician in getting well.

The sick role is intended to be a temporary one. But for the long-term or permanently disabled person there is no immediate recovery in the sense of being restored to one's original physical condition. Because the disability is often an irrevocable part of his/her existence, the disabled person, as a result of the sick role, begins to accept not only his/her condition but also his/her own very personhood as "aberrant" and "undesirable." Moreover, he/she begins to accept the dependency prescribed under the sick role as normative for the duration of his/her disability. Thus, the sick role removes from the disabled person the obligation to take charge of his/her own affairs.

The Impaired Role

This critique of the sick role is affirmed in the concept of the "impaired role" articulated by Gordon[31] and by Siegler and Osmond.[32] The impaired role is ascribed to an individual whose condition is not likely to improve and who is unable to meet the 1st requirement of the sick role, the duty to try to get well as soon as possible. Occupants of the impaired role have abandoned the idea of recovery altogether and have come to accept their condition and dependency as permanent. In the words of Siegler and Osmond,[32] the impaired role "carries with it a loss of full human status":

> ... the impaired role does not require the exertions of cooperating with medical treatment and trying to regain one's health, but the price of this idleness is a kind of second-class citizenship.

The impaired role is not a normative one or one prescribed by the medical model, but is a role a disabled person is allowed to slip into as the passage of time weakens the assumptions of the sick role.

The impaired role is fictionalized in Thomas Mann's Nobel Prize-winning *The Magic Mountain*,[33] a novel about patients living at the Berghof, an international tuberculosis sanitarium for the well-to-do. Here patients abandon the sick role for the impaired role. Siegler and Osmond's[32] description of the impaired role at the Berghof is informative:

> The impaired role has a lower status than the sick role, but in return for this childlike status, they are allowed to spend their days as children do, playing card games, taking up hobbies, having meals served to them, "playing" with each other, or, most often, doing nothing at all.

Mann's fictionalized account of the Berghof presents us with 1 variant of the impaired role as it is found in a particular institutional setting. His account provides a glimpse of the tendencies toward childlike dependency inherent in the impaired role.

The IL movement rejects the behavioral expectations created by both the sick role and its derivative, the impaired role, by saying that the disabled do not want to be relieved of their familial, occupational, and civic responsibilities in exchange for a childlike dependency. In fact, this "relief" is considered tantamount to denying the disabled their right to participate in the life of the community and their right to full personhood.

Deinstitutionalization/Mainstreaming/Normalization

The dependency-creating features of the medical model and the impaired role are most pronounced in institutional settings. Institutions are self-contained social systems that allow house staff and various practitioners to exercise a substantial measure of social control with little outside interference.

Prolonged institutionalization is known to have harmful effects:

> Patients are encouraged to follow instructions, rules and regulations. Compliance is highly valued, and individualistic behavior is discouraged. The "good"

patient is the individual who respectfully follows instructions and does not disagree with staff. On the other hand, the patient who constantly asks for a dime for the pay phone, a postage stamp, or a pass to leave the institution on personal business, tends to be treated as a nuisance or labeled "manipulative." Patients do not make their own appointments, keep their own medical charts, or take their own medications. Responsibility for these things is legally vested in the institution. Yet on the day of discharge, the patient is expected suddenly to assume control of his own health care and life decision making.[34]

The trend to deinstitutionalize is one that cuts across many disabling conditions. The best-known deinstitutionalization effort is the community mental health movement, which has allowed many individuals—often with the use of psychotropic drugs—to leave institutional confinement or remain in the community. Similar examples can be found in other areas such as geriatric care and juvenile correction.

The deinstitutionalization movement has been backed by the political argument that institutional care is expensive and that community care will save taxpayer money. Proof of this argument has been hard to establish, especially when studies overlook the ever-present tendency of institutions to increase utilization to meet capacity.

Severely physically disabled persons and their advocates are understandably latecomers to the deinstitutionalization thrust. Unlike mentally impaired persons or ex-offenders, their disability is more difficult to conceal. Moreover, the deinstitutionalization of the severely physically impaired requires substantial environmental or architectural modifications not required by others.

The IL movement has adopted many of the same money-saving arguments for deinstitutionalization used by other groups. The only problem is that many of these arguments are beginning to wear thin with representatives of the taxpaying public who have not witnessed any significant decrease in human service expenditures. As latecomers to the deinstitutionalization thrust, severely physically disabled persons are less likely to benefit from the money-saving argument. Public cynicism about deinstitutionalization may prove to be yet another barrier to independent living.

Closely related to the deinstitutionalization movement are the concepts of normalization and mainstreaming. These concepts have been discussed mainly in connection with developmentally disabled children and young adults. At one time it was thought that the interests of disabled children were best served by confining them to institutions or segregating them into special education classes. Now, the thinking is that a disabled child or young adult becomes more "normal" when "mainstreamed" with able-bodied counterparts. However, normalization goes beyond mere deinstitutionalization. According to Dybwad,[35] it assumes that

... normal on our earth is trouble and strife, trial and tribulation and the handicapped person has the right to be exposed to it. Normalization ... includes the
dignity of risk ...

Hence normalization takes deinstitutionalization a step further to include
the possibility of failure—a fact which the deinstitutionalization movement
has not always been prepared to accept.

The dignity of risk is what the IL movement is all about. Without the
possibility of failure, the disabled person is said to lack true independence
and the mark of one's humanity—the right to choose for good or evil.

INDEPENDENT LIVING AS AN ANALYTIC PARADIGM

Social movements eventually find their expression in public policy or professional practice. While neither policy nor practice may totally embrace
all the tenets of a movement's philosophy, a significant impact can be discerned. The IL movement is no different. We began our discussion by saying that independent living is more than a social movement seeking new
rights and entitlements for disabled persons, but is also having an impact
on disability professionals. The movement, as we said, is reshaping the manner in which the problem of disability is being defined and encouraging new
interventions. What we are witnessing in American disability policy is the
emergence of a new "paradigm" that is redirecting the thinking of disability professionals and researchers alike.

Kuhn's Conception of Paradigm

My use of the word paradigm is borrowed from Kuhn's oft-cited work, *The
Structure of Scientific Revolutions*.[36] As a historian of the natural sciences,
Kuhn observed that scientific facts did not emerge by simple accumulation
or evolution, but were the products of new ways of thinking—new scientific paradigms. Paradigms define reality for the scientist. They provide the
framework by which problems are identified and solved. A paradigm also
prescribes the technology needed to solve a given problem.

Kuhn's historical frame of reference is not only applicable to the natural
sciences but is appropriate to public policy and professional practice as well.
The concept of a paradigm can be useful here in helping to understand the
debate that has been precipitated by the IL movement.

Two other concepts are important in Kuhn's analytic frame of
reference. First is the concept of an *anomaly*—an event or observation that
cannot be adequately explained by the dominant paradigm of the time.

When a sufficient number of anomalies appear, a crisis is precipitated, and disaffected individuals begin to search for an alternative explanation or paradigm. Second is the concept of *paradigm shift*—when 1 paradigm is discarded for another. Anomalies do not automatically cause individuals to renounce 1 paradigm for another. A paradigm shift does not occur unless there is a new paradigm to replace the old. "[A] scientific theory is declared invalid only if an alternate candidate is available to take its place."[36] Both these concepts are useful to our inquiry here.

The Rehabilitation Paradigm

The dominant paradigm in disability policy today is the rehabilitation paradigm, which is evident in both medical and vocational rehabilitation. It could be argued that there are sufficient differences between medical and vocational rehabilitation to speak of 2 paradigms, but there are also a sufficient number of similarities to consider them as one. Since my main interest is to contrast rehabilitation and independent living as paradigms, the differences between medical and vocational rehabilitation are less important.

In the rehabilitation paradigm, problems are generally defined in terms of inadequate performance in activities of daily living (ADL) or in terms of inadequate preparation for gainful employment. In both instances, the problem is assumed to reside in the individual. It is the individual who needs to be changed. To overcome his/her problem, the disabled individual is expected to yield to the advice and instruction of a physician, a physical therapist, an occupational therapist, or a vocational rehabilitation counselor. The disabled individual is expected to assume the role of "patient" or "client." While the goal of the rehabilitation process is maximum physical functioning or gainful employment, success in rehabilitation is to a large degree determined by whether the patient or client complied with the prescribed therapeutic regime.

The Severely Disabled Person as an Anomaly

In recent years anomalies have appeared that cannot be explained by the rehabilitation paradigm. The most important anomaly was the fact that very severely physically disabled persons were achieving independence without the benefit of, or in spite of, professional rehabilitation. In fact, some were considered too disabled to significantly benefit from rehabilitation services. It became evident that cooperation with professional rehabilitation was not a prerequisite for independent living. As a result, an increasing number of individuals, particularly among the most severely disabled, have become disaffected and have sought an alternative paradigm.

The IL Paradigm

The IL paradigm has emerged, in part, as a response to the anomaly of the severely physically disabled person. According to the IL paradigm, the problem does not reside in the individual but often in the solution offered by the rehabilitation paradigm—the dependency-inducing features of the physician-patient or professional-client relationship. Rehabilitation is seen as part of the problem, not the solution. The locus of the problem is not the individual but the environment that includes not only the rehabilitation process but also the physical environment and the social control mechanisms in society-at-large. To cope with these environmental barriers, the disabled person must shed the patient or client role for the consumer role. Advocacy, peer counseling, self-help, consumer control, and barrier removal are the trademarks of the IL paradigm (see Table 2).

Although the IL paradigm is now well beyond the embryonic stage of development, the rehabilitation paradigm remains strong. We can expect the IL paradigm to strengthen as movement leaders continue to refine its basic principles. In this period of paradigm shift, we see individuals with loyalties to both paradigms. There are some rehabilitation professionals who have introduced IL concepts within their practice but have not totally abandoned the rehabilitation paradigm for the IL paradigm. This analysis differs somewhat from Kuhn's.[36] He argues that "[the] decision to reject one paradigm is always simultaneously the decision to accept another." The analysis here suggests that the shift or transition to another paradigm is not necessarily abrupt or exclusive.

Table 2. *Comparison of Rehabilitation and Independent Living Paradigms*

Item	Rehabilitation Paradigm	Independent Living Paradigm
Definition of problem	Physical impairment/ lack of vocational skill	Dependence on professionals, relatives, etc.
Locus of problem	In individual	In environment; in the rehab. process
Solution to problem	Professional intervention by physician, physical therapist, occupational therapist, voc. rehab. counselor, etc.	Peer counseling Advocacy Self-help Consumer control Removal of barriers
Social role	Patient/client	Consumer
Who controls	Professional	Consumer
Desired outcomes	Maximum ADL Gainful employment	Independent living

Implications for Disability Research

Paradigms not only define problems and the range of appropriate interventions; they also determine what is relevant for purposes of research. Kuhn holds that there is no such thing as research in the absence of any paradigm. Underlying each paradigm is a theory of causation spelling out the relevant set of dependent and independent variables.

In traditional rehabilitation research, the emphasis has been on outcomes such as gains in carrying out ADL, mobility, and employment. The intervening variables thought to be critical have generally centered around patient/client characteristics and various kinds of rehabilitation therapies. Patient/client characteristics typically include age, sex, physical impairment, and the psychological makeup of the individual. The inclusion of these characteristics reflects the assumption in rehabilitation research that the problem to be addressed resides in the individual. The issue for rehabilitation research is not whether rehabilitation works, but which therapy or intervention works best for which groups of patients or clients.

Independent living as a paradigm of research has only begun to emerge. Much of the research incorporating IL concepts has yet to find its way into the published literature. Nonetheless, given the values and assumptions posited by the IL movement, we can at least begin to identify some of the variables considered relevant for research.

The theory of causation implicit in the IL paradigm asserts that environmental barriers are as critical as, if not more so than, personal characteristics in determining disability outcomes. This theory of causation is implicit in Trieschmann's[37] conceptual framework attempting to explain the behavior and outcomes of spinal cord injured persons. Trieschmann hypothesizes that behavior is the function of 3 sets of variables — person variables, organic variables, and environmental variables, as shown in Table 3. According to Trieschmann,[37,38] disability research must give more consideration to the effect of environmental variables, and their impact measured by psychological tests "have not accounted for a large proportion of the variance in behavior."[38] Her list of environmental variables is not exhaustive but does illustrate the research directions proposed by the IL paradigm.

Moreover, the IL paradigm differs from its rehabilitation counterpart in defining outcome variables relevant for research. While rehabilitation has stressed the importance of self-care, mobility, and employment, independent living has emphasized a larger constellation of relevant outcomes. In addition to the 3 outcomes considered desirable in rehabilitation, independent living has emphasized the importance of living arrangements, consumer assertiveness, outdoor mobility, and out-of-home activity. In some instances the IL paradigm would reject the significance of self-care as an outcome variable. The fact that a disabled person needs more assistance from a

Table 3. Trieschmann's Hypothesis of Behavior Functions
in Spinal Cord Injury $(B = f(P \times O \times E))$

P = Person Variables	E = Environmental Variables	O = Organic Variables
Repertoire of habits	Hospital milieu	Age
Personality style	Stigma value of disability	Severity of disability
Types of Rewards	Family and interpersonal	Medical complications
Internal versus	support	Congenital anomalies
external locus of	Financial security	Strength
control	Social milieu	Endurance
Method of coping	Urban versus rural residence	
with stress	Access to medical attention	
Self-image	and equipment repair	
Creativity	Access to educational,	
	recreational, and	
	avocational pursuits	
	Socioeconomic status	
	Architectural barriers and	
	availability of	
	transportation	
	Legislation	
	Cultural and ethnic	
	influences	

human helper does not necessarily imply that he/she is more dependent. If a person can get dressed in 15 minutes with human assistance and then be off for a day of work, that person is more independent than the person who takes 2 hours to dress and remains homebound.

The challenge for disability researchers is to operationalize the concepts introduced by the IL paradigm. In particular, we need to operationalize both the outcomes and intervening variables deemed important by the IL paradigm. In terms of outcomes we need to identify and weight a set of variables that are most reflective of IL values. In terms of intervening environmental barriers we need to define meaningful measures of environmental constraint.

One might ask whether the consideration of environmental variables belabors the obvious. "Ask any disabled person," one might say. While the importance of environmental variables appears to be self-evident, we are not certain about the relative contribution of each environmental constraint in explaining IL outcomes. Nor do we know the collective importance of these environmental variables relative to individual characteristics. We need to go beyond mere statistical significance to show what percentage of the variance in outcome can be explained by variables considered important by the IL paradigm.

But there is a more important reason to consider the impact of environmental variables. There is a growing public debate about the extent to which society should subsidize the removal of environmental constraints — inaccessible public transportation, architectural barriers, unmet personal care needs, and others. If it can be empirically demonstrated that these barriers are predictive of disability outcome, then the IL movement will be considerably strengthened in making its case before various public forums.

Environmental variables, unlike individual characteristics, can be rectified through legislative and administrative action. In his follow-up study of spinal cord injured veterans, Eggert, in an unpublished dissertation, makes this observation:

> Environmental and individual characteristics . . . have qualitatively different degrees of potential manipulation. Demographic characteristics such as age, sex, and race cannot be altered. Other individual characteristics, such as degree of independence in ADL are subject to slight modification through a program of physical therapy. The nature and level of veterans benefits, an environmental variable, is subject to drastic alteration by the stroke of a pen on a piece of federal legislation.[39]

Traditional rehabilitation research that belabors the significance or insignificance of individual patient/client characteristics has little policy relevance — and in many instances, has little clinical relevance as well. As a paradigm of research, independent living offers us an opportunity to steer away from the myopic preoccupation with unalterable individual characteristics that divert our attention from the larger institutional and environmental context in which disabled people live. The institutional and environmental context has for too long been accepted as given.

THE FUTURE

In a mere 7 years, the IL movement has grown from a small band of disabled persons struggling for simple rights to a significant political force shaping the future of disability policy. With its meteoric rise, can we predict how the movement is likely to shape the future of disability policy? Can we predict what the movement will look like in another decade? While these questions cannot be answered directly, we can discern some trends and issues.

The Role of the IL Paradigm

The concept of paradigm can be useful in predicting how the IL movement is likely to affect disability policy. Paradigms are more than analytic frames of reference; they also serve important latent social functions. They prepare students, scholars, and practitioners for membership in a particular discipline, help to define the boundaries of professional practice, and help to confer legitimacy upon professional groups.

Up until now the field of disability policy (for physically impaired persons) has been the captive of the rehabilitation paradigm and rehabilitation professionals whose limited frame of reference in many ways narrowed the options available to disabled persons. The emphasis on one-to-one clinical practice often excluded the contributions of other disciplines. By broadening the problem of disability to include a wide variety of environmental variables, the IL paradigm is opening the field of disability policy to other disciplines. The emphasis on rights and entitlements is encouraging the participation of legal professionals; the matter of architectural barriers is stimulating new interest on the part of architects; and the problem of work disincentives arising from various public assistance programs is sure to invite economists who have plowed similar ground in income transfer programs geared to nondisabled groups.

Furthermore, the infusion of new perspectives precipitated by the IL movement will undoubtedly invigorate the field of rehabilitation and enlarge its awareness of related areas. For example, it may lead vocational rehabilitation counselors to learn more about the rest of the human service system with resulting benefit to their clientele.

The Role of Able-Bodied Persons

One of the most vexing issues in the future will be the role of able-bodied persons in the movement. In some quarters, there are strong feelings that only disabled "consumers" should hold the majority of leadership positions. The issue is reminiscent of the civil rights movement when whites were asked to relinquish their leadership roles in black-advocacy organizations. The debate on this issue is likely to intensify over the next few years. The issue of consumer involvement will become less controversial as able-bodied persons begin to realize the significant role they have outside movement organizations, especially in the development of public policy affecting disabled persons.

Another unresolved issue is the question of who is a "consumer." This question is particularly relevant to parents of disabled children. Parents have often identified themselves as surrogate consumers on behalf of their children. The movement has been somewhat antiparent, since parents of disabled children often perpetuate childhood dependency into adult life. The movement has often viewed parents as a major barrier to independent living.

New Legislation

The new authorizations for IL services under PL 95-602 present both opportunities and risks for the movement. The new law gives an opportunity to strengthen existing IL programs and to extend IL services to parts of the nation where none exist. The new law also affirms the political credibility of the movement. The risk is that new funding could bureaucratize the movement and blunt its cutting edge as it becomes involved in organizational maintenance activities at the expense of advocacy. Moreover, IL funds may be diverted into activities that are only marginally associated with independent living, thus diluting the meaning of what independent living is all about. Finally, since new funding will come through the Rehabilitation Act, there is the danger that the movement may become a captive of the rehabilitation establishment.

We can also expect new legislation on other fronts. Legislation has been pending in the Congress to remove certain work disincentives for disabled persons receiving benefits under the Social Security Disability Insurance and the Supplemental Security Income programs. Disincentives under these programs are most serious for severely disabled persons, who not only lose their income benefits but also their related medical and social service benefits when becoming gainfully employed. If passed, the legislation should enable many disabled persons to become more independent through gainful employment. As of this writing, it appears likely that Congress will pass some legislation in this area. This problem has been in existence for some time and has compromised the ability of state vocational rehabilitation agencies to move severely disabled persons toward gainful employment. Yet, rehabilitation professionals have, until recently, ignored the disincentives problem as a serious disability policy issue—even though the disincentives facing disabled persons have been far more serious than those facing persons participating in other more controversial welfare programs. The disincentives issue illustrates how the IL movement may liberate the formation of disability policy from the assumptions that have governed the rehabilitation establishment.

CONCLUSIONS

The IL movement represents a new chapter in American disability policy. Considering its brief history, its accomplishments in legislation, services, and raising of consciousness have been truly remarkable. But the movement has only begun. We can expect it to reach out to new disability groups and to enlarge its base as its initial adherents grow older. We can also expect it to produce a growing and sophisticated disability literature as it continues to redefine its concepts, programs, and services.

The movement's most significant contribution is that it has given disabled persons a voice in their own future and has fostered a new sense of dignity and pride that for too long has been denied them. This will continue to be its most important contribution in the years to come.

REFERENCES

1. Turner R: The theme of contemporary social movements, BR J Soc, 20 December, 1969, p 321
2. National Center for Health Statistics: Health characteristics of persons with chronic activity limitations, United States, 1974; Vital and Health Statistics Series 10 No. 112; DHEW Publication No. (HRA) 77-1539. Washington, D.C.: U.S. Department of Health, Education and Welfare, October, 1976, p 11
3. Brown BM: Second generation: West Coast. Am Rehabil, 3, July–August, 1978, p 24
4. Stoddard S: Independent living: Concepts and programs. Am Rehabil, 3, July–August, 1978, pp 2–3
5. Corcoran P, Fay F, Bartels E, McHugh R: The BCIL report. Peter Reich, ed. Boston; Tufts-New England Medical Center, Rehabilitation Institute, July, 1977
6. Urban Institute: Report of the Comprehensive Needs Study. Washington, D.C.: U.S. Department of Health, Education and Welfare, Office of Human Development, RSA, June 23, 1975, pp 4–10
7. Parsons MC, Counts R: Historical development of the independent living movement. Omaha, Nebraska: mimeo, May, 1978, pp 1–6
8. Withorn A: To serve the people: An inquiry into the success of service delivery as a social movement strategy. Unpublished dissertation, Brandeis University, Waltham, Massachusetts, 1977
9. Back KW, Taylor, RC: Self-help groups: tool or symbol. J Appl Beh Sci, 12, July–August–September, 1976
10. Hurwitz N: The origin of the peer self-help psychotherapy group movement. J Appl Beh Sci, 12, July–August–September, 1976
11. Levy LH: Self-help groups: types and psychological processes. J Appl Beh Sci, 12, July–August–September, 1976
12. Reissman F: How does self-help work? Soc Pol, 7, September–October, 1976
13. Durman EC: The role of self-help in service provision. J Appl Beh Sci, 12, July–August–September, 1976
14. Levin L: Self-care: An international perspective. Soc Pol, 7, September–October, 1976
15. Sidel VW, Sidel R: Beyond coping. Soc Pol, 7, September–October, 1976
16. Tax S: Self-help groups: Thoughts on public policy. J Appl Beh Sci, 12, July–August–September, 1976
17. Illich I: Medical Nemesis: The Expropriation of Health. New York, Random House, 1976
18. Coe RM: Sociology of Medicine. New York, McGraw-Hill, 1976
19. Fox RC: Illness. International Encyclopedia of Social Sciences, New York, The Free Press, 1968
20. Fox RC: The medicalization and demedicalization of American society. Doing Better and Feeling Worse: Health in the United States, John H. Knowles, ed. New York, W. W. Norton, 1977
21. Freidson E: Profession of Medicine: A Study of the Sociology of Applied Knowledge. New York, Dodd, Mead, 1970
22. Mechanic D: Health and illness in technological societies. Hasting Center Studies, 1, Number 3, 1973

23. Pitts J: Social control. International Encyclopedia of Social Sciences, New York, The Free Press, 1968
24. Twaddle AC: Illness and deviance. Soc Sci Med, 7, 1973
25. Zola I: Medicine as a system of social control. A Sociology of Medical Practice, C. Cox and A. Mead, eds. London, Collier-Macmillan, Ltd., 1975
26. Blauner R: Bureaucraticization of modern death control. Psych 29, 1966
27. Buckingham RW: Living with dying. Can Med Assoc J, 115, 1976
28. Kalish RA: The aged and the dying process: The inevitable decisions. J Soc Iss, 21 October, 1965
29. Kron J: Designing a better place to die. New York Magazine, March 1, 1976
30. Parsons T: The Social System. Glencoe, IL, The Free Press, 1951, pp 428–79
31. Gordon G: Role Theory and Illness: A Sociological Perspective. New Haven, College and University Press, 1966
32. Siegler M, Osmond H: The sick role revisited. Hasting Center Studies, 1, Number 3, 1973
33. Mann T: The Magic Mountain. New York, Random House, 1927
34. Corcoran P: Annual progress report. Boston, Medical Rehabilitation Research and Training Center No 7, Tufts-New England Medical Center, 1978, pp 60–70
35. Dybwad G: Is normalization a feasible principle of rehabilitation? Models of Service for the Multihandicapped Adult. New York, United Cerebral Palsy of New York City, 1973, p 57
36. Kuhn T: The Structure of Scientific Revolutions. Chicago, University of Chicago Press, 1970, p 77
37. Trieschmann RB: The psychological, social, and vocational adjustment in spinal cord injury: A strategy for future research—final report. Los Angeles, Easter Seal Society, April 30, 1978
38. Trieschmann RB: The psychological, social, and vocational adjustment in spinal cord injury: A strategy for future research—executive summary. Los Angeles, Easter Seal Society, April 30, 1978
39. Eggert G: Post rehabilitation experience of a population of spinal cord injured veterans. Unpublished dissertation, Brandeis University, Waltham, Massachusetts, 1973

Part II

Disability:
The Child and the Family

Disability may be present congenitally, or it may be acquired at any time during the life span of a person. Part II focuses on the impact of disability on children, adolescents, and families. In addition, suggestions are presented for rehabilitation and therapeutic interventions.

In a chapter focusing upon socialization, Battle examines the dynamic relationship between the young child with a handicap and significant others. Emphasis is upon the relationship of the child with the mother and upon the important developmental tasks to be acquired by children with handicaps. In addition, alternatives to overcoming social barriers are suggested.

The developmental tasks of adolescence, primarily individuation and sexual identity, and problems in their attainment for handicapped youth are the major themes of Chapter 6 by Goldberg. Rehabilitation programs that have been designed for adolescents, with attention to their unique problems, are recommended and reviewed.

The final chapter in Part II, by Versluys, is a comprehensive analysis of the dynamics of the family engaged in the process of physical rehabilitation of a family member. Presenting a developmental approach, this article explores stages of adjustment, critical issues, and counseling guidelines that are helpful for those working with families of the disabled.

5

Disruptions in the Socialization of a Young, Severely Handicapped Child

Constance U. Battle

In addition to the usual developmental tasks, a handicapped child must make unique, complex adjustments to himself, to his handicapping condition, and to his immediate world. It is likely that a few of the additional burdens he faces include the adjustment to numerous medical examinations and hospitalizations, and an exposure to a larger-than-usual group at an early age for evaluation of his condition. Other adjustments must be made to parents and to a world disturbed about his condition, people who may be curious or ridicule him. Finally, part of coping involves acceptance of his functional limitations, his state of dependency, constant frustration in attempting tasks and in communicating, and occasionally physical discomforts from procedures, treatments, immobility, and changes as a result of physical growth and development. The effects of a physical handicap influence all aspects of the child's growth and development, all areas of his life.

Richardson[24] alludes to the commonly held but erroneous concept of a neat, single effect of disability. A physical disability may in fact impair not only motor functioning but also one or several of other functional capacities — sensory, intellectual, behavioral, and social. Although the most obvious handicap of a child with cerebral palsy might be in the area of gross motor disability (for example, his inability to walk), he may also have equally significant or worse problems resulting from sensory impairment, so that he does not appreciate where his leg is; or he may have poor depth perception, or difficulty chewing, or speaking, or attending to someone. What often happens, unfortunately, is that all efforts to restore or maximize function of the child are focused on the system most involved or the most easily assessed system.

The handicapped child, it is clear, is prevented from taking part in the

From *Rehabilitation Literature*, 35(5) (1974), 130–140. Copyright© 1974 by the National Easter Seal Society for Crippled Children and Adults. Reprinted by permission of the Editor.

normal course of human interaction that comprises the process of socialization of any child because of two barriers or obstacles. The first barrier results from the *physiological limitations* inherent in the condition, e.g., the child can't walk or can't talk. The second barrier is a consequence of the *psychological and social limitations* on the part of the child himself as a result of the blunting effects of a handicap mentioned by Richardson,[26] and a consequence as well of the spontaneous illogical, negative reactions on the part of others (normal) to the child with a handicap, his different appearance and behavior. Some like Shaffer[34] believe that evidence suggests that it is unlikely that social attitudes toward the handicaps and deformities of cerebral-palsied children contribute to the frequency of psychiatric disturbances shown by them. More plausible to him is the likelihood that brain injury in some children may result in a deficiency of social perception, which may in turn distort the child's pattern of social interactions. Richardson's viewpoint[26] represents, perhaps, the middle ground, since he does consider the intrinsic and extrinsic blunting effects of a handicapping condition of a child and has studied with others in considerable detail the attitudes of normal boys and girls to handicapped children, and to handicapping conditions in abstract considerations.[13,25,27,29] The findings of M. O. Shere's study[37] of 30 twin pairs (one twin had cerebral palsy, the other did not) suggest that the condition of cerebral palsy does not necessarily cause social and emotional maladjustment. The parental behavior toward the child was found instead to be instrumental in setting the pattern of the child's behavior.

The purpose of this paper will be to review certain aspects of both categories of barriers that interfere with normal socialization from the moment of birth through the beginning of the school years, the time period to be discussed here. A child with profound neuromuscular impairment, such as seen in cerebral palsy, will be considered as an example, since his impairment presents one of the most global handicapping conditions seen in childhood. From this point on, the term *handicap* will be used with the distinctions set forth by Susser and Watson.[39]*

THE SOCIALIZATION PROCESS IN THE INFANT

A brief review of some fundamental aspects of the process of socialization in the normal child will be presented, along with indications of points where disruptions in that process in the life of a child with a handicap might

---

*Susser and Watson distinguish three components of *handicap*: organic, functional, and social. *Impairment* is the organic component, a static condition of the process of disease. *Disability* is the functional component, or the limitation of function imposed by the impairment and the individual's psychological reaction to it. *Handicap* is the social component, the manner and degree in which the primary impairment and functional disability limit the performance of social roles and relations with others. It is this third component that most closely suits the purposes of this paper.

occur. A definition of *socialization* cited by McNeil[20] from a psychological dictionary by English and English will suit the purposes of this paper well:

> socialization: the process whereby a person (esp., a child) acquires sensitivity to social stimuli (esp., the pressures and obligations of group life) and learns to get along with, and to behave like, others in his group or culture; the process of becoming a social being. . . .[8]

Kagan[15] presents a similar, fuller definition, indicating in detail which behaviors and values are socialized. It will become clear that both the mandatory relationships (parental) in the first years of life and the voluntary social relationships from age three through the school years are influenced significantly by the existence of a physical disability.

Harriet Rheingold[22] has put forth several assertions about the normal newborn infant contrary to those generally held, in maintaining that the human infant begins life as a social organism, that he socializes others more than he is socialized, and that he behaves in a social fashion while very young. These assertions would also seem to hold true for the handicapped newborn. The infant is a social being by biological origin, since he is in contact with other organisms from the moment of birth. He is at the very least a member of a dyad composed of himself and his mother and is probably a member of a much larger group. Assuming that the handicapped child is not ill as a newborn, i.e., is normal and well except for the handicapping condition, then at least one member of the dyad, the mother, is in disequilibrium during the perinatal time. The mother is experiencing shock, deep sadness, depression, guilt, anger, embarrassment, revulsion, personal responsibility, uncertainty about personal worth and about managerial ability because her creative products are defective.[9,14,16,19,21,31,38] The ritual surrounding the child's birth may be upset. The family cancels religious or family celebrations because of their distress or their sense of embarrassment. The larger group may stay away because of their own sense of embarrassment or uneasiness about seeing the baby, about "what to say," "how to act." The larger social group around the handicapped child as a newborn, then, may be "restricted" by the wishes of the larger group itself or the wishes of the family. Richardson[24] points out that there are no generally known alternative patterns of behavior for use by the family of the newborn handicapped child during the weeks immediately after birth.

The assertions of H. Rheingold alluded to above are qualified to apply to infants during the first year of life or so, until that time when effortless locomotion is achieved. Since the handicapped child under consideration will never achieve locomotion, one may perhaps translate these observations to the handicapped child. The newborn infant and the young handicapped child are much alike in several ways. They are both totally dependent on others, since they cannot locomote, cannot grasp an object, and thus can do little if anything for themselves. Such infants must be fed, cleaned, moved, stimulated not to fret, protected from danger. During the first year of life, society does not expect the infant to acquire any social skills. He is not expected to cooperate, to be altruistic, or to demonstrate behavior appropriate to his sex. There is another similarity, since society most likely does not expect acquisition of social skills of the handicapped child either, and he perhaps senses this attitude. Not only is he slow in acquiring social skills in managing relationships with normal persons, but their treatment of him also can retard the socialization process.

It must be noted, even when one is trying to stress that the infant is a socializer, that the infant's behavior is modified by what social encounters he has. The infant is socialized and is responsive to people because they have become associated with satisfactions resulting from certain care-taking operations. His social behavior, in turn, has been reinforced by the responses of people to his responses to them. One can compare this aspect of socialization in the handicapped child. If the handicapped child is easily cared for, then even the most profoundly physically impaired child can be socialized to this degree. If, on the other hand, it is difficult in the first few months for the mother, particularly if the handicapped child is a first baby, to feed the infant, to cuddle him, to get him to sleep, to position him, to keep him entertained, to learn to respond to his cues successfully, there is the likelihood that the handicapped child and his mother will be socializing one another on this elementary or basic level but not in a desirable fashion.

Commenting on the lack of studies of mother-child interaction in the earliest days of life, Campbell[3] suggested that sucking might be a suitable measure of the mother-child relationship, since it has been studied extensively and is recognized as varying with external stimuli. Food intake is known to be influenced by maternal handling. Each infant and mother must acquire sucking and feeding skills, respectively, and can influence or modify the behavior of the other significantly. The handicapped child with severe cerebral palsy has poor sucking, swallowing, and feeding mechanisms, never allowing the mother to acquire skill in feeding him. Feeding her infant successfully is one skill that a mother views as central to her "mothering" process. The mother may be puzzled or even frightened by her infant's behavior patterns, which she recognizes are not normal. Adding to her uneasiness is the expectation of society that this time should be a rewarding one for mother and child. At this time another reason for the uneasiness of the mother of a handicapped child occasionally seen may be the mother's observation that there is some other person (a grandmother, friend, or baby-sitter) who is essentially not emotionally involved and who is the only person who can make her difficult child feel totally satisfied or who has some success in feeding him.

Freeman[11] noted that the rhythmicity of certain functions may not be so readily established in the handicapped child and may further interfere with smooth mother-child interaction. Certain characteristics manifested as personality traits, but which may be a direct consequence of the handicapping condition, such as excessive passivity or placidity, or restlessness and demanding behavior, may bother some mothers in a child's first year of life. When she is bothered, the mother's response to her infant's responses may be negative.[36] The handicapped infant will sense his world as chaotic, uncomfortable, unsatisfying, inconsistent as a consequence, at that time in life when the normal child is developing a sense of basic trust that his needs will be met. Other external disruptions to the socialization process in the first year occur when the handicapped child has to be hospitalized for any acute illness, or diagnostic or therapeutic procedures necessitated by the handicapping condition. The hospitalization results in two traumatic experiences for the infant: separation from the mother, and exposure to various frightening and painful experiences.

Many of the disruptions to the socialization process have been alluded to above. Each one of these disruptions interferes in itself with the infant's ability to socialize and be socialized. Not only do such factors as the mother's not being able to cuddle the baby interfere with his socialization process, but her fatigue from the stress and the additional attention and care needed by the child as a result of the physical impairment prevent her from devoting time and energy to the child's intellectual and social development. A study conducted in Israel revealed that characteristically both *distant* and *involved* mothers of severely handicapped children with cerebral palsy overlooked the role they should play in providing their child with sufficient opportunities for object-contact in their child's cognitive development.[35] These mothers of children who had outgrown the infancy phase, but yet were as helpless as very young infants, did not provide toys or other objects for play, or did not place toys where they could be reached easily.

A dramatic example of how a multihandicapping condition in an infant can disturb the mother-child relationship has been presented by Freedman and others,[10] who reviewed the first 18 months of life of a baby multihandicapped due to maternal rubella. Since the mother of this infant had three earlier successful experiences in rearing her first three sons, it was reasonable to assume that she was able to operate effectively in the "average" expectable mother-child relationship. She was not, however, prepared for the complications of the task of mothering a rubella baby. Since the infant's condition was considered contagious for a while, his care fell exclusively on her. The infant showed a tendency for particular postures. As a result, it was difficult to carry, not to mention cuddle, a baby who persisted in keeping his head retracted and his back arched. As is the usual case when multiple systems are affected, he experienced a decrease in environmental stimulation, which did, in fact, result in sensory deprivation. In addition to having an absolute reduction and qualitative alteration of sensory input due to defective end organs, he was also ill much of the time and was difficult to feed as well as to handle.

Not only was the neonatal period frustrating for his mother, but as he grew older his problems required a proportion of the mother's time considerably greater than what she had spent on the other children at his age. Because of poor feeding, she had to feed him round the clock every three hours for the first three months of his life. It was necessary for her to hold him to nurse until he was 14 months of age. At 18 months of age, he still had to be held in his mother's lap to be fed solids. At the time of the report, the mother was taking him twice a week to various medical clinics, which were part of the rubella program where they lived.

Although, as is readily seen, the mother spent a great deal of time with the child, it was clear to the observers that the care of this child was carried out in a perfunctory manner. She was described as willing to attempt what the professional team asked of her. When the child failed to respond to her ministrations or opposed them with irritation, she was quickly discouraged. Much was done *for him,* but little *with him,* according to Freedman. The child's response to his mother's attention provided the mother with no incentive to act otherwise. Well in advance of his first birthday, the mother characterized the child as one of those children who don't like to be bothered. This fact was verified by the observers.

Such a single example is dramatic. It is likely that a similar situation of parent-child interaction when the child is severely handicapped is not at all so unique or uncommon. In this instance the child had a significant degree of mental retardation superimposed upon his many complicated system malformations and dysfunctions. It is quite possible for the identical picture to exist in a child with a severe handicapping condition in whom there is no mental retardation or only slight mental retardation, and consequently the potential exists for some degree of normal socialization.

A normal infant, especially if he is the first child, socializes his parents in two obvious ways: He causes definite rearrangement of the parents' psychological world, as well as a rearrangement of the family's living quarters. Becoming a parent emotionally causes marked psychological shifts. Acquisition of baby furniture and finding an undisturbed spot for the baby to sleep cause shifts of equal magnitude in the physical world of the family. The baby profoundly affects the parts of the mental lives of the parents that hold their wishes, dreams, and fears about his future appearance, health, intellect, and personality, and about the extent to which he will fulfill their expectations. This process is intensified when the child is handicapped, and the parents' psychological extension in the child is thwarted.

In addition, Richardson[24] points out that when a physical abnormality is identified at birth there is some evidence that the parents' initial attention to the baby's bodily appearance and functions will be enormously intensified as well by constantly looking at the baby, talking abou the problems, and attempting to cover up the problem. It is suggested that this preoccupation may provide a reason for avoiding a more human relationship with the child, or it may result from feelings of guilt for having produced a handicapped child.

The normal infant's powerful socializers are his smile, his cry, and to a lesser extent his vocalizations. Noting that one frequently observes "answering" social and, in particular, vocal play between mother and child, Rheingold and others[23] investigated whether the adults' responses may therefore play an important part in maintaining and developing social responsiveness in the child. The results of this study of 21 infants with a median age of 3 months suggest that the social vocalizing of infants and, more generally, their social responsiveness may be modified by the responses adults make to them. The smile is a delight to the parents. The cry has been called a social signal by which the infant insures his own survival. Since the cry is so aversive, originated by the infant, it cannot be ignored. If the handicapped child or child with a birth injury cries excessively or with a disturbing, high-pitched cry or cannot be comforted, the mother-child relationship is further distorted. Vocalizations also have importance as the beginnings of speech, an additional tool in the service of socialization. The infant up to a year, until he begins to walk, is somewhat helpless physically, not socially, as has been demonstrated.

Socially, the handicapped infant as well as the normal infant is responsive to and initiates social response from others. He also has three powerful tools: the smile, the cry, and the contented babbling, to insure that his needs are met. Unlike the normal child, the handicapped child may remain at this stage much longer, for several or all his years. Current social-psychological theory of behavioral exchange suggests that the single most powerful reinforcer in social interaction is social approval. The assumption has been made here that the parents truly love their handicapped child but have difficulty in relating to him for the various reasons mentioned. Of course, the problem becomes severe if the parents withhold their love or withdraw their love, acknowledged as the most powerful socializing agent there is during early childhood.

It is not clear whether impoverishment of social relationships or opportunities for socialization have more important consequences at one age level or another. Is there a critical period for the formation of basic social relationships? The question has been reviewed recently by Connolly.[5] There is good evidence of the existence of sensitive periods for the establishment of primary social bonds in many species. Studies in humans in which the mother-child relationship did not develop or was disrupted provide evidence in support of the basic contention for sensitive periods during which the human infant is maximally sensitive to social contacts with its mother, contacts that will lead to the cementing of an affectional bond. Do the parents of a handicapped child need guidance and assistance to modify any abnormal responses very early? Do they, on the other hand, have to originate alternative ways or opportunities for socialization if these cannot be experienced in the usual way? Is it all right to allow the child to progress in socialization at his own pace? Is there, in fact, anything that can be done? These are some of the questions raised by a consideration of the disruptions in the interpersonal relationships of the child during his first year of life which result from a handicapping condition.

SOCIALIZATION PROCESSES IN THE YOUNG CHILD

The very early aspects of socialization, involving mainly aspects of the mother-child relationship, have been reviewed above. Similarities and dissimilarities were noted between the socialization process in the normal and handicapped child. The next portion of this paper will be concerned with the socialization process in the young child. The following topics will be covered: mechanisms of socialization; aspects of human behavior in the normal young child that must be socialized; biological needs and socializations; general modes of interacting with the environment; dependency and independence; emergence of a clear body-image, of self-concept, or self-esteem; role-learning, particularly the sex role; imitation; relationships with the siblings and with the peer group; and opportunities for play and for participation in interpersonal relationships. Each of these aspects of early childhood socialization is markedly altered in the child who is handicapped.

Kagan[15] has reviewed the four major mechanisms of socialization, which, he notes, are similar for all cultures, although the content of what is socialized differs across cultures. Each of the four mechanisms—desire for reward, fear of punishment, identification, and imitation—is strongest at different periods of development and facilitates different aspects of the socialization process. Kagan asserts that acquisition and suppression of values and beliefs are less likely to be facilitated by watching others behave and more likely to be the product of identification with a desirable model. The process of *identification* is seen in the desire of the child to be similar to particular persons he has grown to respect, love, and admire.

After the first year of life, there are five aspects of human behavior in the normal young child that must be socialized: feeding and weaning, toileting and elimination, sex needs and practices, aggression needs and practices, and, finally, dependency needs and behavior.[17] Most of these aspects, if not all, cannot be socialized in the usual way in the handicapped child because his body structure and its functions are not normal. He cannot suck, swallow, or chew well. He cannot sit up steadily or walk, or defend himself or his toys. He is unable to learn about sex differences by exploration or learn about his sex role through play and imitation. He may not be able to handle his own bathroom needs. He must remain dependent on others for help in all areas of his life.

Many lists have been compiled of biological and universal needs, such as thirst, hunger, comfort-seeking, freedom from pain, aggression, and probably activity, curiosity, or the need for exploration.[17]

This last need system, the need for exploration, mentioned by McCandless, is the one need that can never be satisfied by the child with severe cerebral palsy, which limits markedly his exploration, so important for certain pleasures in life, for the acquisition of knowledge, and for achieving independence. Some needs are satisfied without social dependency, or, indeed, interaction, such as air-hunger, while other needs must be satisfied within a social setting, such as hunger, elimination, and aggression. McCandless points out that it is these socially conspicuous needs in all likelihood that are important in personality and social development.

In reviewing Bruner's three general modes of interaction with the environment, McCandless[17] infers that the socialized individual must have mastered all three systems. The first mode of interaction with the environment involves the near-receptors — the how-to-do-it mechanisms — the hands. Next, the child must consolidate his vision and other distance receptors; he must learn how to perceive, coordinate, and anticipate. Finally, the fabric of language or symbolic mastery of the environment must be mastered. Each of these three modes is characteristic, respectively, of the years in preschool, elementary school, and the onset of adolescent years. The implications for the handicapped child become clear. He cannot interact with the environment with his hands. The hands of the child with cerebral palsy will not go where he wants them to, will not grasp a toy effectively, or will not hold on to a toy he has succeeded in grasping. By contrast, he may grasp effectively through his eyes; he may interact through his eyes. Sometimes, eye contact is his only path for communication. Some children with cerebral palsy, though, lack depth perception, have strabismus, or perceive the world visually in strange ways. Often these children are fearful in this incorrectly perceived world.

One five-year-old boy, crying in his wheelchair, was asked why he was crying. He responded that he was afraid of the floor. Another child performed well in his special education classroom but broke out into a panic when he had to accompany the class into a large auditorium for gymnastics. He screamed and walked close to the walls until he could be allowed to leave. When back in the small classroom with windows, which he could use to align himself, he again performed well.

Often the child with cerebral palsy cannot speak at all or speaks in a highly unintelligible manner, even though he may have a normal or even high intelligence quotient. All three of these modes of interaction with the environment may be distorted or unattainable for the handicapped child.

Another area that is to be mastered by all children was alluded to earlier—the complete dependence of the infant. Complete dependence must be established early by giving the infant immediate, generous, and consistent rewards for all his demands so that in this loving atmosphere he can establish trust. In turn, the bliss of complete dependence must be dissipated later through the child's fear of the loss of parental love and support and by reinforcing independent behavior. If the infant's needs are not gratified at once, he learns that he is not the center of the universe, but is subject to forces outside himself. This realization is the child's first awareness that other persons are important. The child must achieve independence in order to live a satisfying adult life. The parents through highly selective reinforcement can encourage the child toward independent behavior and help him to seek influence of others besides themselves, in particular the influence of the child's peers. Parents of normal children can unfortunately also reinforce dependency behavior such as crying, whining, lap-sitting, and attention-seeking. It is not uncommon to see parents of handicapped children reinforcing dependency behavior. E. Shere and Kastenbaum[36] suggest that the ambivalent retaliation/dependency-fostering behaviors seem a poor substitute for normal pleasure in mother-child interactions.

What are the implications for the handicapped child who must gain independence? Is it possible for the child to become emotionally independent when he is in fact totally physically dependent on the parents? Scott[32] argues that institutions for the handicapped blind adult, for instance, coerce the individual to be dependent in return for financial and other help. The person, in point of fact, may not be dependent emotionally but is taught to be dependent. A similar phenomenon may occur early within the family of a handicapped child.

Important in the social development of the child, in fact, the most salient of the child's many social roles, is the individual's sex role. The child comes to learn his sex role through psychological identification with the parent of the same sex and by imitation of that parent through play. The child also models himself in many ways (socializes) after the parent of the opposite sex. This cross-identification, or cross-modeling, is also probably socially useful so long as it goes along with established social patterns. It would seem that the handicapped child can never achieve an awareness of himself as a boy (or as a girl) since his impairment may prevent him from role-playing and imitation opportunities.

There is an extensive literature in social psychology, however, which deals with social learning that occurs independent of any active imitation opportunities. Bandura[1] has reviewed extensively the conceptualizations of vicarious or observational learning. Certain theories would suggest that a handicapped child may learn despite the inability to role-play much in the same way as the normal child described by Bandura does. Most persons, for example, exhibiting snake phobias have never had any direct aversive experiences with reptiles; similarly, children may acquire, on the basis of exposure to modeled stimulus correlations, intense emotional attitudes toward members of unpopular minority groups or nationalities with whom they have little or no personal contact.

Such evidence of no-trial learning is encouraging when translated to the learning processes of the handicapped child. The inability to role-play or to imitate because of the physical limitations of the handicapping conditions may not preclude his learning on a vicarious basis. The physical limitations may not be so major an obstacle as has been thought in the past.

One of the better-studied areas of family structure in the socialization of the normal child is birth order. This topic will not be treated here, since much literature is available on this area, indicating that birth order is probably not a very important factor. The relationship to siblings has additional importance in the socialization of the handicapped child. Intense sibling rivalry may arise because parents often do not apply the same standards to their normal children and their handicapped child. Parents, too, face the dilemma of how to praise their normal children without at the same time increasing the feelings of inadequacy and "differentness" on the part of the handicapped child. Freeman[11] points out the marked reaction of handicapped children between the ages of three and six to being surpassed by their normal younger siblings. At this time the handicapped child also begins to realize that he is different from others.

Second only to the parents (including the siblings) in the socialization of the child is the influence of the peer group. McCandless[17] has listed concisely many generalizations from a review of the literature. The peer group is indispensable in role rehearsal, dimensions of cooperative and competitive behavior, expression of aggression, and dependency. The peer group also supplies important confirmation-disconfirmation of self-judgments of competence and self-esteem, as well as a reference point for self-evaluation of elementary sexuality. If the child does not have a peer group or cannot communicate with his peer group, he is deprived of this aspect of the socialization process.

The opportunity and the ability or skills to *play* become increasingly important in the preschool years. In the normal instance, play enables the child to master anxiety, fears, and passivity and to learn imitative patterns. In a discussion about the socialization of blind children, Scott[33] notes that the primary mechanism by which a child learns to internalize the behavior of others is play. Like the blind child who cannot see the other roles, the handicapped child also has a major limitation in his role-playing, since he cannot walk or make his limbs accomplish some task or talk.

Entering school is a major event in childhood. It has become more common for handicapped children, even those with severe or multiple handicapping conditions, to attend school, because of recently enacted legislation, e.g., Illinois provides for placement of all handicapped children from ages 3 to 21 years. McCandless[17] asserts that in American society competence seems to lead more than anything else to self-esteem, which is the core of adequate personal social adjustment (cf. Edgerton[7]). School is one of the major testing grounds of competence for the child. The handicapped child does not have an opportunity to socialize with the peer neighborhood children because of limitations in ambulation, his mother's overprotectiveness, or rejection by other children on account of his being different. At least, he has the opportunity to socialize and be socialized in the classroom. In general, to the present, the development of social skills in the classroom for the handicapped child has not received major emphasis. The major thrust has been in developing other skills such as speech and language, learning the three R's.

As Richardson[24] points out, parallels have been drawn between the stigma attached to persons who are handicapped and the stigma of minority groups and are important in school placement of the handicapped child. Differences between the two groups are significant. Persons born into a minority group learn in their socialization from their minority culture how to deal with the majority culture. In addition, because they develop social skills primarily with adults and peers within their minority group, the behavior inhibitions common to minority/majority social interactions are operating only a small part of the time. In contrast, it is most unlikely that the handicapped child will have parents, neighbors, sibs, or peers with the same handicapping conditions from whom he can gain experience in dealing with others. In general, he will be surrounded by nonhandicapped persons and will share the general negative values toward the handicapped. Furthermore, it is unlikely that he will have an opportunity to develop social skills freely with persons who share his handicap, as Richardson further notes.

In summary, it appears that a child with a physical handicap will encounter more difficulty than a child from a minority group in gaining experience in behavioral skills in general, and specifically in the skills for social relationships with the majority group. Such considerations have implications for school placement: Should a handicapped child be placed in a class with normal children insofar as he is able? Should he be placed with peer handicapped children as much as possible? Or should he have opportunity for socialization with both groups? From the above discussion, it seems reasonable to conclude that the last alternative will provide the most satisfactory socialization process.

Since there are good reasons both for placement in the "normal" classroom and for placement in the "handicapped" classroom, a combination would seem to serve the needs of the handicapped child best. He should have the opportunity to be in a classroom with normal children if he can compete academically, for he will have normal models, can interact with normal persons, and can develop certain specialized skills in managing his social relationships with the nonhandicapped; he will be dealing mainly with this group throughout his life. The value of placement with handicapped children, on the other hand, lies in three areas: opportunity for models of persons who have made good adjustments despite the same obstacles, the comfort of being with similar persons, and the opportunity to compete successfully at least occasionally.

Increasing recognition of the value of interaction between nonhandicapped and handicapped children is seen in the trend to include handicapped children in national children's television shows. Fred Rogers, of "Mister Rogers' Neighborhood," is including a youngster with short-leg braces in several filming sequences.[30] "Sesame Street" has selected 10 handicapped youngsters to participate with other nonhandicapped youngsters in the show's street scene.[40]

Occasionally children with handicaps are unfortunately treated as if they are *sick*, with all the social role connotations that are associated with sickness, as Richardson indicates.[24] The parents give the handicapped child less responsibility, place fewer limits on his behavior, have increased tolerance for deviant behavior, and indulge his personal whims, often at the expense of the other children in the family. The effects of each of these alterations in the socialization of the child would seem to have a profound impact.

A study was referred to earlier concerning the inability of mothers of severely handicapped infants to provide play-learning experiences for their infants.[35] In contrast, some parents are able to facilitate the development of their handicapped child. A group of 60 mothers of cerebral-palsied children and 60 carefully matched mothers of normal children from the New York area were compared.[2] One of many important findings was that Jewish mothers provide significantly more social opportunities for their cerebral-palsied children than either Catholic or Protestant mothers. This study in 1959 also showed that mothers of cerebral-palsied children were significantly more overprotective and maritally conflicted than mothers of nonhandicapped children. Mothers of younger handicapped children were found to be socially withdrawn as well. In general, mothers of the handicapped children had some of the following characteristics: guilt, rejection, and unrealistic attitudes. In a later study, Collins[4] administered a set of personality tests to mothers of children with cerebral palsy who had participated in an education program for the parents of a child with cerebral palsy. He concluded that such programs have demonstrated definite evidence of helping mothers of afflicted children to maintain normal personality patterns, since these mothers did not show personality changes leading to feelings of inferiority, introversion, and depression.

It is obvious that a child with a handicap will have less experience in social relationships than a nonhandicapped child. With the passage of time, the child becomes deeply concerned about his physical disability. As isolated as he is, the handicapped child will not be sufficiently isolated or sheltered to prevent his learning about the negative values associated with his physical disability or the depreciation of value of the handicapped person in society. As a result he will tend to deprecate himself. It has been demonstrated that handicapped children are very realistic in their self-descriptions.

Richardson and others[28] have obtained self-descriptions from 107 children with handicaps and 128 nonhandicapped children ages 9 to 11 years at a summer camp. The differences between these two groups appeared to reflect the functional restriction on physical activity, deprivation of social experience, and the psychological impact of the handicap. Although the handicapped children share in peer values, for example, they are aware that they cannot live up to the expectations that stem from the high value placed on physical activities. Gardner,[12] at the 1970 American Academy of Cerebral Palsy annual meeting, described how the child with cerebral palsy is frustrated in his attempts both physically and psychologically. His frustration begins at birth because the condition interferes with satisfactory interaction between parent and child. The result is that the child lacks self-esteem and behaves as if he were alone in the social world and of no personal consequence to it. The reactions of a child with cerebral palsy, according to Gardner, of extreme rage at disappointment or extreme, inappropriate joy over reward stem from this self-esteemless state. The child with cerebral palsy does comprehend that he is abnormal. He may, in fact, perceive his damaged state as a massive rejection of him as a person.

Several studies, reviewed by Richardson,[24] suggest that the nonhandicapped child who is likely to initiate contact with a handicapped child is more likely isolated, has less general social experience, and has learned the values of his peers less. These findings, especially true for boys, suggest that, even when the handicapped child does participate in a social relationship with a peer, there is a chance that the relationship will not be so beneficial as it might be, since children who do initiate contact with him will be those who are less successful in social relationships, those who hold atypical values, those for whom physical disability cues have low perceptual salience, or those who like others to be dependent on them.

Another flaw in the relationship between the handicapped child and the normal child surmised by Richardson from a review of other studies is the fact that the handicapped person does not receive accurate or spontaneous feedback from others, who feel that they must be especially considerate or careful of the feelings of someone who is handicapped. Absence of accurate feedback makes it difficult if not impossible for the handicapped child to learn what others think of him, to learn appropriate behavior, and to develop social skills ultimately. Not only does the handicapped child have more difficulty in establishing social relationships, but those he does establish are apt to be imperfect. Awareness of these facts makes it clear that the handicapped does not encounter barriers to establishing social relationships only initially. Barriers exist for him at every turn in a relationship.

As Richardson[24] has stated from the evidence that a physical handicap impoverishes the experiences needed for a child's socialization, it appears that there is a cumulative loss in the types of social relationships established (both mandatory and voluntary) in the socialization process of the handicapped child, which results from the obstacles imposed by the physical disability. Thus far, a handicapped child's limitations in establishing a voluntary social relationship with his peers have been considered. In some instances a handicapped child may succeed in establishing a rewarding social relationship with an adult, a teacher, a neighbor, or a relative who is able to view the child as a child with a handicap and not as a handicapped child. From these encounters he may acquire some rewarding experiences and have the opportunity to learn and practice social skills, if his parents are able to facilitate such relationships.

DISCUSSION

It is important that persons dealing with the handicapped child and his family, such as physicians, nurses, teachers, social workers, psychologists, and playground counselors, all persons dealing with children in any way, develop awareness or sensitivity regarding social barriers for the child with a handicap. This review raises more questions than it answers. Some areas are seen to be critical for intervention by the pediatrician and paramedical personnel dealing with the family of a handicapped child. More investigation is needed to attempt to understand the importance of the birth of a handicapped child, the nature of the parental response to learning about the child's condition, and, finally, the resolution or adaptation to many varied, uncomfortable initial feelings.

Some questions must be answered: Are there critical periods for acquiring socialization skills? If so, once past, can intervention reverse the effects of early deprivation in the socialization experience? How can the parents help to enable their handicapped child to play, to establish social relationships and the usual early friendships? Must the parent make special efforts to encourage neighborhood children to visit her house or yard so her child will have opportunities; should the mother resort to bribing children to play with her child at first, with such enticements as her active participation or novelties? On moving to a new neighborhood, one mother invited all the mothers on her block to her house for coffee and cake in order to meet them, to introduce her handicapped child, and to invite them to allow or even to send their children over to play.

Parents should be aided in every possible way, in areas not directly concerned with the handicapping condition, to allow them to be sufficiently free of undue stresses and uncomfortable feelings, so that they do have energies to invest in the socialization of their handicapped child. The implications of Collins' study[4] are important: An education program for parents of a child with cerebral palsy helped mothers to maintain normal personality patterns. If the mother can be assisted in general management problems, if someone will listen to her worries, attend to her fears, help her to anticipate or meet future problem areas, she will be more at ease, more comfortable in the mothering process of a handicapped child.

Often advice for a piece of equipment for moving the child about can make a sufficient difference in the mother's energy level. Guidance for recreational and educational programs on television, or outside the home, such as swimming or summer camp for the handicapped child, must be provided as well for the handicapped child and his family.

Denhoff[6] notes that children with severe cerebral palsy are prevented from participating in after-school activities mainly because of lack of transportation or due to architectural barriers in the playground. According to Denhoff, the Professional Services Program Committee of the United Cerebral Palsy Association has assumed the responsibility to see that transportation and recreational facilities are modified to assist the handicapped child to be with his normal peers more often. Research is under way to modify the concept of the spaceship module to school, playground, and other facilities for opportunity for socialization. Another committee, the Architecture and Engineering Sciences Committee, is exploring behavior-shaping environments, such as outdoor-indoor playgrounds. Similar innovations would help to facilitate the socialization process for the handicapped youngster simply by enabling him to be where other children are.

What about the implications for school placement? Should the child be placed with other handicapped children where competition will be appropriate? Should he have exposure to normal classroom experiences as well as for normal models for behavior? One school initiates its handicapped children slowly into the regular school program by sending the handicapped child to one class period a day, music, with the normal children.

The finding of Collins[4] that the parents of handicapped children may function in a better-adjusted manner if they receive support from some outside group also suggests that facilities dealing with the handicapped child must not isolate him in their thinking from his family. Helping the entire family may be the best or only way to help him. The finding that Jewish mothers provide more social opportunities for their children[2] also merits further study to determine why and how these mothers are able to encourage more socialization in their handicapped children.

A consideration of the three general modes of interaction with the environment alluded to by McCandless[17] has implications in assisting the parents and the teachers of a handicapped child to facilitate the child's ability to interact with his environment. To facilitate *hand mechanisms*, programs of physical and occupational therapy are necessary, as well as simple measures such as providing toys that can be grasped easily or are simple to operate, or building a two-inch railing around the table in front of the child, which will keep the toys within his hand and arm range. Sensory experiences, such as feeling water or sand, smelling a flower, petting a kitten, must be provided for the child who cannot obtain these experiences on his own. It is equally important to develop *eye skills*. The child can be taught to communicate many feelings with his eyes and to communicate even more fully through the use of communication boards.[18] The highest level of interaction with the environment is the *linguistic* or *symbolic* mastery of the environment. In addition to communication board systems, the child can be helped to verbalize a definite "yes" or "no," a simpler yet significant step forward for communication with others.

Perhaps this review will have accomplished enough if it has made us merely consider the magnitude of the social disruptions and barriers for the young handicapped child. Unfortunately, these social barriers increase; as the child grows older, he drops farther and farther behind his normal peers. The basic issue remaining to be determined is: What are the long-term effects of the above-mentioned disruptions in the socialization process of the young handicapped child? It is hoped that this review will move us medical scientists to join with social scientists in answering Richardson's[25] exhortation to study the social conditions that influence children.

REFERENCES

1. Bandura, A. Vicarious Processes: A Case of No-Trial Learning. In: Berkowitz, Leonard, ed. *Advances in Experimental Social Psychology.* New York: Academic Press, 1965.
2. Boles, Glen. Personality Factors in Mothers of Cerebral Palsied Children. *Genetic Psychol. Monographs.* 1959. 59:159–218.

3. Campbell, D. *Sucking as an Index of Mother-Child Interactions.* Paper presented at the Fourth Symposium on Oral Sensation and Perception: Development in the Fetus and Infant. National Institutes of Health, Bethesda, Md., 1972.
4. Collins, Hardin A. Introversion and Depression in Mothers of Cerebral Palsied Children. *Missouri Med.* Oct., 1965. 62:10:847-850.
5. Connolly, Kevin. Learning and the Concept of Critical Periods in Infancy. *Developmental Med. and Child Neurol.* Dec., 1972. 14:6:705-714.
6. Denhoff, Eric. Cerebral Palsy, chap. 43A, p. 997-1025, in: Wallace, Helen M., and others, eds. *Maternal and Child Health Practice: Problems, Resources and Methods of Delivery.* Springfield, Ill.: Charles C Thomas, 1973.
7. Edgerton, Robert B. *The Cloak of Competence: Stigma in the Lives of the Mentally Retarded.* Berkeley, Calif.: University of California Press, 1967.
8. English, Horace B. and English, Ava Champney. *A Comprehensive Dictionary of Psychological and Psychoanalytical Terms: A Guide to Usage.* New York: Longmans, Green, 1958, p. 508.
9. Faigel, Harris C. Small Expectation: The Vulnerable Child Syndrome. *GP.* Sept., 1966. 34:3:78-84.
10. Freedman, David A., Fox-Kalenda, Betty J., and Brown, Stuart L. A Multihandicapped Rubella Baby: The First 18 Months. *J. Am. Acad. of Child Psychiatry.* 1970. 9:2:298-317.
11. Freeman, Roger D. Emotional Reactions of Handicapped Children. *Rehab. Lit.* Sept., 1967. 28:9:274-282.
12. Gardner, Riley W. Evolution and Brain Injury: The Impact of Deprivation on Cognitive-Affective Structures, chap. 14, p. 241-251, in: Sapir, Selma G., and Nitzburg, Ann C., eds. *Children with Learning Problems: Readings in a Developmental-Interaction Approach.* New York: Brunner/Mazel, 1973. Reprinted from: *Bull. Menninger Clinic.* Mar., 1971. 35:2:113-124.
13. Goodman, Norman, and others. Variant Reactions to Physical Disabilities. *Am. Sociological Rev.* June, 1963. 28:3:429-435.
14. Howell, Sarah Esselstyn. Psychiatric Aspects of Habilitation. *Pediatric Clin. of North America.* Feb., 1973. 20:1:203-219.
15. Kagan, Jerome. Personality Development, chap. 7, p. 282-349, in: Talbot, Nathan B., Kagan, Jerome, and Eisenberg, Leon, eds. *Behavioral Science in Pediatric Medicine.* Philadelphia: W. B. Saunders, 1971.
16. Kennedy, James F. Maternal Reactions to the Birth of a Defective Baby. *Social Casework.* July, 1970. 51:7:410-416.
17. McCandless, Boyd R. Childhood Socialization, p. 791-819, in: Goslin, David A., ed. *Handbook of Socialization Theory and Research.* Chicago: Rand McNally, 1969.
18. McDonald, Eugene T. and Schultz, Adeline R. Communication Boards for Cerebral-Palsied Children. *J. Speech and Hearing Disorders.* Feb., 1973. 38:1:73-88.
19. MacKeith, R. Physician's Aid for Parents of the Handicapped. *Medical Tribune.* Sept. 22, 1971. p. 18.
20. McNeil, Elton B. The Nature of Socialization, in: McNeil, Elton B., ed. *Human Socialization.* Belmont, Calif.: Brooks/Cole, 1969.
21. Menolascino, Frank J. Parents of the Mentally Retarded: An Operational Approach to Diagnosis and Treatment. *J. Am. Acad. of Child Psychiatry.* Oct., 1968. 7:4:589-602.

22. Rheingold, Harriet L. The Social and Socializing Infant, p. 779–790, in: Goslin, David A., ed. *Handbook of Socialization Theory and Research.* Chicago: Rand McNally, 1969.
23. Rheingold, Harriet L., Gewirtz, Jacob L., and Ross, Helen W. Social Conditioning of Vocalizations in the Infant. *J. Comparative and Physiological Psychology.* Feb., 1959. 52:1:68–73.
24. Richardson, Stephen A. The Effect of Physical Disability on the Socialization of a Child, p. 1047–1063, in: Goslin, David A., ed. *Handbook of Socialization Theory and Research.* Chicago: Rand McNally, 1969.
25. Richardson, Stephen A. Patterns of Medical and Social Research in Pediatrics. *Acta Paediat. Scand.* 1970. 59:265–272.
26. Richardson, Stephen A. Some Social Psychological Consequences of Handicapping. *Pediatrics.* Aug., 1963. 32:2:291–297.
27. Richardson, Stephen A., and others. Cultural Uniformity in Reaction to Physical Disabilities. *Am. Sociological Rev.* Apr., 1961. 26:2:241–247.
28. Richardson, Stephen A., Hastorf, Albert H., and Dornbusch, Sanford M. Effects of Physical Disability on a Child's Description of Himself. *Child Development.* Sept., 1964. 35:3:893–907.
29. Richardson, Stephen A. and Royce, Jacqueline. Race and Physical Handicap in Children's Preference for Other Children. *Child Development.* June, 1968. 39:2:467–480.
30. Rogers, Fred. Personal communication, 1973.
31. Roos, Philip. Psychological Counseling with Parents of Retarded Children. *Mental Retardation.* Dec., 1963. 1:6:345–350.
32. Scott, Robert A. *The Making of Blind Men: A Study of Adult Socialization.* New York: Russell Sage Foundation, 1969.
33. Scott, Robert A. The Socialization of Blind Children, p. 1025–1045, in: Goslin, David A., ed. *Handbook of Socialization Theory and Research.* Chicago: Rand McNally, 1969.
34. Shaffer, David. Psychiatric Aspects of Brain Injury in Childhood: A Review. *Developmental Med. and Child Neurol.* Apr., 1973. 15:2:211–220.
35. Shere, Eugenia S. Patterns of Child Rearing in Cerebral Palsy: Effects upon the Child's Cognitive Development. *Pediatrics Digest.* May, 1971. p. 28.
36. Shere, Eugenia and Kastenbaum, Robert. Mother-Child Interaction in Cerebral Palsy: Environmental and Psychosocial Obstacles to Cognitive Development. *Genetic Psychol. Monographs.* May, 1966. 73:2:255–335.
37. Shere, Marie Orr. The Socio-Emotional Development of the Twin Who Has Cerebral Palsy. *Cerebral Palsy Rev.* Jan.–Feb., 1957. 18:1:16–18.
38. Solnit, Albert J. and Stark, Mary H. Mourning and the Birth of a Defective Child, p. 523–537, in: *Psychoanalytic Study of the Child,* vol. 16. New York: International Universities Press, 1961.
39. Susser, Mervyn W. and Watson, W. *Sociology in Medicine,* ed. 2. London: Oxford University Press, 1971.
40. There's More Than Counting on "Sesame Street" Now. *UCP Crusader.* 1973. No. 2, p. 5.

6

Toward an Understanding of the Rehabilitation of the Disabled Adolescent

Richard T. Goldberg

INTRODUCTION: THE TASKS OF ADOLESCENCE

Adolescence presents a series of developmental tasks that are mastered with difficulty by the able-bodied youth. The challenge of breaking away from dependence on family and the counter pull of maintaining ties with home may disrupt the hitherto tranquil path from child to adult status. Adolescent turmoil is normal. When a young person in late adolescence (age 17–20) shows no signs of rebelling against parental authority, then we may suspect in American culture delay in normal development.[1] Persistent clinging to family, loss of affect in peers, and schizoid withdrawal from interests outside the home should be cause for referral to a mental health provider. Too often families ignore the incipient symptoms of emotional disorder in the compliant, passive, conformist youth, whereas they may seek help for a rebellious, acting-out counterpart.

The tug-of-war between independence and dependence is complicated by the reemergence of basic instinctual drives of aggression and sexuality. The delicate balance between the expression of drives and the formation of conscience is tipped by the primal urge of biology. Adolescents become preoccupied with the internal process of their own bodies. "Bad" thoughts concerning sexual exploration of the body, masturbation, desire and fear to explore the bodies of other persons, parents, siblings, of the same sex or

From *Rehabilitation Literature*, 42(3–4) (1981), 66–74. Reprinted with permission. Published by the National Easter Seal Society, 2023 W. Ogden, Chicago, IL 60612.

This paper was presented in part at the annual meeting of the American Psychological Association, Symposium on Handicapped Children and Adolescents, Montreal, Canada, September 3, 1980.

of the opposite sex, may dominate a large portion of the adolescent's day-dreams and reveries. Coming to terms with one's own sexuality will lead to the formation of an adult personality.

The twin processes of individuation and sexual identity are necessary to the completion of other adolescent tasks. The making of an educational plan after secondary school presupposes that an adolescent can make an independent choice of future schooling with the help of a knowledgeable adult. The making of a realistic vocational plan leading to an adult career presupposes that an adolescent can accept individual responsibility for a career choice. Finding a suitable lover or mate or choosing to remain single (and, perhaps, celibate) presupposes that an adolescent has formed a stable sexual identity.

Other tasks confronted by the adolescent in American culture are the development of a comfortable body image and feelings of positive self-esteem.[2] The worship of the beautiful body and the cult of physical attractiveness are reinforced by the media paid by the advertising industry. For the able-bodied adolescent it is often difficult to develop an adequate body image that can withstand the taunts of one's peers. Flat chest, thin legs, underdeveloped testes, minimal secondary sexual characteristics, and small stature may threaten the able-bodied youth's concept of one's self as a man or a woman.[3]

Finally, the successful formation of identity may lead to socialization. The adolescent may take a place in the adult world as a worker, lover, parent, or active community leader. Once the dangerous shoals of adolescence are passed, the individual may fuse an identity with others in the greater organic body of the community.[4] The inability to form a strong ego identity in adolescence leads to role confusion in the Eriksonian sense, and to regression.

APPLICATION TO REHABILITATION

Although never easy for the able-bodied youth, the tasks of adolescence, when superimposed upon the burdens caused by chronic physical or mental disability, are laden particularly by conflict and strife. Any rehabilitation program established for the disabled adolescent must first attend to the resolution of normative developmental tasks. It is premature to provide vocational rehabilitation programs for adolescents who are functioning at the developmental level of preadolescence. Too frequently disabled youths who have reached employable age (16 or above) are referred to state rehabilitation agencies and then determined to be ineligible for service because of lack of previous social preparation.

In an attempt to learn more about the transition from child to adult status among disabled youths, several studies of adolescents with a variety of disabilities and with different levels of social competence have been analyzed. Mindful of the developmental tasks of adolescence, the impact of chronic disability, hospitalization, and medical treatment upon their lives will be explored. What follows is an attempt to understand the special problems of disabled adolescents and to recommend rehabilitation programs to meet their needs.

PROBLEMS OF SEPARATION

For the able-bodied adolescent, the problems of separation from the family may be difficult to resolve. For the disabled adolescent, prolonged medical treatment and chronic hospitalization intensify the conflict of separation. Adolescents in a hospital setting are especially rebellious against the constraints of having to take doctors' orders, comply with medications, and abide by hospital rules. At a time in life when they want to become independent, they are required to be dependent for long periods. Hospitalization reinforces their dependency needs, as the adolescent must depend on the doctor, nurse, or therapist to carry out daily tasks. The adolescent may express anger toward the hospital staff as a way of coping with separation. If they are angry, they can justify rebellion. If they are angry toward the parents, they can separate from them more easily.

The problems of separation are even greater when the adolescent has a mental illness. Anxiety over separation may provoke a sudden flight into independence. Sometimes this flight from family succeeds and the adolescent works through the developmental crisis. In many cases, however, the individuals may have to experience a transient schizophrenic episode over and over again until strong enough to stand on their own. This may explain, in part, why brief psychotic episodes may be rolled up in the adolescent turmoil state.[5]

PROBLEMS OF BODY IMAGE

Every adolescent must come to terms with body image. The cultural ideal of physical wholeness and physical attractiveness sets a standard, which visibly physically disabled persons find difficult to meet. Disabilities with visible disfigurement have more social stigma attached to them. In a comparative study of the adjustment of children with congenital heart disease and facial disfigurement, we found that an invisible congenital defect with severe physical limitations had a less deleterious effect upon social and vocational adjustment than a visible disfiguring handicap with slight physical limitations.[6] Cystic fibrosis presents another disability with slight social handicap due to minimal visible disfigurement.[7]

For adolescents with obvious physical handicaps, such as paraplegia, spina bifida, and muscular dystrophy, the problem of incorporating a distorted body image into their self-concept becomes crucial. A wheelchair, a brace, a crutch becomes part of the adolescent's body image. Too frequently physicians and other helping persons emphasize the negative aspects of the disability by concentrating on what the adolescent *cannot* do. Children who have been placed in casts for orthopedic handicaps develop a negative body image as they compare themselves with their able-bodied peers. Dembo, Leviton, and Wright, in a study of persons with amputation, suggested the necessity for a change in values so that the personal assets of the disabled individual may be substituted for a comparative value based upon physical appearance.[8]

PROBLEMS OF ACHIEVING INDEPENDENCE

The disabled adolescent has the special problem of achieving emotional and financial independence despite marked dependence upon parents, friends, and health professionals for the treatment and care of the disability. Society has encouraged the disabled child to remain dependent in sheltered situations at home and school.[9] The pattern of learned helplessness may hinder the disabled adolescent from taking those steps required to prepare for independent living in the community.

Repeated hospitalization for chronic illness reinforces dependency. Adolescents with cystic fibrosis, congenital heart disease, and muscular dystrophy may spend many months in treatment. Their growing sense of isolation, their feelings of helplessness that they will never get out, their anger at parents for placing them in treatment—all these factors tend to diminish their independence.

Adolescents who have been hospitalized since early childhood may learn to become overly compliant. In a study of institutionalized patients at the Massachusetts Hospital School in Canton,[10] it was found that adolescents in the age group 14 to 17 tested two years below their able-bodied counterparts in acceptance of responsibility for making educational decisions. When institutionalized adolescents are required to leave school, they may become frightened, anxious, and withdrawn. After many years of enforced dependency, they are ill prepared to meet the tasks of career building or future training.

The hiatus between special school and the vocational rehabilitation agency is marked by career indecision. Until the recent passage of P.L. 94-142, few states provided guidance services for the group of adolescents who had finished high school and who were considered "not ready" for rehabilitation services. Yet it is just this group that needs intensive guidance.

PROBLEMS OF SEXUAL IDENTITY

Every adolescent has the problem of attaining a stable sexual identity. Erikson points out that the danger of the stage between childhood and adulthood is role confusion. "Where this is based on a strong previous doubt as to one's sexual identity, delinquent and outright psychotic episodes are not uncommon."[4] Able-bodied adolescents learn to explore their sexual parts through the normal course of sexual play. As adolescents begin to show an interest in the sexual parts of their friends, there are normal opportunities for sexual exploration at school dances, at private homes, at the beach, and at athletic events. The formation of sexual identity also involves much time for conversation with the opposite sex (or same sex), since one's ego ideal is reflected in the eyes of another.[4] The wedding of human sexuality with the deeper, more mature expression of love may come in late adolescence or young adulthood.[11]

The disabled adolescent has special problems in resolving the developmental task of sexual identity. Some of the problems are attributable to cultural restraints, taboos, and myths. Some problems are specific to the disability. Still others are caused by social isolation, institutionalization, and chronic, intermittent hospitalization.

Parental attitudes toward their disabled children have been repressive and controlling.[12] Many parents consider their disabled children to be asexual and to have no chance to marry, reproduce, and lead a normal sexual life. They especially consider children disabled from birth to be incapable of ever developing sexual relationships. The disabled child may learn from the reaction of the parents that his or her body is ugly and sexually unattractive. In high school, the disabled adolescent may be excused from classes on sex education because the school principal considers sex education irrelevant for the disabled person.

Attitudes of medical personnel have been no less negative. One physician told his adolescent patient with spina bifida that she should never contemplate having normal sexual relations because she could have no vaginal sensations.[13] Although spina bifida does impair the urogenital system, sexual function may be present and limited genital sensation may be aroused.[14] In adolescent boys with spina bifida, 75 percent are able to obtain erections. In a series on 26 males and 26 females with spina bifida, ages 12 to 30, 80 percent of males and 90 percent of females had poor self-images. The uncertainty about sexual function contributed greatly toward their poor self-image.

The achievement of sexual identity is especially difficult for adolescents with intellectual disabilities. For many years it was felt that mentally retarded persons should be restrained from sexual activity lest they procreate a child whom they cannot raise. Sex education for the mentally retarded is a recent innovation fraught with fear by parents and community.[15] In a recent study of 430 mentally retarded persons exposed to a sex education program, it was found that many students showed positive changes toward their sexual feelings and were more open about communicating their feelings. In another study of adolescents with learning disabilities, consisting of a hetero-geneous group of young men and women (ages 16 to 22) with cognitive and behavioral problems, students' responses to sex education workshops varied from acceptance to anxiety.[16]

Adolescents with sensory disability have particular difficulty in learn-ing sexual roles and functions. Blind persons have to be taught to explore sexual parts by touching. Hearing impaired individuals may feel comfortable in discussing sexual issues with their peers. Deaf adolescents in high school may feel isolated from their able-bodied peers because of communication problems. Group counseling may provide a comfortable setting for discus-sion of sexuality among deaf adolescents.[17] Deaf-blind adolescents have great difficulty in interpreting sensations from their bodies. Deaf-blind children must be helped to become acquainted with their body and with the bodies of siblings and parents.[18]

PROBLEMS OF AGGRESSION

During the adolescent years the aggressive drive is reinforced by changes in the endocrine system and accelerated physical development.[5] Moreover, the capacity to implement the aggressive drive is greatly increased during adolescence. Severe acting-out behavior, alcoholic binges, delinquent of-fenses, promiscuity, and drug-related offenses are more prominent in ado-lescence. Frequently, the adolescent acts out aggression in an antisocial way in order to assert independence of parental and community authority. Anti-social acts may eventually bring the adolescent into conflict with the court. At that point rehabilitation programs may be offered the adolescent to help resolve problems in a socially acceptable way and adjust the person's aggres-sion to the needs of society.

The full-blown syndrome of antisocial personality may develop in the adolescent years. The antisocial personality, according to Hudgens,[19] begins in childhood, persists in adolescence, and tends to be resistant to treatment. The disorder is chronic when it includes at least four symptoms, including school problems, poor work history, excessive drug use, excessive alcohol use, three or more nontraffic arrests, habitual physical aggression, sexual promiscuity or perversion, suicide attempts, habitually impulsive behavior, and lack of guilt. The adolescent with an antisocial personality is the most likely individual to come to the attention of school authorities, the police, the courts, and the community. This type of psychiatric disorder may get treated in the correctional system or in the mental health system, depending on whether the behavioral offense leads the individual to confrontation with the law. Even when the adolescent is treated vigorously, this disorder may develop into a lifelong pattern of criminal and antisocial acts.

PROBLEMS OF DEPRESSION

The most serious problem of psychiatric illness in the adolescent years is attempted suicide. This is more common in girls than in boys, and is more often attempted than completed. Although adolescents are less likely to complete suicide than are depressed adults, the figures are large enough to warrant immediate attention. Suicide is the fifth leading cause of death among adolescents.[19] Suicide prevention centers, "hot lines," and emergency rooms of general hospitals are flooded with calls from emotionally disturbed adolescents. There are few centers that specialize in counseling the physically disabled youth who is threatening suicide, yet this group is enlarging as more children with chronic severe handicaps survive life-threatening illness and trauma.

PROBLEMS OF EDUCATIONAL AND VOCATIONAL DEVELOPMENT

The educational and vocational development of adolescents is linked inextricably with the formation of sexual identity. The reason why many rehabilitation programs for the disabled adolescent fail is that they concentrate exclusively on the specific problems of vocational training and finding a job. Vocational rehabilitation should be considered the end product of many internal and external forces impinging on the adolescent's life. The aforementioned problems of separation, independence, body image, sexual identity, aggression, and depression must be resolved before a vocational choice can be made. Amid all the turmoil of adolescence, the able-bodied/disabled youth cannot be expected to make a realistic choice without a great amount of help.

Able-bodied adolescents attempt to resolve the problems of vocational development by making choices that are consistent with their concept of who they are. Vocational choice defines a person's career goals; it is a summing up of abilities, interests, and values on one side, and the opportunities of the labor market on the other side. When the choice is made realistically, it represents a compromise between aspiration and reality.[20,21]

But the disabled adolescent may lack the experiences at play, school, and part-time work that are helpful in making vocational choices. The disabled adolescent may have unrealistic fantasies or goals, may deny physical or mental limitations, or may overestimate the effect of these limitations upon a vocational choice.

In a recent study of five groups of handicapped children compared with a group of able-bodied children in grades 6 to 12, it was found that handicapped children tested significantly lower than normal children on all measures of vocational development.[10] The rank order of handicapped adolescents by group was as follows: cystic fibrosis, congenital heart disease, orthopedic handicaps, facial burns, and juvenile delinquency. Only the group with cystic fibrosis approached the high score of the able-bodied group. Children with cystic fibrosis and congenital heart disease were hospitalized at a private hospital and came from a higher social class. Children with facial burns and delinquency came from the lower socioeconomic class. All children had a lack of occupational information about curricula and jobs, and few had been exposed to vocational counseling while in the hospital, clinic, or school. By the time they were referred to a vocational rehabilitation agency, they were significantly lagging behind their normal age and grade peers in educational and vocational planning.

Our expectations for disabled adolescents are based on the premise that they can perform normally once their disability is circumvented and their abilities are harnessed through training. However, any training program is bound to fail unless the handicapped youth is ready to accept vocational guidance. Our research and clinical experience show that the handicapped youth must be helped to resolve the developmental problems of adolescence before entering vocational training programs.

REHABILITATION PROGRAMS FOR DISABLED ADOLESCENTS

The aforementioned problems must be met by specific rehabilitation programs. Until recently rehabilitation programs have focused primarily on adults. In a comprehensive search of the literature, a few programs that deal exclusively with youth were located. The majority of these programs focus on educational and vocational problems.

School and Work Programs

Hunter and Zuger[22] discussed the establishment of a summer work program for severely physically disabled youth at the Institute of Rehabilitation Medicine, New York, in conjunction with the New York State Office of Vocational Rehabilitation. The objectives were to provide a summer work experience in the private sector, to enhance the vocational development of handicapped youth, and to introduce a group of handicapped youth to private employers who might later employ them. As a result of the program, 71 high school and college students were placed in a variety of jobs, ranging from file clerk to editorial assistant. A pilot study has been undertaken on nine students to determine the long-range outcome on their vocational development. The results thus far on work values, vocational maturity, job awareness, and change in goals have been equivocal. One problem is that statements about significant change cannot be made without an adequate control group. Nevertheless, this pilot program presents an interesting exploratory model that other agencies might replicate and test with a statistical control group.

The use of an alternative school for both able-bodied adolescents and adolescents with emotional disturbance has been advanced in recent years. The alternative school may provide a limited academic program, up to three hours a day, in a self-contained classroom. Class size is small and the teacher-student ratio is reduced. The alternative school emphasizes basic skills necessary to obtain work. The remainder of the day may be spent in apprenticeship in local industry and avocational interests. One study by Strathe and Hash showed that early adolescents developed greater self-esteem, as measured by the Coopersmith Self-Esteem Inventory, as a result of an alternative school experience, although older adolescents showed no change.[23]

At the Human Resources Center (Albertson, Long Island, New York), a special program provides career alternatives for physically disabled persons. Project PREP (Programmatic Research on Employment Preparation),[24] jointly funded by the Rehabilitation Services Administration and the Bureau of Education of the Handicapped, provides a program in which a high school student is brought through a process from career awareness—in which knowledge of the self, ability for independence skills, and career opportunities are explored—to placement in industry. The curriculum includes bringing in successful career models who relate their experiences and inform students about their careers; business ventures, where students participate in various phases of a business experience; field trips to work sites; a work experience program, where youth engage in paid work experience; and a transitional living experience, where youth have the chance to live without parental or custodial authority in a barrier-free residential setting. The most important element is the integration of the regular curriculum with work experience.

Social Programs

The concerns of adolescents extend beyond the development of educational and vocational skills. Yet few programs emphasizing the development of social skills are available to them. Abramson and others[25] propose three solutions to the problems that handicapped youth must face in everyday life. The first is modeling. As developed by Bandura, modeling requires a teacher or a set of films that demonstrates correct social behaviors to be learned by the handicapped adolescent. These behaviors might include school work and sexual encounters. Most human beings learn social behavior through imitation. Since handicapped youth often are denied access to the most fundamental social behaviors —for example, sex play—it is necessary to provide them with models. A second solution is role playing. The handicapped adolescent is encouraged to assume the role of worker, college student, or sexual partner with controlled conditions. Role playing can be facilitated in a group setting under a trained leader who knows how to reduce anxiety. A third solution is self-instruction, in which the adult model first performs the task while talking aloud; the youth then performs the same task under the direction of the model, and learns to perform the task while talking first aloud, then in whispers, and finally by private speech. Of the three proposed solutions, the authors consider the last to be the most promising.

At the New York University Medical Center, Institute of Rehabilitation Medicine, a new program has been developed to meet the special needs of mainstreamed physically disabled adolescents.[26] Although the public schools attempt to meet some of these needs, the public school program primarily meets academic needs. Therefore, the Institute of Rehabilitation Medicine has begun to develop and coordinate after-school programs in New York City that already exist, such as YMCA and YWCA boys' and girls' clubs, and to explore programs to provide sexual counseling, extensive prevocational planning, and social and interpersonal skills.

Sexual Counseling

Since problems of achieving sexual identity are prominent among disabled adolescents, programs of sexual education and counseling must be provided when they reach sexual maturity. Sexual counseling can be provided either in groups or in individual sessions. Mayers[12] described a program of sexual counseling following spinal cord injury and a variety of chronic physical disabilities. Group membership consisted of 10 disabled individuals, one able-bodied husband of a disabled woman, and a psychologist. Although members of this group ranged in age from 22 to 39 years, they focused on many problems that were encountered with their parents. Those who had been disabled from birth or early childhood recalled that their parents would not acknowledge their sexuality, would not discuss sex with them, and dissuaded them from having sexual relationships with other disabled children. In the group, disabled young adults were encouraged to deal with their sexuality in a manner that was denied them while adolescents.

Often sexual programs for able-bodied, as well as disabled, persons focus almost exclusively on the anatomy, physiology, and function of the sexual parts. What is needed is a program that permits the open expression of feelings. Too often disabled adolescents have bottled up their feelings about sex, just as they have repressed their feelings about their disability. Along with the sexual revolution of the 1960's and 1970's, there has come the revolution of the rights of handicapped individuals to enjoy *their* sexuality. Expression of sexuality is perceived as recreation as well as procreation. As one author put it, "it is an activity people choose to engage in, during their leisure time, for enjoyment and personal satisfaction."[27] Sexual relationships are also a way of meeting people, developing adult interests, and fitting in socially.

Vocational Rehabilitation Programs

Until passage of the Rehabilitation Act of 1978, vocational rehabilitation programs for disabled adolescents under age 16 were minimal or nonexistent. Therefore, in reviewing the literature, criteria were broadened to include vocational training programs for students still in high school or college.

Cooper[28] described a small, structured occupational training program for severely handicapped persons in the public schools of Atlantic County, New Jersey. Two full-time vocational counselors worked with 38 students, evaluated their vocational potential, and placed 17 of them in private industry. Close contact with business leaders in the local community and with the New Jersey Rehabilitation Department was very instrumental in obtaining jobs. Results indicated that 25 students were placed once, four students were placed a second time, and four a third time. While in training, the New Jersey Rehabilitation Department supported 17 students. Although this project began before the passage of the Rehabilitation Amendments of 1978, the results showed that a public school can be coordinated with a local division of vocational rehabilitation and other private agencies for the purpose of job placement in the community. This project foreshadows a model for special education and rehabilitation.

Kohring and Tracht[29] reported the introduction of a work evaluation program for severely handicapped high school students in Chicago. The group consisted of students from two schools, one a special unit for deaf and hearing-impaired individuals, populated mainly by black, male, ungraded students. Students were evaluated at a nearby Goodwill Industries training unit, and were given practice in taking tests, filling out application forms, and exploring vocational areas. The third phase of the program provided a "hands on" work experience in one of Goodwill's training areas. Periodic staff conferences were held at the school and joint planning took place between Goodwill and the school authorities. Results indicated that 12 of 18 students evaluated at Goodwill were able to enter a vocational training program at Chicago's Rehabilitation Institute. Four of 21 graduates who finished public school in June, 1976, are working and one is in college. The program illustrates how a community rehabilitation agency and a public school can jointly plan a vocational evaluation of a student with severe handicaps prior to completion of high school.

The vocational development of the disabled adolescent requires a rehabilitation program that provides a continuous series of vocational tasks analogous to the developmental tasks of adolescence. This means that vocational rehabilitation programs should provide experiences of separation, independence, and identity formation. Separation from parents can be encouraged by providing work experiences in supervised settings away from home. The able-bodied youth may find summer employment in an overnight camp or in after school work situations. Disabled youth should be provided with work opportunities in settings where parental protection is replaced by adult supervision. Camp counseling, sheltered workshops, and transitional living environments made possible by independent living centers would be helpful. Since problems of separation and independence must be resolved by late adolescence, rehabilitation programs must provide opportunities for transitional living in conjunction with work.

Until now, Goldberg,[30] Super,[31] Tiedeman,[32] Hershenson,[33] and others have been calling for a vocational developmental sequence that emphasizes a logical series of vocational phases. As applied to disability, Goldberg[10] has shown that disabled adolescents do not always go through successive phases of development, and that when they do, they tend to score an average of two years below their age and grade peers. For 30 years the field of vocational psychology has been focusing on questions of vocational choice, aspiration, interests, adjustment, and satisfaction. These questions, no doubt, are important. Nevertheless, important problems of adolescence have been left out. Adolescents cannot make choices without first resolving the problems of separation, independence, and sexual identity. What I suggest is that the field of vocational psychology break away from its moorings. Let us begin a new line of empirical research on the developmental problems of adolescence that must be resolved before vocational choice can take place. A new model of vocational development emphasizing independence and risk taking needs to be created. With the advent of independent living centers for persons with disabilities and the advent of alternative schools and lifestyles for able-bodied individuals, there has been created a possibility for studies of adolescence that are relevant to *their* real-life problems.

Long-Term Adjustment

Few programs provide long-term counseling and adjustment services to adolescents after they leave high school. Yet long-term services are required by many disabled adolescents, especially those with mental illness, mental retardation, and severe physical disability. Adolescents with mental illness require the services of day hospitals, social clubs, and half-way houses to ease the transition between hospital and community. Adolescents with mental retardation require lifelong counseling and advocacy services to help them become integrated with the community. Studies of long-term adjustment of mentally retarded persons carried out at the Waisman Center[34] have shown that a large group of retarded students disappear from community contact after leaving school. This group frequently have greater difficulty in social adjustment since they lack rehabilitation services. Rehabilitation services offered to retarded students after high school are minimal at best. The real cost to the retarded young adults is that they do not get placed on jobs quickly or suitably for their limitations. Many of those eventually found by the Wisconsin studies are on SSI or general relief and live in community shelters in urban centers.

Rosenberg[35] found that 79 graduates of a public school for orthopedically handicapped persons attained a higher level of full-time employment and income when they were moderately handicapped and received vocational training after high school leading to a position protected by antidiscriminatory legislation. Of the 79 students, 64 percent entered college, 18 percent entered vocational training programs, and 18 percent sought employment. The relationship between college education and higher-status employment held only for a few college graduates who had professional status. The normal relationship between college education and employment status did not hold for this population. The more severely handicapped individuals went to college, thereby postponing the time when they would have to seek employment.

IMPLICATIONS OF RECENT LEGISLATION FOR DISABLED ADOLESCENTS

The passage of the Rehabilitation Act of 1973 and the Rehabilitation Amendments of 1978 has ensured the provision of services to disabled children and adolescents. One important change is that rehabilitation services are no longer restricted to vocational rehabilitation. This change means that disabled adolescents in need of social skills and vocational development can receive comprehensive services for independent living as part of their rehabilitation program. These services may be given to any individual who is so limited by the severity of the disability that comprehensive services "are required to improve significantly either his ability to engage in employment or his ability to function independently in his family or community."[36] Comprehensive services may include counseling, housing, transportation, attendant care, recreational activities, job placement, physical rehabilitation, therapeutic treatment, prostheses, and health maintenance. These services may be used to meet the needs for independence and sexual identity that are so urgent in adolescence. At the same time, vocational needs are not ignored, as counseling and job placement are provided.

The new amendments make possible counseling throughout the life span of disabled individuals. Adolescents before age 16 may obtain prevocational services through an integrated program of special education and rehabilitation services. As disabled individuals proceed through secondary school to post-graduate training, they may obtain vocational services. When individuals reach retirement age, they may obtain independent living services in order to remain independent, at home, and in control of their own life. Rehabilitation counseling programs should introduce training for life span counseling.[37] These programs should emphasize the coordination of special education, vocational rehabilitation, and welfare services for persons with permanent disabilities. Prevention of additional disability by timely medical and social services may be encouraged by the independent living amendments. Students in rehabilitation counseling should be placed as interns in educational settings and pediatric hospitals. As counselors, pediatricians, teachers, and school social workers get to work with each other, there will be smoother cooperation. An individualized educational plan needs to be integrated with an individualized rehabilitation plan. The transition from school to vocational training can be made a little easier when a multidisciplinary approach is taken.

The question remains whether the integration of special education and vocational rehabilitation will continue to be pushed by the Congress. At present there is hardly enough money to fund each program separately, and hardly enough money to provide independent living services for disabled adults. Although the Rehabilitation Amendments of 1978 call for independent living programs, the Congress has provided a pittance for this activity. When the political pressures of disabled adults are added to the political pressures coming from special educators, parents of disabled children, and disabled adolescents themselves, then it is clear that there are inadequate funds for equal shares of the federal "pie."

We who are concerned with the rehabilitation of the disabled adolescent need to advocate special funding for this group. A section of the rehabilitation act should be earmarked for this group. Without special funding, money tends to get diffused throughout the system. One of the purposes of placing rehabilitation in the Department of Education was to integrate education for the handicapped with vocational rehabilitation. Let us make this possible by a strong amendment to the next Rehabilitation Act.

REFERENCES

1. Friedman, Ruth. The Vicissitudes of Adolescent Development and What It Activates in Adults. *Adolescence*. Winter, 1975. 10:40:520–526.
2. Zeltzer, Lonnie. Chronic Illness in the Adolescent. In: *Topics in Adolescent Medicine*, by Shenker, I. Ronald (ed). New York: Stratton Intercontinental Book Corp., 1978.
3. Schonfeld, William A. Body Image in Adolescents: A Psychiatric Concept for the Pediatrician. *Pediatrics*. May, 1963. 31:845–855.
4. Erikson, Erik H. *Childhood and Society*. New York: W. W. Norton, 1950.

5. Solomon, Philip, and Patch, Vernon. *Handbook of Psychiatry.* Los Altos, Calif.: Lange Medical Publications, 1974.

6. Goldberg, Richard T. Adjustment of Children with Invisible and Visible Handicaps: Congenital Heart Disease and Facial Burns. *J. Counseling Psychol.* 1974. 21:5:428–432.

7. Goldberg, Richard T.; Shwachman, Harry; and Isralsky, Marc. Rehabilitation with Cystic Fibrosis: From Utopia to Reality. *Rehab. Lit.* Sept.–Oct., 1980. 41:9–10:218–228.

8. Dembo, Tamara; Leviton, Gloria; and Wright, Beatrice. Adjustment to Misfortune: A Problem of Social-Psychological Rehabilitation. *Artificial Limbs.* 1956. 3:4–62.

9. Abramson, Marty; Ash, Michael; and Nash, William. Handicapped Adolescents—A Time for Reflection. *Adolescence.* Fall, 1979. 14:55:557–565.

10. Goldberg, Richard T., and Johnson, B. Delia. A Comparative Study of Five Groups of Handicapped Children in Vocational Rehabilitation. *Scandinavian J. Rehab. Med.* 1978. 10:215–220.

11. Masters, W. H., and Johnson, V. E. *Human Sexual Response.* Boston, Mass.: Little, Brown, 1966.

12. Mayers, Kathleen S. Sexual and Social Concerns of the Disabled: A Group Counseling Approach. *Sexuality and Disability.* Summer, 1978. 1:2:100–111.

13. Sexual Attitude Reassessment Seminar, Boston University School of Medicine, Apr. 12–13, 1980.

14. Wabrek, Alan; Wabrek, Carolyn; and Burchell, R. Clay. The Human Tragedy of Spina Bifida: Spina Myelomeningocele. *Sexuality and Disability.* Fall, 1978. 1:3:210–217.

15. Kempton, Winifred. Sex Education for the Mentally Handicapped. *Sexuality and Disability.* Summer, 1978. 1:2:137–146.

16. Rothenberg, Gloria; Franzblau, Susan; and Geer, James. Educating the Learning Disabled Adolescent About Sexuality. *J. Learning Disabilities.* Nov., 1979. 12:9:10–14.

17. Laitman, Emily. Group Counseling: Sexuality and the Hearing Impaired Adolescent. *Sexuality and Disability.* Fall, 1979. 2:3:169–177.

18. Neff, Jan. Another Perspective on Sexuality and Those Who Are Deaf and Blind. *Sexuality and Disability.* Fall, 1979. 2:3:206–210.

19. Hudgens, Richard W. The Antisocial Personality and Similar Disorders. In: *Psychiatric Disorders in Adolescence,* by Hudgens, R. (ed). Baltimore, Md.: Williams & Wilkins, 1974.

20. Ginsberg, Eli; Ginsburg, S. W.; Axelrod, S.; and Herma, J. L. *Occupational Choice.* New York: Columbia University Press, 1951.

21. Blau, Peter M.; Gustad, J. W.; Jessor, R.; Parnes, H. S.; and Wilcock, R. C. Occupational Choice: A Conceptual Framework. *Industrial Labor Relations Rev.* 1956. 9:531–543.

22. Hunter, Patricia N., and Zuger, Rosalind R. Easing the Transition from School to Work for Students with Severe Physical Disabilities. A Summer Work Experience. *Rehab. Lit.* Oct., 1979. 40:10:298–308.

23. Strathe, Marlene, and Hash, Virginia. The Effect of an Alternative School on Adolescent Self-Esteem. *Adolescence.* Spring, 1979. 14:53:185–189.

24. Victor, Jack. "Career Educational Alternatives for the Physically Disabled." Presented at the American Psychological Association Symposium on Handicapped Children and Adolescents. Montreal, Canada, Sept., 1980.
25. Abramson, Marty; Ash, Michael; and Nash, William. Handicapped Adolescents—A Time for Reflection. *Adolescence.* Fall, 1979. 14:55:557–565.
26. Haraguchi, Rosemary S. "Programs Meeting the Special Needs of Physically Disabled Adolescents." Paper presented at the American Psychological Association Symposium on Handicapped Children and Adolescents. Montreal, Canada, Sept., 1980.
27. Nigro, Giovanna. Some Observations on Personal Relationships and Sexual Relationships Among Lifelong Disabled Americans. *Rehab. Lit.* Nov.–Dec., 1976. 37:11–12:328–334.
28. Cooper, Bruce S. Occupational Help for the Severely Disabled: A Public School Model. *Rehab. Lit.* Mar., 1977. 38:3:66–74.
29. Kohring, Curt, and Tracht, Vernon S. A New Approach to a Vocational Program for Severely Handicapped High School Students. *Rehab. Lit.* May, 1978. 39:5:138–146.
30. Goldberg, Richard T.; Bernstein, Norman; and Crosby, Roberta. Vocational Development of Adolescents with Burn Injury. *Rehab. Counseling Bul.* Mar., 1975. 19:140–146.
31. Super, Donald. *The Psychology of Careers.* New York: Harper & Row, 1957.
32. Tiedeman, David V., and O'Hara, Robert P. *Career Development: Choice and Adjustment.* New York: College Board, 1963.
33. Hershenson, David. A Life Stage Vocational Development System. *J. Counseling Psychol.* 1968. 15:23–30.
34. Garber, Howard. "Study of the Mentally Retarded At-Risk for Post-Secondary School Adjustment." Paper presented at the American Psychological Association Symposium on Handicapped Children and Adolescents. Montreal, Canada, Sept., 1980.
35. Rosenberg, Janet. The Relationship of Types of Post-High School Education to Occupation and Economic Independence of Physically Handicapped Adults. *Rehab. Lit.* Feb., 1978. 38:2:45–49.
36. Rehabilitation Amendments of 1978, Public Law 95-602, Title VII, Comprehensive Services for Independent Living.
37. Fortess, Esther. "Preparing Counselors for Implementation of Recent Legislation." Paper presented at the American Psychology Association Symposium on Handicapped Children and Adolescents. Montreal, Canada, Sept., 1980.

7

Physical Rehabilitation and Family Dynamics

Hilda P. Versluys

The role of the family in rehabilitation is crucial. The family's response to the injured or ill person may determine the patient's motivation to tolerate painful procedures and long-term treatment, to face irrevocable losses, and to accept major lifestyle changes. The nuclear family is ill equipped as an organization to deal with stresses and tasks of a severely disabled member. Family size and age distribution of its members limit the role substitutions possible.[1]

Excellent treatment programs may never realize their potential, due to the collapse of a concerned but overwhelmed family. One family solution to such a crisis may be alienation and withdrawal from a relationship with the patient. Even a stable family may be disrupted by a consideration of the stresses involved in caring for the disabled patient.[2] The treatment of choice should involve not only the patient in collaboration with the rehabilitation team, but the family members as well, in programming and individual consultations that meet their needs.

FAMILY REACTIONS TO STRESS

The Role of The Family

An adequately organized family can meet the multiple emotional needs of its members and deal with the stresses and uncertainties of life. Such a family can resolve stress through interfamily action. For example, family members can (1) temporarily decrease their own personal ambitions to deal with family crisis, (2) work out new role patterns to carry on family func-

From *Rehabilitation Literature*, 41(3-4) (1980), 58-65. Reprinted with permission. Published by the National Easter Seal Society, 2023 W. Ogden, Chicago, IL 60612.

tions, and (3) develop collective goals in time of emergency and work toward them cooperatively.[3]

These families usually have previous experience and success in mediating crisis; they have the ability to adapt to change, there is affection among the family members, a good marital adjustment, and a family history of meeting problems through interfamily discussion and problem solving.

An inadequately organized family is vulnerable to crisis, because family roles are inadequate to deal with stress, member behaviors tend to precipitate more problems, and the flexibility to reorganize or to role share in an emergency is lacking. Such families have difficulty in making consistent commitments and in supporting the patient. Their interactions with staff and the patient may impede or prevent rehabilitation success.[2,3]

Family responses can be positive and supportive; for example, family willingness to reestablish and maintain the patient's valued roles, the involvement of the patient in family decision making, and family understanding of the kind of support useful to the patient. The family responses can also be negative and pathological, leading to overprotection, encouragement of dependency, neglect, avoidance of future planning, denial of the diagnosis, excessive and inappropriate demands, and punitive action toward the patient.[1,4,5]

Patients do not make accommodations to physical illness or disability independently of their families. Even intrapsychic processes, such as the movement from denial into mourning or the renegotiation of early fears (such as the fear of abandonment or destruction of self), may be influenced by family attitudes or values. Influencing factors may include family attitudes of rejection or hostility and continued denial of a disability's permanence.

Stages of Family Adjustment

Resolving stress is an interfamily task, and the family's success or failure in coping with crisis is prognostic. Intervention at crisis points by rehabilitation staff is assistive in reaching treatment goals and is based on an understanding of the adjustment process.

The therapist needs to note initial reactions to stress on the part of the family during the first few weeks, allowing for normal responses to crisis. Kaplan indicates that early case finding and intervention reduces the incidence of family disorder and breakdown. The crucial time for the development of healthy coping patterns is during the first 3–4 weeks.[4]

Christopherson outlines the chronological order of rehabilitation as follows: initially the family is vaguely aware of the implications of the illness or disability, and their responses will depend on the quality of relationship within the family. During the reconstruction stage, the patient works to regain function through surgery or a physical/medical regimen. At this point, modification of social, sexual, vocational, and economic roles begins either on a temporary or permanent basis. When all rehabilitation measures available have been utilized, the plateau stage begins. This may be the most difficult time in terms of family relationships, since all hope for a complete recovery is gone, economic and emotional resources have worn thin, and future decisions must be made concerning placement. Both the patient and family may experience severe emotional reactions at this point.[6]

Coping tasks to reduce stress vary significantly with each disease or disability. Reversing a trend to maladaptive coping and facilitating adaptive tasks requires knowledge of the disease process and patterns of adjustment specific to each.[4]

Initial and Continued Reactions

Brodland, in his study of burn patients, outlines both initial and continued reactions to a medical crisis.[7] Initial reactions relevant to physical disability and medical illness include:

1. Relief that the patient did not die or was not more severely hurt.
2. A primary concern for the recovery of the patient.
3. Fear and anxiety in dealing with patient behaviors, such as depression or hostility, the delirium of a brain injured patient, or the regression of the patient after surgery.
4. Distrust and hostility toward medical staff (concerning the diagnoses, the pain, the loss of the person as they know him/her).

Continued reactions include:

1. Family disappointment at results that the medical staff may consider very good (appearance of grafting in burn cases, return of some function in persons with spinal cord injury or cerebral vascular accident).
2. A struggle for psychological preparation for the future (beginning to look at lifestyle change for the total family).
3. Concerns about continued pain, difficult treatment procedures.
4. Trying to deal with the patient's disclosure of feelings such as frustration, grief (the family may discourage such ventilation to preserve its own comfort).
5. The family may cling to unrealistic optimism.

DISORDERED FAMILY DYNAMICS

Family Relationships

Families who are overprotective, are highly anxious, and encourage dependent behaviors may prevent total rehabilitation. For example, a mother whose family is reared but enjoyed the mothering role may be tempted to encourage dependency in a handicapped adolescent or young adult.[8]

Litman found that the existence of close family ties and willingness of others to take care of the disabled often discouraged achievable levels of independence.[9] When the family sees the disabled as being more dependent or sicker than he/she is, efforts toward independence are discouraged. The patient is reinforced to behave according to family expectations, which often discourages the disabled from undergoing the rigors of treatment. This kind of overprotection by family members leads to gradual deterioration and loss of rehabilitation gains. Families may feel they know what is best for the family member and impose their plans and opinions without consideration of the patient's interests or personal goals. Such family responses result in patient regressions, depression, and feelings of helplessness and anxiety. A cross-fire situation exists when the family, staff, and patient differ in their perceptions of the patient's ability to be independent.[9]

Families may hold certain attitudes and values toward disease and illness. They may equate cancer with death, hysterectomy with total eradication of a woman's role,[10] or brain damage as producing a permanent child-like state with no hope for a useful life. It may be difficult for the family to adjust and change their view of the patient as he or she progresses and gains independence and adaptive skills. Cultural or religious beliefs may prevent the patient or family from accepting the recommended treatment. They may view medical systems as untrustworthy and seek advice from lay consultants. Safilios-Rothschild states that the family may regard the disability or injury as punishment for a sin or evidence of guilt and thus may punish the patient by withdrawal or subtle criticism.[9]

A family may already be in crisis due to long-standing resentments or interfamily control issues and anger at past wrongs (such as a spouse's infidelity). They may be punitive toward the patient, take control and prevent the patient from resuming major roles, or reject the relationship altogether. A traumatized family member may be unable to manage and may seek so much support from the patient that his/her emotional equilibrium is in jeopardy. They may absorb staff time to a deleterious degree or become ill themselves and demand equal treatment.

Versluys states that the patient can be placed in the position of dealing with personal adjustments and also supporting his or her family in their denial or anxiety states. The patient is sometimes put in a position of helping others, both family and friends, to relate to the new disability. Some families completely deny the permanence of the disability even after the patient has recognized the permanence of the handicapping or medical condition. Rather than hurt the family, the patient allows the deception.[8]

Critical Family Issues

A critical dynamic occurs when family members do not support the medical regimen (ignoring dietary restrictions in diabetic or cardiac patients or bans on smoking and prescription for weight loss). Jaffe suggests that noncompliance to medical prescriptions is a family problem. In studies of coronary patients who continued to ignore risk factors like diet, exercise, smoking, and lack of relaxation, he found that spouses had not been meeting their husbands'/wives' medical needs, and they were encouraged to assist their spouses in change through family treatment.[11]

Flights into activity accompany the inability of the family to face realities of illness, and to grieve. The family members may become involved in new activities, make changes in the family composition, move to a new home, take on a new job, and spend money on travel or unnecessary purchases. These activities support the denial, increase the family burdens, and absorb both emotional and physical resources needed to contend with stresses of illness and disability.[4]

Problems develop within the family constellation and affect the patient's morale when (1) the family fills the patient's roles on a permanent basis, (2) the patient gets mixed messages concerning the continuation of a role, and (3) the patient returns home and finds his/her roles distributed among family members, given away to others with no place of meaning left.[2,5,6] For example, the spouse finds another role partner or another child.

Kaplan speaks of discrepant coping in which the family members take opposing views concerning the long-term goals for the patient, including telling the patient the diagnosis, caring for the patient at home, handling of continued crisis, and even the values and meaning of medical treatment.[4] Family members may base decisions about the acceptance of rehabilitation or medical treatment goals on the advice of lay consultants. Such coping methods produce a lack of communication, prevent grieving, weaken and undermine family relationships, facilitate denial, and encourage avoidance behaviors. In addition, family members may not feel they are supported by other members during a crisis, leading to resentment and hostility.

Jaffe states that the family has a role in creating an environment which may either prevent or encourage exacerbation or maintenance of illness (as in systematic, neurological, cardiac disease). Individual response to psychosomatic disease may be influenced by family relationships and interfamily behavior patterns. Stressful family processes and life events are important causal factors in illness and health.[11]

In a review of studies on personality and family variables in relation to cancer, many studies supporting the association between cancer and loss of a person or object that is emotionally significant can be found. Thomas and Duszynski report that long-term data suggests that certain childhood family patterns can be linked with certain types of emotional and physical illness occurring many years later.[11]

Secondary Gain

Jaffe feels that secondary gain is present in the majority of illnesses and thus contributes to a reluctance or inability to get well and to the delayed recovery.[11] Minuchin suggests that a sick child plays an important role in the family pattern of conflict avoidance and that this is an important reinforcer of symptoms. The sick child may keep a couple from having to spend time together or keep a wife from her husband, since she needs to spend time nursing the child. Thus, the ill member can absorb the family's energy concentration and assist in conflict avoidance. Secondary gains for the patient may include care, affection and attention, the avoidance of responsibility, a desired dependent status, and control over the family.[8] Simonton and Simonton offer examples of the association of secondary gain with poor responses to cancer treatment.[11]

Other Problem Areas

1. Morbid preoccupation with the disease or disability such as cancer or paralysis, with lack of focus on remaining assets and skills.[4,8]
2. Denial of the reality of the diagnosis and avoidance of those who refer to the facts and try to deal with them—for example, hostility toward staff.[9]
3. Efforts of some family members to prevent grieving in the service of denial.
4. Family suspicion toward medical staff, distrust of medical advice, and possible termination of treatment.[1,8] Such responses may be cultural or religious in nature and part of the family value system.
5. Family efforts (sometimes extreme) to keep diagnostic implications from the patient. This may be due to their own fear and inability to accept diagnostic implications.[4]
6. Family behaviors of open rejection. For example, missing treatment sessions, neglecting home care, refusal to seek out community resources, and avoidance of future planning with the patient[4] (such

as refusal to order a wheelchair and necessary orthotic equipment, or neglecting to make the home accessible).
7. The displacement of family anger and resentment onto the physician and other professionals.

ADAPTIVE FAMILY DYNAMICS

Functional Attitudes

Lowery states that the quality of the interpersonal relationships within the family is far more important than the disability itself.[1] Others suggest that reaction of the family is the crucial determinant of the extent of rehabilitation from chronic illness.

Families who communicate attitudes of essential worth to the patient help to stabilize the self-concept, foster a positive attitude toward the future, and facilitate maintenance of rehabilitation gains.[1,9] Lewis and Bloom state that the presence of a supportive individual early in the diagnosis/treatment phase of breast cancer appears critical to psychological rehabilitation.[12] Hackett states that a good result in a myocardial infarction patient getting prompt treatment and good follow-up care is due to "the executive wife."[13] Dyk and Sutherland report a study of cancer surgery (colostomy) that indicates that the quality of the emotional response and support experienced by the patient within his/her family (especially the spouse) is the important factor in restoration of self-esteem, acceptance of the colostomy, and resocialization.[14]

The family's willingness to maintain or reestablish the patient's roles is an important motivator in rehabilitation. The family can influence the patient's maintenance of roles by (1) their ability to continue to relate to the patient and to see him/her in a major family role, thus contributing to the stability of the patient's self-concept, (2) the willingness to carry out role tasks to allow the patient to continue in a major role, (3) their communication of the patient's value in the organization of the family, and (4) their identification of important and necessary roles the patient can contribute to, within the limits of dysfunction.

Barckley states that "families wonder what to bring the patient, but in the end the greatest gift comes from a loving heart and an understanding mind and an attitude that nothing can happen to the patient that the family's compassion and concern can't alleviate."[15]

FAMILY RESPONSE TO LONG-TERM CARE

Issues around Discharge

An interesting area for further study is how the family absorbs the patient and what assists them in doing so. The patient's personality, strength, and original social role in the family appear to be the best predictors of home success. The patient is more likely to return home if there are valid and responsible roles that can be performed.[16]

Safilios-Rothschild states that married women with children, even if severely disabled, are usually taken back by the family unit because they can maintain part of their usual role functions. The role tasks of the homemaker in planning, organization of family activities, participating in decision making and problem solving, and enabling and encouraging other family members makes their presence a benefit. Active homemaking tasks can be carried out by others.[9]

Research shows that the single disabled person tends to be more independent in activities of daily living functions than the married disabled person. The greater the necessity to perform tasks and roles, the greater the probability the disabled will use all their abilities to do so and will find ways to become as independent as their disability permits.[9]

The first year at home is critical for both the patient and the family. For example, both a spinal cord injured patient and the family may become depressed as they face the problem of mobility, isolation, and time restrictions due to extensive nursing care. Families may find their personal freedom restricted by responsibility for the patient and may find it difficult to meet needs for attention and companionship. Families may withdraw and isolate themselves. They may have their own negative feelings about the disability and may try to protect the patient and themselves from contact with others and possible rejection.[1,4,17] Diller states that there tends to be behavioral disruption when a patient having a cerebral vascular accident (CVA) returns home; the spouse or family has to adapt to new role responsibilities, there are problems finding economic support, there is a void in leisure time activities, and there is difficulty in working alone to maintain physical function.[17] Family members may become overloaded, absent themselves from home, neglect any companionship roles, or exclude the patient from family gatherings.

When the patient is discharged, even a stable family may be overwhelmed by the magnitude of the disability. We cannot assume that families always have the intelligence, values, education, motivation, or interest to enable them as a unit to proceed as cooperative members of the rehabilitation team. For example, there is a higher incidence of wives deserting their husbands who are severely disabled, especially when there is an inability to perform vocational, economic, and sexual roles.[9]

Alienation and negative family attitudes may be due to emotional, economic, and energy drains and the need for support, empathy, and assistance with problem solving. Families run out of energy both physically and psychologically in a constant effort to be adequate. Some families have fewer resources than others and lower thresholds of tolerance to crisis and frustration. Such families may, with support and counseling, still be able to play a role in the lives of their disabled member.

Communication Patterns

Interfamily communication patterns may omit the disabled.[1,18] Upon discharge, the patient may find that the family has developed a system where communication of vital family business takes place outside his/her presence. This alienates the patient from full family participation. Defective communication may be due to an effort not to burden the disabled member or resentment that the patient is no longer contributing to family role responsibilities. The disabled person may become the target for family hostility due to displacement of affection or projection concerning other failures and disappointments. Such secret communication may include planning for the patient without his/her knowledge. The result of these communication practices is to neutralize interfamily communication, since members are afraid to air their own feelings and needs or bring up controversial subjects (family economics, vacation planning, etc.).

Reactions of Family Members

Evidence suggests that spouses of chronically ill persons develop symptoms such as nervousness, fatigue, role tension, and depression to a degree equal to or greater than that of the patient.[9,11] The result may be precipitation of illness in the spouse influencing the patient's chances of returning home.

Spouse responses to patient illness show an increase in symptomatic levels of nervousness, fatigue, and role tension during illness.[12]

Wishnie, Hackett, and Cassem state that wives of coronary patients suffer from marked inhibition to deal with their feelings when the patient is discharged. They are unable to express the hostility that is a by-product of tension, fatigue, and lack of attention to their personal needs. They may feel guilty about the heart attack and about their personal needs and feelings and hold back grievances and frustrations in fear that such expression might bring on another myocardial infarction. The resulting behavior may be in the form of reaction formation such as overprotection or controlling behavior of a punitive nature. Such reactions result in familial discord.[19]

Dependent wives need to reverse lifelong patterns of overreliance upon their husbands. For example, they may insist that husbands with recent CVA incidents with aphasia continue to make important family decisions when they are incapable of doing so.

A spouse may grow to enjoy the leadership role and feelings of total control to the extent that the psychological growth of the patient is neutralized. The spouse may reinforce dependent, infantile behaviors and discourage resumption of major roles, resulting in a parent-child relationship. For example, the spouse of an aphasic patient will "speak" for him/her and totally control all family activities. In addition, children, out of mistaken kindness, may insist on meeting every parental need and thus encourage dependency.[18]

WAYS THE PROFESSIONAL CAN HELP

Jaffe feels that treatment for disordered family dynamics should not be confined to the psychotherapist's office; rather, it should be an integral part of comprehensive medical care offered through members of the medical team. Treatment goals are to change the way the family works together, and to help individual family members change the parts of their lives that contribute to stress, hinder rehabilitation, or lead to interfamily conflicts.[11]

Kaplan and Mearig see informal problem solving as the best way a professional can help. Their research project of providing a family support system through home visits and consistent interaction with the family allowed the staff to grasp the reality of "how would I deal with this situation in their place?"[20] Minuchin's strategy in treating psychosomatic illness in children is to help the patient to become more independent, as well as to convince the family to be less concerned, less intrusive, and to focus less on the patient's physical status. Family members should also be encouraged to get back to normal functions and personal outlets and interests.[11] Diller suggests that spouses or families of aphasic stroke patients need to see value in small-term goals. They need to see changes that occur in small specific functions of daily living as stepping stones vital to the progress of the patient. Such attitudes can be transmitted to the family by the therapist.[17]

Staff Reactions

Rehabilitation staff are nurturing people. The intensity and the commitment demanded in long-term rehabilitation require the ability to give and to care. Staff may also develop rescue fantasies concerning certain patients. They tend to go into competition with the family. Staff may make value judgments concerning family relationships, note neurotic tendencies, or call attention to the refusal to make necessary home adjustments or to order equipment on time. A stressed, hostile family may evoke counterhostility.[1,8]

The staff, while caring for the patient and understanding the individual's process of accommodation, develops a tendency to expect the family to show instant ability to cope with the problems and adjustment of having a disabled family member.

Family Reactions

Families vary in their ability to assess the situation and make compromises in life plans. For example, the transfer of the patient from an acute setting to a rehabilitation unit may signal to the family that this is the end of their worries and the patient is getting better (or in reverse, that the doctors have given up). Families need better information — including explanation of the purpose of treatment procedures, operation of the rehabilitation unit, simple facts about the injury, understanding of the roles of each professional, where they may get important questions answered, and what approach would be most helpful to the patient in the rehabilitation process. The family may have mixed feelings toward the patient, such as guilt, hostility, grief, and feelings of having lost a valued family member as they knew him/her. Not all families have the strength, resources, maturity, or stability to care daily for the severely disabled patient.[1,4,7]

Families may find they are in the way on the wards and in the treatment areas. Busy staff have little time for questions, anxieties, and fears. They may find the family intrusive or dependent, and feel that the patient/family interaction is harmful and not in the patient's best interests.

Families should not be made to feel guilty about their perceived inadequacies, or they will be driven away from any involvement with the patient. Even if the family does not have the emotional or physical resources to take the patient into the home and even if the patient needs to be cared for in an institution, aspects of family relationships can be maintained. The family can be encouraged to visit and to take the patient home for weekends and holidays.

It is unrealistic to expect families to deal with these problems unaided. Families need help in thinking through values, broadening their outlook on the meaning of function and dysfunction, and recognizing that disability does not affect all capacities.[21] The family is also traumatized and should be treated simultaneously with the patient.

Counseling Guidelines

- Be available and therapeutic with the family.
- Identify and appreciate their feelings (grief, disappointment, etc.).[4]
- Encourage ventilation of "hidden" feelings without turning them off or judging.
- Counsel the family to stay in a holding pattern and not to undertake flights of activity.
- Keep the focus on the real crisis.[7]
- Deliver basic information useful to the family and patient.[7]
- Help the family to see that their feelings are normal and acceptable.
- Provide praise for small accomplishments.[17]
- Create bridges to appropriate community support systems.[7]
- Explore the family's and patient's ideas for coping with problems. It is not always necessary to be the authority.

— Provide programs and services that are responsive to family/patient reactions in the early stages of adjustment.
— Discuss alternatives with the family that are realistic but focused on hopeful possibilities.
— Provide information concerning procedures, simple facts about the injury, and the purpose of treatment methods.[7]
— Work to prevent family rejection of the patient or alienation.
— Discuss realistic aspects of being at home again.[19]
— Listen without offering false hope; suggest that you are concerned with how they manage and how they feel.
— Identify what is essential for the patient's welfare and what is not.
— Help with setting limits for the patient and in understanding and dealing with difficult patient behaviors.[4]
— Understand and respond to the family's fear of another incident (or another myocardial infarction, etc.).

Goals of treatment programming are to influence the remedial, supportive, and communicative skills within the family group. Programming objectives include (1) the development of a social/play arena where interpersonal relationships between patient and family can be strengthened through mutually shared activities and where relatives can learn to relate to their family member's change in health status, (2) group problem-solving sessions combining one or more families and focused both on the practical and emotional aspects of rehabilitation, (3) groups combining one or more families focusing on encouragement of expression of patient/family feelings, and (4) task-oriented groups focused on identifying and practicing new living skills through task assignment, within the hospital or in the community.[22]

Treatment Model Examples

D'Afflitti and Weitz designed a treatment group for stroke patients to focus on the difficulties of patients and their families in adjusting their lives to chronic disability, especially when it came time for discharge. The patients were engaged in treatment programs, but the family members had difficulty with emotional acceptance of the patient's disability. This resulted in strained family relationships and negatively influenced discharge planning.

Goals of the family and patient group included (1) interfamily communication concerning feelings about the impact of the disability on family life, (2) counseling to gain more realistic perceptions about the real limitations of the disability, (3) encouragement of patients to share their feelings about the stroke (patients' fear of loss of control, loss of family, feelings of inadequacy), (4) promotion of constructive adjustment to the disability, and (5) encouragement of family and patients to use appropriate community resources and support systems.[23]

This treatment group model can be implemented within the hospital before discharge or as a follow-up group on an outpatient basis, located either at the hospital or at the homes of patients and their families. The model can be activity-oriented and organized around social experiences. Handicapped role models or successful functioning family groups are facilitating.

Hoffman and Futterman describe an outpatient family support group developed by a psychologist and occupational therapist in an outpatient pediatric cancer treatment clinic. The therapeutic goals were to influence family coping tasks required in facing serious and possibly terminal illness in children. Initial goals included reinforcing the cohesiveness of the stressed family unit, preventing isolation and withdrawal, encouraging involvement, and sharing with other families to facilitate a supportive environment. A play group was designed for the children/patients to counteract the oppressiveness of treatment, increase feelings of mastery, reaffirm identity, reduce feelings of vulnerability, provide an outlet for expression of anxiety, and release tension.[24]

This group model is applicable to other diagnostic groups, such as in stroke or spinal cord injury follow-up clinics. Family task-oriented groups are interhospital groups with the goals of maintaining family role relationships. Emphasis is on programming to provide opportunities for families to interact with the handicapped member. Families are involved in dialogue concerning the adjustments to the disability, treatment issues, planning for discharge, and social and recreational activities. Activities planned by staff, patients, and families help to reduce the tension a family feels on relating to the patient in an altered physical form or with a severe medical illness. Bridging activities include dinners prepared by patients or family, trips, game nights and parties, and entertainment by family and friends. These experiences allow the family to observe how the staff relates to the patient and what they expect in independent behavior.

Jaffe discusses the value of family support groups in maintaining interfamily change; for example, fostering good health regimens such as weight loss, loyalty to prescribed diets, new communicative patterns, and role tasks. Family patterns may be rigid and resistant to change. Supportive family groups reinforce positive change.[11] Other areas ripe for the expansion of family and patient programming services include adult or geriatric day treatment centers, community clubs for the handicapped, the visiting nurses' association, and community sponsored agencies delivering health services to the physically disabled, aged, and homebound.

SUMMARY

Literature indicates that even concerned and stable families can be overwhelmed and alienated from the patient by the residual effects of physical injury and the long-term, progressive, and disabling results of chronic disease. Disordered and disorganized families can, with support and counseling, maintain contact with the patient and contribute to the maintenance of rehabilitation gains. Staff identification of functional and dysfunctional family dynamics as influencing remediation is of diagnostic significance and provides information for the development of treatment goals and programming. The staff, while caring for the patient and understanding trauma and behavioral reactions, should make allowances for the stressors that impinge on family structures.

REFERENCES

1. *The Source Book: Rehabilitation of the Person with Spinal Cord Injury.* Washington, D.C.: Superintendent of Documents, U.S. Government Printing Office, n.d. (Stock No. 4100-00063)
2. Kutner, B. The Social Psychology of Disability. In: Neff, Walter S., ed. *Rehabilitation Psychology.* Washington, D.C.: American Psychological Association, 1970.
3. Hill, R. Social Stresses on the Family: Generic Features of Families under Stress. *Social Casework.* 1958. 39:139–150.
4. Kaplan, David M.; Smith, Aaron; Grobstein, Rose; and Fischman, Stanley E. Family Mediation of Stress. In: Moos, Rudolf H., ed. *Coping with Physical Illness.* New York: Plenum Medical Book Co., 1977.
5. Weissman, Roe, and Kutner, Bernard. Role Disorders in Extended Hospitalization. *Hosp. Admin.* 1967. 12:1:52–59.
6. Christopherson, Victor A. The Patient and Family. *Rehab. Lit.* Feb., 1962. 23:2:34–41.
7. Brodland, Gene A., and Andreasen, N. J. C. Adjustment Problems of the Family of the Burn Patient. In: Moos, Rudolf H., ed. *Coping with Physical Illness.* New York: Plenum Medical Book Co., 1977.
8. Versluys, Hilda P. Psychological Adjustment to Physical Disability. In: Trombly, Catherine Anne, and Scott, Anna Deane, eds. *Occupational Therapy for Physical Dysfunction.* Baltimore, Md.: Williams & Wilkins, 1977.
9. Safilios-Rothschild, Constantina. *The Sociology and Social Psychology of Disability and Rehabilitation.* New York: Random House, 1970.
10. Williams, M. A. Easier Convalescence from Hysterectomy. *Am. J. Nursing.* 1976. 438–440.
11. Jaffe, D. T. The Role of Family Therapy in Treating Physical Illness. *Hosp. & Comm. Psychology.* 1978. 29:169–174.
12. Lewis, F. M., and Bloom, J. R. Psychosocial Adjustment to Breast Cancer: A Review of Selected Literature. *Internatl. J. Psychiatry in Med.* 1978. 9:1–17.
13. Hackett, T. P. Lecture on cardiac rehabilitation. Boston, Mass.: Sargent College of Allied Health Professions, Boston University, 1977.
14. Dyk, R. B., and Sutherland, A. M. Adaptation of the Spouse and Other Family Members to the Colostomy Patient. In: American Cancer Society. *Psychological Impact of Cancer.* New York: American Cancer Society, n.d.
15. Barckley, V. Families Facing Cancer. *Cancer News.* Spring/Summer, 1970.

16. McDaniel, James W. *Physical Disability and Human Behavior.* New York: Pergamon Press, 1969.
17. Diller, Leonard. Hemiplegia. In: Garrett, James F., and Levine, Edna S., eds. *Rehabilitation Practices with the Physically Disabled.* New York: Columbia University Press, 1973.
18. Wepman, Joseph M. Rehabilitation and Language Disorders. In: Garrett, James F., and Levine, Edna S., eds. *Rehabilitation Practices with the Physically Disabled.* New York: Columbia University Press, 1973.
19. Wishnie, Howard A.; Hackett, Thomas P.; and Cassem, Ned H. Psychological Hazards of Convalescence Following Myocardial Infarction. In: Moos, Rudolf H., ed. *Coping with Physical Illness.* New York: Plenum Medical Book Co., 1977.
20. Kaplan, Deborah, and Mearig, Judith S. A Community Support System for a Family Coping with Chronic Illness. *Rehab. Lit.* Mar., 1977. 38:3:79–82, 96.
21. Wright, Beatrice A. *Physical Disability: A Psychological Approach.* New York: Harper & Row, 1960.
22. Cogswell, Betty E. Self-Socialization: Readjustment of Paraplegics in the Community. *J. Rehab.* May–June, 1968. 34:3:11–13, 35.
23. D'Afflitti, Judith Gregorie, and Weitz, G. Wayne. Rehabilitating the Stroke Patient through Patient-Family Groups. In: Moos, Rudolf H., ed. *Coping with Physical Illness.* New York: Plenum Medical Book Co., 1977.
24. Hoffman, Irwin, and Futterman, Edward H. Coping with Waiting: Psychiatric Intervention and Study in the Waiting Room of a Pediatric Oncology Clinic. In: Moos, Rudolf H., ed. *Coping with Physical Illness.* New York: Plenum Medical Book Co., 1977.

Part III

The Personal Impact of Disability

The personal response to disability, at any given time, can vary on a continuum from denial of its existence to exaggeration of its consequences. This response is dependent upon a number of variables, including environmental, social, and psychological characteristics of the respondent.

In attempting to explain psychological reactions to physical disability, Shontz indicates that recent theories ascribe maladjustment to environmental rather than personal causes. His review of trends in theories provides current and valuable insights into disability's personal impact.

The relationship between disability and psychological adjustment is the theme of the second chapter by Shontz. Six important principles that refute many commonly held beliefs about physically disabled persons are provided. Shontz concludes that "the understanding of psychological reactions to physical disability requires the understanding of individual human beings in all their complexity."

In the final article of Part III, Hughes compares the grief reaction following a physical disability with the grief reaction following losses after death. The need to resolve grief and the consequences of a failure to do so are emphasized in the reading. Many suggestions useful to disabled persons and rehabilitation workers are provided.

8

Psychological Adjustment to Physical Disability: Trends in Theories

Franklin C. Shontz

Rehabilitation maintains a long-standing interest in improving its understanding of human behavior. In part, this interest derives from the need to assure that the expense and effort of rehabilitation do not go to waste because of patients' poor psychological adjustments to their physical conditions. To state the matter more positively, it stems from the desire to apply psychological insights to improve service delivery and to help patients gain maximum benefit from rehabilitative care. In addition, people who work in rehabilitation recognize that relations between patients and staff profoundly affect treatment outcomes. Assumptions about the causes of human behavior directly influence patient-staff interactions; therefore, it is important that rehabilitation professionals be sensitive to current thinking on the subject.

Over the years, ideas about the causes of psychological maladjustment to physical illness and disability have undergone considerable growth and development. Emphasis upon the mental traits of patients or the somatic properties of disabilities has diminished. At the same time, progressively greater emphasis has been placed upon physical and social environments as critical factors that shape patients' psychological reactions to their conditions.

Subsequent sections of this paper trace the evolution of this change in emphasis. Space limitations preclude providing elaborations of specific points of view or a complete bibliography. However, selected references are provided to facilitate further examination of the issues by readers who desire more detail.

From *Archives of Physical Medicine and Rehabilitation*, 59 (1978), 251–254. Reprinted by permission.

The author thanks Martha Thorp for her helpful criticisms and suggestions.

EARLY ASSUMPTIONS

Before serious study of the psychological aspects of physical disability began in the late 1940s, the fundamental cause of psychological disturbance
in persons with disabilities seemed obvious. Common sense supported the
belief that the primary source of distress in reactions to illness or to disability was the illness or disability itself. If a person with paraplegia had psychological problems, the evident cause of the problems was the spinal cord
injury and the logical solution was to restore neural functioning. Failing that,
alternatives were devised to help the person bypass or overcome the effects
of his condition by providing therapy and necessary equipment such as
braces, a wheelchair, and similar devices. It followed that, once a disability
was removed or circumvented, its associated psychological disturbances
should have disappeared along with it.[1]

But as the rehabilitation movement expanded and matured, especially after World War II, the realization grew that this conception of the cause
of problems in persons with chronic physical illnesses or disabilities was too
simple. Failures in rehabilitation often occurred, even with people whose
chronic diseases had been arrested or whose disabilities had been overcome,
and who possessed marketable vocational skills. Many such failures could
be attributed to psychological factors. For example, some patients continued
to insist they were ill or unable to work when all medical evidence indicated the contrary. Others neglected self-care and thereby brought on additional physical incapacitation. Apparently, removal or circumvention of disability alone was not always enough to insure success in rehabilitation.

MOTIVATION

In the search for an explanation of such failures, the idea grew that the problem stemmed from a deficiency within the clients. Adopting a concept from
the popular "dynamic" psychology of the day, experts began to describe people who did not respond favorably to rehabilitation as "unmotivated." This
term conveys the belief that certain individuals lack the necessary energy
or drive to take advantage of the opportunities provided them.

Before the concept of motivation became prominent, psychologists and
counselors in rehabilitation had typically been concerned exclusively with
evaluating clients' vocational aptitudes and providing training in work skills.
As the new theoretical developments took place, however, psychologists and
counselors began to engage in a variety of additional clinical and therapeutic activities intended to increase patients' effective levels of motivation. Results soon required another redefinition of the problem. In actual practice,
few patients truly lacked motivation; the problem was not usually a deficiency of psychological energy, but a blocking or misdirection of it.[2] A pa-

tient who rebels against treatment is obviously strongly motivated; from a treatment point of view the important question is why the patient's motives fail to correspond to those of the treatment staff.

PSYCHOANALYSIS

To answer that question, it became necessary to apply more complex theories of personality and adjustment. At the time, a great deal of effort was being expended in psychiatry and psychology to study and to treat abnormal mental states. Therefore, when rehabilitation took up the notion that patients who were uncooperative were psychologically maladjusted, its action was in accord with popular opinion among qualified professionals. Lack of motivation became transformed into a problem of mental health, and the theories that were subsequently adopted were those being generally used at the time to explain neuroses, psychoses, and character disorders.

Psychoanalytic theory was the obvious choice. Among other things, it contributed the idea that physically ill patients and persons with disabilities could be divided into the same personality types as mentally ill patients. Psychoanalytic theory identified such groups as the oral, compulsive (or anal), hysterical, masochistic, paranoid, narcissistic, and schizoid types.[3] Furthermore, it seemed sensible to presume that persons with physical illnesses use the same psychological defense mechanisms as persons with mental illnesses. Efforts were therefore made to describe patients' reactions to illness and disability in terms of repression, projection, regression, displacement, reaction formation, and other familiar defensive strategies.[4]

Although psychoanalysis and its derivatives are still employed in many treatment and rehabilitation settings, these theories have become less popular in the past decade or two. Perhaps the most important reasons for their decline were that psychoanalytic treatment methods were too time-consuming and expensive, and practitioners of psychoanalysis were too scarce to be employed in settings that deal only with medical conditions or physical disabilities.

OTHER MENTALISTIC THEORIES

The current influence of psychoanalysis and its derivatives is perhaps most obvious in psychosomatic theories which emphasize the concept of the body image or which assert that specific emotional conflicts and personality types are associated with specific diseases or disabilities. It is also evident in somatopsychological theories which assert that physical illness and disability cause a parallel mental illness called grief or mourning.[1]

Mentalistic theories often view psychological problems in illness and disability as reactions to the loss of a body part or function that affects the whole personality by virtue of its potent symbolic significance.[5] Reflecting the influence of certain forms of existentialism, a few such theories seem to suggest that the ultimate disability is death and that reactions to lesser states may be thought of as merely less intense reactions to the prospect of total annihilation.[6,7]

SOCIOLOGICAL CONCEPTS

Decline in the dominance of mentalistic theories was caused further by the growing recognition that practical reality hampers rehabilitation more severely and more often than do the mental problems of individuals. Psychological maladjustment may be crucial for a few patients, but everyone in rehabilitation is impeded by architectural barriers, prejudice, and public apathy toward the problems of persons with chronic illnesses and disabilities. To take all causal influences into account requires dealing with the physical and social settings in which the patient must eventually function as well as the somatic and mental aspects of the patient's condition. For example, rehabilitated clients' failures to get jobs may stem less from lack of skills or from emotional conflicts than from employers' attitudes of rejection or from physical inaccessibility of job settings.

Recognition of the importance of social attitudes is evident in developments that took place in the field of sociology. In this regard, Parsons'[8] concept of the "sick role" and Mechanic's[9] concept of illness behavior have been highly influential. These theories identify illness and disability as socially defined statuses or roles rather than as objective states of the body. The theories tend to treat the behavior of sick or disabled persons not as responses to physical conditions or inner psychological states, but as conformity to social norms which require people who are labeled as sick or disabled to act in certain ways.

The main contribution of the sociological approach has been to focus attention upon the environment rather than upon the inner experiences of sick persons. In extreme form, this approach emphasizes the external world as exclusively as the orthodox psychoanalytic view emphasizes the internal world. Although each type of theory (sociological and mentalistic) provides a needed counterpoise for the other, neither presents a comprehensive view of the psychological relationship between personality and illness or disability.

INTEGRATIVE FIELD THEORIES

Most attempts to integrate the subjective (internal or mental) and objective (social or environmental) aspects of the problem of adjustment to illness and disability have grown out of Lewin's[10] concept of the "life space" and his formulation that behavior is a function of the person in relation to the environment:

$$B = f(P,E)$$

The most completely developed integrative theory of reactions to physical disability has been promulgated by Wright.[11] This theory is both social (environmental) and personal because it proposes that behavioral reactions are integrated responses to environmental pressures on the one hand, and internal mental processes on the other. Although the theory identifies favorable personal adjustment with subjective states, such as high self-esteem and positive self-regard, it stresses the formative influence of the physical and interpersonal environment as determinants of the extent to which inner adjustment successfully takes place.

Meyerson[12] also followed the Lewinian theoretical line. He undertook the task of integration by pointing out that psychological maladjustment in a person with a disability is not due to the disability itself. It occurs only when the person accepts devaluation imposed by others because of his or her physical state. The environment enters into this principle by way of social attitudes which encourage devaluation of atypical people. The internal state of the person enters into it by way of acceptance of the devaluation. The relational quality of the formulation is present in the idea that both factors must be operative—the absence of either social devaluation or personal acceptance precludes the possibility of maladjustment.

SOCIAL ENVIRONMENTALISM

An additional feature of Meyerson's explanation is that it accepts the sociological view that disability and illness are not states of the body but social judgments based on normative standards of health, disease, and handicap. In fact, though Meyerson's presentation of his theory started out as an apparent attempt at integrating social and personal points of view, he ultimately blamed society for problems of adjustment to disability. In the final analysis, it is society which defines disability and puts pressure upon the disabled to accept personal devaluation.

A similar argument has been put forth by Monbeck,[13] who wrote about blindness but whose ideas are applicable to persons with any disabling condition. The major premise of this argument is that people without disabilities react irrationally and unrealistically to disabilities because they respond to the symbolic rather than to the real meanings of handicapping conditions. Directly or indirectly, this implies that persons who feel uncomfortable about disabilities are psychologically maladjusted. Consequently, their reactions cannot be changed by appeals to reason alone, any more than a neurosis can be cured by appeals to logic. The theory implies that when a person who has a disability learns to recognize this irrational behavior, that person has taken a first step toward successful personal adjustment to disability.

Dembo[14] recently crystallized the issue by pointing out the need for reconciling the disparate and often contradictory viewpoints of insiders (sufferers; persons with disabilities) and outsiders (professional staff; theorists; scientific investigators). Her argument stresses the need for outsiders (who are components of the environment, from the sufferer's point of view) to adapt and change in such a way as to incorporate the views and values of sufferers into research and therapeutic practice. Like Meyerson and Monbeck, Dembo feels more difficulty is caused by environmental neglect of sufferers' needs than by sufferers' psychological inabilities or unwillingness to conform to environmental demands.

BEHAVIORISM

At the furthest extreme of recent theorizing are the views that have been extrapolated into clinical practice from experiments on animals in the psychological laboratory. Most important is the doctrine of operant conditioning. In its extreme form, operant behaviorism shares with other forms of environmentalistic views its virtual abnegation of concern for mental states or conditions of the body. All that matters is that desirable patient behavior be identified and that conditions (reinforcement contingencies) be designed and controlled to bring about that behavior as rapidly as possible.[15,16]

For example, a recent study rejected as unscientific the concept that pain is an inner (mental) experience. Instead, it defined pain as a set of observable behaviors (such as saying "ouch," grimacing, groaning, and taking certain types of medicines). A complex treatment program was then developed to extinguish the occurrence of pain by operant methods alone.[17] The results of the study were inconclusive, though it did demonstrate that medication levels could be decreased and physical activity increased when selected patients suffering chronic pain were exposed to carefully controlled reinforcement contingencies.

Not all behaviorists are so radical that they treat patients merely as objects that emit behavior. More current forms of behaviorism acknowledge the need to take learners' internal psychological processes into account and to admit patients into the treatment process as coparticipants.[18-20] These newer types of behaviorism, however, have not yet been applied extensively in rehabilitation or in medical practice. They will probably become more influential in the next few years as behavior theory merges with cognitive psychology and as practical experience with behavioristic methods accumulates.

SUMMARY AND CONCLUSION

Since about 1950, there has been a progressive tendency for psychological maladjustment to physical illness and disability to be attributed to environmental rather than to personal causes. In some places the pendulum has swung almost completely from mentalistic doctrines to a radical form of operant behaviorism which rejects mental experience altogether and asserts that environmental contingencies are the only causes of patient behavior.

In the long run, it is best not to engage in fruitless arguments over which theories are right and wrong. A better strategy is to learn as much as possible about all theories and to consider each a resource that has utility in appropriate circumstances. Which of many possible points of view a rehabilitation professional adopts in a given instance will depend a great deal upon whether the immediate goal is to merely control specific behaviors in a particular treatment situation or to attempt to understand adjustment to disability in its entirety.

Mentalistic theories are best for dealing with patients whose problems are clearly neurotic in character. But for providing a broad, general understanding of the psychological aspects of disability, integrated social-psychological theories, such as those proposed by Wright[11] or by Meyerson,[12] have more to offer. Being conceptually rather than technologically based, these theories do not produce automatically specific recommendations for treatment of specific behavior problems. Nevertheless, they often have broad practical implications. For example, Wright has used her concepts of the coping and succumbing frameworks to derive recommendations for designing and conducting fund-raising, health-care, and public education campaigns.[20]

For manipulating particular activities in well-controlled environments, such as therapy rooms and sheltered workshops, operant methods may be more to the point; however, just as psychoanalysis or an integrative field theory lacks the ability to produce automatically specific plans of action which solve concrete problems of limited scope, operant approaches can be simplistic and deficient in providing an appreciation of the full range and complexity of the personal-social problem of adjustment to physical illness or disability. The goal toward which future theoretical development is oriented should be a truly comprehensive psychological approach which requires that mentalistic, integrative, and behavioristic theories be made to work together in a mutually supportive and enhancing relationship.

REFERENCES

1. Shontz FC: Theories of adjustment to having a disability. *In* Cruickshank WM (ed): Psychology of Exceptional Children and Youth. Ed 4. Englewood Cliffs, NJ, Prentice-Hall, 1978

2. Shontz FC: Concept of motivation in physical medicine. Arch Phys Med Rehabil 38:635–639, 1957
3. Kahana RJ, Bibring GL: Personality types in medical management. In Zinberg NE (ed): Psychiatry and Medical Practice in a General Hospital. New York, International Universities Press, 1964, pp 108–123
4. Hofmann AD, Becker RD, Gabriel HP: Hospitalized Adolescent: Guide to Managing the Ill and Injured Youth. New York, Free Press, 1976
5. Schoenberg B, Carr AC, Peretz D, Kutscher AH (eds): Loss and Grief: Psychological Management in Medical Practice. New York, Columbia University Press, 1970
6. Schoenberg B, et al (eds): Anticipatory Grief. New York, Columbia University Press, 1974
7. Becker E: Denial of Death. New York, Free Press, 1973
8. Parsons T: Definitions of health and illness in light of American values and social structure. In Jaco EG (ed): Patients, Physicians and Illness: Sourcebook in behavioral science and health. Ed 2. New York, Free Press, 1972, pp 107–127
9. Mechanic D: Concept of illness behavior. J Chronic Dis 15:189–194, 1962
10. Lewin K: Principles of Topological Psychology. New York, McGraw-Hill, 1936
11. Wright BA: Physical Disability—Psychological Approach. New York, Harper, 1960
12. Meyerson L: Somatopsychology of physical disability. In Cruickshank WM (ed): Psychology of Exceptional Children and Youth. Ed 2. Englewood Cliffs, NJ, Prentice-Hall, 1963, pp 1–52
13. Monbeck ME: Meaning of Blindness: Attitudes toward Blindness and Blind People. Bloomington, Ind, Indiana University Press, 1973
14. Dembo T: Utilization of psychological knowledge in rehabilitation. Welfare in Review 8:1–7, July–Aug 1970
15. Ince LP: Behavior Modification in Rehabilitation Medicine. Springfield, Ill, Charles C Thomas, 1976
16. Michael JL: Rehabilitation. In Neuringer C, Michael JL (eds): Behavior Modification in Clinical Psychology. New York, Appleton-Century-Crofts, 1970, pp 52–85
17. Fordyce WE, Fowler RS Jr, Lehmann JF, DeLateur BJ, Sand PL, Trieschmann RB: Operant conditioning in treatment of chronic pain. Arch Phys Med Rehabil 54:399–408, 1973
18. Bandura A: Behavior theory and models of man. Am Psychol 29:859–869, 1974
19. Mahoney MJ: Reflections on cognitive-learning trend in psychotherapy. Am Psychol 32:5–13, 1977
20. Wright BA: Analysis of attitudes—dynamics and effects. New Outlook for Blind 68:108–118, 1974

9

Six Principles Relating Disability and Psychological Adjustment

Franklin C. Shontz

Recently, I agreed to write a brief article summarizing the principles that describe the psychological aspects of physical disability and handicap. The article is to appear in a forthcoming professionally-oriented encyclopedia, the readership of which will probably consist of physicians and psychologists who know little or nothing about the topic. My problem was to select the most important things that such a group should know. Although that task seemed impossible at first, I ultimately found that the mass of things that should be said were reducible to six general propositions.

The thought then occurred to me that the propositions might be interesting to people who are professionally identified with rehabilitation psychology, either for their own information or for presentation to others. At the very least, a public statement of the propositions should provoke discussion and stimulate their revision and improvement.

The first two propositions are confutative; they assert that some commonly held beliefs are false. These propositions describe stereotyped ideas that are not confirmed by systematically collected data; in fact, careful observation provides an ample supply of cases that clearly contradict the stereotypes. The other four propositions are affirmative. They assert relations that are probably true, according to the best information and most authoritative opinion currently available.

To people who are familiar with the field of rehabilitation psychology,

From *Rehabilitation Psychology*, 24(4) (1977), 207–210. Reprinted by permission.
Presidential Address, Division 22, Rehabilitation Psychology, American Psychological Association, Washington, D.C., September, 1976.

the propositions may seem to state the obvious. I hope so, for that will mean we agree on several most important points.

CONFUTATIVE PROPOSITIONS

1. *Psychological reactions to the onset or imposition of physical disability are not uniformly disturbing or distressing and do not necessarily result in maladjustment.*

A corollary to this is that *psychological reactions to the removal of physical disabilities are not uniformly or necessarily pleasant and do not necessarily lead to improved adjustment.*

Some consequences of physical illnesses and disabilities on behavior are direct and consistent; for example, completely severing the optic nerves blocks behavioral responses to visual stimuli. Properly speaking, however, direct consequences such as these are *effects of* rather than *reactions to* disabilities, and reactions are the only concern of this proposition. Though many efforts have been made to correlate disability with overall personality maladjustment, no systematic evidence has yet been published to show that reactions involving psychiatric disturbance occur any more frequently within a truly representative sample of people with disabilities than within the general population. In fact, overall personal adjustment improves when disability, or a handicap, solves life problems. The personality resources of an individual may be strengthened, not weakened, when the stresses that disability imposes are successfully managed.

The corollary to the first proposition is supported by reports that removal of physically disabling conditions sometimes increases guilt, anxiety, or maladjustment. Guilt may stem from the belief that one is unworthy, particularly in cases where the beneficiary believes that personal benefit has been gained at the expense of the health or welfare of others. Anxiety arises when a recovered person is forced to face problems that never arose before or that could be successfully avoided during the period of disablement.

2. *Reactions (favorable or unfavorable) to disabilities are not related in a simple way to the physical properties of the disabilities.*

In massed data, studies of persons with physical illnesses suggest that, as a group, such persons show a tendency to experience heightened body anxiety and depression. However, these studies provide no reason to believe that such responses differ from what would occur under equally strong stress of psychological origin. Well-designed research, testing the relationship between degree or type of disability and strengths of personality traits or types of personality organizations, is practically nonexistent. What studies there are have produced no correlations of any appreciable magnitude or dependability. Knowledge of the type or degree of a person's physical disability provides virtually no information about that person's personality.

AFFIRMATIVE PROPOSITIONS

1. *The shorter and less complex the causal linkage between the body structure affected by disability and the behavior in question, the more predictable the latter is from the former.*

When a cause-effect network consists of physiochemical processes alone, the linkage is *direct* and predictability is high. For example, neurological damage usually has fairly consistent and predictable effects on reflexive responses.

When a cause-effect network concerns instrumental skills, such as dressing and ambulation, that involve learned components, linkage is less direct and predictability diminishes accordingly.

Cause-effect networks that affect emotional states are even less direct than those involving instrumental acts, so predictability is correspondingly lower. At this level, the analysis of the psychological aspects of disability crosses the line from being mainly concerned with the effects of disability to being mainly concerned with the person's reactions or adjustment to disability.

Finally, when the cause-effect network involves such complex matters as the meaning of disability in the total life situation of the person or the place of disability in the self-concept, predictability virtually disappears. At this level of analysis, so many factors other than the body state are operative that correlation between disability is not only minimal but would be truly amazing if it occurred.

2. *The less direct the linkage between the body structure affected by disability and the behavior in question, the more appropriate it is to describe the influence of disability as facilitative, rather than as causal or coercive.*

The term facilitative implies that, while a disability may make one particular trait or type of psychological adjustment easier to adopt or more attractive than others, no disability requires any specific type of molar reaction. Suppose, for example, that a person with a spinal cord injury who can no longer engage in conventional sexual activities reacts by becoming bitter or despondent. Reactions like these are made more probable (i.e., facilitated) by the occurrence of spinal cord injury in a person of a certain age and sex who has certain ideas about the importance of sexual identity in the self-concept. But the reactions are not forced upon the person, they do not arise automatically, and they are not a direct product of the spinal cord injury. Teaching persons with spinal cord injuries to find new means to gain sexual satisfaction or intimacy often restores emotional balance, even though it does not remove or alter the physical disability.

3. *Environmental factors are at least as important in determining psychological reactions to disabilities as are the internal states of the persons who have the disabilities.*

Obvious illustrations of the meaning of this proposition are to be found everywhere in the adversities that architectural barriers impose upon the mobility and the educational, vocational, and interpersonal adjustment of persons with disabilities. Barriers such as these contribute to the overall message often communicated to persons with disabilities that they are judged as inferior and will be kept that way. Maladjustment surely follows when someone accepts that judgment as accurate and fair. The effects of attitudes of devaluing pity or of stigmatization are more subtle but are equally important. These lead to the portrayal of persons with disabilities in the media either as miserable, suffering, helpless creatures whose greatest need is for charity or as supercourageous beings who deserve medals merely for traveling from one place to another or attending college. Anyone who is constantly exposed to such ideas about himself will find it extremely difficult to accept himself as a competent, worthwhile, normal person.

4. *Of all the factors that affect the total life situation of a person with a disability, the disability itself is only one, and often its influence is relatively minor.*

This proposition is stated affirmatively. However, it also confutes the commonly held belief that a physical disability is of necessity the most important thing in a person's life. When a disability interferes with, stops, or actually reverses psychological growth, it is a source of worry and concern. It may even lead to maladjustment; however, the forms that maladjustment takes among persons with disabilities do not differ from the forms it takes in others. By contrast, when a disability opens up opportunities for learning, challenges the persons to achieve successfully, in short, promotes ego growth, it is a source of growth and ultimate maturity.

This is the most important of the six propositions. It implies that, in the final analysis, the understanding of psychological reactions to physical disability requires the understanding of individual human beings in all their complexity.

10

Reaction to Loss: Coping with Disability and Death

Fergus Hughes

In recent years there has been a growing interest in death and the grieving process. Books and articles on the subject of dying and the nature of grief (e.g., Hinton, 1967; Kastenbaum & Aisenberg, 1972; Parkes, 1972) have proliferated, and reports of college and even high school courses on death and grief are widespread. Much of the recent interest in death stems from the pioneering work of Elisabeth Kübler-Ross, who began counseling terminally ill patients fewer than 15 years ago. At first, Kübler-Ross was greeted by defensiveness and suspicion in the medical community. Today, however, there are special hospice units to provide physical and psychological services for dying patients and their families in several American hospitals, and articles about about grief counseling appear frequently in medical journals (e.g., Conroy, 1977; Kowalsky, 1978).

STAGES OF GRIEF

Kübler-Ross (1969) found that terminally ill patients pass through a series of stages in the process of mourning. The first, which occurs after the initial shock, is denial. Dying patients are unwilling to believe that they have been singled out to die because death is usually thought of as happening to someone else. The next stage is anger; the patients resent that they must die and often resent others who are fit and healthy. Anger is followed by a bargaining stage, in which patients try to make a deal with God to extend their lives. They may ask for a little more time to see a child graduate from college, or to experience one last birthday or holiday. In the fourth stage, depression, patients face the overwhelming sadness of impending loss. Finally, if patients

From *Rehabilitation Counseling Bulletin*, June 1980, pp. 251–257. Copyright ©1980 by the American Personnel and Guidance Association. Reprinted with permission.

have been able to deal with the other stages, there is acceptance of death — the quiet resolution after the long struggle.

Parkes (1972) observed similar stages of grief in persons who had lost someone close to them. There is the initial alarm and the numbness of shock. There is denial — a refusal to believe that so terrible an event could have occurred. Then there is searching — the attempt to bring back the loved one through memories, dreams, and even visual and auditory hallucinations. There is anger directed toward the deceased, and guilt, often because the mourner was not kinder and more attentive to the person when he or she was alive. There is the terrible sadness and depression of the "pangs of grief," which are periods in which the person can be overcome by feelings of loss, a tightness in the chest, difficulty in breathing, hyperactivity, and sighing.

GRIEF IN THE PHYSICALLY DISABLED

Most discussions of the grief reaction have focused on the processes of dying and bereavement. Much research evidence, however, suggests that the symptoms of grief can be found when a person suffers a major, or even a minor, loss. Falek and Britton (1974) described what they refer to as the coping sequence, which is a "universal reaction to any change in the established steady state great enough to produce stress in the organism, and [it] occurs from infancy through adulthood in response to minor as well as major traumas" (p. 5). The coping sequence consists of four stages: (a) shock and denial, (b) anxiety, (c) anger and/or guilt, and (d) depression. Falek and Britton suggest that perhaps we should consider grief and separation as particular cases of the more general process of coping with the stresses of significant life changes. In reviewing the literature on the types of loss, Falek and Britton observed that all or most of the characteristics of the coping sequence have been found in patients who had a radical mastectomy (Bard, 1952), severe burn victims (Hamburg, Hamburg, & de Goza, 1953), victims of severe poliomyelitis (Visotsky & Hamburg, 1961), paraplegics (Cogswell, 1967), and victims of natural disasters (Wolfenstein, 1957), as well as in the more frequently studied patients with terminal cancer (Kübler-Ross, 1969) and grieving family members (Parkes, 1972; Wiener, 1970).

A recent collection of readings (Schoenberg, Carr, Peretz, & Kutscher, 1970) contains discussions of grief reactions to a variety of physical disabilities. For example, Orfirer (1970) discussed the "overwhelming feelings of loss" experienced by men who are suffering from sexual dysfunction. Blacher (1970) wrote of the grief experienced by victims of chronic illness, reporting that denial is especially common among chronically ill patients, that the denial is more pronounced in cases of more serious illness, and that doctors as well as patients engage in denial to a certain extent.

Parkes (1975) compared 21 widows with 46 amputees in their reactions to loss and found that the symptoms of grief were remarkably similar. About half of the members of each group felt an immediate reaction of numbness and denial. Later both groups experienced periods of great sadness and preoccupation with their losses, elements of disbelief, and visual memories of the departed husband or the limb. The widows grieved specifically for their spouses, whereas the amputees grieved more for the other losses that had befallen them than for the limbs themselves. The amputees had lost not only a part of the body but often their jobs, their companions at work, their athletic skills, and their ability to drive a car. Many of the comments made by the participants in the study strongly reinforce the similarities between reactions to loss of spouse and loss of limb, with several people spontaneously making the connection themselves.

THE NECESSITY OF GRIEF

Grief may be viewed both as a reaction to loss (in the sense that it represents an attempt to return to a previous state of affairs) and as a process of recovery. If a person is to reach the stage of acceptance of his or her loss, then the stages of coping, or grief, must be experienced. The person must recover from the initial shock, must eventually stop denying the unfortunate event, and must endure the sadness and the depression before coming to a full acceptance of reality and beginning to reconstruct his or her life. Pincus (1974) cites many cases of "repressed mourning" in which individuals did not allow themselves to grieve over the death of someone close to them. One couple, unable to share their feelings with each other about the death of their son six years before, experienced depression, hostility toward each other, and sexual difficulties in their marriage. After several marriage counseling sessions, both husband and wife came to realize that they had never exposed or shared their feelings of grief, and it was this refusal to communicate that had created a major communication problem in their relationship.

THE PROBLEM OF DENIAL

Family and community support to help the dying and the bereaved cope with loss is not always adequate, but there is at least a growing realization that in the face of death we need to grieve, and in that grief we often need the help of others. Have we reached the same level of understanding in dealing with the coping process of the physically disabled?

As noted earlier, the patterns of grief are remarkably similar. Orfirer (1970) even suggested that the person who suffers the loss of normal physical functioning may have *more* difficulty working out grief than the person trying to cope with death. This is not because loss through a disability is more stressful than loss through death, but because the grief of physical loss may be especially difficult to share with others. Death reduces us all to an equal level because we view death as part of common human experience. Orfirer noted, however, that even the most sympathetic friends may see the physically disabled person only in terms of his or her loss and, therefore, in a position of inferiority. Most of us have no personal experience with physical loss, as we do with death, and so we may have difficulty sharing the experience with another.

How, then, *do* we respond to the grief reaction of the physically disabled? Orfirer believes that we often encourage denial on the part of the victims. We urge them not to think of their losses and make false promises that they will recover. As noted earlier, Blacher (1970) has observed that even members of the medical community frequently encourage such denial.

When denial is encouraged, when patients are urged not to accept their disabilities, the healing process of grief is retarded. Adams and Lindemann (1974) cite the case of a young athlete who was paralyzed from the waist down in an automobile accident. After the accident the young man continued to insist, despite evidence to the contrary, that he would completely resume his former active lifestyle. His parents too insisted that a miracle could occur and he would walk again if the hospital staff did their jobs properly. Two years of psychotherapy did little to relieve his depression and extreme hostility, and he clung desperately to a false hope of recovery.

In the same article, Adams and Lindemann (1974) also discussed the case of a young man who was injured in a diving accident and experienced immediate quadriplegia. Early in the rehabilitation process he and his parents engaged in denial, frequently expressing the hope that he would walk again. At the same time, however, the parents began adjusting to the young man's disability by remodeling their home so that it would be suitable for use by a person in a wheelchair. Apparently for this family, denial was a stage of coping rather than a permanent condition. Significantly, when the boy eventually went through the stages of anger and depression, he was open enough with the hospital staff to discuss his sadness and his confusion about his future plans.

PERSONALITY FACTORS IN GRIEVING

Adams and Lindemann (1974) described the first patient as perceiving himself as being "sick and disabled," making it difficult for him to develop a positive self-concept. The second patient came to view himself not as "sick" but as "different." The first patient's point of reference seems to have been the past; the second patient was more present and future oriented.

Why do some patients cling tenaciously to their past lifestyles while others accept change and look toward a promising future? One reason is that some have close family members and friends, and perhaps even doctors, nurses, and counselors, who encourage or allow false hopes and denial of reality. Others, like the victim of the diving accident, are surrounded by people who are realistic and future oriented. Even going beyond external supports, there may be basic personality characteristics associated with successful or unsuccessful coping with loss. In their classic study of life satisfaction among the elderly, a population that is constantly subjected to loss and subsequent grief, Neugarten, Havighurst, and Tobin (1968) found that a distinctive characteristic of those who were highest in life satisfaction was flexibility. The "integrated" personality was the one that accepted change rather than resisted it. Even the previously active integrated personalities were realistic; they could not engage in many of the activities that they enjoyed when they were younger, but they simply substituted new activities for old ones. They were high in self-esteem. Somewhat lower in life satisfaction was a group identified as "armored-defended." These people viewed aging as a threat, as something to resist. Some were happy, but only if they could maintain their previous roles or activities. The less active members of this group were preoccupied with loss and fearful that their world might fall apart.

Apparently, some individuals have an easier time than others in dealing with life changes, and the ones who handle change best are the ones who ⟍ adjust by restructuring their lives when necessary rather than denying that a change has taken place. Perhaps the diving accident victim and the victim of the automobile crash had different internal coping mechanisms to begin with, as well as different family support systems.

AFTER DENIAL

Once denial has been put aside, it is important for the disabled person as well as the dying patient to be able to express sadness and depression openly. Perhaps because we are accustomed to being told to "look on the bright side," we are not as comfortable in dealing with the emotion of sadness as we might be. Denial might indicate a desire to avoid what is the next inevitable step in the course of the grief reaction: pining and sadness. Some may actually be ashamed of feeling sadness. Orfirer (1970) described a disabled man who apologized for being childish after he expressed his grief to a nurse. The nurse reassured him that his depression was understandable. He was very relieved and began to speak more openly and freely of his feelings.

Eventually the normal depression will subside, and the periods of overwhelming sadness will become less frequent, but only if the mourner has had the opportunity to work out these feelings and to share them. A grieving person must be allowed to grieve and often needs the support of other people to do so. For the victim of a physical disability there must first be the realization that he or she is, in fact, grieving and that grief can be as difficult to work through as the grief of the individual coping with death. Mourners need to face reality, to avoid prolonged denials, to express their sadness and their rage, and to get on with the business of restructuring their lives.

REFERENCES

Adams, J. E., & Lindemann, E. Coping with long-term disability. In G. V. Coelho, D. A. Hamburg, & J. E. Adams (Eds.), *Coping and adaptation*. New York: Basic Books, 1974.

Bard, M. The sequence of emotional reactions in radical mastectomy patients. *Public Health Report*, 1952, 67, 1144.

Blacher, R. S. Reaction to chronic illness. In B. Schoenberg, A. C. Carr, D. Peretz, & A. Kutscher (Eds.), *Loss and grief: Psychological management in medical practice*. New York:Columbia University Press, 1970.

Cogswell, B. Rehabilitation of the paraplegic: Processes of socialization. *Social Inquiry*. 1967, 37, 11.

Conroy, R. C. Widows and widowhood. *New York State Journal of Medicine*. 1977. 77, 357–360.

Falek, A., & Britton, S. Phases in coping: The hypothesis and its implications. *Social Biology*. 1974, 21,1–7.

Hamburg, D.; Hamburg, B.; & de Goza, S. Adaptive problems and mechanisms in severely burned patients. *Psychiatry*. 1953, 16, 1–20.

Hinton, J. *Dying*. Middlesex, Eng.: Penguin, 1967.

Kastenbaum, R., & Aisenberg, R. *The psychology of death*. New York: Springer, 1972.

Kowalsky, E. L. Grief: A lost life-style. *American Journal of Nursing*. 1978, 78, 418–420.

Kübler-Ross, E. *On death and dying*. New York: Macmillan, 1969.

Neugarten, B. L.; Havighurst, R. J.; & Tobin, S. S. Personality and patterns of aging. In B. L. Neugarten (Ed.), *Middle age and aging*. Chicago: University of Chicago Press, 1968.

Orfirer, A. P. Loss of sexual function in the male. In B. Schoenberg, A. C. Carr, D. Peretz, & A. Kutscher (Eds.), *Loss and grief: Psychological management in medical practice*. New York: Columbia University Press, 1970.

Parkes, C. M. *Bereavement: Studies of grief in adult life*. New York: International Universities Press, 1972.

Parkes, C. M. Psycho-social transitions: Comparison between the reactions to loss of a limb and loss of a spouse. *British Journal of Psychiatry*. 1975, 127, 204–210.

Pincus, L. *Death and the family*. New York: Vintage Books, 1974.

Schoenberg, B.; Carr, A. C.; Peretz, D.; & Kutscher, A. (Eds.). *Loss and grief: Psychological management in medical practice*. New York: Columbia University Press, 1970.

Visotsky, H., & Hamburg, D. Coping behavior under extreme stress: Observations of patients with severe poliomyelitis. *Archives of General Psychiatry*. 1961, 5, 423–448.

Wiener, J. M., Reaction of the family to the fatal illness of a child. In B. Schoenberg, A. C. Carr, D. Peretz, & A. Kutscher (Eds.), *Loss and grief: Psychological management in medical practice*. New York: Columbia University Press, 1970.

Wolfenstein, M., *Disaster*. Glencoe, Ill.: The Free Press, 1957.

The Interpersonal Impact of Disability

In many instances, interactions between disabled and able-bodied persons are not constructive. These interactions may be described as strained or anxiety-provoking for both participants. In some cases, the persons who have disabilities are excluded socially from others. In other cases, they may be intruded upon through stares or questioned out of curiosity. In Part IV, the problems of these interactions are discussed, and suggestions for improvement are made.

In Chapter 11, "Communication Barriers between 'the Able-Bodied' and 'the Handicapped,'" Zola emphasizes the difficulties of both telling and hearing the story of having a disability. He presents a thoughtful analysis of this problem and its deep roots in Western culture. He notes that these communication problems result in *everyone* being deprived of the knowledge, skills, resources, and motivation to promote change.

In a classic study focusing upon the social acceptance of persons with disabilities by able-bodied persons, Ladieu-Leviton, Adler, and Dembo focus upon three main issues: (1) the characteristics of acceptance versus nonacceptance, (2) some of the reaons for nonacceptance, and (3) ways in which some of these difficulties may be resolved. Their response to these issues provides useful, timely information to the rehabilitation practitioner.

Persons with disabilities sometimes lack the social skills necessary to communicate successfully with nondisabled people in the community, particularly about the stigmatizing effects of their disability; furthermore, they are rarely taught these skills. Cogswell, in her study of the problems of paraplegics in their self-socialization, reviews the problems and suggests the sequential ordering of social encounters by increasing difficulty as an alternative to these difficulties. In discussing the practical implications of her model, Cogswell provides useful suggestions for those who work with disabled people.

11

Communication Barriers between "the Able-Bodied" and "the Handicapped"

Irving Kenneth Zola

"Why doesn't anyone understand what it's like?" is a lament of many who try to convey to others the nature of being physically handicapped or chronically ill. It is a story difficult to hear as well as to tell—a difficulty rooted deep in Western culture. Slater put it well:

> Our ideas about institutionalizing the aged, psychotic, retarded, and infirm are based on a pattern of thought that we might call The Toilet Assumption—the notion that unwanted matter, unwanted difficulties, unwanted complexities and obstacles will disappear if they are removed from our immediate field of vision. . . . Our approach to social problems is to decrease their visibility: out of sight, out of mind. . . . The result of our social efforts has been to remove the underlying problems of our society farther and farther from daily experience and daily consciousness, and hence to decrease in the mass of the population, the knowledge, skill, resources, and motivation necessary to deal with them.[3]

It is, however, increasingly less acceptable to exile "problem" bearers in far-away colonies, asylums, and sanitaria. A recent compromise has been to locate them in places which, if not geographically distant, are socially distant—places with unfree access, like ghettos, special housing projects, nursing homes, or hospitals. This, too, is imperfect. So a final strategy makes them socially indistinct. They are stereotyped. But I never fully appreciated

From *Archives of Physical Medicine and Rehabilitation*, 62 (1981), 355–359. Reprinted with permission.

Presented as part of the Interdisciplinary Forum on "Quality of Life: The Costs of Being Disabled—Financial and Psychological" at the 56th Annual Session of the American Congress of Rehabilitation Medicine, Honolulu, November 12, 1979. Excerpted from Dr. Zola's book "The Missing Piece" (Temple University Press, 1981).

the resultant distancing and isolation until it happened to me! I use a cane, wear a long leg brace and a back support, walk stifflegged with a pronounced limp. All in all, I think of myself as fairly unusual in appearance and thus easily recognizable. And yet for years I have had the experience of being "mistaken" for someone else. Usually I was in a new place and a stranger would greet me as Tom, Dick, or Harry. After I explained that I was not he, they would usually apologize saying, "You look just like him." Inevitably I would meet this Tom, Dick or Harry and he would be several inches shorter or taller, 40 pounds heavier or lighter, a double amputee on crutches, or a paraplegic in a wheelchair. I was continually annoyed and even puzzled how anyone could mistake "him" for the "unique me." What eventually dawned on me was that to many I was handicapped first and foremost. So much so that in the eyes of the "able-bodied," I and all the others "looked alike."

But more is going on here than the traditional stereotyping of a stigmatized ethnic group. The social invisibility of the physically handicapped has a more insidious development. Young children care little about skin color, or Semitic or Oriental features. Only as they grow older are they eventually taught to attend to these. Quite the opposite is true with regard to physical handicap. When small children meet a person using a wheelchair or wearing a brace, they are curious and pour forth questions like, "Why are you wearing this? What is it? Do you take it off at night? How high up does it go? Can I touch it?" If, however, there are any adults or parents within hearing, they immediately become fidgety and admonish the children, "It's not nice to ask such things" or "It's not nice to stare at people who are . . ." The feature in question—the limp, the cane, the wheelchair, the brace—is quite visible and of great interest to children, but they are taught to ignore it. They are not, of course, taught that it is an inconsequential characteristic, but with the effect, if not in words, that it is an uncomfortable and all-encompassing one. They are taught to respond globally and not particularistically— to recognize a handicapped person when they see one but to ignore the specific characteristics of the handicap. Is it any wonder that a near-universal complaint is, "Why can't people see me as someone who *has* a handicap rather than someone who *is* handicapped?" Young children first perceive it that way but are quickly socialized out of it.

But why all this effort? Why this distancing of the chronically ill and handicapped? Why are we, the chronically ill and physically handicapped, so threatening that we must be made socially invisible? The answer is found both in the nature of society and the nature of people.

The United States is a nation built on the premise that there is no mountain that cannot be levelled, no river untamed, no force of nature unharnessed. It should thus be no great surprise that we similarly claim that there is no disease that cannot be cured. And so there is a continual series of wars—against heart disease, cancer, stroke, birth defects. They are wars worthy enough in themselves but ones which promise nirvana over the next hill, a society without disease. It is, however, as Dubos has claimed, but a mirage:

> Organized species such as ants have established a satisfactory equilibrium with their environment and suffer no great waves of disease or changes in their social structure. But man is essentially dynamic, his way of life is constantly in flux from century to century. He experiments with synthetic products and changes his diet; he builds cities that breed rats and infection; he builds automobiles and factories which pollute the air, and he constructs radioactive bombs. As life becomes more comfortable and technology more complicated, new factors introduce new dangers. The ingredients for Utopia are agents for new disease.[1]

I am not arguing for any cessation in these campaigns to alleviate suffering. Rather, I am concerned with their side effects. People no longer die. Doctors simply lost the battle to save them. With society so raging against the anthropomorphic killer "diseases," should it be a surprise that some of the anger at the diseases spills on its bearers? In this context, the physically handicapped become objects, the permanent reminders of a lost and losing struggle, the symbol of a past and continuing failure.

Finally, the discomfiting confrontation of the "able-bodied" with the "disabled" is not just a symbolic one. For there is a hidden truth to the statement often heard when such a meeting occurs, the shudder and occasional sigh, " I'm glad it's not me." But the relief is often followed by guilt for ever thinking such a thought—a guilt one would just as soon also not deal with. Thus, the threat to be removed lies not merely in society's failure but in the inevitability of one's own. The discomfort that many feel in the presence of the aged, the suffering, the dying *is* the reality that it *could* just as well be they. For, like it or not, we will all one day get to grow old, and to die. And in high-technology America, this means dying *not* of natural causes and old age but of some chronic disease. But in the United States this is a reality we never tire of denying.

All this, then, is the burden that we, the chronically ill in general and the physically handicapped in particular, carry. In every interaction, our baggage includes not only our own physical infirmity but the evocation of and sense of infirmity in others and the consequent incapacity to deal with both this empirical and symbolic reality.

ON THE DIFFICULTY IN TELLING

The story of having a disability or illness is difficult to tell as well as to hear. There is thus a complementary question to the one with which I opened this paper: "Why can't *I* make anyone understand what it's like to be handicapped?" To me, the different emphasis implies that the spokesperson may be at a loss "to tell it like it is." Part of the problem may lie in the vantage point of these speakers. Erving Goffman once noted that "minority" group spokesmen may occupy that position precisely because they are successful adapters and, thus, in many ways closer to the "normals."[2] Yet to that extent, they are ironically less representative of the group they are supposed to represent. For instance, I and many other "successful mainstream adapters" have not numbered among our close friends and acquaintances *any* handicapped people—an "alienation" from our disability which has escalated almost to the level of an unconscious principle. Moreover, almost every written account about a "successful" handicapped person, as well as every "success" I have met (including myself), usually regards, as a key element, the self-conception: "I never think of myself as handicapped." Yet the degree to which this is true may have made it virtually impossible to tell anyone what it is like to be disabled in a world of normals. In a real sense, we don't know. Thus, what the public learns from our example is decidedly limited.

Franklin Delano Roosevelt is a case in point. To normals as well as the handicapped, he is the ultimate example of successful adaptation. For after being afflicted with polio and left a virtual paraplegic he went on to become President of the United States. What better evidence of success? And yet the newer biographies reveal a man not so pleasant as an individual, not so happy with his lot, and possessed of certain drives and needs that for another person less famous might have been labelled clinically pathologic. Moreover, whatever his political achievements, his social success was a more limited one. The public knew that he had suffered polio, was confined to a wheelchair, and used crutches rarely, but he was careful never to "confront" the public. He never allowed himself to be photographed in a wheelchair or on crutches. He photogenically passed. But few of us can so control, manipulate, and overcome our environment. So too with the other folk heroes of disease. They are not the little people, not the millions, but the few who are so successful that they also "passed"—the polio victim who later broke track records, the one-legged pitcher who made it to the major leagues, the pianist who was blind, the singer who had a colostomy. They were all so good that no one knew or had to be aware of their "handicap" and therein lay part of their glory.

I do not wish, however, to leave the impression that the only impact of the media, particularly television, on the public's view of the handicapped is in the distorted picture of success. The general problem is perhaps more depressing. For the handicapped are rarely portrayed in successful terms. In the most systematic and incisive analysis I have yet seen, Dr. Bonnie D. Leonard claims that the overall TV portrayal of people with a handicap is quite dismal (unpublished data). In a study focused on prime-time shows, she notes that not only are they numerically under-represented but whether the dimension be demographic, economic, social, personal, or interactional, the handicapped are continually depicted as almost irredeemably inferior to or dependent on the able-bodied. They are retrieved from this status only by a miracle — the unflagging persistence of a skilled physician or the undaunted love of a good person. So "one-down" are they that she characterizes their position as "less than human and beyond servility."

But it is the "success" stories which are more familiar to the public and which in some ways are equally destructive A specific example sticks painfully in my mind. I am a sports fan and, as such, an avid watcher of major events. The 1976 Olympics found me glued to my TV set and I was pleasantly surprised by a documentary which related to me quite personally. I think it was called "Six Who Overcame" and told how six athletes had overcome some problem (five were directly physical) and gone on to win Olympic gold medals. One story really grabbed me. It was about Wilma Rudolph, a woman who had polio as a child. Through pictures and words, her struggle was recreated. Love, caring, exercise, and hard work repeated endlessly, until she started to walk slowly with crutches and then, abandoning them, began to run. And there in the final frames she was sprinting down the track straining every muscle. With tears streaming down my face, I shouted, "Go on, Wilma! Do it! Do it!" And when she did I too collapsed, exhausted and exhilarated. But scarcely, 90 minutes later, I was furious. For a basic message of the film sank in. In each case the person overcame. But overcame what? Wilma's polio was not my polio! And all the love, caring, exercise, and hard work could NEVER have allowed me to win a running race, let alone compete in one.

My point is that in almost all the success stories that get to the public, there is a dual message. The first one is very important — that just because we have polio, cancer, or multiple sclerosis or have limited use of our eyes, ears, mouth, and limbs, our lives are *not* over. We can still learn, be happy, be lovers, spouses, parents, and even achieve great deeds. It is the second message which I have recently begun to abhor. It states that if a Franklin Delano Roosevelt or a Wilma Rudolph could OVERCOME their handicap, so could and should all the disabled. And if we fail, it's *our* problem, *our* personality, *our* weakness. And all this further masks what chronic illness is all about. For our lives or even our adaptations do not center around one single activity or physical achievement but around many individual and complex ones. Our daily living is not filled with dramatic accomplishments but with mundane ones. And most of all, our physical difficulties are not temporary ones to be overcome once-and-for-all but ones we must face again and again for the rest of our lives. That's what chronic means!

ON THE STORY TO BE TOLD

Now, this great achievement syndrome blinds not only the general public but also the achievers. We are paid the greatest of compliments when someone tells us, "You know, I never think of you as handicapped." And we gladly accept it. We are asked, "How did you make it against such great odds?" And we answer the question. And yet in both the accepting and the answering we further distance ourselves from the problems of having a handicap. In a sense they become both emotionally and cognitively inaccessible. I am not using these words lightly. I do indeed mean emotionally and cognitively inaccessible.

Let me illustrate with a personal example. I do a great deal of long-distance travelling and, as such, often find my jet flight located on the furthest runway from the entrance. Adjusting to this, I ordinarily allow myself an extra 20 to 30 minutes to get there. I regarded this for most of my life as a minor inconvenience. And if perchance you had asked me then if I experienced any undue tiredness or avoidable soreness, I would have firmly and honestly answered, "No." But in 1977, a new "consciousness" altered all this. Piqued at why I should continue to inconvenience myself, I began to regularly use a wheelchair for all such excursions. I thought that the only surprise I would encounter would be the dubious glances of other passengers, when, after reaching my destination, I would rise unassisted and walk briskly away. In fact I was occasionally regarded as if I had in some way "cheated." Much more disconcerting, however, was that I now arrived significantly more energetic, more comfortable, freer from cramps and leg sores than in my previous decades of travelling. The conclusion I drew was inevitable. I had *always* been tired, uncomfortable, cramped and sore after a long journey. But with no standard of comparison, these feelings were incorporated into the cognitive reality of what travelling was for me. I did not "experience" the tiredness and discomfort. They were cognitively inaccessible.

What I am contending is shockingly simple. The very process of successful adaptation not only involves divesting ourselves of any identification with being handicapped, but also denying the uncomfortable features of that life. To not do so might have made our success impossible! But this process had a cost. One may accept and forget too much.

I remember, however, but fragments of a story. For there is no special world of the handicapped, and herein lies another major problem in telling the story. There are several reasons for this lack. First, while most minority groups grow up in some special subculture and, thus, form a series of norms and expectations, the physically handicapped are not similarly prepared. Born for the most part into normal families, we are socialized into that world. The world of sickness is one we enter only later — poorly prepared, and with all the prejudices of the normal. We think of ourselves in the shadows of the external world. The very vocabulary we use to describe ourselves is borrowed from that society. We are *de*-formed, *dis*-eased, *dis*-abled, *dis*-ordered, *ab*-normal, and most telling of all, an *in*-valid. And most all share, deep within ourselves, the hoped-for miracle to reverse the process — a new drug or operation that will return us to a life of validity.

A dramatic but mundane way of characterizing an aspect of our dilemma is seen by looking at the rallying cries of current "liberation" movements. As the "melting pot" theory of America was finally buried, people could once again say, even though they be three generations removed, "I'm proud to be Greek, Italian, Hungarian, Polish." With the rise of Black Power, a derogatory label became a rallying cry, "Black is beautiful!" And when Female Liberationists saw their strength in numbers, they shouted, "Sisterhood is powerful!" But what about the chronically ill and disabled? Can we yell, "Long live Cancer!" "Up with Multiple Sclerosis!" "I'm glad I had Polio!" Clearly, a basis of a common positive identity based on our disability is not readily available.

For all these reasons, whatever world the physically handicapped and chronically ill inhabit, it is fragmentary in structure and content. It is, thus, difficult enough to integrate into one's own experience, let alone communicate to others. There is a certain inevitable restraint, for what comes out seems like a litany of complaints. And no one—at least in my society—likes a complainer! But it is a reality, my reality, and as such I record it.

Chairs without arms to push myself up from; unpadded seats which all too quickly produce sores; showers and toilets without handrails to maintain my balance; surfaces too slippery to walk on; staircases without banisters to help hoist myself; buildings without ramps, making ascent exhausting, if not dangerous; every curbstone a precipice; car, plane, and theater seats too cramped for my braced leg; and trousers too narrow for my leg brace to pass through. With such trivia is my life plagued. Even for me, who is relatively well off, mobility provides its daily challenges. If I am walking with a companion, he or she must always be on my right, else will inadvertently kick my cane and throw me off balance. My moment-by-moment concerns are even more mundane. For I must be extraordinarily watchful as to where I place both my cane and my leg. If not, inevitably my cane tip will slide on an oil slick or I will stub my toe on an uneven piece of sidewalk, thus lose my balance and fall. In short, I should walk as if looking for pennies.

But I resist impositions which impede social interaction. For if I am constantly looking down to where my foot or cane must be placed, then I cannot look directly at a person with whom I am conversing. And so I pay the price and run the risk, which means I stumble and fall all too often.

The problems of long-distance travel go even deeper. Every departure from home base is fraught with difficulties, from how long one can go without toilet facilities to how long one must sit in a cramped position; from the lack of a special diet to the lack of a special bed; from the absence of familiar and reliable surroundings to the absence of familiar and reliable help. Each slams home our dependency—our sense of "living on a leash." The leash may be a long one but it nevertheless exists.

This was especially hard for me, who had quite successfully repressed "my leashes." Whenever on long-term travel, I automatically packed my spare leg brace and back support, but never on any short-term trip. And then one day the impossible happened. On a trip to New Delhi, India, my brace snapped. And there I was with a piece of steel protruding through my trousers, unable to put my full weight any longer on my right leg, thousands of miles from home and, I thought, from help. Never had I felt so absolutely helpless. Worse, I felt foolish, embarrassed, even guilty, as if I had some role in my brace snapping. I have never experienced such a sense of total panic. It was as if I suddenly felt that I would never be able to move again—that I would forever remain in this spot with my leg dangling.

But I am "blessed" with a certain amount of income and position. Even in New Delhi, India, I can "command," and that is the appropriate word, resources to deal with my problem. What happens to all those without sufficient money or power to alter their environment—those without resources to have railings built or clothes custom-made or sufficient influence to have meetings take place in more physically accessible locations—those without power to command *immediate* repair of their brace or wheelchair? I suspect that they ultimately give up, unable to change or manipulate the world; they simply cut out that part of their life which requires such encounters, all of which contributes to a real as well as social invisibility and isolation.

Most germane to my point about telling it like it is: What happens when none of these unpleasant events occur? What happens when it all goes off without a hitch? With whom can I share the satisfaction that I did not trip, that my brace did not break, that I did not have difficulty with toilet facilities, that I made it by myself? When hospitalized with polio, I was tearful when I first defecated without the aid of laxative. Even more exciting, after months of impotence, was my first erection. My first steps at walking I could share, but not excessively, with my parents and my friends. My bowel movements were at least acknowledged by the medical and nursing staff. But my sexual issues were kept achingly to myself. Even amongst my fellow residents, socialized as they were into the world of the normal, there was only limited access to any sharing. There was an implicit limit on how much "the others" want to hear about your "minor" successes and failings. Too much time and too much affect and one ran the risk of being thought "too preoccupied" or even "hypochondriacal." Thus gradually the lesson was learned that no one, including myself, really wanted to hear the mundane details of being sick or handicapped, neither the triumphs nor the hardships.

I am sure the specific details and hardships of having a handicap or chronic disease vary from person to person. But not the core problem. The story is inevitably difficult to both hear and tell. To the teller, it is especially hard to acknowledge. Indeed, to even think of the world in such a realistic, paranoid way might make it too depressing a reality to tolerate. As such, the only defense, the only way to live, is to deny it. But then it becomes socially invisible to *all*. We are sadly left as Slater[3] has articulated — both those with physical handicaps and those without, *all* are deprived of the very knowledge, skill, resources, and motivation necessary to promote change.

REFERENCES

1. Dubos R. J.: Mirage of Health: Utopias, Progress and Biological Change. New York, Doubleday, 1961, quote is from flyleaf.
2. Goffman E: Stigma: Notes on Management of Spoiled Identity. Englewood Cliffs, N.J., Prentice-Hall, 1963, pp 105–125
3. Slater P. E.: Pursuit of Loneliness: American Culture at Breaking Point. Boston, Beacon Press, 1970, p 15

12

Studies in Adjustment to Visible Injuries: Social Acceptance of the Injured

Gloria Ladieu-Leviton
Dan L. Adler
Tamara Dembo

In exploring the social-psychological problems of the visibly injured, one sees the constant striving of the injured person to combat what he considers the negative implications of his injury. Among these he counts a variety of attitudes and behaviors which the noninjured direct toward him; e.g., they display unwarranted pity, and treat him as an object of curiosity. In general, the injured feels that as a person he is set apart from people at large. What he demands above all is social acceptance.

The gravity of the problem as seen by injured people is epitomized in the statement of one amputee:

> "You can't write an article about it. It can be said in one sentence—There is no acceptance."

From *Journal of Social Issues*, 4 (14) (1948), 55–61. Reprinted by permission of the publishers.

The work described in this paper was done partially under a contract between Stanford University and the Office of Scientific Research and Development, recommended by the Committee on Medical Research, partially under a contract between the Research and Development Board of the Surgeon General's Office of the Army and Stanford University. The Advisory Board of the project included Ernest R. Hilgard (Chairman), Roger G. Barker, Paul R. Farnsworth, George S. Johnson, Donald E. King, Quinn McNemar, and Calvin P. Stone. The research staff included Dan L. Adler, Tamara Dembo, Eugenia Hanfmann, Helen H. Jennings, Gloria Ladieu, Milton Rose, Ralph K. White, and Beatrice A. Wright. We wish to acknowledge the help of Donald Glad, Research Assistant. Special thanks are given to Alice Phillips Rose, Research Assistant, who volunteered to work on the project. We highly appreciate the cooperation of the staff and patients of Bushnell General Hospital and Dibble General Hospital.

Although this is an extreme instance, it reflects in nature, if not in degree, the general problem as seen by the injured man.

When he demands social acceptance, the injured may ask the noninjured to assess concomitants of the injury in a practical way, and to behave accordingly. Thus, the noninjured are to avoid exaggeration and to eliminate misconceptions regarding the limitations set by the injury.

On the basis of interviews[1] with 125 visibly injured persons (see Table 4) we can summarize what, for them, constitutes social acceptance; what obstacles, in their opinion, stand in the way of such acceptance; and what procedures may alleviate or eliminate the negative implications of injury with respect to acceptance.

ACCEPTANCE VERSUS PARTICIPATION

First and foremost, it is important to differentiate between what may be called nonparticipation and nonacceptance. *Nonparticipation* is seen by injured and noninjured alike as a reasonable abstinence from social activities which are limited by the reality of the handicap. Neither the injured nor the noninjured could expect, for example, to have a leg amputee play on a company baseball team which competes with other teams. This injured man might *miss* the activity keenly, but knowing that he cannot meet the physical requirements, he is not apt to see the situation as one of nonacceptance. *Nonacceptance*, from his point of view, is a one-sided affair, rest-

Table 4. *Distribution of Subjects with Regard to Type of Injury*

Amputation:	
Leg	
below knee and Symes	30
above knee	25
bilateral	3
Arm	
below elbow	12
above elbow	9
bilateral	3
One arm and one leg	1
Fingers	4
Plastic Surgery:	
Facial injuries	24
Hand injuries	4
Other visible injuries	10
Total:	125*

*Hospitalized veterans 88
Nonhospitalized veterans 22
Civilians 15

ing primarily upon the negative attitudes of the noninjured. It appears as a resistance or reluctance to admit him to various kinds and degrees of social relationship. Unlike those instances when actual physical limitations exclude him from an activity, it carries with it an aura of ostracism.

Frequently the injured feel that there is a discrepancy between what the noninjured see as the physical, social, and psychological limitations of the injury and the limitations actually present and acknowledged by the injured. Frequently when the noninjured judge that physical limitations preclude an activity, the injured know that some form of participation is possible—that the limitations are not really coextensive with the demands of the situation as seen by the noninjured.

The margin of difference between the two points of view may spell the difference between nonparticipation and nonacceptance of the injured person. Moreover, it often may give the appearance of willful avoidance of the injured on the part of the noninjured, even though this may not be the case. If, however, the difference is resolved, the situation merely becomes an instance of nonparticipation, and the problem of acceptance does not arise.

REASONS FOR NONACCEPTANCE

The injured feel that they cannot be expected to shift *their* attitudes concerning their physical limitations in order to narrow this margin, since they feel that they are the ones who really know the actual reality limitations in their own cases. They feel that it is the noninjured who have to reexamine their attitudes for possible misconceptions, biases, and mistaken beliefs in order to reduce the discrepancy. In the following sections we shall give our attention to these misconceptions as they are pointed out by the injured. They will be discussed under three headings: namely, misconceptions which pertain to the physical limitations of the injured, to the appearance of the injury, and to evaluations of the worth of the injured as a person.

Physical Limitations

A far-reaching misconception is the tendency on the part of the noninjured to overestimate physical limitations imposed by an injury. Some statements taken from the records exemplify this error:

> "Everyone was going dancing. Everyone had dates but I stayed home. . . . The boys thought I couldn't dance. I was quite unhappy for a while."

> "It doesn't follow as night and day that a man with a high AK (above knee amputation) can't go on a hike. . . . I would just invite him and if he declines, well, he will thank me for my kindness in inviting him."

The simplest remedy is clearly indicated in the quotation above. Since the noninjured cannot readily acquire information as to the variable capacities of the injured, they may indicate their willingness to have him participate, and leave to him the judgment of whether or not he will be able to do so. The noninjured may feel that in the event that participation is impossible, it will seem inconsiderate to have even suggested it. The danger of hurting the feelings of the injured, however, will be no greater than in other nonparticipation situations. At the same time the additional distress of apparent rejection will be avoided.

The manner of approach indicated is also of value in minimizing another kind of misconception. This is the failure on the part of the noninjured to realize the ability and willingness of the injured to participate socially by playing a role different from the usual one. Thus, the injured point out:

> "I don't feel bad about not being a fisherman, and I got a kick out of going along and watching. . . . A fellow who can't play basketball quickly resigns himself to being a spectator. . . . I will go out and referee if the kids are playing."

> "I played in *Pride and Prejudice*. Someone said, 'She limped just like an old person.' Ingenue parts—if you can't do that, that doesn't mean you can't do anything."

> "In high school we had a baseball team. I would hit the ball and they would run for me. That was a tremendous thing they did. . . . When they put me on the baseball team that was great. Then I was in the group."

The implication is that the injured person, motivated by his changed circumstances, willingly restructures situations so that he may become a participant. The restructurizations may range from quite simple to rather extensive ones. Since the noninjured lack the strong motivation of the injured, they are less apt to think of such expedients. Accordingly, they are asked to forego any preconceived ideas of "possible" roles for the injured, and provide, instead, the opportunities for his social participation. In this way the injured person may determine the manner of participation which is compatible with both his interests and ability.

In addition to the misconceptions regarding injury-imposed limitations, there are special problems engendered by the reduced ease and speed of performance of the injured. Whether the injured are denied participation or not, they feel that the noninjured emphasize the inconvenience which they must endure. The injured attribute to the noninjured an apparent unwillingness to "bear with him and be patient and all that." A few examples suffice to make their point clear:

"When you go in a public place you don't want to be fiddling around with your overcoat. They don't want to wait for you all the time."

"And when you're hiking you tire out easy. People try to sympathize and wish you hadn't come on the trip and they don't want to associate with you."

Whether these attitudes are actually maintained by the noninjured, or only projections of the injured's fears, the result is the same—a feeling of non-acceptance on the part of the latter.

Assuming that the noninjured wish to include the injured person, it would be well to clarify the degree of inconvenience which the noninjured may be expected to bear. If the inconvenience is slight, they will take it as a matter of course—just as a man will slow his pace in the company of a woman. They will, too, be expected to make slight changes of plans to make easier or less awkward the participation of the injured. An arm amputee suggests, for example, the following:

"Of course, if a person has one arm you don't want to invite him to a steak dinner. Arrange your menu accordingly. Have croquettes or something that can be handled with one hand nicely."

More can be expected of close persons than of casual acquaintances in both these respects. In the main, the performance of the injured may be judged not by their efficiency and smoothness of performance, but in terms of the end achieved—successful participation in a social group.

Appearance of the Injury

The discrepancy between the beliefs of the noninjured, and the facts as they exist, operates relative to the appearance of the injury just as it does relative to injury-imposed limitations. One of its forms seems to be an overestimation of the "unsightliness" of the injury, which prompts the noninjured to avoid the injured man lest they be forced inadvertently to view the injury. Even close family members may contribute to this kind of nonacceptance:

"Mother and Dad were afraid to look. They thought it was wide open. They couldn't understand how it healed so soon."

The noninjured who himself has no "squeamishness" about seeing the injury is, nonetheless, careful to consider the feelings of others who might be more sensitive. He may, for example, hesitate to invite a visibly injured person to a social gathering because of the discomfort it might cause his guests, and secondarily, the injured man. The tendency here is probably in the direction of overestimating the frequency and strength of such negative reactions.

Such generalizations appear to be more the product of anticipation than of realism. With reference to such feelings, the noninjured should remember that the "unsightliness" of the injury cannot be judged until seen. Further, familiarity and social contact with the injured may serve to lessen the feelings of aversion, whether they arise in anticipation or in actuality. Of such contacts the injured say:

> "You are conscious of the thing all the time and the public is too, more so than you are, until they are accustomed to it and then like us they don't even see it. After the public sees it it won't matter any more. I felt that way myself. After you are around them [other injured] a while you don't notice it. You think different and you see different."

> "Pity, repulsion, surprise, horror . . . they have a feeling of distaste — that's the first impression. After they have seen it a while they get used to it, and it doesn't bother them."

Limiting such contacts because of the expectation of aversion stops the educative process which the injured call "getting used to" the injury, and unnecessarily isolates them.

Personal Evaluation

Another important consideration is felt by the injured to militate against their social acceptance. They believe that they are evaluated by the noninjured not only in terms of the physical aspects of their injury, but in terms of presumed psychological concomitants as well. There appears to be a spread of evaluation from characteristics actually affected by the injury, to other characteristics not necessarily so affected. This "halo" phenomenon is considered as generally devaluative or negative. Thus, the injured point out:

> "The majority think, in case a man is injured it throws him completely into another world or something, and it doesn't."

> "I think most people would think it would give a man an inferiority complex. . . . I expect they'd think he'd be shy and sensitive. . . . The people who came expected to see me in a much worse mental state than I was. I was pretty cheerful."

> "If they could just see the morale of these fellows they would feel a lot different. They feel he is disabled and doesn't want to be around anybody."

In similar fashion the injured imply that the spread of evaluation may go so far that the injured person is considered in a position of lower status and unworthy of acceptance.

> "Some people do condescend to the injured. I can't appreciate the basis for that attitude but it does happen."

> "A lot of people feel sorry, think you're a cripple, and look down in a very severe way."

> "You can just tell by the way a person looks. Some women will look at you as though they have a sorry look. Other people will look at you as if in contempt."

When the injured do not feel seclusive, or know that—aside from the injury—they are not "handicapped," it is the noninjured who must shift preconceived and erroneous attitudes. It is they who can best obviate the accusation of "willful" nonacceptance.

APPARENT VERSUS GENUINE ACCEPTANCE

Sometimes, though the injured person is given access to activities and relationships, he feels rejected nonetheless. These are instances in which he attributes to the noninjured unwelcome motivations such as duty or pity or the empty gestures of acceptance devoid of genuine pleasure in sharing the social situations with him. Such acceptance he interprets as "apparent," in contrast to the genuine acceptance which he seeks.

The anxiety of the injured in this regard makes him ascribe unwelcome motives when they do not exist, and makes him seek assurance of genuine rather than apparent acceptance. For example, a noninjured woman reported that a man with whom she had spent an enjoyable evening remarked, "You'll probably be angry but I'll ask you anyway. Did you go out with me only because I am an amputee?"

An injured woman expresses anxiety about her acceptance in this way:

> "There may be a feeling of superiority on the part of the other person, that he is patronizing you in being with you for that hour. It has never happened to me. I imagine it could happen. You would feel he didn't want to bother to be with a handicapped person."

> "I don't think this has ever happened, but I guess it has—they are doing you a favor being with you. It has never happened to me. They might pity you."

> "I would like to know if they feel superior to the other person, whether they

realize it or not, and because of this feeling, if they have it, are they being with you because they feel they owe it to you, the less fortunate?"

Apparent acceptance is then not more welcome than nonacceptance — perhaps even more disturbing. In each, the injured see an underlying inability or unwillingness in others to know them as they actually are.

SUMMARY

This discussion of social acceptance of the injured is limited to the problems as seen by them. Three general questions are considered: (a) what characterizes social acceptance or nonacceptance; (b) what, according to the injured, are some of the reasons which account for their nonacceptance; (c) how may some of these difficulties be reduced or resolved?

In considering these questions we have indicated the distinction between *nonparticipation* and *nonacceptance*, and between *apparent* and *genuine* acceptance. The reasons for nonacceptance of the injured are developed mainly in terms of the misconceptions of noninjured persons relative to the injury and its effects. The discrepancies between points of view of the injured and noninjured are pointed out. Particular reference is made to the noninjured's evaluation of the physical limitations of the injury, its appearance, and its effect on the personality of the injured person. Remedies aimed at correcting misconceptions and reducing the indicated discrepancies are suggested.

NOTES

1. For detailed account of the interview procedure, see: Studies in Adjustment to Visible Injuries: Evaluation of Help by the Injured. Ladieu, G., Hanfmann, E., and Dembo, T., *Journal of Abnormal and Social Psychology*, April, 1947; Studies in Adjustment to Visible Injuries: Evaluation of Curiosity by the Injured. White, R. K., Wright, B. A., and Dembo, T., *Journal of Abnormal and Social Psychology*, Oct., 1947.

13

Self-Socialization: Readjustment of Paraplegics in the Community

Betty E. Cogswell

Paraplegics receive little or no professional help for one aspect of the reha-bilitation process. In the first phase of rehabilitation, medical teams are avail-able for teaching the physical skills necessary for independent mobility and for assisting patients to accept the reality of their disability. In the final phase, rehabilitation counselors are available to assist with occupational choice, training, and placement. No professional assumes explicit responsi-bility, however, for assisting paraplegics to learn the social skills necessary to relate successfully with nondisabled people in the community. Many of these skills are acquired during a middle phase of rehabilitation, after para-plegics leave the hospital and before they resume full-time student or work roles.

Physical disability is potentially stigmatizing, and the salience of stigma increases outside of the hospital. To become successfully rehabilitated, para-plegics must learn to diminish this effect. This, however, occurs through self-teaching, for paraplegics are left to chart their own course. This paper presents findings on one aspect of the process—the way paraplegics sequen-tially arrange their social encounters. It should be noted, however, that the paraplegics studied were essentially unaware that their experiences were se-quentially patterned.

PROCESS OF SOCIALIZATION

Rehabilitation may be analyzed advantageously as a process of socialization. In fact, if rehabilitation had not been conceptualized in this way, the pres-ent findings might have been overlooked. A socialization model focuses at-

From *Journal of Rehabilitation*, 34(3) (1968), 11–13. Copyright © 1968 by the National Re-habilitation Association. Reprinted by permission of the Editor and the author.

The author wishes to acknowledge the helpful suggestions of Professors Harvey L. Smith, Marvin B. Sussman, and Donald D. Weir, M.D. who read an earlier version of this paper.

tention on the processes by which individuals acquire new roles and leads to questions on the development of new self-definitions, skills, activities, and associations. Socialization proceeds through interaction among novices (individuals learning a new role) and agents (individuals responsible for training). In the research reported here, socialization was studied from the perspective of the novices, that is, paraplegics' learning the disabled role. Paraplegics were interviewed at repeated intervals about their experiences after leaving the hospital. They were asked what they did, whom they saw, how they responded to other people, and how other people responded to them. Comparison of the experiences of those studied reveals that the course of socialization was structured in a way that provided opportunities to develop and master social skills for relating to people in the normal world. Medical professionals may give patients gross indications that they will encounter interpersonal problems in the community, but paraplegics mainly discover these problems for themselves and proceed to handle them in their own way. They become their own socializing agents as well as agents for the many people they encounter who are uncertain about proper behavior toward a disabled person.

The data for this paper are taken from a more extensive study which followed paraplegics from the time of injury to the time they resumed roles in the community. Data were collected in a general teaching hospital over a five-year period by means of field observations and interviews with members of a rehabilitation team and with 36 young adult paraplegics. Eleven of these paraplegics were chosen for intensive study through a series of open-ended interviews with both patients and their families. Generalizations were abstracted primarily from the intensive study data. Data on the other 25 paraplegics, however, were used to refine initial hypotheses. The rehabilitation team was composed of physicians, nurses, physical therapists, occupational therapists, and social workers. The study group of paraplegics included both males and females, whites and blacks, and private and staff patients. The subjects' social class ranged from lower class to upper middle.

MIDDLE PERIOD OF REHABILITATION

Paraplegics need a month or more after leaving the hospital to practice the physical skills necessary to function in the normal world. In theory, after this amount of time, they should be physically ready to resume a job or begin job training. A curious finding is that most paraplegics who do eventually resume full-time training or work roles delay for one to several years. The reasons for this delay are of particular concern for rehabilitation practitioners. Some medical professionals note differences in the way patients respond when they first go home and at that time in the future when they become ready to go back to work, but they are unable to give a clear description of these differences. Some suggest that this may be a necessary period of mourning that paraplegics cannot be rushed through.

Compared to pretrauma life, all of the paraplegics upon returning home had a marked reduction in (a) number of social contacts with others in the community, (b) frequency in entering community settings, and (c) number of roles that they played. All of the paraplegics studied eventually showed some increase in these three activities; however, there is wide variation in the extent of increase. If one takes resumption of a work role as a final indicator of rehabilitation, only six of 26 followed regularly at this hospital had reached this level at the time of last contact. (Ten of the original 36 did not return to this hospital for their medical care after completing physical retraining. Of the 26 followed here, one died, two were remaining at home on the advice of their lawyer, and one developed a heart condition which prevented his return to work. All of the paraplegics had either worked or had been full-time students prior to injury. The six subjects who did return to work, five men and one woman, are all from middle class families.) The others who arrested at lower levels along the way appear to have had common socialization experiences up to this point.

All paraplegics face problems which evolve from the stigma of disability. In the hospital, medical personnel help paraplegics develop a self-image of independence and personal worth. Although difficulties are encountered, it is easier to establish and maintain this self-image in the sheltered social environment of the hospital than in the world outside. When paraplegics return to their homes and communities, definitions of their disability as a social stigma reach the height of salience. This common problem apparently orders their course of socialization.

SELF-SOCIALIZATION INTO A DEVALUED ROLE

In our society the disabled role is socially devalued. Effective socialization results through learning to reduce the stigmatizing effects of disability. Paraplegics must learn the physical and social skills necessary to play the role with sufficient ease to prevent contamination of their identity as well as their performance of other roles. (See Goffman, 1963, for a sociological definition of stigma.) Physical disability, like most stigmas, is not equally stigmatizing in all social situations. Salience of disability as a stigma varies with the type of individual encountered and the type of social setting. It also varies with the paraplegic's definition and projection of self as worthy or demeaned and with his skill in managing others' definitions of his disability.

In learning the skills of stigma management, paraplegics become their own socializing agents. Change which occurs during this period is more apt to occur through day-to-day accommodation to problems rather than through systematic goal-directed behavior. Paraplegics have a diffuse image of a final goal—reintegration into the community as persons of inde-

pendence and worth. This image was initiated in the hospital by rehabilitation practitioners. There is, however, no awareness of the intermediate steps
necessary to attain this goal. There is no agent to spell out these steps nor
to structure progress through the sequence.

Paraplegics, seemingly unaware of the long-range process, order their
course of socialization in response to day-to-day problems by avoiding social
situations where negative social response can destroy positive definitions
of self, by seeking out social situations where demands are not beyond their
current level of competence, and by manipulating social encounters to emphasize positive and minimize negative aspects of self. At first, when paraplegics have had little experience in dealing with disability as stigma, the
threat of failure is great. Uncertain of what the responses of others will be,
paraplegics tend to expect the worst. They are quick to interpret any questionable response as derogatory and rapidly withdraw if they perceive the
slightest strain in a social encounter. They are apprehensive that the attention of others may be focused on the disability and that other aspects of self
will be treated as irrelevant.

TIME-STRUCTURING OF SOCIALIZATION

The middle period of rehabilitation begins with a self-imposed moratorium
during which paraplegics remain at home. Uncertain about how to proceed,
they arrest momentarily. Reentry into the community is gradual and is structured simultaneously in two ways: by sequential choice of social settings and
sequential choice of associates. These two sequences begin with social situations which are easiest to handle and proceed to those more difficult. In essence, paraplegics search out the least threatening environments for the trial
of new behavior.

Self-Imposed Moratorium

On returning home, paraplegics become aware that their once familiar
community has become strange. One world is lost, and another is yet to be
gained. They are unclear about their own identity, for they must establish
new self-definitions for the spectrum of social relationships. These range ·
from casual encounters with waitresses, clerks, barbers, filling station attend-
ants, and dentists to more enduring relationships with friends, dates, teachers, and employers. New definitions of self grow through encounters with
others, yet paraplegics are reluctant to resume social contacts. Instead they
stay at home for a time in passive avoidance of the outside world. Pretrauma
conceptions of self do not apply; new conceptions of self have not emerged;
and action is arrested because paraplegics are unable to answer the question, Who am I?

During the first few weeks, a host of friends and neighbors come to visit, but this is not sustained. Very quickly, paraplegics find themselves alone. They describe this period as a time of social isolation and inactivity. When asked, "Whom do you see?" they reply, "Nobody." When asked, "What do you do?" they reply, "Nothing." Since there are few social expectations for the disabled role, paraplegics may stay at home for any length of time without arousing negative reactions from family or others in the community. Family and friends may encourage outings; but if the paraplegic is not responsive, these overtures tend to cease.

Sequential Selection of Social Settings

Paraplegics first enter those social settings which require the least amount of physical and social skill and proceed later to those more difficult. In selecting settings, patients used three criteria: (a) physical accessibility, (b) flexibility for leaving the scene, and (c) salience of stigma.

Physical accessibility may be considered in terms of four types of increasingly difficult settings: (a) those where the paraplegic can go and remain in his automobile; (b) those allowing easy wheelchair maneuvering, where surfaces are level and where there are wide doors and aisles; (c) those that can be easily entered by wheelchair but require the paraplegic to change seats, such as a dentist's office, barbershop, or theater; and (d) those where some physical assistance from another person is necessary, such as climbing long flights of stairs or crossing rough terrain.

Regarding flexibility for leaving settings, paraplegics want the option of leaving quickly if stigma should become salient. They are concerned with the socially acceptable length of time one must remain after entering a setting. Public streets provide the most flexibility. Following in order of decreasing flexibility are stores, places where one may have an appointment which lasts for thirty minutes or longer, visits, and parties. The most lengthy timebinding setting and the last to be reentered is place of work.

Settings vary in the degree to which each paraplegic feels his disability may become stigmatizing. One paraplegic mentioned that "People don't mind you on the street, but they don't like you in their intimate places like bars." Several mentioned that they began going to church and then to church parties long before they had the nerve to go to private parties. They seemed to feel that people in a religious setting had a greater obligation to accept them.

Sequential Selection of Associates

As paraplegics resume social relationship in the community, they choose individuals who will support definitions of them as individuals of independence and social worth. These relationships are sequentially timed. First, paraplegics phase out and seldom resume relationships with pretrauma friends; second, they begin to associate with individuals of lower social status; and third, they begin to associate with new individuals of equal status.

The paraplegics maintained very few friendships that existed prior to their injuries, declaring that they did not like to be with people that they had known before the accident. Pretrauma friends are attached to a conception of the paraplegic as he once was and have difficulty relating to him as a disabled person. Paraplegics find it difficult to establish a new identity with those who view them from a pretrauma frame of reference. These paraplegics mentioned a number of problems which ensued when they tried to maintain old relationships: Expressions of pity frequently contaminated the relationship, the sincerity of overtures made by old friends was questioned, old friends were inclined to offer unneeded physical assistance, and paraplegics felt that old friends made invidious comparisons between the pre- and posttrauma relationship. One of the more articulate paraplegics mentioned the added difficulty in assisting others to readjust to him. In discussing a breakup between him and his girl, he said, " . . . one person can fight it, but to try to carry somebody, to try to rehabilitate them to me at the same time and take the chance on its not working out, that would be a big loss and might make you tend to give up [in your own rehabilitation]."

As paraplegics begin to acquire new friends, they tend to choose people of lower social status than their pretrauma friends. (Fred Davis [1963] found that polio children on returning home established a close friendship with another child whose status and acceptance in the group was marginal.) These friends may be of lower social class, decidedly younger or older than the patient, or less attractive in other ways. By choosing friends of lower status, paraplegics are able to balance the negative definitions of disability against some negative characteristic of the other person. If, in these relationships, paraplegics become successful in projecting themselves as persons of worth and become skilled in eliciting this definition from others, they proceed to more difficult relationships, eventually forming successful relationships with new individuals of equal status. Physical disability will always pose problems for relationships with others, but paraplegics learn to handle these problems with sufficient ease to maintain stable social relationships.

AWARENESS OF PERSONAL CHANGE

Incidents which are here cited as structured in time emerge in interviews as unrelated experiences. Paraplegics do not have a frame of reference for ordering these events into sequences which lead to mastery of the disabled role. Unlike many types of socialization, there were no agents to present the steps involved. Neither was there sufficient contact among paraplegics during this period for them to compare experiences and establish common benchmarks of progress. (Julius A. Roth [1963] used the term "benchmarks of progress" to designate events which occur sequentially in a career and which are indicative of movement toward an end-point.)

From the perspective of the paraplegics, this period of time often lacked meaning: Days often seemed wasted and empty and appeared to lead nowhere. It is useful to contrast this experience with socialization in the hospital. Here medical personnel repeatedly listed for paraplegics the sequence of events necessary to achieve physical independence. Accomplishments which are meaningless from a normal person's perspective—sitting balance, wheelchair maneuvering, transfer, standing balance, walking with braces and crutches—were symbolized by hospital staff as indicators of progress. Paraplegics accepted this symbolic definition and thereby derived tremendous self-satisfaction from mastery of steps which otherwise they might have considered inconsequential. Due to definitions of the situation presented by the rehabilitation practitioners and accepted by the paraplegics, days had meaning and were filled with purposive activity. Paraplegics knew the steps to be mastered and could assess their own progress.

PRACTICAL IMPLICATIONS

Uncertainty is one of the most threatening experiences a person must face. Any framework for ordering expectations is perhaps better than none. Paraplegics now leave the hospital with only a vague impression of what to expect in their local communities. It would be naive to assume that this uncertainty could be eliminated; but it would appear that it could be reduced, and rehabilitation might be enhanced, if each paraplegic left the hospital with a planned sequence of socialization. Obviously this sequence should be geared to the individual life situation of the patient and to his individual goals. Activities appropriate to the lifestyle of a particular paraplegic could be ordered in terms of their increasing social difficulty, and each type of activity could be given symbolic meaning as an indicator of progress toward rehabilitation.

It is perhaps also important to maintain frequent contact with paraplegics during this period. Events since the last contact could be reviewed and assessed. Events for the coming period could be planned and encouraged. The symbolic meaning of social encounters could be reaffirmed. This procedure divides the middle period of rehabilitation into steps of small increments, reducing somewhat the degree of uncertainty. By presenting paraplegics with a framework for ordering this period of socialization and by guiding them through the steps, rehabilitation practitioners might be able to reduce the length of time between hospital discharge and resumption of training or work roles as well as to increase the number of paraplegics who complete the course. Claims for the merit of this procedure, however, must await experimental evaluation.

The findings presented here also have an important implication for present programs of rehabilitation. Rehabilitation counselors should take into consideration that initial stalling by paraplegics is in no way predictive of job success or failure. Some paraplegics stay at home for two to three years, yet eventually they make good social and work adjustments. This suggests that rehabilitation counselors should not despair if a paraplegic is at first unwilling to resume full-time work. It would seem important to maintain contact with this type of client for several years, giving him repeated opportunities for job training or job placement.

These notions on socialization, while applying to young adult paraplegics, may be equally pertinent to other age groups with other types of disabilities. Almost all physical disabilities are potentially stigmatizing, and successful adjustment to these conditions usually requires learning the skills of stigma management. The findings also may have some bearing on the resocialization of released prisoners and psychiatric patients, as well as of alcoholics, drug addicts, and other types of deviants.

This paper has dealt with only one aspect of paraplegics' socialization careers in the community — ordering social encounters by increasing difficulty. As paraplegics' social skills increased, they attempted to enter more difficult social situations. Further research is necessary to specify the skills which are important and to ascertain the manner in which these skills may be learned. Although our present knowledge of resocialization into the community is limited, it would seem worthwhile for the rehabilitation system to consider assuming greater responsibility for this period of adjustment. Research should be encouraged, and the potential role of rehabilitation workers should be evaluated to determine whether professional assistance might enhance rehabilitation.

REFERENCES

Davis, Fred, *Passage through Crisis: Polio Victims and Their Families*. New York: Bobbs-Merrill, 1963, pp. 147–148.

Goffman, Erving. *Stigma: Notes on the Management of Spoiled Identity*. Englewood Cliffs, N.J.: Prentice-Hall, 1963, p. 5.

Roth, Julius A. *Timetables: Structuring the Passage of Time in Hospital Treatment and Other Careers*. New York: Bobbs-Merrill, 1963.

Part V

Attitudes toward Disabled Persons

The societal response to disability is a reflection of the attitudes of others toward disability and toward disabled persons. This attitude is often negative, and it affects the interpersonal relationships between nondisabled and disabled persons, as well as society's attempts to rehabilitate persons with handicaps.

Livneh, in a comprehensive review, traces the origins of negative attitudes toward persons with disabilities and examines numerous variables as possible correlates of negative attitudes. His classification system provides a useful means for categorizing and discussing sources of negative attitudes.

Changing negative attitudes toward disabled persons is the focus of the other two chapters in this section. Wright compares two ways of responding to a disability—coping with it or succumbing to the disability. On the basis of relevant research, disability simulation from the coping as opposed to the succumbing framework is recommended as a means to affect nondisabled persons' attitudes positively.

Based on his survey of the various means of changing societal attitudes toward persons with disabilities, Anthony suggests an experience combining both contact with and information about persons with disabilities. Anthony discusses ways in which broad societal rehabilitation programs might be implemented in the fields of education, employment, and public service.

The articles in Part V enable the reader to have a clearer understanding of attitudes, how they affect the lives of disabled persons, and how they may be changed.

14

On the Origins of Negative Attitudes toward People with Disabilities

Hanoch Livneh

In the past quarter of a century several attempts have been made to categorize the different sources of negative attitudes toward individuals with disabling conditions. Among these attempts, the works of Gellman,[34] Raskin,[63] Siller et al.,[79] and Wright[90] are often singled out. In addition, a plethora of theoretical and empirical work has been directed toward the narrower goal of advancing and supporting a specific cause (often referred to as *root* or *base*) for negative attitudes toward disability (see Goffman,[35] Meng,[54] Parsons,[61] and Schilder[70]).

The main objective of the current article is twofold; to integrate the major approaches in the domain of attitudinal sources toward people with disabilities, and to offer a new classification system by which these attitudes can be better conceptualized and understood.

Of the four main classifications, earlier attempts by Raskin[63] and Gellman[34] were more narrowly conceived. Both offered a fourfold classification system for the roots of prejudicial attitudes toward those who are blind (Raskin) and those who are disabled in general (Gellman). Raskin perceived these attitudes to be determined by psychodynamic, situational, sociocultural, and historical factors. Gellman, on the other hand, viewed the prejudicial roots as stemming from social customs and norms, child-rearing practices, recrudescence of neurotic childhood fears in frustrating and anxiety-provoking situations, and discrimination-provoking behavior by persons with disabilities.

Wright,[90] in a comprehensive literature review, discussed attitudes toward atypical physique according to the following categories: general requiredness of cause-effect relations (i.e., phenomenal causality between certain "sinful behaviors" and disability as an "unavoidable punishment"),

From *Rehabilitation Literature*, 43 (11–12) (1982), 338–347. Reprinted with permission. Published by the National Easter Seal Society, 2023 W. Ogden, Chicago, IL 60612.

negative reaction to the different and strange, childhood experiences, and prevailing socioeconomic factors. Siller et al.,[79] based on their extensive attitudinal study, reported the existence of 13 aversive content categories toward those with disabilities, utilizing both empirical and clinical findings. Their discussion, however, often confuses components of attitudinal correlates (such as functional limitations or attribution of negative qualities) with attitudinal sources (for example, aesthetic-sexual aversion, fear it could happen to self).

The present article attempts to deal exclusively with attitudinal sources. In other words, only approaches—both theoretical and empirical—which can be perceived in terms of cause (attitudinal source or root) and effect (negative or aversive reaction or attitude) relationships will be dealt with. Also, the classification system of the different attitudinal sources combines both process (psychodynamic mechanisms) and content (sociocultural factors) related formulations. It was felt that any attempt to separate the two would be rather arbitrary.

SOCIOCULTURAL CONDITIONING

Pervasive social and cultural norms, standards, and expectations often lead to the creation of negative attitudes toward the disabled population. Among the frequently mentioned contributing factors are:

1. Emphasis on concepts such as "body beautiful," "body whole," youth, health, athletic prowess, personal appearance, and wholeness. These highly stressed societal standards are often institutionalized into cultural customs, which are to be conformed to by members of society.[34,66,90]

2. Emphasis on personal productiveness and achievement. Individuals in most Western countries are judged on the basis of their ability to be socially and economically competitive.[38,69]

3. Prevailing socioeconomic level. The importance of socioeconomic factors in creating an atmosphere within which attitudes toward individuals with disabilities are often nourished was emphasized by Safilios-Rothschild.[69] The level of societal development (Jordan and Friesen[44]), the rate of unemployment, beliefs concerning the origins of poverty, and the importance attached to the nation's welfare economy and security are all contributing factors affecting attitudes toward people with disabilities.

4. Society's delineation of the "sick role" phenomenon. Whereas the occupant of the "sick role" is exempt from normal societal obligations and responsibilities, the length of a disabled person's remaining in this role is associated with negative attitudes.[60,61,81]

5. The status degradation attached to disability. The social deviance and inferred stigma of having a physical disability bears heavily on society's attitudes toward those affected (see Davis,[15] Freidson,[33] Goffman,[35] Safilios-

Rothschild,[69] Wolfensberger,[86,87] Worthington,[88] and Yamamato[91]). The cultural values held by members of society are often based on the perception of any form of "imputed deviancy," including disability, as a sign of marginal status. The person with a disability is, therefore, viewed as an "outsider," an "offender," or as "different."[5,36,46] Wolfensberger[86,87] regards the devalued or deviant status as a negative role imposed on the stigmatized person and views the sources of this deviancy as stemming from physical, behavioral, and attribution-based characteristics. Yamamato[91] goes as far as to suggest that society needs the deviates as a symbol of evil and intangible dangers.

CHILDHOOD INFLUENCES

The importance of infancy and early childhood experiences, in terms of both child-rearing practices and early parental influences (verbal and behavioral) is often stressed.[34,90] The impact of early experiences and their related emotions and cognitions have a major role in influencing the growing child's belief and value system. Parental and significant others' actions, words, tone of voice, gestures, and so forth are transmitted, directly or indirectly, to the child and tend to have a crucial impact on the formation of attitudes toward disability.

Rearing practices which emphasize the importance of health and normalcy, and which threaten any infringement of health rules with sickness, illness, and long-term disability, result in aversion toward individuals affected.[34,90] Childhood stages of development (oral, anal, phallic, genital) are wrought with anxiety-laden premises regarding the etiology of certain illnesses; therefore, the association with ongoing disabilities and disabled persons, as past transgressors, is readily made.

PSYCHODYNAMIC MECHANISMS

Several mainly unconscious psychological processes have been advanced in the literature as explanatory mechanisms for the attitudes manifested by the "non-disabled" toward the "disabled." Although most of these mechanisms are apparently sown during early childhood[34,79,90] and may, therefore, be regarded as related to childhood experiences, it was felt that due to their significance in creating and maintaining these attitudes such a separation is warranted.

1. Requirement of mourning. The person with a disability is expected to grieve the loss of a body part or function. He or she "ought" to suffer and slowly adjust to such a misfortune.[16,17,46,80,81,90]

The non-disabled individual has a need to safeguard his or her values, by wanting the disabled individual to suffer, and show the appropriate grieving, so as to protect one's own values of the importance of a functioning body.[16,17] Any attempt on the disabled person's part to deny or reject the "suffering role" is met with negative attitudes. The mechanism of rationalization is clearly operative in this case.

2. Unresolved conflict over scopophilia and exhibitionism. Psychoanalytic thought stresses the importance of vision in early psychosexual and ego development.[8] The significance of sight, both in terms of pleasure of looking at and being looked upon in the pregenital stages, is stressed in the psychoanalytic literature. Any unresolved conflicts related to these developmental stages may be triggered as a consequence of the approach/fascination–avoidance/repulsion conflict often associated with the sight of a disabled person.

3. Negative attributes resulting from the "spread phenomenon." Attributing to those with disabilities certain negative characteristics frequently results when the mechanism of "halo effect" or "spread phenomenon" is in operation.[90] The generalization from one perceived characteristic (e.g., physical disability) to other, unrelated characteristics (e.g., emotional or mental maladjustment) is referred to as "spread" and explains the too often pervasive negative correlates of a pure physical deviance.[46,81]

4. Associating responsibility with etiology. The attribution of personal-moral accountability to the cause of a disabling condition results in negative attitudes. If an individual can be held responsible for an imputed deviance, certain social management approaches are then suggested (punishment, control, "rehabilitation," correction, and so forth), which are frequently embedded with negative connotations.[33,69,91] Again, the operation of a rationalization mechanism is evident here.

5. Fear of social ostracism. Siller et al.[79] suggest this category as an extension of the "guilty by association" phenomenon. The non-disabled person fears that an association with disabled persons may be interpreted by others as implying some psychological maladjustment on his or her own part. The internalization of others' values and beliefs, which tends to weaken one's ego boundaries, coupled with projection onto others of unwanted personal attributes, are the main operating mechanisms.

6. Guilt of being "able-bodied." Guilt of "enjoying" one's body intactness in addition to possible injustices directed toward persons with disabilities (e.g., the belief in the disabled person's responsibility for the condition, lack of involvement in charitable activities) may result in attempts at atonement or further dissociation from the presence of disabled individuals.[79,90]

DISABILITY AS A PUNISHMENT FOR SIN

The triad of sin, punishment, and disability can be conceived as a component of the earlier discussion of psychodynamic mechanisms operating in the creation of aversive reactions toward disability. Due to their importance in elucidating the roots of negative attitudes toward people with disabling conditions and the various versions of their interrelatedness, which are advanced in the literature, it seems justifiable to treat these concepts under a separate heading.

1. Disability as a punishment for sin. Alexander's[1] concept of "emotional syllogism," when applied here,[79,90] stresses the consequential appropriateness between physical deformity and a sinful person. The source of the disabled person's suffering is attributed to either a personally committed evil act or to an ancestral wrongdoing.[72]

2. The individual with a disability as a dangerous person. Meng[54] (reported in Barker et al.[7]) attributed fear and avoidance of those who are physically disabled to three unconscious mechanisms: (a) the belief that a disability is a punishment for a transgression and, therefore, that the disabled person is evil and dangerous; (b) the belief that a disability is an unjust punishment and that, therefore, the person is motivated to commit an evil act to balance the injustice; and (c) the projection of one's unacceptable impulses upon the disabled person, which results in perceiving the latter as evil and dangerous (see also Siller et al.[79] and Thoreson and Kerr[81]). Thus, whereas in the previous section suffering was perceived as being a punishment for an evil deed, in the present section physical deviance is viewed as the cause, the consequence of which is felt to be a sinful and evil act ("a twisted mind in a twisted body").

3. The non-disabled person fearing imminent punishment. If the notion of disability as a punishment is warranted, then the non-disabled person who anticipates, often realistically, retribution for past personal misdeeds avoids the persons with disabilities because of guilt of not being punished or the fear of imminent punishment by association.[34]

4. Vicarious self-punishment offered by the punished disabled person. An extension of the above formula was offered by Thurer.[82] The sinning disabled person, in fiction or reality, is perceived to be an easy target for one's own projections. Since the disabled individual was punished for the sin committed and since the non-disabled person unconsciously identifies with the sin, he or she is also punished, albeit vicariously, and the felt guilt is, therefore, lessened. The externalization of one's inner conflicts upon a punished target assists in controlling them. The result is, therefore, the repelling-gratifying conflict of feelings that ensues as a result of seeing, hearing, or reading about a disabled individual.

ANXIETY-PROVOKING UNSTRUCTURED SITUATIONS

The role of unfamiliar situations in creating anxiety and confusion was stressed by Hebb[39] and Heider.[40] Similarly, upon initial interaction with a disabled person, the non-disabled person is often faced with an unstructured situation in which most socially accepted rules and regulations for proper interaction are not well-defined. These ambiguous situations tend to disrupt both cognitive-intellectual processes as well as the more fundamental perceptual-affective mechanisms.

1. Cognitively-unstructured situations. The non-disabled person interacting with a disabled individual faces uncertain social outcomes engendered by the new and, therefore, cognitively vague situation.[41] The unfamiliarity presents an incongruent cognitive gestalt which disrupts the established basic rules of social interaction and may cause withdrawal from such a situation[91] or create strain in this interaction.[79] The often reported findings in the literature—that the lack of factual knowledge and information about disabling conditions tends to lead to negative attitudes (Anthony,[3] English[21,22,23])—also support this contention.

2. Lack of affective preparedness. There is an apparent fearful and negative reaction, on a visceral level, to the different and strange.[39,40,79] Strange and mutilated bodies trigger a conflict in the observer, because of incompatible perceptions.[39] People tend to resist the strange because it does not fit into the structure of an expected life space[41] and because of a lack of affective readiness.[88,91] Siller et al.[79] perceived it to exemplify their negative atypicality category, which creates in the observer a feeling of distress. Lack of experiential contact and exposure to persons with disabilities is a contributing factor to the origination of such an attitude.[3,21,22]

AESTHETIC AVERSION

The impact of a purely aesthetic-sexual aversion, triggered by the sight of a visibly disabled person, has been stressed by several authors.[41,78,79] These feelings of repulsion and discomfort are felt when non-disabled persons come in contact with certain disabilities (such as amputations, body deformities, cerebral palsy, skin disorders).[64,68,74] The importance of aesthetic-sexual aversion as a basis for negative attitudinal formation was also reported in Siller et al.'s study,[79] in which the felt aversion referred to the direct and conscious reactions experienced on sensory and visceral levels. The role played by aesthetic attractiveness was also demonstrated by Napoleon et al.[56] as a predisposing factor in judging a person's degree of mental illness.

THREATS TO BODY IMAGE INTEGRITY

The concept of body image, as the mental representation of one's own body, was originally coined by Schilder.[70] Several related formulations were proposed regarding the importance of the body image concept (i.e., self-image, body cathexis, body satisfaction) as an explanatory vehicle in understanding attitudes toward people with disabilities.

1. Threat to the body image. Schilder[70] argued that, via the mechanism of identification, seeing a person with a physical disability creates a feeling of discomfort because of the incongruence between an expected "normal" body and the actual perceived reality. The viewer's own unconscious and somatic body image may, therefore, be threatened due to the presence of the disabled individual.[55]

2. Reawakening of castration anxiety. The psychoanalytic concept of castration anxiety, as applied to explaining the formation of negative attitudes toward persons with disabilities, stresses the stirring up of archaic castration fears in the presence of analogous situations (such as direct loss of a leg or an eye or an indirect loss of a certain body function).[10,29,51,79,90]

3. Fear of losing one's physical integrity. Profound anxiety about becoming disabled plays a crucial part in forming prejudicial attitudes toward those who are. When faced with a disabled person, the non-disabled individual becomes highly anxious because the original fear of potential bodily harm is rekindled.[68,69] Roessler and Bolton,[66] capitalizing on Gellman's[34] original discussion, believe that non-disabled persons, being fearful of disablement and loss of self-control, feel intense discomfort which arouses additional anxiety when in contact with a visibly disabled person. The result is avoidance of the disabled person and attempts at segregating and isolating them. Similar ideas were advanced by Siller et al.,[79] who viewed the fear that the disability could happen to oneself as a basis for an aversive attitude toward people who are disabled.

4. Separation anxiety. Although somewhat related to castration anxiety and fear of losing physical integrity, separation anxiety, in the sense of object loss, is another unconscious source leading to negative attitudes toward disability.[79] The loss of a body part or function may trigger, in the viewer, narcissistic concerns and unresolved infantile anxieties, which often evolve around possible separation from parental figures.[73]

5. Fear of contamination or inheritance. The fear that social interaction with disabled people may lead to contamination provokes aversive attitudes.[79] This refers to avoiding those with disabilities on both superficial interactive levels (social intercourse) and more in-depth relationships (marriage, having children).

MINORITY GROUP COMPARABILITY

The view that attitudes toward the disabled population parallel those manifested toward minority groups, in general, was advocated by Barker[7] and further elaborated on by Wright.[90] This view holds that disabled people, as a marginal group,[5,80] trigger negative reactions in the non-disabled majority. Being perceived as marginal, or as a member of a minority group, carries with it the same stereotypic reactions of occupying a devalued and inferior status shared by ethnic, racial, and religious groups.[9,13,14,93] The resulting attitude can, therefore, be categorized as being discriminatory and prejudiced in nature, and as advocating isolation and segregation of disabled persons from the remaining population.[69,90]

DISABILITY AS A REMINDER OF DEATH

The parallelism between reactions toward those who are disabled and feelings associated with dying (anxiety, fear, dread) was suggested by several authors.[20,48,49,59,76] The contention is that the loss of a body part or a physical function constitutes the death of a part, which in the past was integrally associated with one's ego.[4] The anxiety associated with death is, therefore, rekindled at the sight of a disabled person. The disabled groups, both literally and symbolically, serve as a denial of our primitive, infantile omnipotence[28] and as a reminder of our mortality.

PREJUDICE-INVITING BEHAVIORS

Gellman[34] and Wright[90] discussed the effect of certain provoking behaviors, by persons with disabilities, on discriminatory practices toward them. These provoking behaviors may be categorized into two general classes:

1. Prejudice by invitation.[66] Specific behaviors by disabled individuals (being dependent; seeking secondary gains; acting fearful, insecure, or inferior) create and strengthen certain prejudicial beliefs in the observer. Wright[90] similarly traced these behaviors to the physically disabled person's expectations of being treated in depreciating ways, and as a result set themselves up in situations in which they will be devalued.

2. Prejudice by silence. Lack of interest on the disabled person's part or lack of effective public relations campaigns or self-help groups representing the interests and concerns of specific disability groups to combat the public's ignorance is a way of fostering stereotypic and negative attitudes on the latter's part.

THE INFLUENCE OF DISABILITY-RELATED FACTORS

Several disability-connected variables were reported in the literature as affecting attitudes toward disabled persons. The association of these variables with certain negative perceptions was both empirically studied[6,74] and theoretically discussed.[33,69]

Among the major reported variables can be found:

1. Functionality versus organicity of disability. Barker[6] found that a dichotomy exists between the public's perceptions regarding certain personality traits attached to functional (alcoholism) or organic (blindness, cancer) disabilities. Siller[74] concluded that those disabilities having the least functional implications were also those reacted to least negatively. Similar conclusions were reached in the context of occupational settings where employers preferred physically disabled individuals (for example, those with paraplegia) to the more functionally impaired persons (such as those who were mentally retarded or emotionally disabled).[6,65,69]

2. Level of severity. Usually the more severe a disability is, the more negatively it is perceived.[69,71,74] Severity is, of course, related to level of functional limitation involved.

3. Degree of visibility. Generally, the more visible a disability is, the more negative an attitude it tends to trigger.[69,71,74]

4. Degree of cosmetic involvement. Generally, the more the cosmetic implication inherent in the disability, in terms of aesthetic characteristics (see also "Aesthetic Aversion"), the less favorably it is reacted to.[74]

5. Contagiousness versus non-contagiousness of disability. Safilios-Rothschild[69] discussed the influence of contagious disabilities on the degree of prejudice directed toward them. The more contagious a disability is, the more fear of personal contraction is aroused and the more negative, therefore, is the ensuing reaction.

6. Body part affected. The importance of the body part affected by the disability, in terms of both personal and social implications, was suggested by Safilios-Rothschild[69] and Weinstein et al.[84]

7. Degree of predictability. The factor of imputed prognosis or probability of curability was studied and discussed by Freidson,[33] Safilios-Rothschild,[69] and Yamamato.[91] On the whole, the more curable and therefore predictable the disability is, the less negatively it is perceived.

The final category to be briefly discussed includes the association of certain demographic and personality variables of the non-disabled population with negative attitudes toward disabled persons. Since this category has been the target of extensive empirical research in the past years and since most of these studies are correlational rather than causal in nature, discussion will only revolve around their main findings. It should be noted that although the conclusions drawn by the studies' authors are only suggestive and cannot be generalized beyond their participating populations, most authors regarded the respondents' personal variables under study as determinants of attitudes toward disability due to their enduring and deeply ingrained qualities (such as sex, intelligence, self-concept, anxiety level).

DEMOGRAPHIC VARIABLES ASSOCIATED WITH ATTITUDES

Several major reviews of studies investigating demographic correlates of negative attitudes toward people with disabilities[21,53,67] have reached these conclusions concerning the following variables:

1. Sex. Females display more favorable attitudes toward individuals who are physically disabled than males.[9,32,74,75,94]

2. Age. There appear to be two inverted U-shaped distributions when age-related differences toward persons with disabilities are measured.[67] Attitudes are, generally, more positive at late childhood and adulthood, and less favorable attitudes are recorded at early childhood, adolescence, and old age.[67,74,77,79]

3. Socioeconomic status. Higher income groups manifest more favorable attitudes toward the emotionally and mentally disabled than lower income groups[21,43]; however, no differences were found regarding physical disabilities.[19,21,50,85]

4. Educational level. In spite of age-confounding research difficulties, most studies concluded that educational level is positively correlated with more favorable attitudes toward persons with disabling conditions.[42,43,75,83]

PERSONALITY VARIABLES ASSOCIATED WITH ATTITUDES

Research on the association of several personality traits and characteristics in the non-disabled population with respect to negative attitudes toward disabled people was summarized and reported by several authors (e.g., English,[21] Kutner,[46] McDaniel,[53] Pederson and Carlson,[62] and Safilios-Rothschild[69]). Major findings include the following:

1. Ethnocentrism. Chesler,[9] Cowen et al.,[13,14] Lukoff and Whiteman,[50] Noonan,[57] Whiteman and Lukoff,[85] and Yuker,[93] following Wright's[90] formulation of the comparability between attitudes toward persons with disabilities and attitudes toward ethnic and religious minorities, in general, found that high ethnocentrism was related to lack of acceptance of the disabled population.

2. Authoritarianism. Jabin,[43] Lukoff and Whiteman,[50] Noonan et al.,[58] Tunick et al.,[83] and Whiteman and Lukoff[85] reported a positive correlation between accepting attitudes toward disabled persons and low authoritarianism (see also Dembo et al.'s[16] theoretical discussion).

3. Aggression. Meng's[54] original hypothesis suggested that the projection of one's aggressive and hostile desires upon those with disabilities will

lead to the belief that disabled persons are dangerous and, as a result, to prejudicial attitudes toward them. Jabin,[43] Siller,[75] and Siller et al.[79] confirmed this hypothesis in independent studies, concluding that less aggressive individuals express more positive attitudes toward this group.

4. Self-insight. Siller[75] and Yuker[92] reported findings which suggested a moderate relationship between the need for introspection, as a measure of insightfulness, and empathic understanding of people who are disabled.

5. Anxiety. The degree of manifest anxiety was found to be associated with attitudes toward disabled persons. Jabin,[43] Kaiser and Moosbruker,[45] Marinelli and Kelz,[52] Siller,[75] Siller et al.,[79] and Yuker et al.[94] demonstrated that a high level of manifest anxiety is positively correlated with rejection of disabled individuals.

6. Self-concept. Several studies (e.g., Epstein and Shontz,[24] Jabin,[43] Siller,[75] Yuker,[92] and Yuker et al.[95]) reported a relationship between positive self-concept and a more accepting attitude toward disability. It seems that persons who are more secure and confident in their own selves also tend to feel more positive and accepting of disabled persons.

7. Ego strength. Similarly to self-concept, ego strength was found to be related to attitudes toward people with disabilities. Siller[71,72,73,74] and Siller et al.[79] reported on the relationship between ego weakness and rejection of the disabled, while Noonan et al.[58] found a trend in this direction, albeit not statistically significant.

8. Body- and self-satisfaction. Several studies (Cormack,[12] Epstein and Shontz,[24] Fisher and Cleveland,[31] Leclair and Rockwell,[47] and Siller[73]) concluded that lack of satisfaction with one's own body (low "body-cathexis" score) is related, and probably a contributing factor, to the development of negative attitudes toward physically disabled persons. Siller,[73] Siller et al.,[79] and Yuker et al.[95] expanded the body-cathexis concept to successfully argue that a positive perception of one's self is related to the acceptance of disabled individuals. People with positive and secure self-concepts tend to show more positive and accepting attitudes toward those with disabilities, while people with low self-concepts often reject them (see also section on "Threats to Body Image Integrity").

9. Ambiguity tolerance. The ability of non-disabled persons to better tolerate ambiguity was found to be positively correlated with acceptance of physically disabled persons.[27]

10. Social desirability. The need for social approval and acceptance by others was positively associated with acceptance of people having disabilities.[18,26,43,79]

11. Alienation. Alienated individuals tend to be more hostile toward, and rejecting of, disabled persons.[43]

12. Intelligence level. English[21] tentatively concluded, from his review of related studies, that there may be a relationship between the non-disabled intellectual capacity and acceptance of disability.

SUMMARY AND CONCLUSIONS

The present article has attempted to outline a classification system according to which a number of sources of negative attitudes toward people with disabilities was categorized and discussed.

The major categories included were (a) conditioning by sociocultural norms that emphasize certain qualities not met by the disabled population; (b) childhood influences where early life experiences foster the formation of stereotypic adult beliefs and values; (c) psychodynamic mechanisms that may play a role in creating unrealistic expectations and unresolved conflicts when interacting with disabled persons; (d) perception of disability as a punishment for a committed sin or as a justification for committing a future evil act, which triggers unconscious fears in the non-disabled person; (e) the inherent capacity of unstructured social, emotional, and intellectual situations to provoke confusion and anxiety; (f) the impact of a basic aesthetic-sexual aversion, created by the sight of the visibly disfigured, on the development of negative attitudes; (g) the threat to the conscious body and unconscious body image triggered by the mere presence of physically disabled individuals; (h) the devaluative and stereotypical reactions fostered by the marginality associated with being a member of a minority group; (i) the unconscious and symbolic parallelism between disability and death as a reminder of man's transient existence; (j) prejudice-provoking behaviors, by persons with disabilities, that result in discriminatory practices toward them; (k) disability-related factors (e.g., levels of functionality, visibility, severity) which may contribute to specific negative attitudes; and (l) observer-related factors, both demographic (sex, age) and personality-connected (ethnocentrism, authoritarianism), which may foster the development of negative attitudes.

The classification system suggested suffers one major drawback. There is a certain degree of overlap among several of the categories (e.g., castration anxiety, viewed here as a threat to body image, may well be conceived as belonging to the childhood influences category; or anxiety provoked by unstructured situations may be regarded as just another psychological-operated mechanism if viewed phenomenologically rather than environmentally based). It should be noted, however, that due to the often highly abstract and conjectural nature of several of these categories, at present there is no escape from resorting to a certain level of arbitrariness when attempting to adopt such a classification model.

No attempt was made in the present discussion to suggest the matching of certain attitude-changing techniques (informative, experiential, persuasive) with the categories discussed. Several excellent articles have been written on strategies to combat negative attitudes toward people with disabilities and toward minority groups in general (see Allport,[2] Anthony,[3] Clore and Jeffrey,[11] English,[22] Evans,[25] Finkelstein,[30] Hafer and Narcus,[37] Kutner,[46] Safilios-Rothschild,[68] and Wright[89,90]).

It seems to this author that due to the complexity of the interacting factors which contribute to the creation of negative attitudes toward this group, any attempt at change, in order to be successful, must first be cognizant of the fact that since attitudes are learned and conditioned over many years, any experimental study of short duration, hoping to change attitudes, is futile at best. Attempts to modify the prevailing negative attitudes have been generally unsuccessful.[66] They will probably continue to follow such an inevitable course as long as researchers and clinicians look for quick and easy results and solutions.

REFERENCES

1. Alexander, Franz G. Remarks about the Relation of Inferiority Feelings to Guilt Feelings. *Internatl. J. Psychoanalysis.* 1938. 19:41–49.
2. Allport, Gordon W. *The Nature of Prejudice.* New York: Addison-Wesley, 1954.
3. Anthony, William A. Societal Rehabilitation: Changing Society's Attitudes toward the Physically and Mentally Disabled. *Rehab. Psych.* 1972. 19:117–126.
4. Bakan, David. *Disease, Pain and Sacrifice: Toward a Psychology of Suffering.* Chicago, Ill.: Univ. of Chicago Press, 1968.
5. Barker, Roger G. The Social Psychology of Physical Disability. *J. Soc. Issues.* 1948. 4:4:28–38.
6. Barker, Roger G. Concepts of Disabilities. *Personnel & Guidance J.* 1964. 43:4: 371–374.
7. Barker, Roger G.; Wright, Beatrice A.; Meyerson, Lee; and Gonick, Mollie R. *Adjustment to Physical Handicap and Illness: A Survey of the Social Psychology of Physique and Disability* (rev. ed.). New York: Social Science Research Council, 1953.
8. Blank, H. Robert. Psychoanalysis and Blindness. *Psycho-Analytic Quart.* 1957. 26:1–24.
9. Chesler, Mark A. Ethnocentrism and Attitudes toward the Physically Disabled. *Personality & Soc. Psychol.* 1965. 2:6:877–882.
10. Chevigny, Hector, and Braverman, Sydell. *The Adjustment of the Blind.* New Haven, Conn.: Yale University Press, 1950.
11. Clore, Gerald L., and Jeffery, Katharine M. Emotional Role Playing, Attitude Change, and Attraction toward a Disabled Person. *J. Personality & Soc. Psychol.* 1972. 23:1:105–111.
12. Cormack, Peter A. The Relationship between Body Cognition and Attitudes Expressed toward the Visibly Disabled. *Rehab. Counseling Bul.* 1967. 11:2:106–109.
13. Cowen, Emory L.; Bobrove, Philip H.; Rockway, Alan M.; and Stevenson, John. Development and Evaluation of an Attitudes to Deafness Scale. *J. Personality & Soc. Psychol.* 1967. 6:2:183–191.
14. Cowen, Emory L.; Underberg, Rita P.; and Verrillo, Ronald T. The Development and Testing of an Attitudes to Blindness Scale. *J. Soc. Psychol.* 1958. 48: 297–304.

15. Davis, Fred. Deviance Disavowal: The Management of Strained Interaction by the Visibly Handicapped. *Social Problems*. 1961. 9:2:121–132.
16. Dembo, Tamara; Leviton, Gloria L.; and Wright, Beatrice A. Adjustment to Misfortune—A Problem of Social Psychological Rehabilitation. *Artificial Limbs*. 1956. 3:2:4–62.
17. Dembo, Tamara; Leviton, Gloria L; and Wright, Beatrice A. Adjustment to Misfortune—A Problem of Social Psychological Rehabilitation. *Rehab. Psychol.* 1975. 22:1–100.
18. Doob, Anthony N., and Ecker, Barbara P. Stigma and Compliance. *J. Personality & Soc. Psychol.* 1970. 14:4:302–304.
19. Dow, Thomas E. Social Class and Reaction to Physical Disability. *Psychol. Reports*. 1965. 17:1:39–62.
20. Endres, Jo Ellen. Fear of Death and Attitudinal Dispositions toward Physical Disability. *Dissertation Abstracts International*. 1979. 39:7161A *(University microfilm No. 79-11, 825)*.
21. English, R. William. Correlates of Stigma toward Physically Disabled Persons. *Rehab. Research & Practice Rev.* 1971. 2:1–17.
22. English, R. William. Combatting Stigma toward Physically Disabled Persons. *Rehab. Research & Practice Rev.* 1971, 2:19–27.
23. English, R. William, and Oberle, J. B. Toward the Development of New Methodology for Examining Attitudes toward Disabled Persons. *Rehab. Counseling Bul.* 1971. 15:2:88–96.
24. Epstein, Seymour J., and Shontz, Franklin C. Attitudes toward Persons with Physical Disabilities as a Function of Attitudes towards One's Own Body. *Rehab. Counseling Bul.* 1962. 5:4:196–201.
25. Evans, John H. Changing Attitudes toward Disabled Persons: An Experimental Study. *Rehab. Counseling Bul.* 1976. 19:4:572–579.
26. Feinberg, Lawrence B. Social Desirability and Attitudes toward the Disabled. *Personnel & Guidance J.* 1967. 46:4:375–381.
27. Feinberg, Lawrence B. "Social Desirability and Attitudes toward the Disabled." Unpublished manuscript, Syracuse, N.Y., Syracuse University, 1971.
28. Ferenczi, Sandor. Stages in the Development of the Sense of Reality. In: S. Ferenczi (ed.), *Contributions to Psychoanalysis* (rev. ed.). New York: Dover, 1956.
29. Fine, Jeffrey A. "Castration Anxiety and Self Concept of Physically Normal Children as Related to Perceptual Awareness of Attitudes toward Physical Deviance." Unpublished doctoral dissertation, New York, New York University, 1978.
30. Finkelstein, Victor. *Attitudes and Disabled People: Issues for Discussion*. International Exchange of Information in Rehabilitation, Monograph No. 5. New York: World Rehabilitation Fund, 1980.
31. Fisher, Seymour, and Cleveland, Sidney E. *Body Image and Personality* (2nd rev. ed.). New York: Dover, 1968.
32. Freed, Earl X. Opinions of Psychiatric Hospital Personnel and College Students toward Alcoholism, Mental Illness, and Physical Disability: An Exploratory Study. *Psychol. Reports*. 1964. 15:2:615–618.
33. Freidson, Eliot. Disability as Social Deviance. In: M. B. Sussman (ed.), *Sociology and Rehabilitation*. Washington, D.C.: American Sociological Association, 1965.

34. Gellman, William. Roots of Prejudice against the Handicapped. *J. Rehab.* 1959. 40:1:4-6, 25.
35. Goffman, Erving. *Stigma: Notes on Management of Spoiled Identity.* Englewood Cliffs, N.J.: Prentice-Hall, 1963.
36. Gove, Walter R. Societal Reaction Theory and Disability. In: G. L. Albrecht (ed.), *The Sociology of Physical Disability and Rehabilitation.* Pittsburgh, Pa.: University of Pittsburgh Press, 1976.
37. Hafer, Marilyn, and Narcus, Margery. Information and Attitude toward Disability. *Rehab. Counseling Bul.* 1979. 23:2:95-102.
38. Hanks, Jane R., and Hanks, L. M. The Physically Handicapped in Certain Non-Occidental Societies. *J. Soc. Issues.* 1948. 4:11-20.
39. Hebb, Donald O. On the Nature of Fear. *Psychology Rev.* 1946. 53:259-276.
40. Heider, Fritz. Social Perception and Phenomenal Causality. *Psycholog. Rev.* 1944. 51:358-374.
41. Heider, Fritz. *The Psychology of Interpersonal Relations.* New York: Wiley, 1958.
42. Horowitz, Leola S.; Rees, Norma S.; and Horowitz, Milton W. Attitudes toward Deafness as a Function of Increasing Maturity. *J. Soc. Psychol.* 1965. 66: 331-336.
43. Jabin, Norma. Attitudes towards the Physically Disabled as Related to Selected Personality Variables. *Dissertation Abstracts.* 1966. 27:2-B:599.
44. Jordan, John E., and Friesen, Eugene W. Attitudes of Rehabilitation Personnel toward Physically Disabled Persons in Columbia, Peru, and the United States. *J. Soc. Psychol.* 1968. 74:151-161.
45. Kaiser, P., and Moosbruker, Jane. "The Relationship Between Attitudes toward Disabled Persons and GSR." Unpublished manuscript, Albertson, N.Y., Human Resources Center, 1960.
46. Kutner, Bernard. The Social Psychology of Disability. In: W. S. Neff (ed.), *Rehabilitation Psychology.* Washington, D.C.: American Psychological Association, 1971.
47. Leclair, Steven W., and Rockwell, Lauralee K. Counselor Trainee Body Satisfaction and Attitudes toward Counseling the Physically Disabled. *Rehab. Counseling Bul.* 1980. 23:4:258-265.
48. Leviton, Don. "Education for Death or Death Becomes Less a Stranger." Paper presented at the American Psychological Association convention, Honolulu, Hawaii, Sept., 1972.
49. Livneh, Hanoch. Disability and Monstrosity: Futher Comments. *Rehab. Lit.* 1980. 41:11-12:280-283.
50. Lukoff, Irving F., and Whiteman, Martin. "Attitudes toward Blindness." Paper presented at the American Federation of Catholic Workers for the Blind meeting, New York, 1964.
51. Maisel, E. "Meet a Body." Unpublished manuscript, New York, Institute for the Crippled and Disabled, 1953.
52. Marinelli, Robert P., and Kelz, James W. Anxiety and Attitudes toward Visibly Disabled Persons. *Rehab. Counseling Bul.* 1973. 16:4:198-205.
53. McDaniel, James W. *Physical Disability and Human Behavior.* New York: Pergamon Press, 1969.
54. Meng, Heinrich. Zur sozialpsychologie der Körperbeschädigten: Ein beitrag zum

problem der praktischen psychohygiene. *Schweizer Archives für Neurologie und Psychiatrie.* 1938. 40:328–344. (Reported in Barker, R. G., et al., 1953.)

55. Menninger, William C. Emotional Adjustments for the Handicapped. *Crippled Children.* 1949. 27:27.

56. Napoleon, Tony; Chassin, Lauri; and Young, Richard D. A Replication and Extension of "Physical Attractiveness and Mental Illness." *J. Abnormal Psychol.* 1980. 89:2:250–253.

57. Noonan, J. Robert. "Personality Determinants in Attitudes Toward Disability." Unpublished doctoral dissertation, Gainesville, Florida, University of Florida, 1967.

58. Noonan, J. Robert; Barry, John R.; and Davis, Hugh C. Personality Determinants in Attitudes toward Visible Disability. *J. Personality.* 1970. 38:1:1–15.

59. Parkes, C. Murray. Psychosocial Transitions: Comparison between Reactions to Loss of Limbs and Loss of a Spouse. *Brit. J. Psychiatry.* 1975. 127:204–210.

60. Parsons, Talcott. *The Social System.* Glencoe, Ill.: The Free Press, 1951.

61. Parsons, Talcott. Definitions of Health and Illness in the Light of American Values and Social Structure. In: E. G. Jaco (ed.), *Patients, Physicians, and Illness.* Glencoe, Ill.: The Free Press, 1958.

62. Pederson, Linda L., and Carlson, Peter M. Rehabilitation Service Providers: Their Attitudes towards People with Physical Disabilities, and Their Attitudes towards Each Other. *Rehab. Counseling Bul.* 1981. 24:4:275–282.

63. Raskin, Nathaniel J. "The Attitude of Sighted People toward Blindness." Paper presented at the National Psychological Research Council on Blindness, March, 1956.

64. Richardson, Stephen A.; Hastorf, Albert H.; Goodman, Norman; and Dornbusch, Sanford M. Cultural Uniformity in Reaction to Physical Disabilities. *Am. Soc. Rev.* 1961. 26:2:241–247.

65. Rickard, Thomas E.; Triandis, H. C.; and Patterson, C. H. Indices of Employer Prejudice Toward Disabled Applicants. *J. Applied Psych.* 1963. 47:1:52–55.

66. Roessler, Richard, and Bolton, Brian. *Psychosocial Adjustment to Disability.* Baltimore: University Park Press, 1978.

67. Ryan, Kathryn M. Developmental Differences in Reactions to the Physically Disabled. *Human Develop.* 1981. 24:240–256.

68. Safilios-Rothschild, Constantina. Prejudice Against the Disabled and Some Means to Combat it. *Intern. Rehab. Rev.* 1968. 19:4:8–10, 15.

69. Safilios-Rothschild, Constantina. *The Sociology and Social Psychology of Disability and Rehabilitation.* New York: Random House, 1970.

70. Schilder, Paul. *The Image and Appearance of the Human Body.* London: Kegan Paul, Trench, Trubner, 1935.

71. Shontz, Franklin C. "Body-Part Size Judgement." *VRA Project No. 814, Final Report.* Lawrence, Kansas: University of Kansas, 1964. (Reported in McDaniel, J. W., 1969.)

72. Sigerist, Henry E. *Civilization and Disease.* Ithaca, N.Y.: Cornell University Press, 1945.

73. Siller, Jerome. Reactions to Physical Disability by the Disabled and the Non-

Disabled. *Am. Psychologist, Research Bull.* 1964. 7:27–36 (American Foundation for the Blind).

74. Siller, Jerome. Reactions to Physical Disability. *Rehab. Counseling Bul.* 1963. 7:1:12–16.
75. Siller, Jerome. Personality Determinants of Reaction to the Physically Disabled. *Am. Foundation for the Blind Research Bul.* 1964. 7:37–52.
76. Siller, Jerome. Attitudes toward Disability. In: Herbert Rusalem and David Maliken (eds.), *Contemporary Vocational Rehabilitation.* New York: New York University Press, 1976.
77. Siller, Jerome, and Chipman, Abram. Factorial Structure and Correlates of the Attitude towards Disabled Persons Scale. *Educ. and Psychol. Meas.* 1964. 24:4: 831–840.
78. Siller, Jerome, and Chipman, Abram. "Perceptions of Physical Disability by the Non-Disabled." Paper presented at the American Psychological Association meeting, Los Angeles, Sept. 1964. (Reported in Safilios-Rothschild, C., 1970).
79. Siller, Jerome; Chipman, Abram; Ferguson, Linda T.; and Vann, Donald H. *Studies in Reactions to Disability: XI. Attitudes of the Non-Disabled Toward the Physically Disabled.* New York: New York University, School of Education, 1967.
80. Sussman, Marvin B. Dependent Disabled and Dependent Poor: Similarity of Conceptual Issues and Research Needs. *The Social Service Rev.* 1969. 43:4:383–395.
81. Thoreson, Richard W., and Kerr, Barbara A. The Stigmatizing Aspects of Severe Disability: Strategies for Change. *J. Applied Rehab. Counseling.* 1978. 9:2:21–25.
82. Thurer, Shari. Disability and Monstrosity: A Look at Literary Distortions of Handicapping Conditions. *Rehab. Lit.* 1980. 41:1–2:12–15.
83. Tunick, Roy H.; Bowen, Jack; and Gillings, J. L. Religiosity and Authoritarianism as Predictors of Attitude toward the Disabled: A Regression Analysis. *Rehab. Counseling Bul.* 1979. 22:5:408–418.
84. Weinstein, S.; Vetter, R.; and Sersen, E. "Physiological and Experiential Concomitants of the Phantom." *VRA Project No. 427, Final Report.* New York: Albert Einstein College of Medicine, 1964.
85. Whiteman, Martin, and Lukoff, Irving F. Attitudes toward Blindness and Other Physical Handicaps. *J. Soc. Psychol.* 1965. 66:135–145.
86. Wolfensberger, Wolf. *The Principle of Normalization in Human Services.* Toronto, Canada: National Institute on Mental Retardation, 1972.
87. Wolfensberger, Wolf. The Normalization Principle. In: Sheldon A. Grand (ed.), *Severe Disability and Rehabilitation Counseling Training.* Washington, D.C.: National Council on Rehabilitation Education, 1976.
88. Worthington, Mary, E. Personal Space as a Function of the Stigma Effect. *Environment and Behavior.* 1974. 6:3:289–294.
89. Wright, Beatrice A. Developing Constructive Views of Life with a Disability. *Rehab. Lit.* 1980. 41:11–12:274–279.
90. Wright, Beatrice A. *Physical Disability: A Psychological Approach.* New York: Harper & Row, 1960.
91. Yamamato, Kaoru. To Be Different. *Rehab. Counseling Bul.* 1971. 14:3:180–189.

92. Yuker, Harold E. *Yearly Psycho-Social Research Summary.* Albertson, N.Y.: Human Resources Center, 1962.
93. Yuker, Harold E. Attitudes as Determinants of Behavior. *J. Rehab.* 1965. 31:1: 15–16.
94. Yuker, Harold E.; Block, J. R.; and Campbell, W. J. *A Scale to Measure attitudes Toward Disabled Persons: Human Resources Study No. 5.* Albertson, N.Y.: Human Resources Center, 1960.
95. Yuker, Harold E.; Block, J. R.; and Younng, Janet H. *The Measurement of Attitudes toward Disabled Persons.* Albertson, N.Y.: Human Resources Center, 1966.

15

The Coping Framework and Attitude Change: A Guide to Constructive Role-Playing

Beatrice A. Wright

Current efforts at mainstreaming in the schools and at affirmative action in places of employment can benefit from knowledge derived from theory and research on the problem of influencing attitudes. The body of literature on this topic continues to grow and the findings continue to vary. Some studies show positive effects of the change attempts, some negative, and others no change. These variable effects can be better understood if the meaning of positive attitudes is conceptualized in terms of constructive views of life with a disability.

THE COPING VERSUS THE SUCCUMBING FRAMEWORKS

I shall begin by presenting the main components of two basically different frameworks that define contrasting views of the significance of disability (Wright, 1975a). Briefly, the succumbing framework concentrates upon the difficulties and heartbreak of being disabled and not the challenge for meaningful adaptation and change. Emphasis is on what the person can't do; what is denied the person; the problems that weigh the person down. The disability is seen as central, as overriding everything else about the person. The person as an individual, with a highly differentiated and unique personality, is lost.

The coping framework, on the other hand, represents the constructive view of life with a disability. It orients the perceiver to appreciate the individual as having abilities that have intrinsic value. People with disabilities are seen as having an active role in attempting to live their lives constructive-

From *Rehabilitation Psychology*, 25(4) (1978), 177–183. Reprinted by permission.

ly, not as being passively devastated by difficulties. The problem of managing difficulties has a double focus. One focus is upon environmental change, that is, changing those alterable conditions that add to the person's handicap, such as architectural and attitudinal barriers, discriminatory practices, lack of employment opportunities, family problems, and inadequate housing and transportation. The second focus is directed toward change in the person through medical and psychological procedures that reduce disability, through education and training that lead to new skills, and through value restructuring that facilitates acceptance of the physical condition as nondevaluating. As for the suffering associated with disability, the coping framework is oriented toward seeking solutions and discovering satisfactions in living. It recognizes the disability as only one aspect of a multifaceted life that includes gratifications as well as grievances.

RESEARCH ON MODIFYING ATTITUDES

Misguided Role-Playing

Simulating a disability as a way of directly experiencing "what it is like to be disabled" is increasingly being recommended for teachers and students (Glazzard, 1979), for employers and workers, for government officials, and for ordinary citizens. The hope is that such experience will help eliminate prejudice and promote better understanding of handicapping conditions. My concern is that role-playing can enhance, not only understanding of some problems, but also pervasive pity and devaluation. How this occurs is revealed by examining the following research.

In one study (Wilson & Alcorn, 1969), college students simulated blindness, deafness, or an orthopedic disability for eight consecutive hours. Results comparing the experimental groups with a non-role-playing control group showed no significant change on a pre- to postintervention measure of "Attitudes toward Disabled Persons." However, the frustrations and insights described by the subjects in narrative accounts raise a serious question. That the frustrations were many is not surprising, especially since the assignment directed the subjects to give "special note to specific frustrations." Rather, it is the nature of the insights that alerts concern. All but one of the 18 most frequent types of "new insights gained into the feelings of the disabled" revealed *negative* emotional reactions (Tables 2–4, p. 305–6). These were, for example, for blindness: loneliness, fear, helplessness; for deafness: tendency to withdraw, depression, fear of others talking about him or her; for orthopedic disability: dependence on others, irritation at self, embarrassment. The only constructive insight listed was "greater use of other senses" in the case of blindness. A basic question is: Does not the impact of a simulated disability, solely or even predominantly in terms of frustrations and negative feelings, fit precisely within the succumbing framework? Where is there recognition of abilities, of coping strategies, of efforts at environmental change, of satisfactions?

A second study (Wilson, 1971) concentrated on the simulation of deafness (using wax and fiber ear plugs and masking the sound in the room). Subjects simulating deafness engaged in activities with hearing persons during 2½ hours of directed activities. As in the previous experiment, no significant difference between the role-playing and control groups was found on a scale measuring attitudes toward deaf persons. However, on a measure dealing more specifically with the affective component of attitudes, namely semantic differential ratings of persons who are deaf, the role-playing group revealed *less* positive feelings than the controls.

A third study (Clore & Jeffrey, 1972) investigated the effects of wheelchair simulation. A group of students spent about an hour in a wheelchair going from a campus building to the refreshment area where they were to eat at a snack bar. As compared to a control group, the simulators were more favorable to a series of issues concerning disabled students immediately after the experiment. They also were more favorable, four months later, to using unspent student fees for facilities for disabled students than were the control group. However, ratings on semantic differential scales indicated that their predominant feelings while in the wheelchair were "weak, bad, anxious, and empathic." Surely, most people who must use a wheelchair in real life would view these terms not as typical descriptions of themselves, but as capturing their feelings only some of the time, under some circumstances. They would argue that not only negative terms, but also positive terms are needed to describe their lives.

These three studies give cause for concern that simulating a disability in a novel and contrived situation will lead to a projection of the person's dispirited feelings onto the entire life of people who have a disability. A counselor in training wrote, "After this day in a wheelchair, I can better understand the rehabilitation problems of a person who is handicapped in this way because, for a short period of time, I shared their feelings of inferiority, in their lack of confidence and their general feelings of helplessness." Actually, feelings of inferiority, lack of confidence, and helplessness hardly need role-playing, for these are common stereotypes of people with disabilities held by the outsider. Instead of being immersed in these feelings, would it not have been far better if the counselor also had appreciated the person's hope of being able to lead a good life, the person's striving to come to terms with what has to be faced, the person's efforts to improve his or her own circumstances and those of others in similar situations? Such constructive aspects of life with a disability, represented by the coping framework, are not even touched upon in the usual role-playing experience.

That one must become wary of role-playing in awareness training is further seen in the following incident. Paul is a child with cerebral palsy who uses a wheelchair. An assistant teacher, eager to promote independence in her pupils, persisted in her attempt to get him to open the restroom door by himself, despite the fact that the head teacher had pointed out that the tight clearance made it impracticable for Paul to do so. The head teacher then suggested that her assistant try to do it herself while using the wheelchair. In writing about this incident, the head teacher reported: "My assistant was shattered by the restriction the chair created. It was cumbersome, impossible to control. She caught her hand in the door, which was painful. *Unfortunately, she did not see the need to change the door.* Rather, she pushed Paul to the room—something she had never done before. She helped him the rest of the day. I might not have noticed the unnecessary help if I hadn't been aware of the simulation downfall. My assistant and I sat down and discussed this effect. I feel better. She has not pampered Paul again" (Labine, Note 1).

Constructively Guided Role-Playing

Role-playing can be employed with greater assurance when attention is directed toward *improving* the situation. Consider the following studies. One concerned empathy training for medical corpsmen (Anthony & Wain, 1971). The training consisted of repeated role-playing of patient-corpsmen interactions intended to shape the trainees' responses toward increasingly high levels of empathy, plus weekly home assignments in which the trainee wrote responses to patient statements provided by the trainers. A control group received no specific empathy training, although they met for the same period of time to discuss problems in their work and role-played *unguided* patient-corpsmen interactions occasionally. Significant effects of the empathy training were revealed on two outcome measures. Ratings of the corpsmen's written empathic responses to a taperecording of 15 patient expressions before and after the experiment showed significant improvement for the trained group but not for the untrained group. More importantly, the trained group received a significantly higher rating on their actual work one month after the experiment than did the control group, although initially there had been no difference between the groups. What remains unanswered is whether the guided role-playing alone or the home assignment alone would have produced these positive effects.

A second study was explicitly directed toward awareness of environmental conditions that contribute to difficulties experienced by elderly persons with sensory losses (Pastalan, 1974). The subjects were four doctoral students in architecture specializing in environmental problems. Simultaneous sensory losses involving vision, hearing, olfaction, and tactility were simulated by each subject. For example, tactile impairment was created by applying a liquid fixative to the finger tips, visual loss by wearing lenses to simulate light scatter and glare. Each subject, while experiencing the four sensory deficits, spent at least one hour each day in one of three standardized settings: a dwelling unit, a senior center, and a shopping center. An entire experience cycle took three days; this cycle was repeated for a period of six months. The subjects kept a daily log of their experiences and periodically held meetings to compare their observations. The discussions elicited unanimous agreement on a number of sources of environmental difficulties, with implications for reducing them. For example, with respect to visual loss: "If only a single intense artificial light source is used for illumination, rather than several, the chances of inducing uncomfortable glare is increased" (p. 359). For auditory loss: "Some combination of carpeting, acoustical ceiling, and draperies absorb too much sound and make functional hearing still more problematic" (p. 359). The daily log also recorded the trials and sense of loss experienced by the simulators. Thus, they referred to tactile difficulties with fine muscle control in turning pages and gripping objects. But the point is that the experience of loss was oriented toward how to adapt and how to modify the environment. In fact, the simulation was purposefully extended over a period of half a year to allow the person to overcome the "shock-value associated with 'instant' sensory deprivation" so that, "after ceasing to be preoccupied with the deficits" the person could begin "to perceive the environment" (p. 359). This is the kind of role-playing that is consistent with the coping framework. The difficulties and loss are experienced. But so are *the possibilities for personal adaptation and environmental change.*

Assertive role-playing is another form of role-playing that can be recommended (Williams, Note 2). In this case, two people from the group simulate antagonistic roles, one that of a person with a particular disability, and the other of a person who denies him or her access to a needed opportunity. The following example of a person with multiple sclerosis and a personnel manager illustrates this method of confrontation:

The person who is to assume multiple sclerosis is given the following profile: "You have a high school diploma and a certificate from an area vocational-technical school in clerical and business machine skills. You are trying to return to the work force, but have recently been diagnosed as having multiple sclerosis."

The person assuming the role of personnel manager is given a series of statements that pose objections to hiring a person with multiple sclerosis. Thus, he or she begins by saying: "I'm impressed with your credentials, but our insurer insists that it screen all applications, and you are not acceptable as an employee because you are a bad health insurance risk."

The person simulating multiple sclerosis is then asked to respond. Others in the group are encouraged to chime in until an understanding of how best to deal with this problem is reached.

The personnel manager then escalates the confrontation further by stating: "I notice that you need rest periods every few hours, but we only give a 10-minute break in midmorning and midafternoon, so I'm afraid you just won't work out." Again the person simulating multiple sclerosis is asked to respond, and others in the group join the effort to demolish the validity of this argument.

Depending on the available time, a number of prepared typical encounters with attitudinal barriers can be role-played, using different simulated disabilities. The confrontation is designed to force members of the group to assert themselves in meeting the challenge of overcoming barriers to equal opportunity.

Role-reversal is still another form of role-playing that can be especially useful when the object is to discover how an interpersonal helping relationship can better meet the needs of a person with a particular problem. Two studies will be described, one involving a feeding situation, the other a walk (Wright, 1975b). The members of the group are first paired off. In the feeding situation, one member of the pair feeds the other, who is simulating arm paralysis. The partners are instructed to consider how the feeding situation could be made more pleasant for both of them. After the meal is consumed, the roles are reversed, the feeder now becoming the one fed. The entire group then discusses the problems encountered in each role and offers suggestions for amelioration. For the person fed, mention is made of various irritations, embarrassment, and unwanted dependency. For the feeder, boredom and aversion to unsightly mastication emerge as problems. Suggestions for improvement pour forth. They concern size of portion, tempo of feeding, attention of the feeder, optimal distance between the two parties, the responsibility of the person being fed to inform the feeder of his or her wishes, the importance of conversation of mutual interest, etc.

The second study involves pairs of subjects who take turns simulating being a blind person and a sighted guide while taking a walk. Recommendations to future guides, based on experience when in the role of the blind person, come readily: e.g., letting the blind person know whether stairs are ascending or descending, informing the blind person of the name of the individual with whom they stop to talk, being more sensitive to pacing, etc.

Notice that the method of role-reversal differs from ordinary simulation procedures insofar as the person experiences the position of the insider (the person with the particular problem) and the outsider consecutively, a juxtaposition that makes more real the awareness that direct knowledge of both can be useful in improving the helping relationship. It should also be noted that this form of instructed role-playing, by focusing on ameliorating problems, makes it less likely that the person will be impressed only with the succumbing aspects of disablement. At the very least, emphasis on the active participation and responsibility of both parties in improving the situation can be expected to contribute to constructive views of life with a disability.

BASIC CONCERNS AND RECOMMENDATIONS

Role-playing tends to give rise to a number of forces that make the emergence of the coping framework difficult. To begin with, simulating disability represents a new situation, one in which the disability necessarily looms as the main feature. The immediate contrast with the temporarily abandoned able-bodied state tends to bring out the negatives without the balance of sustaining forces that come with having to live with a disability. Moreover, new situations are generally conducive to heightened emotionality, and the role player may indulge in the frustrations of the temporary situation, feeling reassured by the prospect of relief. What is of special concern is that the process of reevaluation, or reordering priorities and values, so necessary in living on satisfactory terms with a disability, takes more time than is accorded in simulation situations.

In a word, the main danger of role-playing is that the essence of life of people with a disability will be perceived in negative terms. Although some aspects of life are assuredly disturbing, others are neutral, and still others are gratifying, but role-playing does not easily lend itself to appreciating the latter two. That is why members of self-help groups understand rehabilitation problems far better than did the earlier mentioned counselor in training. Many if not most of these members have worked through the succumbing framework and have gradually replaced it with the coping framework, in which striving and ability combine to meet the challenge of personal and environmentally imposed limitations. They do not remain stuck within the mire of inferiority and helplessness, role-playing projections notwithstanding.

That people who are directly affected by a difficult situation in real life are inclined to perceive more positives in their situation than do those who are more detached has research support (Hamera, 1977; Hamera & Shontz, 1978). In this study, three groups of subjects, varying in closeness to life-threatening illness, responded to a questionnaire about possible effects of disability and illness. The closest group, adult patients with cancer, endorsed more positive aspects than the next closest group, parents of children with cancer, who in turn endorsed more positive aspects than nonmedical hospital employees, the most removed group. Endorsement of negative items followed a reverse order.

Whether the forces in role-playing that underexpose the person to the constructive, positive, and coping side of living with a disability can be offset by special instructions has to be explored further. We have proposed that guiding the simulation in terms of the coping framework (where the role-player is oriented toward problem solving and toward social and personal events that are gratifying, and not only those that are disconcerting) may help turn role-playing into a constructive experience. Discussing the limitations of role-playing with the participants in advance of the experience also may help to counteract the spread of perceived negative effects of disability. Finally, discussion following the role-playing enactment would appear to be useful in providing a forum for strengthening those aspects of the experience that lead to constructive views of life with a disability.

REFERENCE NOTES

1. Labine, J. Graduate student who had been exposed to the pitfalls of role-playing, University of Kansas, 1979.
2. Williams, R. Demonstration of assertive role-playing for workshop on disabilities, sponsored by Personnel Services, University of Kansas, 1979.

REFERENCES

Anthony, W. A. & Wain, H. J. An investigation of the outcome of empathy training for medical corpsmen. *Psychological Aspects of Disability*, 1971, *18*, 86–88.

Clore, G. L. & Jeffrey, K. Emotional role playing, attitude change, and attraction toward a disabled person. *Journal of Personality and Social Psychology*, 1972, 23, 105–111.

Glazzard, P. Simulation of handicaps as a teaching strategy for preservice and in-service training. *Teaching Exceptional Children*, Spring, 1979, 101–104.

Hamera, E. K. *Positive and negative effects of life threatening illness*. Doctoral dissertation, University of Kansas, 1977.

Hamera, E. K. & Shontz, F. C. Perceived positive and negative effects of life-threatening illness. *Journal of Psychosomatic Research*, 1978, 22, 419–424.

Pastalan, L. A. The simulation of age-related sensory losses: A new approach to the study of environmental barriers. *New Outlook for the Blind*, 1974, 68, 356–362.

Wilson, E. D. A comparison of the effects of disability simulation and observation upon attitudes, anxiety, and behavior manifested toward the deaf. *The Journal of Special Education*, 1971, 5, 343–349.

Wilson, E. D. & Alcorn, D. Disability simulation and development of attitudes toward the exceptional. *The Journal of Special Education*, 1969, 3, 303–307.

Wright, B. A. Social-psychological leads to enhance rehabilitation effectiveness. *Rehabilitation Counseling Bulletin*, 1975a, 18, 214–223.

Wright, B. A. Sensitizing outsiders to the position of the insider. *Rehabilitation Psychology*, 1975b, 22, No. 2, 129–135.

16

Societal Rehabilitation: Changing Society's Attitudes toward the Physically and Mentally Disabled

William A. Anthony

Physically and/or mentally disabled individuals, who bear such labels as the mentally ill, physically handicapped, or mentally retarded, often are the targets of prejudice and discriminatory practices. Researchers have shown that this discrimination is least apparent in relatively impersonal situations and most blatant in contemplating either close interpersonal or business situations, such as marriage and employment (McDaniel, 1969; Rusk and Taylor, 1946; Whatley, 1959). It would appear that society is least tolerant of the disabled individual in areas of functioning which in our culture are of critical importance to mental health.

   With the growing interest in preventive or community psychiatry, mental health professionals have increased their concern about the impact of the community's negative attitudes on the mental health of the mentally and physically disabled (Bindman and Spiegel, 1969; Caplan, 1964; Caplan, 1970; Iscoe and Spielberger, 1970; Lamb, Heath, and Downing, 1969). Various researchers have theorized that society's attitudes and expectations for the disabled may be of critical importance in maintaining the mental health of the physically handicapped and in restoring quickly the mental health of the mentally ill (Anthony, 1970; Centers and Centers, 1963; Roehrer, 1961; Scheff, 1963; Spitzer and Denzin, 1968; Yamamato, 1971). If society's attitudes are indeed so crucial to the functioning of the physically and mentally disabled, it would seem incumbent upon mental health professionals to attempt to influence these attitudes in a positive direction.

   In this survey *societal rehabilitation* refers to efforts which attempt to reduce the general public's prejudicial attitudes toward the disabled indi-

Reprinted from *Rehabilitation Psychology, 19* (3) (1972), 117–126. Copyright © 1972 by the American Psychological Association. Reprinted by permission of the publisher and author.

vidual. *Societal rehabilitation* is to be distinguished from *individual rehabilitation*. The latter is designed to restore or reintegrate the disabled individual into society (Jacques, 1970).

Although efforts at societal rehabilitation have been varied, it seems both possible and legitimate to group these attempts into three broad categories on the basis of the procedures emphasized: (a) contact with the disabled individual, (b) information about the disabled individual, and (c) a combination of both contact and information.

CONTACT

One procedure designed to induce attitude change is to arrange contacts between the general public and members of a disabled group. Studies investigating the contact dimension do so in two different ways. One method is to divide the subjects into groups simply on the basis of their self-reports about the amount of contact which they have had with a member of a disabled group, and to determine if differences exist in the attitudes of subjects differing in amount of self-reported contact. The second method exposes the subjects to a specific contact experience and assesses the effects of this observable contact experience on the subjects' attitudes.

Results of studies of the first type are fairly divergent. If one struggles to find a consensus, it appears that individuals who report contact tend to have slightly more favorable attitudes than those who report no contact. Evidence of the facilitative effects of contact has been provided by Semmel and Dickson (1966), who found that as the amount of contact reported by college students increased, attitudes toward handicapped people became more positive. Another study also provided evidence of a moderate tendency toward more favorable attitudes by individuals who said they had had contact with the physically disabled (Gaier, Linkowski, and Jacques, 1968). A further example of the mild effects of contact was provided by Jaffe (1967). He found that high school students who reported some contact with the mentally retarded showed a more positive attitude on one of three attitudinal measures.

Slightly negative effects of contact also have been reported (Cowen, Underberg, and Verrillo, 1958). These researchers found that individuals who had had contact with the blind tended to have more negative attitudes than individuals reporting no contact.

A recent monograph summarized the results of over 20 studies of the relationship between reported contact with the physically disabled and attitudes toward physically disabled persons. Similar to the results presented previously, the studies exhibited a wide range of findings, but a slight majority of studies reported a significant relationship between amount of contact and favorableness of attitude (Yuker, Block, and Younng, 1966).

These retrospective contact studies are methodologically deficient in several important ways that may account for their conflicting results. First, it is the individual subject who defines what is meant by *contact*: The type of contact experience no doubt varies from subject to subject. Also, the contact experience for many subjects may have contained informational components as well, and the independent effects of contact and information may not be isolated.

These deficiencies are overcome in the more experimental type of contact study, and as a result the divergent findings disappear. Studies of the effects of specific contact experiences with a wide variety of disabled groups consistently have found no consistent changes in the subjects' attitudes as a result of their contacts with disabled persons.

Physically Disabled

Anthony and Cannon (1969) found no effect on physically normal children's attitudes toward physical disability as a result of attendance at a 2-week summer camp with physically handicapped children. The findings indicated a nonsignificant tendency for children who had negative attitudes to become even more negative. Similarly, Centers and Centers (1963) found that children who attended class with amputee children had significantly more rejecting attitudes toward the amputee children than toward a matched group of nonhandicapped children. In a study of adult attitudes, Granofsky (1966) was unable to improve the attitudes of volunteer hospital workers toward the physically disabled by arranging eight hours of social contact between the volunteers and a group of physically disabled men.

Mentally Retarded

Studies which attempted to change attitudes toward the mentally retarded through contact experiences have met with equally discouraging results. These studies typically involve assessing the attitudes of school children toward mentally retarded classmates who have been integrated into the non-mentally-retarded children's class or school. The findings are unanimous in indicating that contact is not sufficient to produce positive attitudes toward mentally retarded children (Lapp, 1957; Rucker, Howe, and Snider, 1969; Strauch, 1970).

Mentally Ill

The unique effects of a contact-only experience with mental patients recently has been investigated (Spiegel, Keith-Spiegel, Zirgulis, and Wine, 1971). College students visited mental patients for 1–3 hours per week for a semester but received no supervision or information. At posttesting the students saw the typical mental patient as significantly more depressed and irritable, less neat, and less interested in socialization. Their scores on the Opinions about Mental Illness scale (OMI) changed on only two of the five scales — the students became significantly less authoritarian but also less benevolent toward the mentally ill.

Of peripheral interest is one other study which examined the specific effects of contact with the mentally ill (King, Walder, and Pavey, 1970). Rather than assessing attitude change, this investigation assessed pre-post personality changes in college students who volunteered for a semester-long companion program in a mental hospital. While some personality change did occur, it was more circumscribed than the changes brought about by a similar contact-plus-information experience to which it was compared.

In summary, while a dearth of experimental studies on the effects of contact exists, those that have been done are in general agreement — contact in and of itself does not significantly change attitudes toward persons with a disability. The unique effects of contact on changing attitudes toward the physically handicapped, mentally retarded, or mentally ill have yet to be demonstrated.

INFORMATION

Attempts also have been made to change attitudes by providing the nondisabled person with information about disabled people. This information may take the form of a book, a course lecture or discussion, or a film or institutional tour. General agreement seems to exist in the literature that regardless of the way in which the information is presented, the power of information alone to produce positive attitude change is negligible.

Several studies investigated the attitude change of college students enrolled in an abnormal psychology course (Altrocchi and Eisdorfer, 1961; Costin and Kerr, 1962). The first study compared students in classes of abnormal psychology, personality development, and industrial management. As would be expected, abnormal psychology students increased their information about mental illness; however, their attitudes toward mental illness as measured by a semantic differential did not change.

Costin and Kerr (1962) compared students in an abnormal psychology class with a comparable group of controls. They reported some changes for the abnormal psychology students on the OMI, but these changes appeared to reflect informational increases rather than attitudinal changes. For example, the students increased their belief that mental illness is caused by interpersonal experience (Interpersonal Etiology scale), but they did not change their opinion about how different the mentally ill are from normals (Mental Hygiene Ideology). Furthermore, their scores on a scale of benevolence toward mental patients decreased.

Semmel and Dickson (1966) compared seniors in elementary education who had taken a course in special education with those who had not. No significant difference was found in attitudes measured by the Connotative Reaction Inventory, a scale designed to assess how comfortable a person says he would be in 10 social situations with a physically disabled person. Two studies on the combined effects of contact plus information have used as a control group an information-only sample—typically psychology majors or introductory psychology students (Chinsky and Rappaport, 1970; Smith, 1969). Neither study reported significant, positive changes in attitudes as a result of didactic course-work in psychology.

Another way to present information about disabled people is by means of a film or institutional tour. Staffieri and Klappersack (1960) examined the effect of viewing a favorable film on cerebral palsy on college students' attitudes. The authors found no change in attitudes as measured by a social distance scale. An attempt to modify high school and college students' attitudes toward the mentally retarded by providing them with a tour of a state school for the mentally retarded did result in attitude changes, "but not necessarily of a positive nature" (Cleland and Chambers, 1959). While the students became more open in praise of the institution and employees, they tended to see the mentally retarded children as "better off in the institution."

Sarbin and Mancuso (1970) recently reviewed various educational programs designed by mental health professionals which attempted to influence the general public to consider mental illness with the same nonrejecting attitudes as somatic illness. Similar to the results of the informational studies reviewed in this survey, they concluded that mental health education campaigns have been notably unsuccessful in their objective.

In conclusion, it would appear that providing individuals with information about disabled people has demonstrated only the obvious effect—it increases a person's knowledge about disabled people. However, merely having more and more information about persons with a disability does not enable the nondisabled persons to evaluate the disabled persons more positively. An as yet untested possibility remains that the information presented by the professionals is faulty and that some other kind of information would be effective in facilitating attitude change.

CONTACT PLUS INFORMATION

Many researchers have attempted to change attitudes toward disabled individuals by combining the contact experience with some type of information about the disability. The findings of these studies appear to be remarkably consistent: Regardless of the type of disability studied, and seemingly independent of the type of contact and information experience provided, all studies reported that a contact-plus-information experience had a favorable impact on the nondisabled person's attitudes.

Physically Disabled

Anthony (1969) studied the attitudes of counselors employed at a summer camp for handicapped children. The camping experience provided the counselors with information conveyed by the professionals on the camp staff as well as continuous contact. The findings indicated that at the beginning of the camping experience new counselors had significantly less positive attitudes than counselors who had worked at the camp previously, and that by the end of the summer the new counselors had significantly improved attitudes toward physically disabled persons.

In a cross-sectional study of the effects of rehabilitation counselor training, Anthony and Carkhuff (1970) found that advanced students, who generally had more contact and information about physical disability, had more positive attitudes toward physically disabled individuals than beginning students, whose attitudes did not differ from graduate students in a nonhelping profession.

Rusalem (1967) attempted to change the attitudes of a group of high school girls toward the deaf-blind. A unique aspect of this study was that the students were preselected from a larger group to form two groups: one with the most positive attitudes and one with the least positive. In addition, the students did not volunteer but were required to participate in the research. The contact and information experience consisted of six 1-hour group sessions that involved information about deaf-blindness, instruction in the manual alphabet, and the opportunity to communicate with deaf-blind individuals. Measures of attitude change were self-reports, a sentence completion test, and behavior.

Results showed that students with the most positive attitudes did not change on the self-report or the sentence completion test, probably due to a ceiling effect, but that the group with the poorest attitudes improved on both the attitude and behavioral measures. Measures of behavioral change included self-initiated volunteer work and reading about deaf-blindness.

Mentally Ill

The studies concerned with changing attitudes toward mental illness have used only two groups of subjects — student nurses in psychiatric training and college students concurrently working part-time in a mental hospital and enrolled in courses which provided them with an opportunity to discuss their work. The college students were participants in programs which ranged from 30 hours (Chinsky and Rappaport, 1970) to 2 years (Smith, 1969) and varied in intensity from 40 hours per week (Kulik, Martin, and Scheibe, 1969; Schiebe, 1965) to several hours per week (Holzberg and Gewirtz, 1963; Keith-Spiegel and Spiegel, 1970). Using a variety of measures such as the Adjective Check List, the OMI, and the Custodial Mental Illness Ideology Scale, all of the above studies reported favorable effects on attitudes toward the mentally ill.

Of related interest, some researchers also investigated the effects of contact-plus-information experiences on volunteers' descriptions of themselves. The results have been inconsistent. Both positive effects (Scheibe, 1965; Holzberg, Gewirtz, and Ebner, 1964) and no effects (Chinsky and Rappaport, 1970) as a result of the contact-plus-information experience have been reported.

The effects of psychiatric-nurse training on the attitudes of student nurses have been investigated repeatedly (Altrocchi and Eisdorfer, 1961; Hicks and Spaner, 1962; Lewis and Cleveland, 1966; Smith, 1969). Within a time span of 8–16 months, the psychiatric nursing experience provides the student nurses with extensive opportunities for contact as well as exposure to the professional literature in psychopathology. The research has shown consistently that this type of experience has positive effects on attitudes toward mental illness.

Mentally Retarded

A study of attitudes toward mental retardation, while not a pre-post test design, compared a group of student teachers and teachers of the mentally retarded with teachers and students in general education and professionals in other fields. The findings indicated that student teachers and teachers of the mentally retarded had the most positive attitudes (Efron and Efron, 1967). If one can assume that training to teach the mentally retarded involves both contact and information, this result is consistent with the previously reported positive effects of a contact-plus-information experience.

CONCLUSIONS AND IMPLICATIONS

1. The attitudes of nondisabled persons toward persons with a disability can be influenced positively by providing the nondisabled individual with an experience which includes contact with disabled persons and information about the disability. Neither alone is sufficient, significantly and consistently, to have a favorable impact on attitudes toward disabled persons. It appears that without information contact has only a limited positive effect or may even reinforce existing negative attitudes. Similarly, information without contact increases knowledge about the disability only but appears to have little or no effect on attitudes.

The consistency of the research is all the more remarkable when one considers that the present survey examined attitudes toward three different disability groups assessed with a variety of attitudinal measures. In addition, the type of contact-plus-information experience varied from study to study. While it is conceivable that a researcher could deliberately arrange a destructive contact-and-information experience and obtain negative results, it is impressive that of the variety of contact-plus-information experiences which researchers have so far investigated, all have yielded positive results.

2. The research conclusions on the contact-plus-information experiences must be limited, because almost all the studies have been done on either college students who volunteered to undergo a contact experience or trainees in the helping professions. A dearth of research exists on other age groups, nonhelping professionals, and nonvolunteers.

3. Little is known about how much time is needed to change attitudes. The programs presented in this survey varied in length from 6 hours to 2 years. Smith (1969) suggested that attitude change occurs early in a semester-long contact-plus-information experience. The fact that Rusalem (1967) was able to bring about both attitude and behavioral change toward the deaf-blind in only 6 hours suggests that an extremely short but intensive contact-plus-information experience is capable of producing favorable attitude change.

4. Professionals involved in community mental health and rehabilitation possess sufficient knowledge to begin to design broad societal rehabilitation programs based on a contact-plus-information experience. Mental health professionals who work in the schools could devise a societal rehabilitation program consisting of a required course at the high school level, similar to the kind of program conducted by Rusalem (1967). Such courses should include contact with physically disabled and formerly mentally disabled individuals, as well as reading and discussions which facilitate student understanding of their reluctance to interact with disabled persons. College instructors of abnormal psychology courses also might include a contact-plus-information experience as part of their course requirements.

Other professionals could run programs designed to change the attitudes of employers. Perhaps such a course could be required in-service training for personnel directors of government agencies. The attitudes of private employers might be changed by training disabled persons to conduct job development interviews, thus insuring a contact-plus-information experience for each employer interviewed.

All of these societal rehabilitation programs should be based on the principles of program development which emphasize the development of simple steps to achieve a complex goal such as attitude change (Carkhuff, Friel, and Berenson, 1972). In addition, such programs must evaluate their efforts not just in terms of attitude change but ultimately in terms of behavioral criteria. For example, if the attitude change program was directed at employers, the real measure of success might be the number of disabled persons subsequently hired. Or, if the target population was high school and college students, behavioral measures might include variables such as the number of individuals who subsequently volunteered to work in agencies serving disabled persons, or the amount of information about disabilities obtained on the students' own initiative, or the frequency of contact with disabled persons.

REFERENCES

Altrocchi, J. and Eisdorfer, C. Changes in attitudes toward mental illness. *Mental Hygiene*, 1961, 45, 563–570.

Anthony, W. A. The effect of contact on an individual's attitude toward disabled persons. *Rehabilitation Counseling Bulletin*, 1969, 12, 168–171.

Anthony, W. A. The physically disabled client and facilitative confrontation. *Journal of Rehabilitation*, 1970, 36(3), 22–23.

Anthony, W. A. and Cannon, J. A. A pilot study on the effects of involuntary integration on children's attitudes. *Rehabilitation Counseling Bulletin*, 1969, 12, 239–240.

Anthony, W. A. and Carkhuff, R. R. The effects of rehabilitation counselor training upon trainee functioning. *Rehabilitation Counseling Bulletin*, 1970, 13, 333–342.

Bindman, A. J. and Spiegel, A. D. (Eds.) *Perspectives in commmunity mental health.* Chicago: Aldine, 1969.

Caplan, G. *Principles of preventive psychiatry.* New York: Basic Books, 1964.

Caplan, G. *The theory and practice of mental health consultation.* New York: Basic Books, 1970.

Carkhuff, R. R., Friel, T., and Berenson, B. G. *The art of program development.* Amherst, Mass.: Human Resource Development Press, 1973.

Centers, L. and Centers, R. Peer group attitudes toward the amputee child. *Journal of Social Psychology*, 1963, 61, 127–132.

Chinsky, J. M. and Rappaport, J. Attitude change in college students and chronic patients: A dual perspective. *Journal of Consulting and Clinical Psychology*, 1970, 35, 388–394.

Cleland, C. C. and Chambers, W. R. Experimental modification of attitudes as a function of an institutional tour. *American Journal of Mental Deficiency*, 1959, 64, 124–130.

Costin, F. and Kerr, W. D. The effects of an abnormal psychology course on students' attitudes toward mental illness. *Journal of Educational Psychology*, 1962, 53, 214–218.

Cowen, E. L., Underberg, R. P., and Verrillo, R. T. The development and testing of an attitude to blindness scale. *Journal of Social Psychology*, 1958, 48, 297–304.

Efron, R. E. and Efron, H. Y. Measurements of attitudes toward the retarded and an application with educators. *American Journal of Mental Deficiency*, 1967, 72, 100–107.

Gaier, E. L., Linkowski, D. G., and Jacques, M. E. Contact as a variable in the perception of disability. *Journal of Social Psychology*, 1968, 74, 117–126.

Granofsky, J. *Modification of attitudes toward the visibly disabled.* Unpublished doctoral dissertation, Yeshiva University, 1966.

Hicks, J. M. and Spaner, F. E. Attitude change and mental hospital experience. *Journal of Abnormal and Social Psychology,* 1962, 65, 112–120.

Holzberg, J. D. and Gewirtz, H. A method of altering attitudes toward mental illness. *Psychiatric Quarterly Supplement,* 1963, 37, 56–61.

Holzberg, J. D. Gewirtz, H., and Ebner, E. Changes in moral judgment and self-acceptance as a function of companionship with hospitalized mental patients. *Journal of Consulting Psychology,* 1964, 28, 299–303.

Iscoe, I. and Spielberger, C. D. (Eds.) *Community psychology: Perspectives in training and research.* New York: Appleton-Century-Crofts, 1970.

Jacques, M. E. *Rehabilitation counseling: Scope and services.* Boston: Houghton Mifflin, 1970.

Jaffe, J. Attitudes and interpersonal contact: Relationships between contact with the mentally retarded and dimensions of attitude. *Journal of Counseling Psychology,* 1967, 14, 482–484.

Keith-Spiegel, P. and Spiegel, D. Effects of mental hospital experience on attitudes of teenage students toward mental illness. *Journal of Clinical Psychology,* 1970, 26, 387–388.

King, M., Walder, L. O., and Pavey, S. Personality change as a function of volunteer experience in a psychiatric hospital. *Journal of Consulting and Clinical Psychology,* 1970, 35, 423–425.

Kulik, J. A., Martin, R. A., and Scheibe, K. E. Effects of mental hospital volunteer work on students' conceptions of mental illness. *Journal of Clinical Psychology,* 1969, 25, 326–329.

Lamb, H. R., Heath, D., and Downing, J. J. (Eds.) *Handbook of community mental health practice.* San Francisco: Jossey-Bass, 1969.

Lapp, E. A. A study of the social adjustment of slow learning children who were assigned part-time regular classes. *American Journal of Mental Deficiency,* 1957, 62, 254–262.

Lewis, D. L. and Cleveland, S. E. Nursing students' attitudinal changes following a psychiatric affiliation. *Journal of Psychiatric Nursing,* 1966, 4, 223–231.

McDaniel, J. W. *Physical disability and human behavior.* New York: Pergamon Press, 1969.

Roehrer, G. A. The significance of public attitudes in the rehabilitation of the disabled. *Rehabilitation Literature,* 1961, 22, 66–72.

Rucker, C. N., Howe, C. E., and Snider, B. The participation of retarded children in junior high academic and non-academic regular classes. *Exceptional Children,* 1969, 35, 617–623.

Rusalem, H. Engineering changes in public attitudes toward a severely disabled group. *Journal of Rehabilitation,* 1967, 33(3) 26–27.

Rusk, H. A. and Taylor, E. J. *New hope for the handicapped.* New York: Harper, 1946.

Sarbin, T. R. and Mancuso, J. C. Failure of a moral enterprise: Attitudes of the public toward mental illness. *Journal of Consulting and Clinical Psychology,* 1970, 35, 159–173.

Scheff, T. J. The role of the mentally ill and the dynamics of mental disorder: A research framework. *Sociometry,* 1963, 26, 436–453.

Scheibe, K. E. College students spend eight weeks in mental hospital: A case report. *Psychotherapy: Theory, Research, and Practice*, 1965, 2, 117-120.

Semmel, M. I. and Dickson, S. Connotative reactions of college students to disability labels. *Exceptional Children*, 1966, 32, 443-450.

Smith, J. J. Psychiatric hospital experience and attitudes toward "mental illness." *Journal of Consulting and Clinical Psychology*, 1969, 33, 302-306.

Spiegel, D., Keith-Spiegel, P., Zirgulis, J., and Wine, D. B. Effects of student visits on social behavior of regressed schizophrenic patients. *Journal of Clinical Psychology*, 1971, 27, 396-400.

Spitzer, S. P. and Denzin, N. K. *The mental patient: Studies in the sociology of deviance*. New York: McGraw-Hill, 1968.

Staffieri, R. and Klappersack, B. An attempt to change attitudes toward the cerebral palsied. *Rehabilitation Counseling Bulletin*, 1960, 3, 5-6.

Strauch, J. D. Social contact as a variable in the expressed attitudes of normal adolescents toward EMR. *Exceptional Children*, 1970, 36, 495-500.

Whatley, C. D. Social attitudes toward discharged mental patients. *Social Problems*, 1959, 6, 313-320.

Yamamato, K. To be different. *Rehabilitation Counseling Bulletin*, 1971, 14, 180-189.

Yuker, H. E., Block, J. R., and Younng, J. H. *The measurement of attitudes toward disabled persons: Human Resources Study No. 7*. Albertson, N.Y.: Human Resources, 1966.

Part VI

Sexuality and Disability

The sexual realities of persons with disabilities have traditionally been given little recognition by professionals, although currently this is a major area of concern. It has been suggested that sexual functioning is a subject area that is frequently avoided by professionals working with clients. Part of this neglect undoubtedly stems from taboos against the discussion of sex; another reason for avoidance is the lack of education and information about sex as it relates to people with physical disabilities. The articles in Part VI have been selected to assist in overcoming both attitudinal and informational problems.

In his general discussion of sexuality and disability, Diamond presents the views of the client, the professional, the agency, the family, and the person on whom the client's sexual attention is focused. Following a discussion of these perspectives, Diamond examines specific problems and issues related to sexual functioning and provides guidelines for improving the sexual relationship.

The psychosocial aspects of sexuality in disabled and nondisabled people and the role and reactions of the rehabilitation team in assisting to overcome problems related to sexual functioning of patients with cardiovascular disorders, spinal cord injury, and amputation are presented in Chapter 18 by Griffith and his associates. The importance of understanding a patient's premorbid lifestyle as it related to sexual functioning is emphasized.

A step-by-step approach designed to facilitate the sexual adjustment process of severely disabled persons is the focus of the chapter by Shrey, Kiefer, and Anthony. Disabled persons with sexual adjustment difficulties often share a common barrier—they lack the knowledge and skills to overcome deficits in sexual functioning. Rehabilitation professionals interested in facilitating their clients' improved sexual functioning should benefit from the information provided in this chapter.

17

Sexuality and the Handicapped

Milton Diamond

Professional recognition of the sexual problems and concerns of the handicapped has been developing and expanding for the last several years. To date, however, little has been formalized in print, and what has been done is primarily directed toward making the professional aware of the area as one of legitimate concern. For this presentation, I would like to formalize some specific matters to be considered, offer specific recommendations for handling problems, and develop a directness in dealing with some of the more controversial issues involved. This is now appropriate, since during the past several years many excellent people have contributed their knowledge and efforts to make the sexual problems of the handicapped a respectable issue of concern and have awakened many to the disrespect that must be attached to ignorance and nonconcern with the subject (e.g., Comarr; Gochros and Schultz; Kempton). These positive efforts have further engendered a desire for professionals to have working models and ideas to follow the general attitudinal changes stressed previously.

My presentation will be divided into several portions. First, I will indicate how the perspectives of various individuals or groups color the way this subject is treated. Then I will deal with some specific problems and issues in sexual expression and follow this with recommendations for handling problems that fall into associated areas. My concluding comments will contain several general rules for improving sexual functioning that are pertinent for all, able-bodied and handicapped, but more so for the handicapped.

First, I would like to make clear just how many levels I think are involved with sexuality and how these must be distinguished. It must be understood that when one considers sexuality, one must not think only of genitals or bedroom activity, although that it usually what first comes to mind. At least two broad areas must be considered: public and private sexuality.

From *Rehabilitation Literature*, 35 (1974), 34–40. Copyright © 1974 by the National Easter Seal Society for Crippled Children and Adults. Reprinted by permission of the Editor.

Public. How does the person act in public; what role is played by these actions? Will a handicap interfere with the individual's personal or public appraisal of his or her masculinity or femininity? For example, can a telephone lineman with a paralyzed leg accept, without loss of masculinity, the job of a telephone operator? Can the arthritic housewife accept the loss of her hands and deft touch without considering it a reflection of her femininity?

Sexual patterns and roles are our public demonstration of socially recognized sexual expressions. Public concerns may manifest themselves in the choice of how the individuals interact with society.

Private. Here we refer to the genital sexual responses and those inner problems not usually discernible. This includes the ability to maintain an erection, have orgasm, receive and give genital and sensual pleasures, and reduce sexual tensions in oneself or partner.

Naturally, these public and private concerns might be combined.

Next, I would like to make clear that we must not confuse genital satisfaction, love, reproduction, and marriage. These four areas are quite distinct, although they may go together or be related. We must clearly keep them separate in our own minds and in the minds of our clients, certainly to insure just what is being communicated. The four areas of genital satisfaction, love, reproduction, and marriage offer different rewards and present different problems. For example, a client wanting genital satisfaction doesn't necessarily want marriage, and one wanting marriage doesn't necessarily want children or sex. If this seems like too radical a concept, just recall that it is only a few generations back when our ancestors had marriages that were arranged so sex and marriage were started without love; most present-day marriages are not entered into by virgins; and birth control and family planning are facts of life. In a very practical vein, we must insure that children are to be considered on their own merits not as visual proof of masculine or feminine abilities; reproduction is not sexual identity and neither is genital gratification. A handicapped person might be more disadvantaged than an able-bodied person in having a child who is not wanted for himself but rather as an affirmation of masculinity or femininity.

It is appropriate here to distinguish between the different stages during which persons may become handicapped. These may be considered: prepubertal, adolescent, marriageable, married, separated, divorced, widowed, and senescent. A teenager is obviously involved with different concerns than is a senior citizen, and obviously the attendant concerns of one with memories of the past and lost demonstrated abilities would differ from those of one who never had experiences to draw from. While this will not be dealt with in detail now, it is well to reflect on how each stage has its specific concerns.

PERSPECTIVES AND ISSUES

At least five different perspectives have to be considered in any professional situation. These viewpoints are those of (1) the client; (2) the professional dealing with the client; (3) the agency represented by the professional; (4) the family in which the client resides; and (5) the "second person" involved, i.e., the individual on whom the client's attention is or might be focused.

These five different perspectives all have a similar focus, but they may differ quite markedly. There may even be many areas of wide disagreement and friction among these five factions, although theoretically they should all be working together.

Client

The client generally looks at his or her problem as quite personal and private. The client may consider the sexual situation as separate from the handicap or part of the handicap but generally thinks it's a problem to be borne in silence and one that should not concern the professional. This is doubly so for the handicapped compared to the able-bodied. Both the able-bodied and handicapped have, first of all, been taught that sexual matters are private and not to be honestly discussed, so this is a common problem. But the handicapped person also has or is given the feeling that any interest or effort that doesn't focus most directly on the handicap should be considered minor. For example, the blind should worry only about seeing and the paralyzed only about walking.

Professional

The professional quite often looks at sexual problems as outside both the professional's scope and the client's area of legitimate concern. The professional's training has generally been toward getting the individual back on the job, capable of caring for a family, and generally self-supporting. Regardless of whether the professional has been trained as a physician, psychologist, social worker, or other type of therapist, until quite recently sexual counseling was never considered as within the legitimate scope of activities. Therapists were not taught the clues to which to attend in this area. Often, even if the client does bring up concern regarding the subject, the professional quite often avoids the issue entirely by not replying to the clues or defends himself by saying words to the effect of, "You should be worried about not being able to walk or not being able to see or not being able to hear rather than worrying about your sexual concerns." It's as if the sexual concerns have to be of lower magnitude than the other abilities. The professional more than anyone must realize that meeting an individual's sexual concerns can go a long way in reestablishing or establishing a general feeling of self-worth conducive to general rehabilitation.

It must be mentioned here, in contrast with what I've just said, that an overzealous professional should in this area, as in others for which he has been trained, be careful to be attuned to client sensitivities. One should not project concerns on patients that are not there, since many handicapped handle their sexual concerns quite well.

Agency

Agencies, most often, are interested only in those factors that they consider leading to job placement or getting the person functioning in the home. They think in terms of productivity or income, and their distance from the client makes them even less aware than the professional counselor of some of the human sexual concerns of the client. Agencies change even more slowly than do individual professionals. So, even though the professional (physician, social worker, counselor, or psychologist) might be interested in the individual client's sexual abilities, the agency frequently takes a dim view of these concerns. Often, the agency is most concerned with image and thinks that being concerned with an individual's sexual problems is inappropriate for a state, foundation-supported, or religion-affiliated organization. Again, I think these views are changing, and it's slowly becoming apparent, to both the professional and the agency, that, once an individual's worth as a complete person is reestablished, he or she is much more apt to be educable, hireable, and content with himself and his situation.

Family

Next, we have the family perspective. Here the issue is quite different. To be sure, the family, too, thinks the sexual problems are private and not to be discussed in public. They think they are also outside the province of the agency or professional dealing with the client, yet the family is quite often ambivalent about the situation. While they recognize that these are valid issues, they generally wish the sexual concerns to be ignored; they want them to sort of "go away," since they are ill at ease dealing with them, and don't really know how to handle the issues. They, too, are beset with the societal value that sex is private and not to be discussed in public.

Quite often, the family would imagine that if, especially in younger people, sex is not discussed, it would never come up in a person's experiences. As with the able-bodied, they don't know how to deal with overt sex, whether it be masturbation or displays of affection toward possible sexual partners. They have strong conflicts. On the one hand, they want to consider the handicapped family member like everyone else and thus allow all opportunities. On the other hand, they don't want to, as they consider it, raise false expectations and hopes. Lastly, it is difficult for the family to recognize that children or parents can be sexual. Regardless of age, elderly parents are often considered "beyond it" and children "not yet ready."

Second Person

Last is the "second person." This is the perspective of the one on whom the client focuses his or her sexual attention. This is also considered to be personal and private, but here the individual definitely is concerned with how the handicap may be involved, although the concern may not be shown. There is the question of just what the partner can do or not do, and can this be discussed openly, or will the issue be too sensitive for probing? Often both of the parties involved seek advice and counsel from others, lay and professional, instead of speaking with each other about sexual feelings, concerns, capabilities, and expectations.

SPECIFIC ISSUES

With my broad introduction and talk of perspectives, I will now present three specific issues that must and can be dealt with within these perspectives. These issues are (1) performance and expectations, (2) guilt, and (3) communication. While my remarks are directed mainly toward dealing with the concerns of the handicapped, it will be obvious that they apply equally as well to the able-bodied.

Performance and Expectations

Too many individuals view their sexual expression as a performance to be rated and graded on some sort of consensually agreed-upon scale. It is as if there were a "right" and a "wrong" way to be sexual and anything less than "right" is to be criticized. Our society certainly fosters these expectations and we live with them in Archie Bunker fashion every day. For our clients, in a realistic and nonjudgmental manner, we have to realign the performance expectations with performance capabilities, so that the only allowable criteria for concern are based on what the couple or the individuals prefer within their abilities. The capabilities naturally will limit the expectations, but it must be made clear that the value systems that an individual puts on a particular type of love relation, or sexual relation, or reproduction relation, or marriage relationship, should be on an individual level or a couple level, so long as public society is not disturbed. Private acts have no standards that are immutable or written in stone. As we ourselves don't ask society's blessings on our private activities, let's help our clients to be encouraged in arriving at their own acceptable solutions with our blessings. Not only should we sanction their solutions, regardless of how novel, but we must encourage experimentation so that many possibilities are attempted to achieve a maximum of satisfaction.

Guilt

Here it is appropriate to introduce the issue of guilt. Too often the clients have enough problems with considering themselves different. In the area of sexuality, we must honestly stress that being different may be of small actual matter, because what one does in the privacy of the bedroom is of concern only to the individuals involved. If the function of sexual expression is private genital satisfaction, then that takes precedence over public approval, and, if the purpose is to give or receive love, then that is not dependent upon certain formulas of performance or public acceptance.

With these concepts, the client should realize that guilt is an inappropriate feeling, not because the individual is less able, but because no standards for anyone, able-bodied or not, are legitimately imposed. One needn't worry about being different sexually, because anything goes that is functional and mutually acceptable. Oral-genital stimulation, manual stimulation, anything that the couple or the individual can find satisfaction in doing is okay, and we as professionals and agencies have to make our permission and sanction (because we have the power to grant such) very clear. We must not put a negative value on any practice found acceptable, whether it involves masturbation, oral-genital relations, a female superior position, or anything else that satisfies the couple.

For this we have to train ourselves against being judgmental and considering some practices preferable to others. This doesn't mean that we have to force on any client any practice he or she may find objectionable. We also shouldn't force our own or society's guilt-laden values on the person or couple. We may encourage experimentation into previously personal or societally taboo areas. We should do all we can to help remove whatever inappropriate guilt feelings may exist in the achievement of sexual satisfaction.

Communication

Lastly, here it is appropriate to talk about communication. There are practically no sexual concerns or situations that cannot benefit from increased communication by and between the individuals involved. Expectations and performance capabilities can be more realistically appraised with good communication, and false impressions can be minimized. The handicapped, as do many able-bodied, often attach a magnified value to certain suspected deficiencies without ever testing the reality of the situation with the "second person." For example, in the realm of sexuality, most of us are concerned with something in our physical makeup. In this regard the handicapped and able-bodied again are alike. Consider that an individual may be concerned personally with being bald, having small breasts, or being deaf, blind, or elderly. Only by communication with the "second party" can one find out if the concern is mutual or the magnitude of the concern. Communication between the individuals involved will reduce hesitancy in finding out just what is and is not possible and what is or is not acceptable.

As professionals, we must thus encourage open, frank discussions of sexual matters as legitimate topics of conversation (often this means removing guilt in talking about sex). We must realize, parenthetically, that communication may be nonverbal as well as verbal. A touch, glance, smile, or grimace may speak loudly. However, for most, an adequate vocabulary still provides the best means of transmitting ideas and feelings. Regrettably, not everyone has an adequate vocabulary and we as professionals may help in providing one. For the deaf, for example, we might remedy the lack in acceptable universal signs for many sexual and reproductive ideas. We hope a satisfactory vocabulary is available soon.

We then come full circle. Good communication can help the other issues, linking performance and expectations and reducing guilt as well as helping in its own way. With this brief introduction, I'd like to present a dialogue and see how it exemplifies some of the issues at hand. (See Note at end of chapter.)

JERRY: Well, I don't really think that I had any idea that things were going to be so different after the operation on my back. I thought my sexual life was going to be the same as it always was, and it turned out to be completely different.

MICKIE: I think at first I felt a sense of desolation that the emotional side of my life was all over with and that I've been condemned to the life of a robot or a zombie.

FRANCIS: I feel embarrassed when I talk to girls, because I drool a lot, and I spit when I talk. And during the conversation, I keep on drooling; I feel like a waterfall.

GEORGE: A heart attack is a massive insult to the body, and to myself as a person. And because of this, the relationship between myself and others—the alienation, the depression—is a whole area of related phenomena that we ought to study very carefully; an area of which we know very little about.

BILL: I've been paralyzed for over 20 years and it's been so long ago that I've forgotten what "normal" sex was. But as I recall, it had to do with sex being pretty much equated with an orgasm. But since I've been paralyzed and had a few chances of sex, I've realized that orgasm is not so important in sex; in fact, it actually hinders the enjoyment of it, because when you don't worry about the orgasm and don't think about the orgasm, sex just continues on and on, and it's never over.

DR. DIAMOND: When we think of the functions that sex serves, we have to think in terms of giving and getting pleasure, of reducing tension, of sharing intimacies. If we keep that in mind we can remove ourself from the stereotype that "good" sex involves only an erect penis in a vagina; that that's the only way or right way. Do you feel that the value of an orgasm is part of the myth, Bill?

BILL: Well, very much so. In fact, before, you kinda work up to something, and then it's over. This way, you just keep going on and on.

DR. DIAMOND: What do you find the most pleasurable thing now?

BILL: Well, still touching the penis, but just touching the nipples and breasts and the sides. I'm very sensitive under the arms.

DR. DIAMOND: So you could find your own way of giving and getting pleasure and that solves your own needs.

BILL: Yeah, but it's much better when somebody else does it.

DR. DIAMOND: Well, that's what I assumed.

BILL: You just have to try—find the right partner, and I guess the right partner is just about anyone who shares your feelings toward each other.

DR. DIAMOND: Mickie, how about yourself?

MICKIE: Well, since being paralyzed and getting out of the more severe part of it, I find that I am perfectly normal except that the mechanics of the thing are different. My legs and back are totally paralyzed. As far as feelings are concerned, if anything, they're heightened because the type of polio I had made me hypersensitive. I find that it's just mostly the mechanics that interfere. And, of course, the preconceived idea that, because you're in a wheelchair, "Don't bother with her—she can't do anything anyway."

DR. DIAMOND: Well, we find that even able-bodied persons begin to find that there is more than one way to skin a cat and probably the handicapped find this out a lot quicker. George, how about you and your heart condition?

GEORGE: Well, I feel like there isn't that comfort that I'm getting from the rest of the people here about my relationship with sexuality. When I had my heart attack, the doctor told me to stop having sex for awhile, but he never told me when to come on again. I feel a profound kind of lack of knowledge and hesitancy . . .

MICKIE: George, do you feel a sense of fear in this area?

GEORGE: Oh, yeah. I think that the fear that accompanies this kind of activity is very profound because it's a deep insult to the body. There's a great hesitancy and I think this leaves a feeling of separation.

DR. DIAMOND: How about with your wife? Obviously, you can look at it both ways. You may want love, but she doesn't want to lose you. Francis, how about yourself with cerebral palsy? How do you see your condition now?

FRANCIS: Well, I'd like to be like any normal guy. I had this cerebral palsy since back in my preschool years. There came a time when the doctors over there wanted me to progress and I didn't progress rapidly. Now, I could do almost anything any normal person could do.

DR. DIAMOND: But now, are you dating now? Are you married now?

FRANCIS: Oh, no. I'm still dating girls.

DR. DIAMOND: Jerry, how about yourself with your back condition?

JERRY: With me, it was a problem, I believe, of creating a new self-image. I thought that I had to be the virile male and live up to my wife's expectations (which she didn't have) of me. She was perfectly satisfied with what I was able to give her after the accident, but I was always trying to do more, and finally I just sat back and enjoyed it, and it was great!

DR. DIAMOND: Why couldn't it have been this way before?

JERRY: Yeah, why did I have to go through all this misery of thinking that I wasn't performing and that I had lost my capabilities?

DR. DIAMOND: Isn't that a problem with all of us—we become spectators, rather than participants. We ask, "What am I supposed to be doing?" rather than, "What can I do?" Shouldn't we concentrate on what we have, rather than on what we don't have?

BILL: This business about fear—it can be emotional fear, too. With fear that, once you are handicapped, you're not going to be able to live up to the expectation that you've been taught in the past other people have of you and you have of yourself. Being in a wheelchair, they don't have the same expectations; they kind of wonder if you can or you can't. Once you show that you can have intercourse, you can also show them what would normally be progressing steps to intercourse. You can show them that you've had good experiences and pleasurable experiences, and the orgasm doesn't become important anymore—or the typical intercourse methods.

DR. DIAMOND: Did you have different experiences as you went through different ages? Many of you have had your handicaps for quite some time.

MICKIE: I've had a rather different type of life. I lost my first husband because of my illness. He couldn't face up to having a disabled wife and two small children. The second time around, it was great. However, before my husband died, he was, for the last two or three years, so very ill that for us there was no more sex as most people think of it. But there was still a deep affection between us. I built my life around different types of activities, so I can't say that I really felt too great a lack in my life, because he was still very affectionate, very sweet to me, and showed me lots of love and attention, and I tried to do the same for him. That was important. The fact that we no longer had typical sexual relations just ceased to be of any importance to either one of us.

DR. DIAMOND: Do any of you get the feeling that either the spouses or lovers, or what have you, are hesitant in initiating sex because of the handicap? How do you overcome that?

GEORGE: I feel that one of the greatest difficulties with my whole family is lack of being able to say it's all right. We begin to have a profound doubt of our own feedback mechanism. You know what I mean—an acceptance. That I'm okay where I'm at is kind of cut off because of this regression. You know, when you're on your own, you lose that trust in yourself.

DR. DIAMOND: Is there anybody that you can communicate with? Your physician or your spouse?

GEORGE: Somewhat; I think more would be helpful.

DR. DIAMOND: Francis, whom do you talk to when you have problems?

FRANCIS: I sometimes talk to my parents, counselors, or probably with the girl I'm dating. I find that the girls are understanding. I talk about the problems that I have, and they feel compassion about my problems, and I feel that they understand.

DR. DIAMOND: What is your biggest problem that you think you've had and overcome? Jerry, how about that?

JERRY: I really believe that the biggest problem was living up to an expectation that wasn't expected at all.

DR. DIAMOND: But now you don't worry about it at all?

JERRY: No, I don't worry about it. That's just the way it is. My wife is a wonderful woman. She's very loving and we've established a new relationship on a different level.

DR. DIAMOND: You just don't have the movements.

JERRY: Right.

DR. DIAMOND: Bill, how about yourself?

BILL: I agree with that. That the most important thing is to get your own self-confidence and just do what comes naturally when you're with your girl.

DR. DIAMOND: How do you do that?

MICKIE: Well, you throw your inhibitions out the window and let it all hang loose.

DR. DIAMOND: How do you do that though? How do you throw out your inhibitions if you've got them?

BILL: It's just a matter of confidence. The first time you may not take advantage of what you later perceive to be the girl's willingness, then you verbally kick yourself in the rear end. The next time, by God, you're not going to make the same mistake twice! You're going to go ahead and do it.

DR. DIAMOND: Mickie, you said something I think is crucial about getting rid of your inhibitions. How about those feelings with guilt? That you may be doing something that somebody else says is not normal?

MICKIE: That is a very hard thing to overcome, but you've got to make up your mind; either you're going to take happiness now while it's there waiting for you or forget it because you're not going to come back and do it again. You know—it's that simple. It isn't like having a piece of cheese in the "refrig" and a week later going and getting it out. There's no way that you're going to be able to do that. So you've got to say—maybe we'll try something else.

DR. DIAMOND: Sex, in terms of genitals, is important but, in terms of personal worth, getting along with somebody and self-worth are perhaps more important.

MICKIE: Oh, I think so!

What does this discussion illustrate? The dialogue demonstrates how the separation of expectations and capabilities is narrowed when guilt feelings are lessened. It goes further, as we must, in reducing guilt and lessening the gap between expectations and capabilities by legitimately doing away with false expectations. For example, we do away with the "myth," which, in essence, states that the only satisfactory means of expressing oneself sexually and achieving satisfaction is with an erect penis in a well-lubricated vagina. For the able-bodied as well as the handicapped, sexual satisfaction is possible without these practices and, in fact, may even be more satisfying. Hands, mouth, feet, any body part may be used any way to achieve satisfaction, and one means is not, a priori, to be preferred over another. Presenting this concept in a positive way can be very helpful to clients.

Further, we should do away with the "marriage manual" formula and concept, which views some activities as foreplay, some as afterplay, and only coitus as "the real play," each "play" with a prescribed time allotment and sequence. We must advocate that anything goes, for however long or in whatever sequence. This is as true for those whose motor functions are compromised as for those with a sensory loss. Persons should be encouraged to maximize the use of those functions that remain, rather than bemoan the nonuse of those functions that are lost.

We can do even more to lessen the gap between capabilities and expectations by suggesting the use in sexual expression of some of the same types of devices we would offer to lessen the gap in job performance between capabilities and expectations. I'm referring to the use of prostheses. We certainly encourage the use of and recommend artificial arms, legs, or eyes where they will serve a function, even a cosmetic one. We can do similarly in a sexual situation. While the use of false breasts has become common for women with mastectomies, we might encourage or at least recommend the use of dildos, vibrators, or anything that the client might find usable, functional, or cosmetic in his or her sexual relationships.

While this might strike some as inappropriate, I think we have to realize that the same reasons other prosthetics are used in normal, everyday life apply to their sexual use. This actually should be seen as quite appropriate for the handicapped, since many able-bodied use them routinely; in fact, the able-bodied provide the major market for their present use. The aged and arthritic and hand amputees can certainly use vibrators where they have lost hand function, and an artificial penis or vagina also has its use, for either solitary or mutual pleasure.While it may take some education on the part of both the client and the partner to accept these devices, with professional encouragement they can accept or reject them without the connotations of guilt that might otherwise go along with their use of consideration. It is to be emphasized that these devices are presently available and are most often used by the able-bodied, so they should not carry a special stigma for the handicapped. These should legitimately be sold in surgical supply stores as freely as in the porno supply shops, where they are presently sold.

Prostheses help those with motor problems. For those with a sensory loss, I will offer a suggestion that is also helpful for those with reduced motor abilities, i.e., maximize the use of all possible senses. If a person is deaf or blind, then obviously maximal use is made of other input means. A soft touch or caress or kiss on a sensitive area may be quite stimulating, and we can increase or multiply the use of available senses by reading or viewing explicit, sexually oriented material or pornography, by the use of perfume, good food, fancy candles, music, and the like. Certainly it should be reiterated here that talking and touching, the most basic means of communicating, must be increased. Eye contact and language are to be encouraged. Novelty and spontaneity also have erotic overtones that should be exploited for maximum sexual satisfaction.

The dialogue also stressed another major point made earlier. That is, satisfaction is quite different from orgasm. Further, sex is, itself, usually used as a means of communicating deep feelings. These feelings can be provided with simple touches, glances, and personal interchanges, which don't require elaborate gymnastics or idealized anatomy. Satisfaction is most often a result of good sexual communication and shared intimacy and is independent of orgasm. Satisfaction and orgasm may be simultaneously sought after but separately achieved. If we make this idea acceptable to our clients, I think we will have helped them in a major way.

In conclusion, I would like to apologize for not discussing, in detail, special problems associated with pregnancy or contraception, or dealing with the special issues and concerns of the mentally retarded. These must await a subsequent publication. What I did hope to do, however, is alert your attention to (1) the difference between public and private sexuality; (2) the separate concerns attendant to genital satisfaction, love, reproduction, and marriage; (3) these aspects as different, dependent upon the client's life stage; and (4) sexuality as viewed from various perspectives. Further, I tried to show how to deal conceptually with several overriding issues for the handicapped, i.e., expectations and performance, guilt, and communication. Lastly, I tried to provide some specific ideas to help meet these issues.

I would reiterate that everyone's sexual life can be improved by (1) increased communication; (2) decreased guilt with anything mutually satisfying; and (3) education and ease in dealing openly with sexual issues, so that expectations are more realistically in line with performance capabilities. All of this serves the human need for satisfaction in self-assessment and interpersonal relationships. This satisfaction is seen as the first stage in a person's successful road to rehabilitation specifically, but contentment with life's lot generally.

What I am offering for you to master are concepts that don't take a large budget or special, elaborate training. What it does take is empathy, and those in rehabilitation, by virtue of the career choice, have usually demonstrated an ample supply of this.

NOTE

At the 1973 regional National Rehabilitation Association conference in Hawaii, a half-hour video recording of various participants discussing sex and the handicapped, made with the aid of the Rehabilitation Association of Hawaii, was presented. This dialogue is a slightly modified portion of the tape. A full copy of the tape is available from the Public Television Library, 512 E. 17th St., Bloomington, Ind. 47401, under the title *When Illness Strikes, Program 21* of the *Human Sexuality Series*, moderated by Dr. Milton Diamond.

18

Sexual Dysfunctions Associated with Physical Disabilities

Ernest Griffith, Compiler

Roberta B. Trieschmann   **Jerome S. Tobis**
George W. Hohmann   **Victor Cummings**
Theodore M. Cole

This paper is an abridgement of six addresses, the first three of which are concerned with the psychosocial aspects of sexuality in normal and physically disabled individuals and with the reactions of a rehabilitation team to sexual problems of patients. The remaining three addresses outline principles of management of sexual dysfunctions associated with three types of physical disability: cardiovascular disorders, spinal cord injury, and amputation.

Sex, Sex Acts, and Sexuality

Roberta B. Trieschmann

Sexual function is a complex matter; therefore, it is important to distinguish among sex, sex acts, and sexuality.

Sex is one of the four primary drives, the others being hunger, thirst, and avoidance of pain. These drives originate in the subcortex but are modified by learned responses originating in the cortex. Thus the cortex governs the methods, occasions, opportunities, and expressions of the primary drives.

From *Archives of Physical Medicine and Rehabilitation,* 56 (1975), 8–13. Copyright ©1975 by the American Congress of Rehabilitation Medicine and the American Academy of Physical Medicine and Rehabilitation. Reprinted by permission of the Managing Editor.

A majority of these learned patterns are regulatory, inhibitory, or prohibitory, deriving historically through church and state laws.

Sex acts are behaviors involving the secondary erogenous zones and genitalia, sexual intercourse being only one kind of sex act. The term *sex act* does not indicate the relationship of the people involved, their emotions, or their attitudes.

Sexuality is the combination of sex drive, sex acts, and all those aspects of personality concerned with learned communications and relationship patterns. This learned, regulated communication and relationship process occurs at many levels, for example, conversation, shared activities and interests, and various expressions of affection, including sexual intercourse.

Learning of controls, prohibitions, and regulations may produce many attitudes, anxieties, and misconceptions about sexuality which interfere with communication and relationships among people. Attitudes vary according to age, race, sex, social class, and religion. Some examples of the prohibitory, regulatory attitudes that influence the expression of sexuality include:

Sex before marriage is wrong, or sinful, or both.
A good woman is sexually innocent before marriage.
It is acceptable for men, but not women, to be sexually experienced before marriage.
Sex for other than procreation is sinful.
Masturbation is sinful, harmful, destructive.
Genital-genital contact is the only proper form of sexual contact. Perversion is anything other than genital-genital contact.

Such attitudes are complex interactions of an intellectual concept with an attached emotion; therefore, they are not always easily changeable through reasoning alone. These attitudes can create anxiety and guilt about having sexual urges and about how those urges are to be expressed. They may inhibit communication and the genuine expression of love. Functional sexual dysfunctions occur because certain of these attitudes inhibit behavior sufficiently so that the person is unable to exper ,nce pleasure, satisfaction, and relaxation during sexual interactions.

Some of these attitudes may inhibit the effectiveness of any member of a treatment team who deals with individuals who have a sexual dysfunction. These attitudes may hinder the adaptations that a disabled individual must make if he (she) is to regain a reasonably satisfactory relationship with the partner.

The communication process during sexual activity may be considered in the context of the sexual response cycles of men and women described by Masters and Johnson. Men and women differ somewhat in the timing, intensity, and duration of their sexual excitement, a situation requiring communication if mutual satisfaction is to be experienced.

A man can reach the plateau phase and orgasm fairly rapidly. After the orgasm, he is incapable of further sexual reaction until a period of time has elapsed, the time varying according to the individual and his age. This one pattern is fairly typical of most men. But a woman's sexual response is more complex, less predictable, and more susceptible to interruption. One pattern is that of gradual progression from excitement and plateau phases to a series of orgasms. Other women progress to the plateau stage and hover at that level without achieving an orgasm. And some women progress rapidly to the plateau phase, attain an orgasm, and rapidly lose sexual interest.

During the excitement and plateau phases, communication becomes critical because interruptions or other changes can alter the level of sexual excitement of either partner and interfere with satisfaction. A comfortable couple, sensitive to one another, will coordinate these response cycles for their mutual enjoyment. By superimposing upon his normal situation the attitudes and inhibitions that may be learned, one can appreciate how difficult the communication process can be. If an individual has a large number of inhibiting attitudes, there is a higher probability that he or she will have a less satisfactory sex life than one who does not have as many of these attitudes. Furthermore, a physical disability may introduce additional complications of mobility limitations, neurological impairment of the sex organs, and chronic pain or discomfort.

Therefore, we must recognize that the onset of a physical disability does not eliminate sexual feelings any more than it eliminates hunger or thirst; there are many different kinds of sex acts available for satisfaction, and a disability may interfere with only a certain number of these; and the sexuality of the disabled individual must be evaluated in terms of his particular pattern of relating to others. We must consider this human being in terms of who he is, what attitudes he has learned about sexuality, and what his premorbid sexual functioning was. Therapeutic efforts must include the disabled individual's partner, since both must learn new patterns of behavior. Thus, evaluation of the partner in terms of his or her concept of sexuality and attitudes toward sexual functioning is essential.

Reactions of the Individual with a Disability Complicated by a Sexual Problem

George W. Hohmann

The many taboos and prohibitions surrounding all three aspects of sex (sex drive, sex acts, and sexuality) intensify the threat imposed by assault on the sexual ability of the physically disabled person. This generates a severe and immediate anxiety in the person. The assumption is generally made by the patient, his family, and the professional staff that his sex drive and sexuality are essentially nonexistent. Anxiety is intensified by attitudes, misapprehensions, and misunderstandings in several areas on the part of these same people. The patient's anxiety is further increased by a lack of responses to his questions, an unwillingness to listen to his problems, a postponement of discussion of his anxiety, an inability to perceive his unasked questions. He is met by innuendos communicating to him that he is an asexual being, that neither he nor anyone else should be concerned about any aspect of his sexual functioning.

What then does the disabled person expect from the staff in helping him deal with feelings, anxieties, and attitudes about his sexuality? He has a right to expect a lack of judgmental attitudes on the part of the staff. He expects the staff to be relatively free from enforcing on him the major prevailing cultural attitudes. He expects assistance in overcoming his misapprehensions regarding his sexuality and taboos of things that he would like to do. He has a right to expect a willingness to provide the information requested in a spirit of comfort, sensitivity, and truthfulness.

The person expects to discuss sexuality with someone with whom he has a meaningful relationship. It is someone with adequate knowledge about sexual function in the normal person, and sexual function in the particular disability state (and associated medical disorders) which the individual has. It is someone who, if not free of sexual hangups, does not impose them on the disabled person.

The patient wants counseling that will help him and his partner establish a meaningful relationship in the area of sexuality, sex acts, and sex drive and enable them to come to some decision as to how they will function in their sexual relationship. In order to discuss what a person is to be told about sexuality, several definitions of sex can be considered:

1. A buildup of striated and autonomic muscle activity culminating in orgasm.

2. A method of procreation.
3. A way of building flagging self-esteem.
4. A way of manipulating and controlling other people.
5. An expression of tenderness, mutual concern, love, and affection.

The patient wants to develop attitudes so that he is free to engage in whatever sexual behavior is organically possible and psychologically acceptable to him and his partner.

What can the patient expect to do? Genital intercourse is possible for an overwhelming majority of disabled people. Foreplay of various types can be an extremely gratifying experience. Body contact is possible for most individuals. Stimulation of the secondary erogenous zones may prove gratifying and pleasurable whether or not genital function is possible. The use of prosthetic appliances has been acceptable to many people. Many marriages have been based on casual expressions of self-esteem, affection, and love.

The patient may ask about what he can expect in the way of gratification from his sexual life. Regardless of type and degree of disability or physical condition, his sexuality can be used to weld a relationship with another human being. He can please a partner; he can experience empathic gratification. He can enjoy the excitement of stimulating the secondary erogenous zones and achieve feelings of adequacy from giving pleasure to another person.

A few precautions should be considered in counseling:

1. Do not put a person in conflict with his God.
2. Avoid extreme pressure on the patient to discuss sexuality.
3. Avoid forcing your morality and convictions on the patient.
4. Do not threaten the patient with your own sexuality.
5. Do not make sex an all-or-none sort of experience.
6. Do not assume that once the topic is discussed that you can leave it alone.
7. Do not conclude that there is only one way to convey information.
8. Be sure that the conjoint nature of sexual relationships is held parallel.
9. Do convey the notion that all relationships, including the sexual one, are a matter of compromise.

Help the patient understand and work on this kind of premise in negotiating his sexual relationships.

Reaction of the Rehabilitation Team to Patients with Sexual Problems

Theodore M. Cole

In considering the title of this discussion, most rehabilitation professionals would first focus on the word *sexual*. To them, it may mean that they are being asked to reveal something of themselves, perhaps to deal with their own sexuality, to yield some of their own preciously guarded privacy. A second reaction may be to the word *problems*. What are this patient's problems, his physiological and anatomic limitations, the things he can and can't do? Only on the third time around may we finally consider the patient, his partner, and especially their feelings. These three reactions are often overcast with the morality of the professionals on the rehabilitation team. There may be a sense of rightness and wrongness about human sexuality. For most of us, these reactions are also overcast with a general ignorance about human sexuality. For many, these reactions are weighted with sexual guilt, fear, and titillation.

Some of the reactions of the rehabilitation team to patients with sexual problems include:

1. I will leave the discussion of sex to someone who is effective because I don't want to hurt the disabled person.
2. I will leave the discussion of sex to the specialists because I do not know enough about it myself.
3. My primary responsibility is to help people achieve a better state of health, and sex is separate from health.
4. I will deal with sexuality in people who became employed and act responsibly because they need the information more than the homebound person.
5. If I introduce the discussion of sexuality, it may become unmanageable.
6. There should be hospital rules about sexuality; and if patients break these rules, they should be reprimanded or dismissed.

In contrast to the above, it is time to consider sexuality as a legitimate part of the rehabilitation process. Team members should try discussing sexuality with colleagues and with disabled patients. Disabled people can take it and will appreciate your sensitivity and interest. Sexuality is a proper dimension of health care delivery and thus should be discussed with the appropriate information given. In this manner, professionals can play a meaningful role by endorsing the concept of sexuality to disabled patients. Rather than equating sexuality with employability, information on sexuality should be made available to all physically disabled patients, since it is a part of us all and should not have to be earned through work. Furthermore, hospitals should provide the opportunity for privacy in addition to the opportunity to interact with others. We should encourage sexual rehabilitation in the hospital as well as outside of it.

There is a need for practical information which can help people develop the competence which is an important part of human sexual expression. But much more important is the inherent permission to be sexual. If sexual confidence can be reestablished, more will feel that they dare try reentry into the world of vocation, self-respect, and responsibility. A frank and personal approach helps to desensationalize the sensitive aspect of physical disability. It humanizes the disabled in the eyes of the able-bodied treater or counselor, for it is difficult for the treater to regard a client as less than he if he knows that the client has access to and skills with one of the most powerful aspects of human behavior, human sexuality.

Cardiovascular Patients and Sexual Dysfunctions

Jerome S. Tobis

It is questionable whether the findings that Masters and Johnson obtained in a somewhat laboratory-type situation have validity to cardiac stress. Their estimates of pulse rates rising to 170 and 180 per minute must have been influenced by the fact that the partners were being monitored. This certainly must have influenced the emotional and autonomic responses of the participants. One of the really valuable contributions made in this area is that of Hellerstein and Friedman. They reported on 91 male subjects who had participated in a YMHA physical fitness program. These 91 individuals, 48 of whom had myocardial infarctions and 43 of whom were healthy but coronary-disease prone, were subjected to an extensive questionnaire concerning their sexual behavior. Eighteen of 43 respondent subjects with coronary artery disease indicated that they developed one or more symptoms during sexual relations. Most common of these symptoms was excessively fast heartbeat. In some 20% of those with coronary disease, there were symptoms suggestive of angina. The interval between the coronary event and resumption of sexual activity was approximately 14 weeks. The impact of a coronary event on sex was great during the first six months after the acute episode but by the end of the first year was minimal.

Curiously, this finding is at odds with other reports in the literature. Tuttle reports that some 10% of people who were involved in a work-evaluation unit were totally impotent long after their acute episode and Weiss stated that some 30% of his subjects reported impotence. Whether this represents a skewed population that Hellerstein and Friedman were dealing with, that is, a predominantly Jewish population of middle-class businessmen, or whether the physical fitness program improved their sexual performance, is open to question and deserves further study. It was the impression of Hellerstein and Friedman that those who participated in the exercise program improved relative to their sexual behavior in terms of quality and frequency of sexual activity. These authors found that the physiological cost for sex in the middle-aged male, married approximately 20 years or longer, was less than the requirement for carrying out the Master's Two Step Test. They estimated that approximately 6 kilocalories per minute was required for a maximum of perhaps 30 seconds, with a heart rate of less than 120 beats. Obviously, these variables depend on who the partners are; those involved in extramarital relationships presumably require considerably higher energy costs. The frequency of the occasional cardiovascular catastrophies during extramarital intercourse has never been well established. If cardiac patients are capable of climbing one or two flights of stairs or walking a block briskly without difficulty or complaint, they are likely able to participate in the sex act.

Another factor that should be considered is the wife's attitude. Often her fear and anxiety that sexual activity may be disastrous for the patient will mitigate against a normal relationship. Many of the antihypertensive drugs may contribute to some degree of impotence. Serious depression associated with fear and anxiety concerning the disease may be a factor. Another consideration is the effect of exercise. Isometric exercise has been shown by Donald and his colleagues to raise blood pressure significantly and produce additional stress on an already impaired heart. Under such circumstances, the person with significant heart disease should avoid the prone position, and instead use the side-lying position or other postural modifications. Certainly the cardiac patient should avoid heavy eating or heavy imbibing of alcohol prior to participation in sex.

Spinal Cord Injury Patients and Sexual Dysfunction

Theodore M. Cole

What do we know about how a paraplegic or quadriplegic person responds to sexual stimulation? The research on paraplegic women is abominably lacking. We know of no literature that describes the secretions from the wall of the vagina during sexual arousal in a woman with complete cord transection. Nor does the literature tell us what happens to the swelling and opening of the labia, contracting of the uterus, and ballooning and expanding of the vagina. We know that the clitoris may become reflexly tumescent; the nipples may indeed swell, as may the breasts. Breathing, blood pressure, and pulse rate may increase. Muscles may go into spasm, and a characteristic sex flush can occur.

What about the paraplegic or quadriplegic man with complete cord transection? His penis may become erect; his nipples may erect. His muscles may develop spasms; his blood pressure, pulse, and respiration may increase. The skin of his scrotum may tense. He may develop a skin flush. However, it is unusual for him to have an emission or ejaculation. Thus, the spinal cord patient is capable of most of the sexual responses of the able-bodied.

Still, we tend to think of the paraplegic or quadriplegic person as somehow drastically different from the able-bodied. Coupled with that is the fact that we tend to regard information about the sexuality of spinal-cord-injured people as drastically different from other medical information we may obtain. We have divided medical information into at least two packages: general medical information and sexual information. Masters and Johnson have suggested that the reason the sexual history has been separated from routine history-taking is that all of us take sexual functioning out of its natural context of everyday living. Our difficulty in assigning sexual function an honorable role as a basic physiological process stems from a physical characteristic unique to this form of physiology. Sexual functioning can be delayed indefinitely or even denied for a lifetime. One cannot say the same for other natural functions.

I talk with a patient about his spinal cord injury and his sexuality together within the context of the total problems faced by him or her. Several principles guide me: I am no longer frightened or put off by the person in the bed; most people can take what I am going to say. I try to be understanding and to use a lot of eye contact. I sanction sexuality as a positive aspect of life. I set expectations for activity and gratification, and say that I will return for further discussion. Shortly after the patient's injury, when there is still concern about his survival, is not an opportune time to begin the discussion. However, when the time comes that you would consider appropriate for such discussion, you can be assured that the patient has already been thinking about it.

What do I talk about? First, I talk about his losses: I ask about physical, occupational, recreational, and self-image types of losses. As he responds, I learn what he considers to be a loss. I must remember that those things I consider losses may not be so to him. Then I talk about activity or performance. What can he do, not just sexually, but also in regard to other kinds of activities? I inquire about his or her partner: "Do you have a partner? Do you have a relationship going? How is this person going to interact with you in your home life, your work life, and in your sex life?" I talk about the future. "What kinds of adjustments do you think are necessary, sexual and other than sexual?" I talk about communication: "How are you going to communicate with people? How are you going to communicate with your sexual partner?" Then I end an interview by coming back to the present with discussion of general concerns such as nursing procedures. Finally, I set the expectation that I will be back to talk later. I am not done; I will return to continue discussion of this subject.

Amputees and Sexual Dysfunction

Victor Cummings

Those of us in the health professions who treat patients with major limb amputation, either congenital or surgical, ordinarily do not include sexual problems when considering the functional problems that they must face during and after prosthetic rehabilitation. One can guess at the reasons that little attention has been given to sexual problems among amputees. First of all, the majority of amputees who find their way to organized clinics are usually in the older age group. Even if they were not amputees, many physicians would feel that probing into their sex lives would be a waste of time, and a source of irritation and embarrassment. Secondly, if the amputee is younger and in good health, one might assume that he or she has no sexual problems, so why bother asking? It is the rare amputee who will spontaneously imply that he or she has sexual problems, and it is very rare that he or she will ask direct questions about sex problems. Finally, it is only relatively recently that the health professions have become sensitized so that some attention is paid to the physiology, pathology, and psychology of sex. Unfortunately for the amputee, it is the patient with emotional, cardiac, and neurological problems who receives the most attention. Speaking about the surgical amputee then, what kind of problems does he or she face with regard to sex? There is the obvious emotional trauma: the depression and mourning period, the distortion of body image, and the perception of self as not whole, or as ugly, or as no longer feminine or masculine.

Although an amputation obviously creates a profound psychological impact, there may be quite a difference between the sexes with regard to the kind of impact it produces. In the male, the impact is usually similar to castration: that is, the loss of limb is equated to the loss of manhood. But the impact on a female psyche may be quite another thing. In their study, Weinstein and associates have demonstrated that the bodily part preference of men and women differs considerably. They reported that the largest majority of men between the ages of 20 to 40 years rated the penis as the part of the body to be most valued, while the majority of women between the ages of 20 to 70 years rated the tongue as the most important organ.

Phantom sensation, whether painful or not, can present problems. This phenomenon is almost always present in patients who have undergone amputation. A painful phantom can be disturbing or disastrous when performing the sex act.

The mechanics of body positioning during sex play and intercourse have presented difficulties. Balance, movement, or lack of either may be a problem. Some problems can be solved simply: for example, by suggesting to the upper extremity amputee to switch sides of the bed with the partner so they have their normal arm free in the side-lying position. Change of position during the sex act might be necessary. In some cases, change from the male superior to the female superior position might be indicated.

Often the disease causing the amputation causes additional problems. The male patient with a diabetic neuropathy may be unable to ejaculate, or have an erection, or both. Similarly, the male who has undergone bilateral lumbar sympathectomy may be unable to ejaculate, or may ejaculate retrogradely. Vascular disease can add to the difficulties. Erection can be interfered with due to inadequate blood flow. The most classic example of this is the Leriche syndrome, which causes impotence and high intermittent claudication. Enforced isolation because of limited mobility can impose added difficulties. If a man and woman who are not amputees do not get along, and cannot resolve their differences, one or the other can walk out and find another mate. But in many instances, a severely handicapped amputee cannot walk out, or for that matter cannot walk anywhere, particularly if living in a walk-up apartment or tenement.

Another aspect of sexuality of the amputee is somewhat unusual in nature. It concerns the nonamputee who is sexually aroused by an amputee of the opposite sex. This sexual variance, which is a form of fetishism, occurs, to my knowledge, in men only. These men have gone so far as to form organizations. They look down upon the female amputee who covers her stump with a prosthesis, referring to such a woman as one who "tries to pass." They call themselves hobbyists, and write stories or draw pictures about their fantasies.

There is far less known about congenital amputees, and much clinical research must be done to identify their problems so that we in the health professions can sort them out and go about finding some answers.

SUMMARY

Those who treat sexual dysfunctions of the physically disabled should be aware of the distinctions among sex drive, sex acts, and sexuality. Although a disability may impose alterations in sex acts, sex drive and sexuality remain intact. Before initiating treatment, the therapist should know both patient and sexual partner as people whose sexuality and sexual function have been shaped by previous specific experiences, attitudes and beliefs.

Anxiety is a frequent early reaction of the patient. He may share the assumption of family and staff that his sex drive and sexuality cease to exist. Patient expectations of counseling include lack of judgmental attitudes and provision of readily accessible, accurate information. Various types of gratification are possible. Precautions in counseling are enumerated.

Early reactions of rehabilitation team members may be concerned with the need to deal with their own sexuality and ignorance, limitations which the disability imposes upon sexual acts and the morality of sex. Examples of conventional approaches in managing sexual problems are presented. Suggestions of alternate strategies and their rationale are offered.

Management of sexual dysfunction in cardiac patients requires familiarity with the study by Hellerstein and Friedman of men with coronary artery disease. Cardiac patients capable of one or two flights of stair-climbing should be able to participate in sex acts. Significant variables affecting sexual activities in these patients are the attitude of the spouse, drugs, depression, exercise, positioning, and dietary intake.

Most of the physiological sexual responses seen in the able-bodied remain in spinal-cord-injured subjects. History-taking and discussions of sexuality should be done in context of the patient's total problems. Principles of interview technique and topics of discussion are reviewed.

Sexual problems of amputees may be related to emotional trauma such as depression and distortion of body image. Additionally, phantom sensations, difficulties in balance and positioning, and associated disease states may alter sexual performance. Immobility may enforce physical isolation.

19

Sexual Adjustment Counseling for Persons with Severe Disabilities: A Skill-Based Approach for Rehabilitation Professionals

Donald E. Shrey
Judith Sterling Kiefer
William A. Anthony

INTRODUCTION

The goal of sexual adjustment counseling for a person with a severe disability is to help the individual feel more positive about himself/herself as a man or woman, and to facilitate this person's ability to make decisions concerning positive relationships with others. Severely disabled persons are those individuals who are significantly inconvenienced because of sensory limitations, and/or a range of disorders which may include musculo-skeletal, cardiovascular, respiratory, digestive, urogenital, endocrine-metabolic, mental, neoplastic, and others.

The need for sexual adjustment among persons with severe disabilities implies that a sexual maladjustment exists. Sexual adjustment problems are often viewed as the result of a physiological impairment or a psychological reaction to a physical impairment, or both. In any event, people who are faced with sexual adjustment problems frequently share one common barrier — they have neither the skills nor the knowledge to overcome their deficits in healthy human sexuality.

The rehabilitation process is directed at increasing the *strengths* and *assets* of people so that they can achieve their maximum potential for a meaningful and satisfying life. Few rehabilitation professionals would question the role of sexuality as an important aspect of normal physical and social

From *Journal of Rehabilitation*, 45(2) (1979), 28–33. Reprinted by permission.

relationships. Sexuality is affected in all that a person is and does (Cole and Glass, 1977). Berkman (1975) described the strong relationship between feelings of sexual adequacy and the individual's self-concept. Anderson and Cole (1975) emphasized the positive relationships between a disabled person's self-esteem, work life, and sex life.

Although much has been written about sexuality and the disabled person, rehabilitation professionals often lack the knowledge, experience, and skills necessary to facilitate adequate sexual adjustment among severely disabled persons. Disabled people frequently report that they have received adequate physical treatment and vocational counseling, but it is difficult to find a professional who is comfortable, understanding, and knowledgeable about sexuality (Glass and Padrone, 1978).

This article offers a step-by-step guide to facilitate the rehabilitation professional's involvement in the sexual adjustment counseling process. There have been several sexual adjustment counseling models presented in the literature (Bockway et al., 1978; Cole et al., 1973; Eisenberg and Falconer, 1978; Eisenberg and Rustad, 1976; Halstead et al., 1977; Held et al., 1975). Guidelines for responding to the sexual adjustment needs of severely disabled clients have also permeated the professional journals (Baxter and Linn, 1978; Cole, 1975a; Cole, 1975b; Miller, 1975; Schneider, 1976). These models and guidelines tend to provide the rehabilitation professional and his/her client with insight into the nature of the problem. However, little is offered regarding 1) how to explore the client's strengths and deficits, 2) how to set goals with the client, and 3) how to systematically implement sexual adjustment goals so that they are realistic, measurable, and attainable. The following guidelines to sexual adjustment counseling go beyond the stage of therapeutic insight. An action component is offered, focusing on the individualized implementation of goals, as they relate to the unique sexual adjustment needs of people with severe disabilities.

SEXUAL ADJUSTMENT:
A PROCESS AND A GOAL

Sexual adjustment is both a process and a goal. The process implies a relationship between the severely disabled person (who needs the knowledge and skills to overcome barriers) and significant others in this person's environment. Significant others may include the rehabilitation counselor, the client's spouse, his/her physician, and other allied health professionals. Sexual adjustment counseling refers to those skilled activities of the rehabilitation professional which facilitate the severely disabled person's attainment of his/her individualized goals.

The sexual feelings and concerns of disabled persons are becoming increasingly apparent as a result of the deinstitutionalization movement. Also, legislative trends such as the Rehabilitation Act of 1978 demonstrate much awareness of the needs for independent living among severely disabled clients. Through the efforts of normalization strategies, devalued people are now being integrated into regular classrooms and work settings (Glass and Padrone, 1978). Those who were once confined to institutional living now reside in group homes and private residences. Along with normalized living, learning, and working arrangements comes the greater likelihood of dating and marriage, as well as increases in interpersonal relationships and sexual activities. New environments require new adjustments among disabled persons.

Rehabilitation professionals and their clients need information and skills concerning the sexual adjustment process. According to Cole (1975b), much misinformation about the sexuality of disabled persons has been generated by society through ignorance and prejudice. This often perpetrates myths which eventually lead to feelings of guilt and shame among many disabled persons. The end result of such ignorance is sexual maladjustment, which is frequently characterized by psycho-social and interpersonal problems.

Rehabilitation professionals are similarly characterized as having skill deficits in the area of sexual adjustment counseling. Both knowledge and skill acquisition regarding the sexual adjustment process are important for the practitioner, so that he/she may facilitate the severely disabled person's attainment of meaningful interpersonal and sexual relationships. Therefore, an important factor in sexual adjustment counseling is the maturity and preparation of the practitioner. Cole (1975b) emphasized that it would be necessary for this person to thoroughly explore and understand his/her attitudes regarding sexuality and disability prior to initiating a sexual adjustment counseling relationship with a severely disabled person. Much of what results from the counseling relationship will depend upon the professional's level of comfort with his/her own sexuality.

SEXUAL ADJUSTMENT COUNSELING: WHEN AND WHERE

The implementation of sexual adjustment counseling skills is seen as appropriate at any point during the rehabilitation counseling and planning process. Although sexual adjustment counseling should be considered early in the rehabilitation process, the initiation of counseling should be gauged according to the client's readiness. Certain aspects of sexual adjustment counseling can be used in controlled or sheltered environments with clients functioning at low levels. For example, the sexual adjustment process can be used to explore what heterosexual socialization experiences might be best for the person with a severe developmental disability. The determining criterion is the point at which it becomes functional for the severely disabled person to begin exploring his/her sexual adjustment needs in a more systematic way.

The rehabilitation professional can initiate sexual adjustment counseling with severely disabled persons in individual and/or group settings. The group context has several advantages as well as some disadvantages. A group approach is more efficient in terms of the professional's time. Groups can provide a forum for sharing sexual adjustment problems and potential solutions (Mayers, 1978). Conversely, the level of the client's readiness to explore his/her sexual adjustment needs may warrant a more private, personalized, and individualized counseling approach.

HOW THE SEXUAL ADJUSTMENT COUNSELING PROCESS IS ACCOMPLISHED

The purpose of this section is to overview the steps involved in the sexual adjustment counseling process. The ultimate goal of this developmental process is for the severely disabled person to implement his/her goals relevant to meaningful interpersonal and sexual relationships.

In order to accomplish these goals, the severely disabled person must proceed through three developmental phases. In the initial *exploration* phase, the rehabilitation professional facilitates the client's awareness of personalized sexual and interpersonal needs. During this phase, the client should also gain an awareness of how other persons perceive sexuality and interpersonal relationships. In particular, the client first explores his/her physiological and psycho-social strengths and weaknesses, as well as personal values related to sexuality. The client then explores these areas as they relate to the sexuality of others. This provides the client with a frame of reference with which to compare his/her knowledge, skills, and values regarding sexuality.

The exploration phase of sexual adjustment counseling leads the client into the *understanding* phase. During this phase, the rehabilitation professional facilitates the client's understanding of information and resources relevant to specific physiological and psycho-social needs, and the client's attitudes and values. The client learns how to use information, resources, and skills to overcome barriers to meaningful sexual and interpersonal relationships. The rehabilitation professional helps the severely disabled person to develop a systematic method for making decisions and developing goals based on the client's acquired information, resources, skills, sexual attitudes, and values.

Finally, the client is prepared to enter the *action* phase of counseling. During this phase, the practitioner facilitates the client's development of a step-by-step plan. This plan should be designed to help the client achieve the goals which he/she developed in the understanding phase.

In order to implement the client's goals, the rehabilitation professional must work with the client to identify in concrete and specific terms the barriers that prevent him/her from overcoming physiological and psycho-social problems. Once these barriers have been specified, the client is helped to identify in concrete, specific, and *achievable* terms the steps needed to overcome these barriers.

EXPLORATION PHASE: INFORMATION AND RESOURCES RELATED TO THE SEXUALITY OF PERSONS WITH SEVERE DISABILITIES

The purpose of this section is to describe three general areas in which the exploration of sexuality information should be considered. These three general areas include (1) physiological deficits and assets, (2) psycho-social deficits and assets, and (3) sexual values and attitudes. The client and the practitioner need to explore where the client is in relation to these areas during the initial stages of counseling.

Physiological Deficits and Assets

Information regarding the relationship between the client's disability and his/her functional sexual capacity can be elicited from the client as well as from others, including the client's spouse, his/her physician, and other allied health professionals. The rehabilitation professional should be sensitive to the confidentiality of such information. Clients' rights and ethical standards should be observed, and information with respect to sexuality issues should neither be disclosed nor pursued without the individual's consent.

The first step in exploring the client's physiological deficits and assets is to initiate an interview with the client. The rehabilitation practitioner should focus particular attention on the following areas and issues:

1. The client's physical mobility
2. The client's physical sensations, i.e., touch, pain, etc.
3. Degree of spasticity, if applicable
4. Levels and areas of pain
5. Continency, including urinary drainage devices
6. Difficulties in seeing and hearing
7. Endurance
8. Balance
9. Reactions to medications
10. Genital and extragenital sexual response, i.e., capacity for erection, ejaculation, etc.

In addition to information ascertained from the client during the initial interview, the practitioner should consider contacting the client's physician and other professionals to obtain information such as the following:

1. Level of fertility
2. Hormonal changes
3. Hereditary and/or genetic factors
4. Residual functional capacity, including cardiovascular status
5. Perceptual difficulties
6. Communications disorders

Psycho-Social Deficits and Assets

It is important for the client and the practitioner to assess the client's emotional well-being in order to identify specific psycho-social deficits as well as assets. Information regarding the client's self-concept, feelings of sexual attractiveness, attitudes toward his/her disability, and the client's potential for interpersonal and sexual relationships with others should be explored.

During the counseling interview, the practitioner and his/her client may explore the following issues:

1. Client's motivation and commitment to explore psycho-social deficits and assets
2. Client's level of psycho-social adjustment to his/her disability
3. Client's premorbid and present coping mechanisms and skills
4. Client's interpersonal skills and behaviors
5. Identifying significant others in the client's world
6. Attitudes of significant others toward client's disability
7. Client's body image
8. Client's level of satisfaction/dissatisfaction with current relationships (interpersonal and sexual)

Sexual Values

The client's sexual values should be explored in order to clarify those factors which are important to the client with respect to his/her sexual needs. Information regarding the client's physical, psycho-social, and personal values should be considered:

1. Religious beliefs and attitudes, i.e., birth control, premarital sexual relationships, etc.
2. Priorities of sexual relationships for the client
3. Cultural beliefs and attitudes

4. Marriage and family priorities and values
5. Preferences in sexual activities, i.e., masturbation, oral-genital sex, manual stimulation, fantasy, and sexual positions
6. Use of physical stimulation appliances, i.e., vibrators
7. Values regarding flexibility of male-female roles
8. Sexual preferences, i.e., heterosexual/homosexual
9. Physical appearance of others and self
10. Preferred areas or locations (environmental) to initiate interpersonal/ sexual relationships

UNDERSTANDING PHASE: ACQUIRING THE KNOWLEDGE AND SKILLS NECESSARY FOR SEXUAL ADJUSTMENT

During this phase, the practitioner and the client develop and choose alternative methods of overcoming the severely disabled person's barriers to sexual adjustment. The client's general knowledge deficits in the area of sexual adjustment may be overcome during the exploration phase, when the client and his/her practitioner explore information and resources related to sexuality issues. The client, however, may also lack the ability to establish individualized goals in a systematic way. For example, the client may not understand enough about what he/she wants to accomplish through interpersonal relationships and sexual activities. Perhaps little is understood regarding potential strategies to reach the client's individualized goals. Finally, although the severely disabled person may have all the needed information, he/she may have no systematic method for using this information to reach his/her goals.

The first step in establishing goals with the client is to identify those areas in which the client has deficits related to his/her sexuality. For example, one physiological deficit may be difficulty in bladder control during sexual activity. A psycho-social deficit may be the client's inability to initiate social contacts with persons of the opposite sex. It may be helpful to rank the client's deficits according to their order of greatest concern, based on the client's values. Thus, the rehabilitation professional and the client would focus on the most important areas of concern first.

The next step is to establish goals based on the client's deficits. Goals are established by identifying the skills needed to overcome these specific deficits. For example, a deficit in the area of physical mobility would result in identifying measurable and attainable skills that the client would need in order to increase physical mobility, or to effectively compensate for his/her lack of mobility.

The final step in the understanding phase is to identify physiological and psycho-social resources in order to facilitate the client's goal attainment.

For example, the client may need resources such as literature, information from his/her physician, or physical devices. Furthermore, the client should be aware of his/her physiological and psycho-social *assets*, as they relate to achieving the goals. (See Table 5 for an example of how to list deficits, goals, and possible resources.)

ACTION PHASE: FACILITATING A STEP-BY-STEP PLAN TO OVERCOME SEXUAL ADJUSTMENT PROBLEMS

The final phase of sexual adjustment counseling involves implementing a step-by-step plan to help the client reach his/her goals. Basically, this means that assets and deficits must be assessed and programs developed to overcome the client's barriers to sexual adjustment. If the practitioner and the severely disabled person have identified specific goals, it is good to recheck the client's assets and deficits in light of these goals to clarify the sexual adjustment plan.

Assessing Present Problem Behavior

Once the problems have been identified, they must be operationalized. Operationalization means to define the client's sexual adjustment problems in observable and measurable terms. This serves to make the problems clear to both the practitioner and the severely disabled person. In order to operationalize problems, it is important to identify (1) *who* is performing the behavior, (2) *what* are the client's skill deficits related to the problems, (3) *how much* of the behavior is performed, i.e., frequency, amount of time or quantity, (4) *when* the behavior is performed, and (5) *where* the behavior is performed.

Assessing the Needed Goal Level

Once the problems have been identified and the client's present problem behavior has been assessed, the next step is to assess the client's needed level of functioning. Assessing the client's goals in observable terms will ensure that both the rehabilitation professional and the severely disabled person will be able to determine when the client's goal has been achieved. This procedure builds accountability into the entire sexual adjustment counseling process. To set the goal, the practitioner helps the severely disabled person to quantify his/her desired level of functioning. In order to assess the client's goal, it may be necessary for the practitioner to consult with people in the client's environment, such as the physician, the client's partner, family

Table 5. Listing Deficits, Goals, and Possible Resources

Deficit	Goal	Possible Resources
1. Pain during sexual intercourse	Decrease pain during sexual intercourse	1. Consultation with physician concerning medications 2. Information on techniques of sexual intercourse that are not painful 3. Consultation with physical therapist on ways to reduce pain 4. Instruction in relaxation techniques
2. Lack of bladder control	Increase bladder control or compensate for loss of bladder control	1. Consult with physician regarding client's urological status 2. Information on drainage devices (if applicable) and techniques of sexual intercourse when one uses drainage devices 3. Meeting with other disabled person who knows ways to control bladder 4. Role-play of ways to explain lack of bladder control to partner
3. Lack of knowledge of ways to have a family when fertility is decreased	Has knowledge of ways to have a family when fertility is decreased	1. Consultation with physician concerning client's level of fertility 2. Referral to fertility clinic (if applicable) 3. Information on adoption and artificial insemination 4. Meeting with other disabled person who knows of ways to deal with decreased fertility

(continued)

241

Table 5. Listing Deficits, Goals, and Possible Resources (continued)

Deficit	Goal	Possible Resources
4. Lack of knowledge of safe birth control with respect to disability	Has knowledge of birth control with respect to disability	1. Consultation with physician or counselor 2. Information on safe birth control 3. Exploring literature on safe birth control
5. Difficulty in meeting persons of the opposite sex	Increased ease in meeting persons of the opposite sex	1. Assertiveness training and/or role-playing 2. Grooming skills 3. Transportation 4. Developing leisure activities 5. Meeting with other disabled persons who have overcome this problem 6. Social clubs available to client
6. Negative body image	Positive body image	1. Developing pleasurable activities 2. Grooming techniques 3. Role-playing 4. Involvement in group counseling with others who have learned to overcome this problem

members, etc. This will ensure that the goals which are set are realistic. (See Table 6 for measuring goal levels.)

Developing Steps to Reach Goals

The next task for the rehabilitation professional is to help the client to implement his/her plans by identifying the steps which must be taken to achieve the goal. First, the client and the practitioner should "brainstorm" the steps involved in reaching the goal. Second, they should order the steps in terms of what comes first, second, third, etc. Finally, *substeps* should be developed to lead to the larger steps, especially if the client does not understand how to initiate the main steps which were identified. It is very important that the client can effectively and successfully do each of the steps. Depending on the client, then, the sexual adjustment plan can range from an outline of what is to be done to a highly detailed program.

Identifying Needed Resources

After the steps to sexual adjustment have been identified, they must be implemented. In developing these steps, the need for the use of community resources may be indicated. Such resources may include either persons or agencies. The rehabilitation professional should work with the client to identify the resources that will be used, so that the sexual adjustment plan will actually be implemented.

Resources can be clearly specified by focusing on the *name* of the agency or person, *where* this resource is located, *who* should be contacted, and *how* the contact should be initiated. Thus, if one of the client's goals were to obtain information regarding birth control, one step might be to identify a person or agency with information on planned parenthood. The client would then identify the specific resources he/she will use to obtain birth control information. Identifying a contact person may require an initial telephone call. However, the extra effort is worth it, since many individuals feel more comfortable if they have a person to contact rather than just an agency.

Assigning Completion Dates

The final step in the sexual adjustment counseling process is to assign completion dates to each of the major steps in the program. Such deadlines provide the rehabilitation professional and the client with a clear indication as to the degree of progress being made. As a result of this final step, further accountability is built into the adjustment plan.

It is important for the practitioner to help the client develop *realistic* completion dates. One mechanism for doing this is to estimate the number

244

Table 6. *Assessment of the Needed Goal Level*

Deficit	Operationalized Statement	Assessment of Present Level	Assessment of Goal Level
1. Lacks information on painless ways of experiencing sexual intercourse	As measured by number of ways of experiencing sexual intercourse that client knows	1	10
2. Lack of bladder control	As measured by number of times client is incontinent a week	6	0
3. Lacks knowledge on having children when fertility is impaired	As measured by the client's knowledge of ways one can have children when fertility is impaired	0	3
4. Lacks knowledge on safe birth control with respect to disability	As measured by the number of safe methods of birth control client can identify	1	4
5. Has difficulty in meeting persons of the opposite sex	As measured by number of persons of the opposite sex that client meets per week	1	5
6. Has negative body image	As measured by number of times per week client goes out in public and feels positively about appearance	0	7

of hours required to complete the task and then to estimate the number of hours per week the client can spend working on the task.

In addition to time lines, it may be necessary to develop differential reinforcements to initiate each step of the plan. That is, if in the rehabilitation professional's judgment the client needs some external consequences to insure the completion of each step, then a positive and negative reinforcer may be assigned to that step or combination of steps.

CONCLUSION

The goal of rehabilitation is to restore to disabled persons their capacity to function in the community. Philosophically, this means that rehabilitation is directed at increasing the knowledge and skills of these individuals so that they can achieve their maximum potential for independent living. Although independent living is loosely defined, human sexuality is a major factor with respect to meaningful relationships in life. The step-by-step approach described in this article is designed to facilitate the sexual adjustment process of those severely disabled persons who have knowledge and skill deficits in the area of human sexuality.

REFERENCES

Anderson, T. and Cole, T. Sexual counseling of the physically disabled. *Postgraduate Medicine*, 1975, 58(1), 117–123.

Baxter, R. and Linn, A. Sexual counseling and the SCI patient. *Nursing 78*, 1978, September, 46–52.

Berkman, A. Sexuality: A human condition. *Journal of Rehabilitation*, 1975, 41(1), 13–15.

Brockway, J., Steger, J., Bemi, R., Ost, V., Williamson-Kirkland, T., and Peck, C. Effectiveness of a sex education and counseling program for spinal cord injured patients. *Sexuality and Disability*, 1978, 1(2), 127–136.

Cole, T. Sexuality and physical disabilities. *Archives of Sexual Behavior*, 1975, 4(4), 389–403. (a)

Cole, T. Sexuality and spinal cord injured. In *Human sexuality: A health practitioner's text*, Green, R. (ed.) Baltimore: Williams & Wilkins, 1975, 147–170. (b)

Cole, T., Chilgren, R., Rosenberg, P. A new programme of sex education and counseling for spinal cord injured adults and health care professionals. *Paraplegia*, 1973, 11, 111–124.

Cole, T. and Glass, D. Commentary on sexuality and physical disabilities. *Archives of Physical Medicine and Rehabilitation*, 1977, 58, 585–586.

Eisenberg, M. and Falconer, J. Current trends in sex education programming for the physically disabled: Some guidelines for implementation and evaluation. *Sexuality and Disability*, 1978, 1(1), 15.

Eisenberg, M. and Rustad, L. Sex education and counseling program on a spinal cord injury service. *Archives of Physical Medicine and Rehabilitation*, 1976, *57*, 135–140.

Glass, D. and Padrone, F. Sexual adjustment in the handicapped. *Journal of Rehabilitation*, 1978, *44*(1), 43–47.

Halstead, L., Halstead, M., Salhoot, J., Stock, D. and Sparks, R. A hospital-based program in human sexuality. *Archives of Physical Medicine and Rehabilitation*, 1977, *58*, 409–412.

Held, P., Cole, T., Held, C., Anderson, C. and Chilgren, R. Sexual attitude reassessment workshops: Effect on spinal cord injured adults, their partners and rehabilitation professionals. *Archives of Physical Medicine and Rehabilitation*, 1975, *56*, 14–18.

Mayers, K. Sexual and social concerns of the disabled: A group counseling approach. *Sexuality and Disability*, 1978, *1*(2), 100–111.

Miller, D. Sexual counseling with spinal cord injured clients. *Journal of Sex and Marital Therapy*, 1975, *1*(4), 312–318.

Schneider, E. Human sexuality and the handicapped. *Personnel and Guidance Journal*, 1976, *54*, 7, 378–380.

Part VII

The Rights, Contributions, and Needs of Disabled Consumers

Until recently, persons with disabilities had little or no involvement in the programs that shaped their lives. Today, however, many clients participate actively in their rehabilitation through self-help groups and as advisory group members, directors, or staff members in rehabilitation agencies and facilities. In addition, many able-bodied rehabilitation workers espouse the concept of comanagement with clients.

In reaffirming its faith in human rights in December 1975, the United Nations proclaimed a Declaration on the Rights of Disabled Persons. This Declaration calls for national and international action to insure a common frame of reference for protecting the rights of, and assuring the welfare and rehabilitation of, physically and mentally disabled individuals. Those who work with disabled persons, as well as disabled persons themselves, should be fully aware of the rights declared in this Declaration, in addition to other rights of disabled persons.

Self-help groups are organized by peers who share a common problem. Jaques and Patterson discuss the development of self-help and its implications for rehabilitation. The self-help service model is compared to the professional service model, and the unique but complementary contributions of each are discussed.

In a moving presentation concerning an international application of a self-help group, l'Arche Movement, Vanier focuses upon the contribution that handicapped people make to humanity. His firsthand experience as founder of the movement, which now encompasses nearly 50 communes of handicapped persons throughout the world, has provided Vanier with a philosophy of life that he sensitively and emotionally shares with the reader.

The final chapter in Part VII, "Women and Rehabilitation" by Thurer, examines several critical rehabilitation issues from a woman's perspective. In this timely chapter, the discussion of employment, psychological concerns, sexual exploitation, and motherhood identifies the needs of women that must be considered in maximizing their rehabilitation potential.

20

United Nations
New York
General Assembly
Resolution 3447 [XXX]
Adopted 9 December 1975:
Declaration on the Rights of
Disabled Persons

The General Assembly,

Mindful of the pledge made by Member States, under the Charter of the United Nations, to take joint and separate action in co-operation with the Organization to promote higher standards of living, full employment and conditions of economic and social progress and development,

Reaffirming its faith in human rights and fundamental freedoms and in the principles of peace, of the dignity and worth of the human person and of social justice proclaimed in the Charter,

Recalling the principles of the Universal Declaration of Human Rights,[9] the International Covenants on Human Rights,[10] the Declaration of the Rights of the Child[11] and the Declaration on the Rights of Mentally Retarded Persons,[12] as well as the standards already set for social progress in the constitutions, conventions, recommendations and resolutions of the International Labour Organisation, the United Nations Educational, Scientific and Cul-

[9]General Assembly resolution 217 A (III).
[10]General Assembly resolution 220 A (XXI), annex.
[11]General Assembly resolution 1386 (XIV).
[12]General Assembly resolution 2856 (XXVI).

tural Organization, the World Health Organization, the United Nations Children's Fund and other organizations concerned,

Recalling also Economic and Social Council resolution 1921 (LVIII) of 6 May 1975 on prevention of disability and rehabilitation of disabled persons,

Emphasizing that the Declaration of Social Progress and Development[13] has proclaimed the necessity of protecting the rights and assuring the welfare and rehabilitation of the physically and mentally disadvantaged,

Bearing in mind the necessity of preventing physical and mental disabilities and of assisting disabled persons to develop their abilities in the most varied fields of activities and of promoting their integration as far as possible in normal life,

Aware that certain countries, at their present stage of development, can devote only limited efforts to this end,

Proclaims this Declaration on the Rights of Disabled Persons and calls for national and international action to ensure that it will be used as a common basis and frame of reference for the protection of these rights:

1. The term "disabled person" means any person unable to ensure by himself or herself wholly or partly the necessities of a normal individual and/or social life, as a result of a deficiency, either congenital or not, in his or her physical or mental capabilities.

2. Disabled persons shall enjoy all the rights set forth in this Declaration. These rights shall be granted to all disabled persons without any exception whatsoever and without distinction or discrimination on the basis of race, colour, sex, language, religion, political or other opinions, national or social origins, state of wealth, birth or any other situation applying either to the disabled person himself or herself or to his or her family.

3. Disabled persons have the inherent right to respect for their human dignity. Disabled persons, whatever the origin, nature and seriousness of their handicaps and disabilities, have the same fundamental rights as their fellow-citizens of the same age, which implies first and foremost the right to enjoy a decent life, as normal and full as possible.

4. Disabled persons have the same civil and political rights as other human beings; article 7 of the Declaration of the Rights of Mentally Retarded Persons applies to any possible limitation or suppression of those rights for mentally disabled persons.

[13]General Assembly resolution 2542 (XXIV).

5. Disabled persons are entitled to the measures designed to enable them to become as self-reliant as possible.

6. Disabled persons have the right to medical, psychological and functional treatment, including prosthetic and orthotic appliances, to medical and social rehabilitation, education, vocational education, training and rehabilitation, aid, counseling, placement services and other services which will enable them to develop their capabilities and skills to the maximum and will hasten the process of their social integration or reintegration.

7. Disabled persons have the right to economic and social security and to a decent level of living. They have the right, according to their capabilities, to secure and retain employment or to engage in a useful, productive and remunerative occupation and to join trade unions.

8. Disabled persons are entitled to have their special needs taken into consideration at all stages of economic and social planning.

9. Disabled persons have the right to live with their families or with foster parents and to participate in all social, creative or recreational activities. No disabled person shall be subjected, as far as his or her residence is concerned, to differential treatment other than that required by his or her condition or by the improvement which he or she may derive therefrom. If the stay of a disabled person in a specialized establishment is indispensible, the environment and living conditions therein shall be as close as possible to those of the normal life of a person of his or her age.

10. Disabled persons shall be protected against all exploitation, all regulations and all treatment of a discriminatory, abusive or degrading nature.

11. Disabled persons shall be able to avail themselves of qualified legal aid when such aid proves indispensible for the protection of their persons and property. If judicial proceedings are instituted against them, the legal procedure applied shall take their physical and mental condition fully into account.

12. Organizations of disabled persons may be usefully consulted in all matters regarding the rights of disabled persons.

13. Disabled persons, their families and communities shall be fully informed, by all appropriate means, of the rights contained in this Declaration.

21

The Self-Help Group Model:
A Review

Marceline E. Jaques
Kathleen M. Patterson

The decade of the thirties saw the beginning of parallel movements in rehabilitative care. One was counseling and psychotherapy, developed on a
traditional base of professional care; the other was a "people's movement"
of self-help. For more than 35 years, these two helping systems have existed
side by side. They have expanded, matured, and grown beyond the expectations of their adherents; yet they have ignored or denied each other, have
rarely communicated, and have gone about their business as if the other
did not exist. Occasionally rumblings were heard, and more often than not
they were critical of the other's practices. A few individuals from each system
showed interest in the practices of the other, but interactions were rare and
superficial. Primarily, each seemed convinced of its "rightness of approach"
and chose not to examine its relationship or be examined.

The questions remain: What do the two approaches have in common?
Is it possible to share or move between the professional and the self-help
model? Or is the self-help process a unique modality of care not now widely known, acknowledged, or accepted by the professions, but a functional
part of a total rehabilitative system?

Recently, the professional world has shown more interest in the self-
help world as it has become progressively more difficult to ignore its growth
in numbers, size, and benefits. The reports of satisfaction by self-help group
members and the pragmatic results they have achieved for themselves have
been impressive, if not disturbing, to some professionals. These reports seem
to be in contrast to the general aura of self-doubt and dissatisfaction permeat-
ing the professionals' helping fields. Hard evidence that the professional serv-

From *Rehabilitation Counseling Bulletin*, 18(1) (1974), 48–58, Copyright © 1974 by the
American Personnel and Guidance Association. Reprinted with permission from the publisher and authors.

ice system works effectively for those seeking help is sparse. Too many persons with problems are either not cared for or cared for in an unsatisfactory manner.

GROUP TYPES AND PURPOSES

There are two basic types of self-help groups: (a) individuals with a certain condition or problem who have suffered a personal-social deprivation, such as Alcoholics Anonymous (AA) and Recovery, Inc., and (b) groups of families or friends of persons who have a condition or problem, such as Al-Anon, Alateen, and Parents of Retarded Children. Groups are also referred to as mutual aid groups. The labels, self-help and mutual aid, state concretely the purpose and method of these groups. Help for each member around specific problem areas is the group goal. Although groups of the first type are usually occupied with their personal problem solving and programs, the group members often fulfill an information-giving function to the interested public. Groups of the second type more often engage in advocacy, social action, and program development.

There seems to be a fine line of demarcation between a families/friends self-help group and a voluntary agency, with no clear-cut criteria of distinction. As the group grows in size it tends to develop structure and add services, usually given by professionals. This, of course, changes the original self-help and mutual aid function. The volunteers who join the group help the programs and support a common cause, though they may not share the problem. Examples are hundreds of college students and persons from all walks of life who volunteer their services as companions, foster grandparents, big brothers and sisters, and in other aspects of planning, program development, public information, and fund raising in large and small private agencies. The self-help and mutual aid may not be as clear-cut, at least not explicitly, although Riessman's helper principle (1965) of receiving therapeutic help in the process of helping others may apply.

Katz (1970) described five phases of development by which some self-help groups evolve a more complex organization: origin by disadvantaged persons and relatives, informal organization spread through friends and acquaintances, emergence of leaders, formal organization through rules and by-laws, and use of professional methods and staff. Zola (1972) described the development occurring in another order from voluntary lay associations of American pioneer days to mutual aid societies with membership based on social characteristics of race, religion, and country of origin. The original mutual aid was of a tangible, material type, like money lending, Zola reported. The tangible aid members gave to each other was followed by "aid of a more social psychological nature" (p. 180).

GROWTH AND DEVELOPMENT OF SELF-HELP MODEL

Self-help groups have undergone an impressive growth, although there is no up-to-date total directory or census. Mowrer (1964) reported that Maurice Jackson developed a directory in 1961–62 entitled *Their Brother's Keepers* and listed 265 different types of self-help groups. A recent survey of self-help organizations for the physically handicapped reported over 1,200 groups nationwide (Massachusetts Council of Organizations of the Handicapped, Inc. 1973). In their most recent directory, Alcoholics Anonymous (1973) reported 600,000 members throughout the world, with 405,858 United States members in 14,037 groups. This is a phenomenal story of growth and development, which began with two members in 1935. The Oxford group movement of that day is credited with providing some background for the AA method, though its tenets were considered too rigid by the AA founders (Alcoholics Anonymous 1955, 1957). AA has been used as a model for the development of other self-help groups, such as Synanon, Gamblers Anonymous, Neurotics Anonymous, Weight Watchers, and Overeaters Anonymous. Recovery, Inc., reported in their 1973 directory that they have 950 groups in 46 states and five Canadian provinces and one group each in Puerto Rico and Israel.

Self-help groups have spread not only across the nation but throughout the world. It is safe to say that more groups exist in the United States and Canada than in other parts of the world. They have spread, at least in contemporary times, from the United States to other countries in the manner of AA and Recovery, Inc. Katz (1964, 1965) reported two quite different self-help programs in England and Poland. The Psychiatric Rehabilitation Association in England has a program of social clubs or groups where numerous self-help functions are carried out for both former and present patients. Although these are done with official support and in official health centers, professionals are in the background, with the patients or clients actually planning, organizing, and directing the programs from counseling to planning job interviews and training. The programs are not limited to professional activities but may include cultural and social functions.

The Polish Union of Invalid Cooperatives exists so that disabled persons and their families may prepare themselves for work through both treatment and training. The cooperatives, not state-owned or managed, are set up on a self-help model. The disabled persons belong to the cooperatives, share in planning, and participate in the rehabilitation programs. Apartments, workshops, and business enterprises, along with counseling, training, and placement, are integral parts of the cooperative program. Participation in the planning and policymaking seems to provide high incentive and motivation toward self-help.

There is no end to the possible number and type of self-help groups. Their potential may be as variable as unsolved human problems or the special needs not met by existing social arrangements. Some behavioral scientists believe that the small group is in fact a new dimension in social organizations, counteracting the isolation of our time and the rigidity of an institution. Rogers (1973) described the emergence of a new kind of person, who uses the small informal group as an alternative to the structured bureaucratic institution. The traditions and structure of AA, for example, permit few organizational structures within or influences from outside. For example, chairpersons rotate monthly, and the work of the group is assumed by members for short periods of time. The group supports itself only by members' small contributions; no contributions from outside are permitted, therefore eliminating a potential source of control.

The Integrity Group movement described by Mowrer (1972) and the Self-Directed Therapeutic Group reported by Berzon and Solomon (1966) are related developments by professionals in counseling and psychotherapy who have used several aspects of the self-help mutual aid model. Frankel and Sloat (1971) described the total process of development of a self-help group for persons with physical, emotional, and social disabilities who wanted group involvement, but existing groups were not available to them. Colbert (1969) reported a program of planned mutual help at the Veterans Administration Hospital at Brentwood, Los Angeles, where the opportunity of giving as well as receiving help was incorporated into the rehabilitation program. This is an example of the use by professionals of a concept long known and practiced by self-help organizations.

EFFECTIVENESS OF THE SELF-HELP PROCESS

The nature of the self-help process has been commented on by a number of authors (Grosz 1972, 1973; Hurvitz 1970; Jaques 1972; Jaques and Perry 1974; Katz 1965, 1967, 1970; Mowrer 1972; Riessman 1965; Wechsler 1960; Wright 1971; Yalom 1970). In most cases authors, usually professionals, have read the sparse literature, attended meetings of self-help groups, collected self-reports of members, and, from an outsider's viewpoint, attempted to be objective, empirical observers. Two survey research projects were reported by Grosz and Wechsler. From the perspective of self-help group participant members, some reports have appeared in their own publications, such as the Recovery Reporter, the AA Grapevine, and Paraplegic News. In addition, an AA survey of its own membership was reported (Bailey and Leach 1965).

Positive aspects to members of self-help groups include the following knowledge, therapeutic, and skill dimensions: (a) gaining facts and knowledge of the condition; (b) social learning of coping mechanisms from those who are successfully living with the condition; (c) motivation and support by communicating with others who have shared a similar life experience; (d) the modeling effect of successful problem-solving behaviors, which provides reinforcement for new members and for long-term members; (e) self-evaluation of progress resulting from feedback and sharing with members at various stages of problem, knowledge, and levels of coping behavior; (f) identification with the group, providing a tangible sense of belonging, of an individual and social nature, and minimizing isolation and alienation; and (g) in the mutuality of the altruistic concern for others, finding self-help.

The self-help mutual aid group cannot be ignored as a system for maintaining rehabilitation gain and preventing deterioration of function over time. Modeling effect is provided by members who are coping with stigma problems and functioning adequately in life roles. Positive impact on social attitudes may be an additional gain from the coping behaviors demonstrated. Too frequently, negative, succumbing aspects of disadvantaged disability are emphasized in the media, particularly for fund-raising purposes (Wright 1969). Observing persons with handicapping problems functioning in the community and living "like other people" cannot help but enhance the quality of life for the able and disabled alike. AA group members report that persons are coming to their groups at earlier ages, which seems to demonstrate a more hopeful and accepting view of the problems presented. And, of course, the value of seeking help early cannot be overemphasized in rehabilitation.

A case study of Recovery, Inc., reported by Wechsler (1960), included the results of two surveys, one of the characteristics and opinions of members and the other of selected psychiatrists, members of the American Psychiatric Association in Detroit and Chicago. The results reported certain potential problem areas which concerned the psychiatrists sampled. These areas included the lack of medical or professional supervision, no system for the screening of members or of training leaders, and certain professional reservations about the Recovery method. The respondents did agree that the group aspect satisfied "the needs of some ex-patients for various forms of group support" (p. 309). The basic criticism resulted from a professional view of services giving little recognition to the validity of the self-help mutual aid group model as part of the total service system.

Recovery, Inc., was founded in 1937 by Abraham A. Low, a psychiatrist (Recovery, Inc. 1973b). Until his death in 1954, Low underwent years of attack and rejection by his colleagues. His biography (Rau and Rau 1971) documented his struggles to establish the self-help method. A recent survey by Grosz (1972, 1973) reflected a change in attitude on the part of the psychiatric profession to the Recovery approach. Grosz related this in part to the general climate of acceptance of the important role of paraprofessionals in mental health. For the last three years, Recovery panels have been a regular event at the annual meeting of the American Psychiatric Association.

OPERATIONAL ASSUMPTIONS

The basic operational assumptions of the self-help group approach are as follows:

1. Individuals come together because they have a specific personal problem or condition which they share (e.g., alcoholism, weight loss, paraplegia).
2. The status of peer relationships is maintained for all members within the group.
3. Peers, sharing the condition or problem, come together with the expectation of helping themselves and each other; that is, both the self-help and mutual aid aspects are central to the group process.
4. Behavior change is expected by and for each member. Learning a new way of life, presumably more satisfying, is undertaken at the individual's own pace.
5. Peers identify with the specific program developed by the group, become committed to its basic beliefs, tenets, and procedures, and actively support the program through practicing its principles in daily life.
6. Although the basic form of interaction is a regularly scheduled group meeting, peers are readily accessible and available to each other as needed outside of group meetings. This interaction is of a one-to-one type relationship, so both group and individual modes of contact are used.
7. The group process consists of actively relating, "owning," and revealing problems; receiving and giving feedback to each other; and sharing hope, experiences, encouragement, and criticism in relation to the day-to-day goals of individual behavior change.
8. Members are held responsible for themselves and their behavior. This involves being honest about themselves, both within and outside the context of the group interaction.
9. Group leadership develops and changes from within the group on the basis of giving and receiving help in keeping with the program's purposes and principles.
10. Status comes from helping and being helped effectively, which in turn provides the validity for the program. Status achieved outside the group is of little, if any, value after joining the group; in fact, if it is used manipulatively, it can work against a member's status within the group.

These assumptions have been experientially derived and remain untested, but they are supported pragmatically by the demonstrated help group members receive. Why and how the self-help methods work for so many individuals are common and challenging questions to the professional. Basic themes of many self-help stories shared in the groups are of past experiences and relationships with professionals which were not satisfactory or helpful with their problems. Part of the cathartic value of self-help groups is in sharing past frustrations with other members who have experienced them, knowing there is hope and help within "their program." The self-help experience was described in the words of one member as "a weight of despair being lifted from my life" and "at last I can experience some joy in living" (personal communication, April 1972). It is a common observation and sometimes a surprise to new members and visitors that self-help group meetings are happy occasions with much humor and laughter shared.

THE PROFESSIONAL MODEL: A LOOK WITHIN

The feeling held by many self-help group members is that their professional experience or contact has not been helpful and, in some instances, even harmful. That these perceptions are not unrealistic has been verified by the experience of many persons, both professional and nonprofessional, who have attested to the ineffectiveness and fragmentation of much service delivery. By and large professionals still ignore, if not downgrade, the self-help model, although there is evidence that a change in attitude is occurring (Wright 1973). Self-help and professional groups alike seem to be increasingly more open, trustful, and appreciative of each other's unique experience and knowledge.

Tyler (1973) referred to a shift on the part of persons needing help away from the professional therapist to others who understand because they have had the same problems. "Alcoholics Anonymous was perhaps the first herald of this change in the manner in which psychological difficulties were to be dealt with" (p. 1022).

The Lasker Award was given to AA in 1951 by the American Public Health Association. The citation stated: "Historians may one day recognize Alcoholics Anonymous to have been a great venture in social pioneering which forged a new instrument for social action; a new therapy based on the kinship of common suffering; one having a vast potential for the myriad other ills of mankind" (Alcoholics Anonymous 1955, p. 573). The role of the helping professional changed from that of a therapist in the medical model to a consultant who suggests rather than prescribes. An equally dramatic change is emerging in the role of the person needing help, from a passive recipient of a service to a consumer who can not only make choices among alternatives, but who also assumes responsibility as the manager of a personal rehabilitative plan. Some problems of professional service delivery may be inherent in the rigid impersonal nature of the bureaucracy and organizations within which agencies exist. Some organizational shifts are apparent in rehabilitation service delivery systems generally, and others are underway (Morris 1973).

Programs of client advocacy have developed over the last decade. The provisions within the Rehabilitation Act of 1973 for consumer participation in program planning and evaluation, a specific client-counselor program planning review process, and program review by a third party make these concerns explicit. They attempt to assure that the clients are truly comanagers of the rehabilitation process. Whether or not the reforms contemplated will be more than paper plans, honestly reflecting humanness and personal concern for individuals with problems in concrete ways, is yet to be tested in practice.

A number of groups have developed statements of need or codes outlining their basic human rights as individuals. Geist and others (1973) called for agencies to develop codes of ethical practices, pointing out the necessity for agency ethic accountability to consumers if individual professional codes of ethical standards are to have real meaning in practice. Clearly, consumer input has already had considerable effect on the service providers, both institutions and professionals' practices, but this is only a small beginning. The professional enterprise itself is in need of careful reexamination. Change in organizations, institutions and service delivery systems will not modify negative or unhelpful professional attitudes and practices, and it is here that the self-help group experience can be most useful. Its essence of helpfulness seems to pinpoint the areas where professional blind spots and insensitivity exist.

History shows that a self-help group appeared where professionals did not or could not help. The self-help movement is a reflection of professional pressure points due, in part, to a lack of knowledge but also due to rigidity in professional behavior and beliefs. Yet at each junction of a new self-help group development, a few professionals out of step with their colleagues and the times, in thinking and practice, turned the tide to a new approach. For example, the founders of AA, a stockbroker and a physician, both hopeless alcoholics, credit the work of three professionals for the ideas and inspiration that brought AA into existence (Alcoholics Anonymous 1957, p. 262): W. D. Silkworth, "benign little doctor who loved drunks," William James' great wisdom in his *Varieties of Religious Experience*, and Carl Jung's statement that "science had no answer for the alcoholic." Abraham Low's persistence against professional attacks, referred to earlier, showed the way to a major self-help movement. Charles Dederich, founder of Synanon, is another example of a person whose beliefs, practices, and courageous struggles were in tune with the needs of persons fighting addiction.

THE RELATIONSHIP OF THE PROFESSIONAL TO THE SELF-HELP MODEL

During the last three years both authors have had occasion to relate to the two systems of self-care and professional care in new and highly personal ways. The first author moved from a primary professional stance to the study and experience of the self-help approach, and the second author from self-help group experience of long standing to graduate training in rehabilitation counseling. A unique opportunity to share and learn from each helping modality resulted. Although the experiences of self-help and the professional process are unique, it is possible to share and move between these systems, but only under certain conditions. For example, a professional cannot be a self-help group member or leader unless the conditions of common problem, peer relationship, and mutual aid exist. Any other arrangement would be a violation of the self-help model. Professionals who do not or choose not to meet these conditions can relate only in the capacity of visitor-observer. On invitation a professional can act as a consultant or speaker. The professional therapeutic skills as such cannot be used inside the self-help group. That, of course, would also be a violation of self-help precepts.

It may be that both parties to the helping contract can learn what to expect and what to ask of each other and how they relate to the total rehabilitation task. For example, self-help groups might be able to ask professionals to help study aspects of the process self-help groups do so well. The variables of effectiveness within the helping system could be more precisely defined and isolated to study the patterns of this process. Some members drop out of groups while others stay. How many are in each category, and what characteristics differentiate them? What are the characteristics of those who return again and again?

Professionals could learn to ask self-help group members for specific and regular feedback on their help-getting experiences. Members' reactions and suggestions, as consumers of these services, could be effective in improving and humanizing the total service delivery functions. A plan for evaluation of each individual service interaction might be initiated just as courses and professors' performance are evaluated by students. Better Business Bureaus exist to protect consumers and monitor practices. Certainly as much vigilance should be given to human-helping services. Plans might be developed for confronting the social and community barriers that plague both groups, such as public understanding of problems of disability, deprivation, and job and other types of discrimination.

Raising these issues and other questions could lead to an openness in communication which does not now exist between helpers and those on the receiving end of service delivery. The feedback from this interaction might significantly modify therapeutic practices, rehabilitation outcomes, and professional attitudes, resulting in help being given and received more effectively to the contractual standards set by both parties. A more humanized service delivery system could result. Clearly, both models, the self-help and the professional, are necessary parts of a total rehabilitation service system.

REFERENCES

Alcoholics Anonymous. *Alcoholics Anonymous: The story of how many thousands of men and women have recovered from alcoholism.* New York: Alcoholics Anonymous World Services, 1955.

Alcoholics Anonymous. *Alcoholics Anonymous comes of age.* New York: Alcoholics Anonymous Publishing, 1957.

Alcoholics Anonymous. *Alcoholics Anonymous world directory.* New York: Alcoholics Anonymous World Services, spring 1973.

Bailey, M. B. and Leach, B. *Alcoholics Anonymous: Pathway to recovery.* New York: National Council on Alcoholism, July 1965.

Berzon, B. and Solomon, L. N. The self-directed therapeutic group: Three studies. *Journal of Counseling Psychology,* 1966, 13(4).

Colbert, J. N. Philosophia habilitatus: Toward a policy of human rehabilitation in the post-institutional phase of disability. *Journal of Rehabilitation,* 1969, 35(5), 18–20.

Frankel, A. and Sloat, W. E. The odyssey of a self-help group. *Psychological Aspects of Disability,* 1971, 18(1), 41–42.

Geist, G. O., Curin, S., Prestridge, R., and Schelb, G. Ethics and the counselor-agency relationship. *Rehabilitation Counseling Bulletin,* 1973, 17(1), 15–21.

Grosz, H. J. *Recovery, Inc., survey: A preliminary report.* Chicago: Recovery, Inc., May 1972.

Grosz, H. J. *Recovery, Inc., survey: Second report.* Chicago: Recovery, Inc., May 1973.

Hurvitz, N. Peer self-help psychotherapy groups and their implications for psychotherapy. *Psychotherapy: Theory, Research and Practice,* 1970, 7(1), 41–49.

Jaques, M. E. Rehabilitation counseling and support personnel. *Rehabilitation Counseling Bulletin,* 1972, 15(3), 160–171.

Jaques, M. E. and Perry, J. W. Education in the health and helping professions: Philosophic context, multidisciplinary team models and cultural components. In J. Hamburg (Ed.), *Review of allied health education,* Vol. 1. Lexington, Ky.: University Press of Kentucky, 1974.

Katz, A. Poland's self-help rehabilitation program. *Rehabilitation Record,* 1964, 5(3), 30–32.

Katz, A. Application of self-help concepts in current social welfare. *Social Work,* 1965, 10(3), 68–74.

Katz, A. Self-help in rehabilitation: Some theoretical aspects. *Rehabilitation Literature,* 1967, 28(1), 10–11, 30.

Katz, A. Self-help organizations and volunteer participation in social welfare. *Social Work,* 1970, 15(1), 51–60.

Massachusetts Council of Organizations of the Handicapped, Inc. *A directory of organizations of the handicapped in the United States.* Hyde Park, Mass.: Author, 1973.

Morris, R. Welfare reform 1973: The social service dimension. *Science,* August 10, 1973, 181(4099), 515–522.

Mowrer, O. H. *The new group therapy.* Princeton, N.J.: Van Nostrand, 1964.

Mowrer, O. H. Integrity groups: Basic principles and objectives. *Counseling Psychologist,* 1972, 3(2), 7–33.

Rau, N. and Rau, M. R. *My dear ones.* Englewood Cliffs, N.J.: Prentice-Hall, 1971.

Recovery, Inc. *Recovery, Inc., National directory.* Chicago, Ill.: Author, January 1973. (a)

Recovery, Inc. *Recovery, Inc., What it is and how it developed.* Chicago, Ill.: Author, 1973. (b)

Riessman, F. The "helper" therapy principle. *Social Work,* 1965, *10*(2), 27–32.

Rogers, C. R. *The emerging person: A new revolution.* La Jolla, Calif.: Center for Studies of the Person, 1973.

Tyler, L. E. Design for a hopeful psychology. *American Psychologist,* 1973, *28*(12), 1021–1029.

Wechsler, H. The self-help organization in the mental health field: Recovery, Inc., A case study. *Journal of Nervous and Mental Disorders,* 1960, *130*(4), 297–314.

Wright, B. A. Activism versus passivism in coping with disability. In Ireland National Rehabilitation Board (Ed.), *Proceedings of the Eleventh World Congress of Rehabilitation International, Community Responsibility for Rehabilitation.* Dublin, Ireland: National Rehabilitation Board, 1969.

Wright, B. A. Changes in attitudes toward people with handicaps. *Rehabilitation Literature,* 1973, *34*(12), 354–357, 368.

Wright, M. E. Self-help groups in the rehabilitation enterprise. *Psychological Aspects of Disability,* 1971, *18*(1), 43–45.

Yalom, I. *The theory and practice of group psychotherapy.* New York: Basic Books, 1970.

Zola, I. K. The problems and prospects of mutual aid groups. *Rehabilitation Psychology,* 1972, *19*(4), 180–183.

22

The Contribution of the Physically and Mentally Handicapped to Development

Jean Vanier

Those who live close to wounded people become rather accustomed to hearing talks about how so-called "normal" people should help their unfortunate brothers and sisters. We rarely ask what handicapped people can bring to others. The very thought rarely comes to mind; it seems so remote and far-fetched.

And yet I feel deeply that handicapped people have an important part to play in the development of the world, in helping it to find its equilibrium. They can insure that development is not just a development of mind and matter, but a development of the total human person, who is certainly intelligence and creativity, activity and productivity, but who is also a heart, capable of love, a seeker of peace, hope, light, and trust, striving to assume the reality of suffering and of death.

I have had the grace and joy to live with mentally handicapped adults over the last ten years. With friends, we have been able to create some forty-five small homes for men and women who were either roaming the streets, locked up in asylums, or just living idly — though frequently in a state of aggression or depression — with families who did not know how to cope with them. These homes of l'Arche are in France, Canada, the United States, England, Scotland, Belgium, and Denmark, as well as in Calcutta and Bangalore in India; our first home in West Africa is just beginning in the Ivory Coast. Each of these homes welcomes and finds work for eight to ten handicapped men and women and for their helpers or assistants. They try to

Published in *"Development and Participation — Operational Implications for Social Welfare":* *Proceedings of the XVIIth International Conference on Social Welfare, Nairobi, Kenya,* 290–297. (Published 1975 for the International Council on Social Welfare by Columbia University Press, New York & London.) Reprinted by permission.

be communities of reconciliation where everyone can grow in activity, creativity, love, and hope. Some of the handicapped people leave us and find total autonomy; others, who are more severely handicapped, will stay with us always.

It is this experience of daily living, working, and sharing with my handicapped brothers and sisters that has made me so sensitive to the question of their contribution to the development of our world. A man or woman can only find peace of heart and grow in motivation and creativity if he or she finds a meaning to life. If they are there only to be helped and can bring nothing to others, then they are condemned to a life of simply receiving, of being the last, the most inferior. This will necessarily bring them to depression and a lack of confidence in themselves. This in turn will push them into anguish and make them aggressive towards themselves and others. For them to find real meaning in life, they must find people who sense their utility, their capacity for growth, and their place in the community and in the world.

The tragedy of humanity is not primarily the lack of development of peoples, or even poverty. It is the oppression, the despisal, and the rejection of those who are weak and in want. It is the horrible and disastrous inequality of wealth and opportunity and lack of sharing. The tragedy of man is his hardness of heart, which makes individuals and nations endowed with the riches of this world despise and consider as inferior those who are poor and handicapped. They not only refuse to help them; they tend also to reject and exploit them.

The tragedy of mankind is the collective national or religious prejudices and pride which close nations and peoples upon themselves, making them think and act as if they were the elected ones and the others enemies to be rejected and hurt, whose development and expansion should be checked. Our world today, with its terrible divisions and hatred, with its continual sounds of war, with its vast budgets being poured into armaments instead of into works for love and justice, is the result of these prejudices and fears.

The tragedy of our world today is that man is still afraid of man. Far from seeing other individuals and peoples as collaborators in the mystery of universal human growth, we see them as enemies of our own growth and development.

It is of course terribly important that misery and starvation be erased from our earth. It is of course terribly important that everyone has access to social and medical benefits. But it is even more important that the hearts of all men open up to universal love and to the understanding of others, to gentle service to mankind and especially to its weaker members. For if we do not work together to create a world of fraternity and of peace, we will sink in wars, economic crises, and national disasters.

There is a continual struggle in all our countries between traditional religious and moral values, lived through family ties, and economic and industrial development. Highly industrialized countries offer a certain financial prosperity, but so frequently this prosperity has been achieved at the cost of the values of community. Competition and the desire for wealth, individual leisure, and liberty have tended to crush compassion and understanding. So it is that we find old people lingering in homes for the aged, handicapped people in large institutions, and a mass of marginal and suffering people unable to work because of alcoholism, drugs, and social ills. We find thousands of children abandoned and given over to social agencies, a frightening rise in delinquency, and prisons which offer only punishment instead of reeducation and so cause the high rise in recidivism. We find mental disease rampant, because in our search for efficiency we have lost our acceptance of "the other" and prefer to label people "mad" rather than to understand them. We condemn more and more people to live like strangers, in terrible loneliness, in our large urban conglomerations. The growing population of our cities, our disastrous housing, and inhuman working conditions bring a real disequilibrium of the human heart in its quest for love, peace, and truth.

In the small villages of Africa and India, or in rural areas of North America and Europe, there are still sturdy people living simply off the land and artisans bound closely to the matter with which they work. There is deep love and commitment among families. There is a spirit of gentleness and openness, sharing and welcome for the stranger, which has often been lost in the big cities. Certainly this is a generalization, for there are also tribal warfares and social injustices and individual anguishes. But we must not forget the values of fraternity and community held by simple people, which are so often crushed with the coming of economic development. We can see the gradual breakdown of these values as the desire for material possessions is stimulated, as the attractions of big-city leisure activities become stronger, and the older generation and its ways are rejected.

Of course, it is essential that people should develop and find the benefits of greater wealth and security. But it is even more essential that this development take place in a human context that safeguards and strengthens the forces of sharing, participation, and responsibility. Where economic development take place in a human context that safeguards and strengthens villages are destroyed, where children are displaced and men obliged to leave their homes for far-off lands, the situation is extremely serious: It can gradually cause the destruction of what makes a human person a person.

In each of us there is a mixture of weakness and strength. Each of us is born in weakness, unable to fend for ourselves, to find nourishment, to clothe ourselves, or to walk. The growth to autonomy is long and slow, and demands many years of loving education. The period of strength and capacity, during adolescence and manhood, the period during which we are able to act efficaciously and to defend ourselves, to struggle against the forces of nature and environment, is in fact short. After it, we all enter a period of weakness, when our bodies become tired and sick, when we are hurt by the trials and sufferings inherent in human life. And all of us are then called to the last and final poverty of death.

The child in his weakness has all the potential of activity which must grow in him. The strongest of men is inherently weak, because he has a mortal body, and also because he is called to love and is vulnerable to the sufferings of love and of infidelity in friendship; he is weak because he is capable of depression and sadness, drowning in the vicissitudes of life.

The society that encourages only the strong and the intelligent tends to forget that man is essentially weak. We are all potentially handicapped, and we are all created to suffer and to die. So often the search for riches, or hyperactivity in work, is a flight from these essential realities which we must all face one day. What is the meaning of our life, and of suffering, and of death? Are we called simply to be active and to gather wealth, or does man find peace of heart, interior liberty, and happiness in the growth of love? Is it not in service to others, sharing, and mutual understanding—which is not mere sentimentality—that we find this inner peace and human fulfillment?

If people do not refind this energy of love and acceptance of their own intrinsic poverty, if they do not discover that joy comes more in giving than in taking, we are heading for more conflict. If we do not grow in the desire to give our lives rather than to exploit and take the lives of others, than we are all doomed to destruction.

In all societies there are vast numbers of weaker brothers and sisters: those who are aged or depressed, those who have been struck by sickness while young and cannot take on a working life. Are these people just misfits who must be gradually eliminated? Are they just people we must try to reeducate so that they become active members of society? Or have they a special place and role in the development of our society? This is the question we must ask ourselves.

My experience of living with the wounded, the weak, is that they have very precious values which must be conserved for the full development of society. Their experience of rejection, their experience of suffering which is a taste of death, has brought them closer to certain realities that others who have not suffered flee and pretend do not exist.

Handicapped people have all the rights of other men: the right to life, to medical and social help, and to work. They are able, when this is recognized, to develop in so many ways. With the right educational and work techniques, many can find their place in the world of work and become totally integrated in that world. I have seen men who at the age of six were judged incapable of any growth, working in a factory at the age of twenty and living quite autonomously. Others who were condemned to asylums, to beggary, or to total inactivity are now finding fulfillment as artisans and enjoying life in the community. With care, loving attention, and the right kind of technical help, many can find their place in society.

Handicapped people, and particularly those who are less "able," are frequently endowed with qualities of heart that serve to remind so-called "normal" people that their own hearts are closed. Their simplicity frequently serves to reveal our own duplicity, untruthfulness, and hypocrisy. Their acceptance of their own situation and their humility frequently reveal our pride and our refusal to accept others as they are.

I had occasion once to appear on television with Helen and some others. Helen has cerebral palsy. She cannot talk, she cannot walk, she cannot eat by herself. She is condemned to a wheelchair for the rest of her life. Her only means of communication is through a typewriter, on which she laboriously expresses her thoughts with two fingers. But Helen has the most beautiful smile. She gives herself through her smile. At one moment in the program, someone asked her if she was happy. She broke out into a big smile and typed: "I wouldn't change my life for anything in the world." Her smile got even bigger, and as the program closed, the camera picked up the last word she was writing: "Alleluia!"

Helen, who has nothing except her joy and her love, revealed to me and to so many who possess the goods of this earth that fulfillment does not come from material riches but from some inner strength and liberty. Through her acceptance of herself and her condition, she showed how poor we are, in all our petty quarrels, pride, and desires.

At a week's meeting with some two hundred people, there was a handicapped man called Glen. He could not use his legs, and he lay on the floor. During the last day, there was a period when each person could express what he felt about the week's activity. Glen propped himself up and just said: "I have only one thing to tell you: I love you all so much." His simple words broke down the barriers of convention and of fear in many of us. He wasn't afraid to talk of love.

So often "normal" people have interior barriers that prevent them from relating with others in a simple way. All of us have deep needs to love and to be loved. All of us are in the conflict of our fear of death and of our own poverty. We so quickly pretend we are more clever, more intelligent, and more powerful than we actually are. So often we flee reality by throwing ourselves into activity, culture, and the struggle for power and prestige. We lose contact with our deep inner selves. Handicapped people do not always have these barriers. In their poverty, they are more simple and loving, and thus they reveal to us the poverty of our riches.

The weaker members of society are total human persons, children of God. They are not misfits or objects of charity. Their weaknesses and special needs demand deep attention, real concern, and continuing support. If we listen to their call and to their needs, they will flourish and grow. If we do not, they will sink into depression, sadness, inward revolt, and a form of spiritual suicide. And we who carry responsibilities will have closed our beings to love and to a strength which comes from God and which is hidden in the smallest and the weakest.

Those who take time to listen to them, who have the inner peace and patience to respond to their silent call, will hear crying in them the great cry of all humanity for love and for peace. A great Dutch psychiatrist has written of the schizophrenic that he is not insane, not made of wood, but is "the loudspeaker from whom the sufferings of our time ring perhaps most clearly" (Foundraine, 1974). The same can be said for all weak and handicapped people who cannot fend for themselves.

If we listen to them, then we, the so-called "normal" people, will be healed of our unconscious egoisms, our hardness of heart, our search for power and for dissipating leisure. We will discover that love, communion, presence, community, and deep interior liberty and peace are realities to be found and lived. We will discover that these can become the inspiration for all men. We will realize more fully that men are not machines or objects to be used, exploited, tyrannized, and manipulated by law and by organizations, but that each one is beautiful and precious, that each one in his uniqueness is like a flower which should find its place in the garden of humanity for the fulfillment and beauty of all mankind.

If each one of us who holds a responsible place in society pays attention to the heartbeats of the smallest, the weakest, and the companionless, then gradually we will make of our countries not lands of competition, which favor the strong and powerful, but lands of justice, peace, and fraternity where all men unite and cooperate for the good of every man.

Then nations will no longer rival each other in their search for power, prestige, and wealth, but will work together. They will turn from fear and from group prejudices and from the creation of large and horribly expensive armies. They will use their intelligence, strength, wealth, and natural resources for the growth of all men throughout the world, and especially for the smallest, the weakest, and the companionless. Mankind will then, through the heart of the poor and those crucified in their flesh, refind the road to unity and universal love, where all can be themselves without fear, growing together in love and in the peace of God, our beloved Father.

REFERENCE

Foundraine, J. *Not made of wood.* London: Quartet Books, 1974.

23

Women and Rehabilitation

Shari L. Thurer

The occurrence of disability is a jolt. To assert that it is more devastating for one gender than another begs the issue: It is a psychosocial shock for most persons. But the fact that the pain of disability is sex-blind does not imply that the issues are the same for males and females. Nor does it imply that rehabilitation service is equitable. To date, there has been very little attention paid to the concerns of disabled women. Public disability policy was originally designed to address the needs of males in the labor force; scientific inquiry into the psychology of disability, especially that concerning sexuality, is most frequently from a male point of view; the special needs of women have not been recognized. This dearth of literature, in itself, suggests a certain bias. The following, then, is an attempt to partially redress this lack of attention by highlighting some of the areas of special concern to disabled women.

EMPLOYMENT

Disabled women are much less likely to have paid employment than men.[2] Levitan and Taggart[11] found that 60 percent of men with disabilities have paying jobs, compared to only 29 percent of women with disabilities. While the weekly wage of employed disabled males averaged 79 percent that of nondisabled males, the ratio for females was lower—74 percent of nondisabled women.[11] Although relatively fewer disabled women seek jobs, these data imply that such women are at a double disadvantage. Employers may be reluctant to hire them because of their disability *and* their gender. Moreover, these statistics suggest that the whole may be greater than the sum of its parts: that disabled women face *more* employer resistance than the

From *Rehabilitation Literature, 43* (7–8) (1982), 194–197. Reprinted with permission. Published by the National Easter Seal Society, 2023 W. Ogden, Chicago, IL 60612.

I wish to extend thanks to Janna Zwerner, counselor, Boston Self-Help, and Sanda Wiper, student at Boston University, for sharing their ideas with me; and to the staff of the Massachusetts Rehabilitation Commission for aid in research.

combination of the factors of gender plus disability can account for. While 70 percent of disabled males who had been working in the year before the onset of their condition were employed in 1966, only 44 percent of former-ly working women had returned to work.[7]

Even a cursory observation of the current employment situation con-firms the implications of these figures. Disabled women are not meaningfully present in the work place. The leaders of the disabled rights movement are, more often than not, male; the rehabilitation establishment is dominated by men. When women with disabilities are trained for jobs, they are fre-quently trained for less skilled jobs because they are female.[2, p. 104]

BENEFITS

Disability policy in the United States was originally tailored to the needs of formerly working males. Only later were individuals with more tenuous ties to the labor market (i.e., females) included. Even today, women receive not only fewer but also less generous benefits from the major programs — disability insurance, supplemental security income, workers' compensation, and vocational rehabilitation.[10] Since eligibility for benefits includes partic-ipation in the labor force for a prescribed period of time, and since disabili-ty insurance benefits correlate with earnings, women in a sense are punished for having been unpaid homemakers prior to the onset of disability. Con-versely, women are overrepresented under supplemental security income, which is a public assistance program that supports disabled individuals *be-low* the poverty level.

One of the most glaring inequities in service delivery to disabled men and women is found in the vocational rehabilitation program, especially with respect to the nature of rehabilitation outcome (i.e., work status and occupa-tion) and its correlate, weekly earnings at closure. Hence, in fiscal year 1976, one woman in three was in a non-wage-earning activity at rehabilitation clo-sure (homemaking and unpaid family work), compared to only one man in 15. The mean weekly wage at rehabilitation closure was $63 for women and $112 for men. Only 2.1 percent of the women, compared to 10.3 percent of the men, were earning $200 or more per week at closure. Also, vocational rehabilitation services may be underutilized by women in the first place — only 47 percent of referrals are female,[13] and the "typical" client that the Division of Vocational Rehabilitation sends for a work evaluation is male.[16]

These data do not incontrovertibly prove sex discrimination, but it is clear that a woman is less likely than a man to receive most kinds of train-ing. As Sachs has written:

> . . . while one woman in three is rehabilitated as a non-wage-earner nationally, it is safe to assume that this proportion is higher in some agencies. These agen-

cies, in particular, should review their placement policies for female clients. Surely, two questions to be answered from such a review would be, "Was the homemaker closure really what the client wanted?" and "Was this closure appropriate to the situation?"[13]

Ironically, women may have a greater need for disability benefits. Kutza examined the Social Security Administration's 1972 *Survey of Disabled and Nondisabled*[8] and found that women represent a greater proportion of persons in the population who report experiencing one or more chronic conditions or impairments. They are more likely than men to be limited or prevented from working because of their disability, and are likely to experience a higher degree of work disability at an earlier age than men. Analyzing data in the Office for Handicapped Individuals' 1979 *Digest*,[4] Kutza found, in addition, that disabled women are more likely to be without a spouse than disabled men.[10] Such a situation naturally deprives them of the benefits that may accrue from the presence of a husband, such as greater income and perhaps greater attention to personal care needs. In short, women with disabilities may tend to be worse off than men with disabilities, and receive fewer benefits. Clearly, disabled women require a more responsive public policy.

THE PSYCHOLOGY OF WOMEN WITH DISABILITIES

That men and women respond differently to disease is rarely questioned, but almost never examined. To be sure, there are isolated studies available, such as one suggesting that injury or deformity which mars aesthetic quality of the body is likely to have more serious significance for a woman than a man. He is more likely to be affected by any chronic illness which enforces dependence on others and interferes with capacity for work.[12] Another study indicates that women are more concerned than men with the effects of their disability on their personal relationships.[9] But these findings, while important, do not go far enough toward providing a thoroughgoing and rigorous understanding of the interaction of gender and handicap.

The issues beg consideration. It is commonly acknowledged that there is a cultural expectation for women to be passive and dependent, and that there are similar expectations for individuals with disabilities. Faced with compound pressure for compliance and docility, how do women with disabilities cope? How may they avoid being psychologically undermined? Recently, the Task Force on Concerns of Physically Disabled Women (1978) reported some of the experiences of women with disabilities. These included issues of body image, dependence, social and sexual vulnerability, intimacy, relationships with parents—all areas special to the experience of being female.[17] Unfortunately, there appears to be very little empirical data to shed light on these areas.

Sexuality is a case in point. The literature is replete with studies of the sexuality of males with spinal cord injury. But only very recently have researchers addressed the female response.[1,3] To date, we have only very imperfect advice to offer disabled women on sexual exploration, orgasm, family planning, menstruation, menopause, and similar important aspects of being female. Indeed, numerous women have reported instances of gross insensitivity by medical staff regarding these matters.[17]

SEXUAL EXPLOITATION

Public lack of awareness notwithstanding, there seems to be an alarming incidence of women with disabilities who suffer from sexual abuse — specifically, harassment, molestation, incest, and rape. While there is almost no attention paid to these matters in the professional or even popular media, they are issues of great concern to disabled women themselves. Recently, women have been voicing their distress at various conferences across America, such as at the workshop entitled "The Disabled Person and Sexual Assault," held at Minnesota's Southwest State University in the spring of 1980[15]; the Eighth Annual Conference on Feminist Psychology, held in Boston in March, 1981; and the Third Annual Symposium on Sexuality and Disability at New York University in June, 1981. Visually impaired women complain of unwanted and objectionable looks as well as contact by men who may deem them unconscious of these acts and/or vulnerable. Mobility-impaired women have spoken of encounters with men who are perversely attracted to their prostheses. Numerous reports of sexual abuse by caregivers are offered by physically and developmentally disabled women and their associates. Sanford, author of *The Silent Children,* indicated that the use of disabled children in pornographic films is becoming more common.[14]

Just why there has been no popular acknowledgment of these issues is speculative. Disabled individuals are often stereotyped as asexual, so perhaps the public does not readily associate them with sexual acts. Law enforcement officials typically do not record whether the victim of sexual abuse is disabled or not. Probably more cases go unreported anyway. Seemingly, the only available data documenting these problems are contained in a startling report by the Developmental Disabilities Project of Seattle Rape Relief. This project recorded over 300 incidents involving sexual exploitation of physically or mentally disabled persons between July, 1977, and December, 1979. These cases include both adult and child victims of rape, incest, and indecent liberties in the Seattle/King County regions of Washington. The study contains speculation that only 25–30 percent of all disabled victims report the event, and its authors also estimate that up to 30,000 cases of sexual exploitation involving disabled persons occur each year in Washington state alone.[5]

Project data also indicate that only 1 percent of reported cases involve sex offenders who are strangers to the disabled victim. Most persons with disabilities are exploited by "friends," acquaintances, or relatives. These offenders include neighbors, boyfriends, staff persons in residential facilities, bus drivers, aides, fathers, and foster fathers. Frequently the victim is in a position of dependency upon the sexual offender.[5] There appears to be a great need for consciousness-raising in this area among both rehabilitation professionals and individuals with disabilities, as well as in the community at large.

MOTHERS

While not readily thought a "women's issue," or even an issue at all, the difficult situation of mothers of individuals with disabilities should be examined. These women often struggle with a relentless grind of caring for an individual who may require feeding, dressing, toileting, frequent medical treatment, and constant supervision. Of course men may be involved in these tasks, but typically it is the female parent who is in charge of vigilantly overseeing the child's care. Sometimes, these mothers have no respite.

Medical and rehabilitation professionals have compounded the problems of such women in a number of ways. By strongly supporting the deinstitutionalization and mainstreaming movements, they have inadvertently reinforced a moral climate suggesting that individuals with disabilities — no matter what their nursing and personal care needs — are best served in the home. This implies care by one's mother; after all, mothers are culturally designated to be at home and do the caretaking. While the deinstitutionalization movement is highly praiseworthy, it may place an undue burden on individual women. Even when deinstitutionalization has not been put into practice and when residential care continues to be publicly provided, the cultural notion that this care is "less good" may be highly guilt-inducing for the mother involved. If and when the child is returned home, the mother may be faced with a life of unremitting servitude. Certainly such a choice should be hers and not the government's.

Ironically, the mother of an individual with disabilities endures not only the pain of loss and the burdens of caretaking, but she is often seen as the cause of the disability. Perhaps she sipped a glass of wine during pregnancy or underwent natural childbirth; or perhaps she did *not* undergo natural childbirth, or averted her eyes for a moment as her child turned on the stove. Mothers of children with emotional disorders may be especially vulnerable to blame. Theories abound which imply that mothers cause mental disease, such as schizophrenia ("the mother herself must have been schizophrenic"), and autism ("the mother is probably cold, humorless, and perfectionistic"). Scientific proof, in these cases, is nonexistent.

Finally, mothers are expected to oversee a treatment plan, no matter how unrealistic in terms of time, energy, money, and the demands on the rest of the family. Sometimes she is expected to do so with little outside support, much conflicting advice from other professionals, and little promise of success—and when things do not proceed smoothly, she is blamed! Should she discourage her child from unnecessary risks, she may be deemed "overprotective"; should she encourage independence, she may be deemed "neglectful" or "rejecting"; should she demur from following any professional advice, she may be called a "saboteur." Featherstone movingly captures the frustrations of the mother's predicament. When told by a well-intentioned nurse to brush her disabled child's teeth three times a day, for five minutes, with an electric toothbrush, this was the mother's response:

> Although I tried to sound reasonable on the phone, this new demand appalled me. I rehearsed angry, self-justifying speeches in my head. Jody, I thought, is blind, cerebral-palsied, and retarded. We do his physical therapy daily and work with him on sounds and communication. We feed him each meal on our laps, bottle him, change him, bathe him, dry him, put him in a body cast to sleep, launder his bed linens daily, and go through a variety of routines designed to minimize his miseries and enhance his joys and his development. (All this in addition to trying to care for and enjoy our other young children and making time for each other and our careers.) Now you tell me that I should spend fifteen minutes every day on something that Jody will hate, an activity that will not help him to walk or even defecate, but one that is directed at the health of his gums. This activity is not for a finite time but forever. It is not guaranteed to help, "it can't hurt." And it won't make the overgrowth go away but may retard it. Well, it's too much. Where is that fifteen minutes going to come from? What am I supposed to give up? Taking the kids to the park? Reading a bedtime story to my eldest? Washing the breakfast dishes? Sorting the laundry? Grading students' papers? Sleeping? Because there is no time in my life that hasn't been spoken for, and for every fifteen-minute activity that is added, one has to be taken away.[6, p. 77]

Mothers of individuals with disabilities need a reprieve. In the frustrating business of trying to rehabilitate seriously disabled individuals, professionals must stop over-identifying with the patient and projecting blame onto the mother. She is entitled to her rage and sadness, even her shortcomings. She needs emotional support, guidance, and consistency, and—probably most of all—actual physical help in caretaking.

That the special needs of women with disabilities and mothers of persons with disabilities have been overlooked is not surprising. Such an oversight is merely part of a larger male-oriented world view. But, as this bias is being corrected in other spheres — literature, media, history, religion — it is time we did the same in the field of rehabilitation. Both women and individuals with disabilities have been demanding and attaining equal rights in recent years. We are now ready for women who themselves have disabilities to receive the same. As rehabilitation professionals we must become more sensitive to the needs of women and to the needs of mothers; we must advocate for affirmative action to assure equal employment and equal benefits, and to eradicate sexual harassment. We are long overdue for consciousness-raising. Sexism in rehabilitation should become a *non sequitur.*

REFERENCES

1. Becker, E. F. *Female Sexuality Following Spinal Cord Injury.* Bloomington, Ill.: Cheever Pub., 1978.
2. Bird, C. *What Women Want.* New York: Simon & Schuster, 1979.
3. Bregman, S. *Sexuality and the Spinal Cord Injured Woman.* Minneapolis, Minn.: Sister Kenny Institute, 1975.
4. Department of Health, Education and Welfare. Office for Handicapped Individuals. *Digest of Data on Persons with Disabilities.* Washington, D.C.: U.S. Government Printing Office, 1979.
5. Developmental Disabilities Project. *Information Concerning Sexual Exploitation of Mentally and Physically Handicapped Individuals.* Seattle, Wash.: Seattle Rape Relief, 1979.
6. Featherstone, H. *A Difference in the Family: Life with a Disabled Child.* New York: Basic Books, 1980.
7. German, P. S., and Collins, J. W. Disability and Work Adjustment. *Social Security Survey of the Disabled,* Report No. 24. Washington, D.C.: U.S. Department of Health, Education, and Welfare, Social Security Administration, 1974.
8. Krute, A., and Burdette, M. E. 1972 Survey of Disabled and Non-Disabled Adults: Chronic Disease, Injury, and Work Disability. *Social Security Bul.* 1978. 41:4:3–7.
9. Kutner, N. G., and Kutner, M. H. Race and Sex as Variables Affecting Reactions to Disability. *Arch. Phys. Medicine & Rehab.* 1979. 60:62–66.
10. Kutza, E. Benefits for the Disabled: How Beneficial for Women? *Sociol. and Social Welfare,* 1983.
11. Levitan, S., and Taggart, R. *Jobs for the Disabled.* Baltimore, Md.: Johns Hopkins University Press, 1977.
12. Lipowski, Z. Physical Illness, the Patient and His Environment. In: S. Arieti (ed.) *American Handbook of Psychiatry,* 2nd ed. New York: Basic Books, 1975.
13. Sachs, F. *Information Memorandum,* RSA-JM-78-62, U.S. Department of Health, Education and Welfare, Office of Human Development, Rehabilitation Services Administration, 1978.
14. Sanford, L. *The Silent Children.* New York: Doubleday, 1980.
15. Stuart, V. W. *Sexuality and Sexual Assault: Disabled Perspective.* Marshall, Minn.:

Health and Rehabilitation Services Program, Southwest State University, 1980.

16. Task Force No. 1. Vocational Evaluation Services in the Human Services Delivery System. *Voc. Evaluation and Work Adjustment.* 1975. 8:7–48.

17. Task Force on Concerns of Physically Disabled Women. *Toward Intimacy: Family Planning and Sexuality Concerns of Physically Disabled Women.* New York: Human Sciences Press, 1978.

Part VIII

Helping Persons with Disabilities

The primary goal of rehabilitation is to help persons with disabilities to overcome, as much as possible, their deficits; to capitalize upon their assets; and to achieve their optimal functioning. Although this help can be provided by a variety of professionals — rehabilitation counselors, nurses, physical therapists, occupational therapists, psychologists, speech pathologists and audiologists, social workers, and physicians — the common denominator in the helping process is the ability to listen and respond effectively in order to assist clients to achieve rehabilitation goals. Therefore, an understanding of varying therapeutic methods is helpful in the fulfillment of team roles and in the adoption of helpful techniques.

McDowell and his associates overview the psychosocial needs of handicapped persons and provide counseling strategies meeting these special needs. Needs relating to self-concept, body image, frustration and anger, and dependency and motivation are presented. Strategies drawn from neo-Freudian, Gestalt, rational-emotive, and behavioral frameworks, designed to meet these needs, are described. The authors highlight the importance of therapeutic flexibility and personalized strategies.

A review of assessment strategies designed to provide meaningful intervention strategies for handicapped persons is the purpose of the chapter by Guidubaldi and his associates. The role of the counselor as a member of a diagnostic team and the importance of individualized planning are emphasized.

In Chapter 26, Lasky, Dell Orto, and Marinelli present Structured Experiential Training (SET) as a systematic and eclectic group model that focuses on the development of resources and skills for persons who are experiencing the rehabilitation and health care process. Descriptions of the various SET stages and of representative structured experiences involved in the stages are two major contributions of this chapter. In addition, the chapter reviews significant publications related to group counseling with physically disabled persons.

The rehabilitation setting can be used to promote or retard reintegration of persons with disabilities into society. Kutner discusses the impact of the total institution on the resocializaton of the adult with disabilities, and suggests milieu therapy to provide the patient with an arsenal of social skills.

Although stress is common to both disabled and nondisabled populations, people with disabilities are generally faced with many additional potentially stressful situations. Goodwin provides a general overview of stress and also discusses specific stress-related problems of disabled people. The "relaxation response" and means of triggering the response are presented as an effective method for rehabilitation workers to combat stress in their clients.

During the last few decades, many behaviorally based treatment modalities have been developed to treat the psychosocial difficulties of disabled and nondisabled persons alike. Self-management, one of these new behavioral technologies, and its application to rehabilitation are discussed in Chapter 29 by Livingston and Johnson. In their model of self-regulation, covert responses, such as thoughts and feelings, are modified (when viewed as debilitating) or are used to modify overt behaviors. The applications of covert processes in rehabilitation situations are described.

24

The Handicapped: Special Needs and Strategies for Counseling

William A. McDowell
Arnold B. Coven
Violette C. Eash

A 35-year-old laborer has had a cerebral vascular accident resulting in hemiplegia with aphasia, from which he has partially recovered. He has lost the use of his left arm and leg. He says that he just wants a job.

Suzie's parents have just been told their daughter is mentally handicapped. They are assured that she is educable and that special services will be provided in the public school system. They are unbelieving, stunned.

John, 23, is a quadriplegic as a result of an automobile accident. After months of treatment he is barely able to lift his finger and flip the switch on his battery-powered wheelchair. He insists it won't be long before his physical functioning returns and he can fulfill his dream to be a mining engineer.

These problems are not atypical in counseling persons who are disabled.* Clients may have obvious physical handicaps, such as blindness or loss of limbs; hidden conditions, such as diabetes or heart disease; and such handicaps as multiple sclerosis, crippling arthritis, or spinal cord injuries. They also may be mentally or emotionally handicapped.

How are these clients different and how are they similar to nonhandicapped clients? What are their problems? How can the counselor assist them in managing their lives? One of the great dangers of trying to express important ideas directly and easily is to oversimplify the extremely complicated. The philosopher A. N. Whitehead remarked, "Seek simplicity — and mistrust it." We are always searching for "the way." We hope that this course, that

From *Personnel and Guidance Journal*, December 1979, pp. 228–232. Copyright © 1979 by the American Personnel and Guidance Association. Reprinted with permission.

*Disabled and handicapped are not intended as holistic descriptions of persons with impairments.

technique, this book, or that professor will provide us with the answer. This article identifies significant psychosocial aspects of disabled people and describes several counseling approaches that deal with the special needs of the handicapped.

PSYCHOSOCIAL NEEDS AND COUNSELING STRATEGIES WITH THE DISABLED

As a disabled psychologist stated, "The psychology of disability is really nothing different than the psychology of being human" (Vash, 1975, p. 147). Shontz (1970) concurred with Wright (1960) that no evidence exists that different physical disabilities are related to particular personality types or that the individual's reaction to disability is related to severity of injury. Whatever we may say about psychological differences of persons with disabilities, we may also say of the nondisabled. No matter what differences there are in our physical bodies, our sensory capacities, or our intellectual abilities, we are more alike than we are different. Every severely disabled person does not necessarily go through a period of depression. All people, not just disabled people, suffer loss.

Although more similar to the nondisabled than different, the disabled person does have to cope with unusual stimuli. A recent booklet, *The Invisible Battle* (1979), illustrates some of these stimuli. The stimulus may be biological; for example, the person may be paralyzed and confined to a wheelchair. The stimulus may be social, as depicted in a scene where two paraplegics in wheelchairs are seated in a restaurant with a friend; the waitress asks the friend, "What would they like for dinner?" Or the stimulus may be economic, as when the handicapped person is not able to get employment because an employer concentrates on disability rather than ability.

Although one cannot detect a unique constellation of personality characteristics that can be attributed to a particular disability, some common problems do tend to exist among those who are handicapped. In fact, there are several special problems that commonly develop in handicapped persons. The reasons are apparent: (a) Handicapped persons tend to experience a disproportionately large number of frustrations and difficulties in their attempts to solve problems; (b) they encounter more situations of nonacceptance, prejudice, and devaluation than the nondisabled majority; and thus (c) handicapped persons, especially children, often have difficulty in developing realistic and healthy self-concepts (Johnson, 1967). Thus several psychosocial needs have been identified as especially important in the psychology of the disabled. Problems of self-concept, body image, frustration and anger, and dependency and motivation will receive special attention in this article.

Self-Concept

The impact of physical impairment on an individual's self-concept, body image, and social interactions is well documented (Hamburg, 1974; Kolb & Woldt, 1976; Linkowski & Dunn, 1974; Litman, 1962; Wright, 1960). Self-concept may be affected, whether the disability is totally or permanently disabling, or moderate in effect.

A major source of how we perceive ourselves, value ourselves, and attempt to enhance ourselves is acquired through our interactions with others. As a consequence, the family is the primary environment for testing abilities and learning about limitations. How individuals cope with stress or disability may reflect how their families react to the situation. The family can be harmful or helpful in the rehabilitation process. The family may never allow a child with cerebral palsy to try sewing or to work with tools, for fear of personal injury. Overprotection can contribute to an inadequate self-concept in many handicapped persons.

The impact of physical impairment on self-concept is also related to the premorbid personality of the client. Therefore, in the case of adventitious disability, it is helpful for the counselor to know something about the client's previous personality. Unless clients, their families, or the referring agency can provide an adequate psychosocial history, the counselor may not be aware of the self-concepts the client had before the trauma. If the client had a history of a poor self-concept and accompanying feelings of inadequacy, the trauma—accident, stroke, or whatever—may intensify those feelings. Similarly, an angry young man who, through his own impulsiveness, suffered a spinal cord injury in an auto accident may manifest exaggerated hostility.

In addition to the case file and information obtained from self-report, the counselor can use the novel, yet probing, technique suggested by McKelvie and Friedland (1978) for defining the client's self-concept. This technique also helps clarify the disabled individual's goals, fears, needs, and environmental perceptions. With this approach, the counselor effectively uses early childhood recollections to collect background information, thereby focusing on a client's life-long self-concept. The following describes and illustrates McKelvie and Friedland's procedures.

> An early recollection is *one specific* incident that occurred roughly before the age of eight and that can be visualized. A report describes a recurring kind of event, e.g., "We used to go to church every Sunday." When you do get a report, ask the client to describe one specific time. It is helpful to require that the memory be like a snapshot—a vivid one-time experience. (p. 85)

One client, when asked to visualize an instant mental picture of his childhood, stated that it was too simple and probably not of value. He was running. When asked if he had a destination, the reply was negative—he was always just running. With some probing and educated guessing, it was learned that this individual is still, in adulthood, a man in a hurry. He always eats fast and frequently gets up and leaves a conversation—with no destination in mind. He would like a job in which he is always on the move.

An example, with a handicapped client, follows:

AGE 8:   I am on the school playground at recess watching the other kids play ball. I can't participate because I have braces and crutches. Nobody's talking to me—I'm just sitting there watching.
FOCUS: Watching the other kids play ball at recess.
FEELING: Alone, isolated, left out.
BECAUSE: I couldn't participate because of my handicap.

If the above is the client's most vivid imagery of childhood, an educated guess would be that he or she still experiences the same feeling. The client wants to be included, to be an integral part of the action, and to avoid being ignored and rejected. Such feelings should especially be kept in mind throughout vocational counseling. If the client has a job that consists of little involvement with other people, it is possible that these same feelings could return and lead to poor personal job adjustment.

In addition to information, the early recollection generates feeling. "Differences in private logic will affect the feeling in a situation; don't try to guess how the client felt" (McKelvie & Friedland, 1978, p. 86). The purpose of recalling early experiences is not so much to inform the counselor about childhood experiences as it is to serve as a foundation for an understanding of the client in the here-and-now. Interpretations must relate to the present, and the client will validate the counselor's assumptions. This method is useful for working with the disabled, to help discern the previous personality and self-concept and the extent to which they have been changed by the trauma of disablement.

Body Image

Theoretically, body image is closely related to self-concept. Body-image proponents do not view them as equivalent, but believe that body perceptions reflect generalized feelings of self (Wapner & Werner, 1965). Body attitudes are often the result and reflection of interpersonal relationships. Handicapped persons have frequently been encouraged to deny their bodies and assume an asexual attitude. Family members may encourage handicapped children to develop intellectual or social skills and to discourage the children's exploration of their bodies. Teenagers who must wear leg braces may be painfully aware of their differences in the summer, when other teenagers are wearing shorts and swimsuits. The resulting emotions associated with body image are often denied by the handicapped individual (Shontz, 1970).

The process of physical restoration and rehabilitation readily brings to the surface conflicts the client experiences in relation to body image. An attractive young woman, a lower-extremity amputee, had three prostheses fabricated because with each one she experienced open sores, blisters, and extreme pain at the points of contact with the stump. The conflict was revealed one day when she touched her prosthesis and exclaimed, "But it doesn't feel like skin." Not until she accepted the prosthesis did her chronic medical problem cease. Following extensive counseling she came into a session, slapped her artificial leg, and smiled as she said, "My leg is doing fine."

The counseling process generally focuses on the disabled individual's resistance to seeing the prosthesis as part of the self. This is particularly noticeable in cases of traumatic disability, where the person who was a healthy, fully functioning individual is now experiencing a different lifestyle. Until insight is developed and frustrations are brought to the surface, the client's "emotional senses" may make it painful even to touch the appliance (Eash & McDowell, 1978).

If counselors are able to encourage clients to explore their bodies and accept the reality of the disability, fear and denial may lessen or disappear. Thus disability would be integrated into the client's total self-concept. Kolb and Woldt (1976) suggest two strategies that can be used in dealing with the body image or physical aspects of a disabled person.

1. Helping disabled persons to contact their physique through fantasy, self-exploration, psychodrama, and modified body-movement patterns, by focusing on areas where sensation is blocked and where it is capable of being perceived (p. 52). For example, the counselor may guide the handicapped person through body-awareness exercises that focus on each part of the body. The counselor can then discuss with the client preconceptions or misconceptions of personal strength and weakness and how these images can restrict or enhance behavior.

2. Encouraging handicapped clients to contact another person through mutual body exploration and nonverbal expressiveness, in order to experience giving and receiving sensory communication. The clients' impasses in physically sharing their feelings with others may be discerned. The clients are encouraged to confront such barriers to expand their potential for body contact, which, in turn, frees others to be spontaneous in physical, emotional interactions with them (p. 52). Simple experiences, such as a "blind walk," where each person in turn shuts his or her eyes and is guided about, offer a unique opportunity for many persons with impairments to have someone physically dependent on them.

Frustration and Anger

Feelings, as well as the body, are affected by a disability. The emotional response of anger may result from a frustrating situation in which the sense of adequacy and security are threatened, or in which a handicapped person perceives that he or she does not measure up to the expectations of others. Able-bodied persons who are uncomfortable with the handicapped often avoid them or view them as helpless, dependent, and unable to care for themselves. In addition to physical stress, such actions by others can engender hostile and aggressive feelings in the disabled. These emotional reactions are often unexpressed by the disabled individuals, because perceptions that they should be strong, patient, and long-suffering are often part of the handicapped individuals' self-concept. Psychological devices, such as denial, withdrawal, or projection, may even keep them unaware of such feelings. Severe mobility and muscular restrictions may also prevent the expression of anger through physical means.

Sometimes the frustration and anger of the disabled are manifested as sarcasm and cynicism. Handicapped persons thus may outwardly discourage peers and potential friendships, which is the exact opposite of what they want to do. They may be so anxious and self-conscious that they constantly make negative references to themselves — on how they hold a glass, or cut meat, or how they get about. The counselor must deal directly, not with the sarcasm and terseness, but with the underlying frustrations that cause the attitude.

Cognitive-based approaches, such as Ellis's rational-emotive therapy, can deal with anger that results from frustrations. The counselor's role becomes one of helping the handicapped person work on irrational ideas, attitudes, and beliefs. A basic technique used by the rational-emotive counselor is to assist a client through a rational self-analysis. An example is that of a paraplegic client who has overturned a wheelchair and is highly embarrassed.

> *Point A. Activating event:* My wheelchair overturned, and although unhurt, I was completely helpless on the floor.
> *Point B. Belief system:* I can't stand being seen helpless like this. I'll always be a helpless invalid.
> *Point C. Consequent affective emotions:* Self-directed anger and other-directed anger.
> *Point D. Dispute irrational beliefs:*
>
> 1. How can I tell myself that I cannot stand having others see me helpless on the floor when I was, in fact, "standing it," even while I was telling myself I could not?

2. "Can't" usually means I refuse to try or I haven't tried. It is inconvenient to require the assistance of others, and I don't like it, but I can stand it.
3. "Always" is certainly an irrational absolute. Change is always possible, as I live in a world of probability where little is beyond the possibility of revision. To rate a few of my abilities and then call that rating my *self* is irrational. Although my injured spinal cord resulted in paralysis of the lower half of my body, I cannot rationally call myself a helpless invalid. Others in my condition, and even worse, have led happy and productive lives. (Wallace & Maddox, 1978)

In this fashion clients are taught to dispute and challenge their irrational beliefs and thereby convert emotional disturbance into mild negative feelings.

In addition to assisting in the reduction of irrational attitudes, the counselor can also help the client with the behavioral expression of feelings. More recent expressive therapies facilitate the release of anger through such techniques as screaming, twisting a towel, or kicking. Psychodrama techniques for venting anger can result in an increased capacity to experience anger and can help the client discover socially useful ways to direct anger (Sacks, 1976). The blocked or disowned anger of the person may be placed in an "empty chair," and the client may be encouraged to have a dialogue between the long-suffering self and the angry self. Once the person is in touch with the anger, several techniques can be used to let it out. The counselor can advise the client to write a furious letter but not mail it, or to telephone the offending person but keep the button down.

Dependency and Motivation

One of the difficulties frequently mentioned by counselors of handicapped individuals is dependency — the lack of involvement and the lack of motivation by the client. Wright (1960) perceived motivating children and preventing dependency as major concerns. DeBlassie and Cowan (1976) viewed the lack of motivation toward independence as a key issue in counseling the mentally handicapped child. Rehabilitation counseling has considered the lack of motivation or resistance of disabled clients as a constant, continuing problem (Coven, in press). Lack of motivation in the handicapped has sometimes been attributed to the system, which often creates a passive role rather than an active role (Morgan, Hohmann, & Davis, 1974; Schlesinger, 1963; Vash, 1975).

Overprotected clients exhibit a degree of fixation at primitive levels of coping. Case files are filled with such statements as "This client is emotionally and socially immature." For this reason, counseling should be a cooperative process involving many other persons in the client's environment.

Physical therapists, vocational instructors, cooks, housekeepers, and others who can help the client achieve independence should be enlisted to help. The common denominator of a comprehensive program for the handicapped is the development of emotional growth, free of neurotic defenses, which will help clients face a society that imposes many demands on them.

The nonmotivated client can be perceived as being ambivalent toward rehabilitation. Coven (1978) presents a Gestalt exercise to help disabled persons recognize their ambivalence. The handicapped person is asked to state three life goals and then to write them down. The act of writing the goals, of placing oneself on paper, involves more of the person's feelings and can increase attachment to goals. The counselor can then have the client write down one need that can be fulfilled today. This helps clients attend to how they are currently fulfilling needs and goals. The counselor then suggests that the person experiment with stating and writing down the opposite of each stated goal. If the client has noted, "I want to be rehabilitated," or "I want to work and be independent," he or she now tries out, "I don't want to be rehabilitated," or "I don't want a job." Such statements of opposite life goals intensify the ambivalence/resistance so that it stands out and is obvious. In addition, this identification with one position and then another facilitates the awareness of the existence of opposite needs and wants. Finally, the client assesses whether current behavior is consistent with the positive or negative goal statements. This evaluation makes it difficult for clients to avoid facing behavioral incongruencies and heightens the awareness and experiencing of avoidance and resistance to the rehabilitation process. The evaluation can lead to a fruitful exploration of how persons behaviorally prevent themselves from reaching objectives. Disabled clients can then assume responsibility for the behavioral resistance and can choose whether to stay the same, or change and behave congruently with the verbalized goal of "I want to be rehabilitated."

CONCLUSION

We have noted that people with disabilities are individuals—individuals who should not be categorized or dehumanized because of their differences. Yet we have also maintained that handicapped individuals face many unusual stimuli, which may lead them to experience special problems with self-concept, body image, frustration and anger, and dependency and motivation. The suggested counseling strategies recognize that the counselor must deal with the total person. The counselor must become involved with how the disability affects every aspect of the client's life. Furthermore, we have stressed that counselors must be versatile, using the tools and techniques that have the most efficacy. In short, counselors must use their resourcefulness, as well as that of others, to assist the client in finding meaning and wholeness in life.

REFERENCES

Coven, A. The application of Gestalt therapy to rehabilitation counseling. In W. A. McDowell & A. Coven (Eds.), *Counseling theories applied to rehabilitation.* New York: Human Sciences Press, 1978.

DeBlassie, R. R., & Cowan, M. A. Counseling with the mentally handicapped child. *Elementary School Guidance and Counseling,* 1976, 10, 246–253.

Eash, V., & McDowell, W. A. The application of psychoanalytic theory to rehabilitation. In W. A. McDowell & A. B. Coven (Eds.), *Counseling theories applied to rehabilitation.* New York: Human Sciences Press, 1978.

Hamburg, D. A. Coping behaviors in life-threatening circumstances. *Psychotherapy and Psychosomatics,* 1974, 23, 13–25.

The invisible battle. Washington, D.C.: Regional Rehabilitation Research Institute on Attitudinal, Legal and Leisure Barriers, 1979.

Johnson, W. I. Guidance for exceptional children. In W. M. Cruickshank & G. O. Johnson (Eds.), *Education of exceptional children and youth.* Englewood Cliffs, N.J.: Prentice-Hall, 1967.

Kolb, C. L., & Woldt, A. L. The rehabilitative potential of a Gestalt approach to counseling severely impaired clients. In W. A. McDowell, S. A. Meadows, R. Crabtree, & R. Sakata (Eds.), *Rehabilitation counseling with persons who are severely disabled.* Huntington, W. Va.: Marshall University Press, 1976.

Linkowski, M. A., & Dunn, M. A. Self-concept and acceptance of disability. *Rehabilitation Counseling Bulletin,* 1974, 18, 28–32.

Litman, T. J. The influence of self-concept and life orientation factors in rehabilitation of the orthopedically disabled. *Journal of Health and Human Behavior,* 1962, 3, 249–257.

McKelvie, W., & Friedland, B. *Career goal counseling: A holistic approach.* Baltimore: F.M.S. Associates, 1978.

Morgan, E. D.; Hohmann, G. W.; & Davis, J. E., Jr. Psychosocial rehabilitation in VA spinal cord injury centers. *Rehabilitation Psychology,* 1974, 21, 3–33.

Sacks, J. M. Shut up! A psychodramatic technique for releasing anger. In P. Olsen (Ed.), *Emotional flooding* (Vol. 1), pp. 41–44. New York: Human Sciences Press, 1976.

Schlesinger, L. E. Patient motivation for rehabilitation: Integrating staff forces. *American Journal of Occupational Therapy,* 1963, 17, 5–8.

Shontz, F. C. Physical disability and personality: Theory and recent research. *Rehabilitation Psychology,* 1970, 17, 51–69.

Vash, C. L. The psychology of disability. *Rehabilitation Psychology.* 1975, 22, 145–163.

Wallace, W. A., & Maddox, E. N. Rational-emotive theory. In W. A. McDowell & A. B. Coven (Eds.), *Counseling theories applied to rehabilitation.* New York: Human Sciences Press, 1978.

Wapner, S., & Werner, H. (Eds.). *The body percept.* New York: Random House, 1965.

Wright, B. A. *Physical disability—A psychological approach.* New York: Harper & Row, 1960.

25

Assessment Strategies for the Handicapped

John Guidubaldi
Thomas J. Kehle
Joseph N. Murray

Assessment of handicapped students has always presented educators, counselors, and psychologists with a major challenge. In addition to more general assessment problems, such as inadequate norming samples, limited predictive validity, and a dearth of good measures of social and emotional adjustment, the person attempting to assess a handicapped child or adult must also deal with a wide variety of physical, emotional, or cognitive limitations of the student that may severely confound the evaluation. Because the justification for assessment lies in its generation of remedial strategies, a further problem is the difficulty in using assessment data to devise interventions that truly make a significant difference in the handicapped individual's adaptive functioning.

Despite difficulties such as these, recent legislative mandates (PL 94-142) have offered reasons for optimism, particularly since assessments of handicapped persons must now be multifactored and based on a team approach. The multifactored directive promotes examination of a wide variety of characteristics rather than allowing intervention decisions to be made on the basis of a single attribute such as IQ. The required team approach increases the probability that teachers, parents, counselors, and other people familiar with the child will be able to contribute meaningful diagnostic input and to share in the design of recommendations.

Considering the greater versatility in both assessment staff and evaluation variables, it is apparent that counselors will be playing a larger role in identifying special children, adolescents, and adults and structuring programs to meet their needs. Consequently, they need to broaden their knowl-

From *Personnel and Guidance Journal*, December 1979, pp. 245–251. Copyright © 1979 by the American Personnel and Guidance Association. Reprinted with permission.

edge of strategies for assessment and devise ways to contribute to the group decision-making process. This expansion of role should begin with an understanding of the domains to be assessed and the strategies for data gathering.

ASSESSMENT DOMAINS

Determining the adequacy of the match between a handicapped person's capabilities and environmental requirements is perhaps the central objective of assessment. This includes not only judgments about current functioning but also projections about ability to adapt to future environmental presses. The individual-environment interaction is, of course, a fluid process with developmentally changing capabilities and increasing environmental requirements. Diagnosticians must nonetheless estimate, on the basis of current assessments, how an individual is likely to function in future tasks.

Ideally, these projections should be based on personal attributes that have known predictive validity, yet most typically assessed characteristics individually account for only a small portion of the variance in later performance. When they are combined in multiple regression equations, however, substantially more powerful predictions are possible. This repeated research finding (e.g., Harper, Guidubaldi, & Kehle, 1978; Perry, Guidubaldi, & Kehle, 1979; Stevenson, Parker, Wilkinson, Hegion, & Fish, 1976) obviously lends support to the multifactored assessment procedures.

In addition to predicting future performance, a comprehensive assessment plan offers a data base for current intervention, specifying strengths and limitations that are pertinent to the immediate learning tasks confronting the individual. Because individuals vary considerably in learning styles, and because handicapping conditions often preclude learning through certain modalities, multifactored assessment is essential in order to prescribe appropriate levels of task difficulty and optimal instructional approaches.

Multifactored assessments of handicapped persons usually include evaluations of ability levels in cognitive, social-emotional, academic, perceptual-motor, and self-help domains. Some of these performance areas are typically given more emphasis than others, and some degree of overlap clearly exists among the categories. The categories also vary in predictive validity, psychometric sophistication of measuring devices, and type of data source. For example, IQ is frequently considered more salient than motor coordination and offers greater predictive validity for academic achievement, yet visual-motor performance is clearly one of the component factors in IQ examinations of young children. Tests of cognitive ability are psychometrically better developed than tests of visual-motor coordination, but in classroom settings cognitive behaviors are more difficult to observe than motor functioning (e.g., Lambert, 1978). Thus, each domain needs to be considered in reference to its importance in the overall evaluation, its forms of assessment, and its data sources.

Cognitive Ability

There is probably no area of psychology that has generated as much controversy as the nature of intelligence and its measurement. The intensity of debate about the plasticity of human intelligence has risen tremendously as our culture has increasingly allocated its roles and resources on the basis of this valued attribute. For several decades, heated debate has periodically been observed in psychological journals, but widespread public awareness of the heredity versus environment and IQ test arguments is a relatively recent phenomenon promoted by massive media exposure and legislative action. The use of IQ tests to evaluate compensatory programs for disadvantaged pupils and to place handicapped individuals in special programs has come under particular scrutiny, and several researchers have recommended that this criterion be deemphasized or abandoned (e.g., Anderson & Messick, 1974; McClelland, 1973; Zigler & Trickett, 1978). Some have even suggested that the IQ score is used as a tool of social injustice and political oppression (e.g., Kamin, 1975).

There is clearly a great deal of confusion about intelligence testing, labeling, legal requirements, and ethical issues. However, some critics of intelligence testing have based their objections on emotional, political, or social arguments rather than on the psychometric properties of the tests themselves. Others are so concerned about elitism that they deny the obvious variability in certain human competencies. While it is socially acceptable to identify and recognize individual differences in such characteristics as athletic or musical ability, it appears to be socially and politically objectionable to acknowledge relative strengths or weaknesses in cognitive capabilities.

Moreover, although one may attribute some of the variance in musical and athletic ability to genetic endowment, the aversion to such explanations of intellectual development is obvious, and many professionals continue to assert that environmental variables are far more important in determining cognitive ability. This assumption of intellectual malleability not only puts the burden of performance on parents, teachers, and other persons charged with shaping the child's environment, but it also generates difficult assessment problems. For example, does an increase in tested IQ reflect a true increase in cognitive ability, or is it a function of improved motivation or other social and emotional factors?

Zigler and Trickett (1978) suggest that such formal cognitive processes as abstract reasoning ability and speed of visual information-processing constitute only one part of the IQ index, and that past achievement and motivational and personality factors also influence the final test score. They and other researchers agree that IQ tests are highly predictive of school achievement and that they are psychometrically sophisticated instruments (e.g., Anastasi, 1976; Clarizio, 1979; Flaugher, 1978; Jensen, 1975; Kaufman, 1979; Sattler, 1974; Thorndike & Hager, 1977).

Clarizio observes that

> It is unlikely, in my opinion, that the search for new, nondiscriminatory assessment measures will come any closer to achieving the goal of non-biased assessment than has been achieved by presently available standardized scales of intelligence. Current IQ tests do what they propose to do, and this is all that the test *per se* can be held accountable for. It is time we move beyond scapegoating the IQ test. (1979, p. 87)

Although Zigler and Trickett (1978) recommend using social competence as an alternative to the IQ criterion, their definition of social competence includes a measure of formal cognitive ability, and they indicate that the IQ would be an acceptable measure of this attribute. They and others (Kohlberg & Zigler, 1967; Mischel, 1968) note that "no other measure has been found to be related to so many other behaviors of theoretical and practical significance" (1978, p. 791).

Counselors involved in the assessment of handicapped persons should acknowledge the importance of cognitive assessments, rather than follow the sometimes politically expedient alternative that disregards valid measures of the construct. They need to recognize that correlations between individually administered IQ tests and school achievement range as high as .70. Among the most valid and reliable instruments are the Stanford-Binet Intelligence Scale, Wechsler Intelligence Scales, Peabody Picture Vocabulary Test, and the Otis-Lennon Mental Ability Test. Specialized tests with norms for some handicapped groups include the Blind Learning Aptitude Test (Newland, 1969); the Hiskey-Nebraska Test of Learning Aptitude (Hiskey, 1966); the Columbia Mental Maturity Scale (Burgemeister, Blum, & Lorge, 1962), and the Leiter International Performance Scale (Arthur, 1950).

Social-Emotional Competence

Within the past 5 years, a considerable amount of interest in assessment of social-emotional competence has emerged. This movement may have been prompted by the washout of long-range IQ gains for disadvantaged pupils who attended compensatory preschool programs, or it may have developed as a response to the disproportionate number of minority group children placed in special education classes on the basis of IQ tests. Whatever its origin, this new focus has yielded some impressive research results that illustrate effective prediction of primary grade academic success by pre-school social-emotional competence measures (e.g., Guidubaldi, 1969; Harper, Guidubaldi, & Kehle, 1978; Kohn & Rosman, 1972, 1974; Perry, Guidubaldi, & Kehle, 1979; Stevenson, Parker, Wilkinson, Hegion, & Fish, 1976).

Attempts to measure social and emotional competence suffer from the lack of well-developed instrumentation. For example, Anderson and Messick (1974) report that a panel of experts called together by the Office of Child Development to try to define social competency included 29 separate attributes in their definition. Unfortunately, well-constructed assessment devices for most of these characteristics have not yet been developed. The authors note that for "the youngest children and for certain classes of variables throughout the age range, tests do not provide a valid basis for inferences about social competency; other measurement techniques must be used" (p. 292). Most published instruments that purport to measure social-emotional variables are based on projective techniques or rating-scale approaches. Examples include the Thematic Apperception Test (Murray, 1943), the Piers-Harris Children's Self-Concept Scale (Piers & Harris, 1969), Human Figure Drawing Test (Koppitz, 1968), the Vineland Social Maturity Scale (Doll, 1965), and the Adaptive Behavior Scale (Nihira, Foster, Shellhaas, & Leland, 1975).

Counselors attempting to assess social and emotional functioning of handicapped students need to recognize that this constellation of attitudes and behaviors may be more influential in determining future success for handicapped individuals than for their unimpaired age-mates. For many handicapping conditions, such specific variables may make the difference between social rejection or acceptance, academic effort or alienation, and satisfactory life adjustment versus discouragement. Development of appropriate behaviors and attitudes expected by others should be accomplished by handicapped children before integration into normal classrooms if mainstreaming efforts are to be optimally successful (Kehle & Barclay, 1979).

Academic Achievement

The use of achievement tests along with informal educational skill inventories is often the counselor's primary responsibility to the interdisciplinary team's analysis (Hatch, Murphy, & Bagnato, 1979). Generally, the assessment of academic achievement in normal populations is accomplished by the counselor through group testing procedures. However, with handicapped students, individual assessment is required both for overall academic ability and the diagnosis of specific academic deficiencies. The Wide Range Achievement Test (Jastak & Jastak, 1965) and the Peabody Individual

Achievement Test (Dunn & Markwardt, 1970) are widely employed with handicapped populations to gain knowledge of the student's overall academic functioning. In the diagnosis of deficits in reading and arithmetic, the Woodcock Reading Mastery Tests (Woodcock, 1973) and the Key Math (Connolly, Nachtman, & Pritchett, 1971) are often the tests of choice.

The assessment of overall academic ability is relatively easily accomplished; however, diagnosis of specific academic deficiencies in such areas as reading and arithmetic implies remediation, which requires the counselor to rely on the expertise of individuals specifically trained in those areas.

In assessing the academic potential of preschool children, counselors may find the Learning Accomplishment Profile (LAP) (Sanford, 1974) useful. The LAP is a developmentally based diagnostic-prescriptive instrument. It provides a simple criterion-referenced profile of the handicapped child's existing skills, enabling counselors to identify appropriate learning criteria and to evaluate progress through the child's changes in the rate of development.

Perceptual-Motor Capabilities

Although there exists little empirical support for the efficacy of using perceptual-motor tests in planning remediation strategies that enhance academic competencies, counselors can effectively use these tests to aid in the assessment of visual-motor integrity (Hatch, Murphy, & Bagnato, 1979). Counselors can choose from a wide assortment of instruments measuring a variety of perceptual-motor behaviors, such as balance, form discrimination, ocular control, attention for detail, eye-hand coordination, spatial relations, figure-ground perception, fine and gross motor ability, memory for detail, and body image. Perhaps the most commonly used instruments are the Developmental Test of Visual Perception (Frostig, Lefever, & Whittlesey, 1964), the Purdue Perceptual-Motor Survey (Roach & Kephart, 1966), the Bender Visual-Motor Gestalt Test (Koppitz, 1975), and the Memory for Designs Test (Graham & Kendall, 1960).

A perceptually based instrument that appears to be relevant to academic programming is the Visual-Aural Digit Span Test (VADS) (Koppitz, 1977), which measures intersensory integration and memory. The VADS assumes "a close relationship between children's reading, spelling, and arithmetic achievement and their functioning in intersensory integration and recall" (p. xi). Supporting this assumption, high positive correlations exist between the VADS and the subtests of the Wide Range Achievement Test (Koppitz, 1977). The VADS can be administered quickly and its diagnostic information can be readily applied to enhance the effectiveness of the individual educational plans.

Self-Help Skills

When assessing self-help skills or adaptive behavior, specific attention should generally be given to those behaviors or skills that allow, disallow, or diminish self-sufficiency and independence.

The AAMD Adaptive Behavior Scale (Nihira, Foster, Shellhaas, & Leland, 1975) can be employed to evaluate the adaptive behavior of children and adults in all settings. Although the scale is primarily designed to rate the behaviors of mentally retarded, emotionally maladjusted, and developmentally disabled individuals, it can be employed to evaluate other handicapped persons as well. The Adaptive Behavior Scale is organized developmentally and assesses 10 behavior domains considered significant to the development of personal sufficiency and independence. In addition, another section of the instrument provides measures of maladaptive behavior related to personality and behavior disorders.

Other normatively based adaptive rating scales commonly employed are the Vineland Social Maturity Scale (Doll, 1965), and the Preschool Attainment Record (Doll, 1966).

Nonnormative information regarding how an individual maintains personal independence in daily living and how he or she deals with the social expectations of the environment can be gained through parent interview. Instruments designed to help counselors structure the parent interview deal with the child's self-maintenance, physical and language development, socialization, and maladaptive behaviors.

A combination of both a normatively based behavior rating scale and informal parent interview data can give the counselor a great deal of information regarding the handicapped individual's abilities in meeting the social expectations of everyday life.

OTHER DATA SOURCES FOR MULTIFACTORED ASSESSMENT

In order to maximize the information base for intervention planning, evaluators of handicapped persons need to broaden their assessment strategies beyond standardized tests. Evaluators of normal individuals may often safely assume that these individuals' test performance is indicative of their functioning in nontest settings. This inference is more tenuous for handicapped persons, however, because their specific impairments may produce markedly different performance outcomes in different situations. For example, an easily distracted youngster may function acceptably in a one-to-one testing environment, but these results may not generalize to classroom settings where there are far more distractions. Thus, multifactored evaluations of handicapped individuals must utilize the full variety of available data sources and procedures.

One way to conceptualize the process is to consider the evaluation as a series of observations of varying duration gathered from different sources, occurring in different locations and with different levels of structure. For example, psychometric tests are observations generally performed in brief time periods by examiners who remove subjects from their normal environments and administer highly structured assessment items. In contrast, observations, rating scales, interviews, and sociometric assessments offer opportunities to increase the range of assessment variables and the validity of final judgments by incorporating observations by parents, counselors, teachers, and peers over longer periods of time in natural settings.

Observations in School Settings

Systematic observational study of children in their natural environments would appear to be an obviously essential element in any meaningful evaluation. Yet, in the past, this form of data gathering has been employed primarily by researchers and only recently by those attempting to evaluate individual students for instructional purposes. Kerlinger (1973) notes that in research designs

> observations *must* be used when the variables of research studies are interactive and interpersonal in nature and when we wish to study the relations between actual behavior, like class management techniques or group interaction, and other behaviors or attribute variables. (p. 554; italics added)

Clearly, this advice also applies when our research efforts are oriented to individual students and their learning capabilities.

Although a good deal of attention is not being given to observational assessment, perhaps the most significant and comprehensive contribution to the observational study of children in natural settings has been made by the Midwest Psychological Field Station established in 1947 by Barker and Wright (Barker, 1968; Wright, 1960). Wright has classified observational approaches into open and closed methods. Open methods stress the recording of all behavior, or as much as is perceived, in a blow-by-blow description of events, and include diary descriptions, specimen descriptions, and narrative accounts. Closed methods record specific behaviors previously decided upon as relevant to a particular theory or hypothesis. They include time sampling, event sampling, trait rating, and category systems. These methods were created to satisfy needs for quantifiable data and observer reliability. Some examples are provided by Kerlinger (1973), Medinnus (1976), and Sackett (1978).

Wright, however, praises the narrative record approach because "it commands the breadth, richness, subtlety, and permanency of the written word, compared with which the best of checklists and rating scales are limited instruments" (1960, p. 81). In this procedure, the observer records everything the subject says and does and also everything said and done to the subject. Interpretations and generalizations are to be labeled as such and kept separate from the objective recording of the stream of behavior. In contrast to closed methods, such as checklists, this procedure allows clear definition of sequencing with antecedent and subsequent events establishing a context in which the specific behavior can be more fully understood. Moreover, it clearly describes environmental conditions, does not require immediate coding decisions, and provides a permanent record available for reanalysis at a later time.

To combine the benefits of both open and closed observational systems, counselors can devise checklist-type scoring systems to be used in scoring previously obtained narrative records. These checklists can be jointly constructed with teachers and other school personnel, and can be designed to assess separate domains for different types of handicapping conditions. Such scoring system flexibility is sorely needed in work with handicapped individuals.

Sociometric Assessment

The term *sociometry* has acquired several meanings over the years as its frequency of occurrence in educational literature has significantly increased. Generally speaking, however, the term has come to mean the study of personal relationships within a group situation — a critical dimension of assessment for handicapped individuals.

Through sociometric procedures, counselors not only evaluate the degree of peer acceptance or rejection of the handicapped individual, but also gain an independent source of data to serve as a validity check on information obtained through other means. Peer nominations of classmates are not limited to popularity variables, but also can include judgments of the individual's friendliness, academic ability, sensitivity to others, et cetera.

Another oversimplification of sociometric procedure relates to data analysis. Contrary to popular belief, sociometric analyses are not limited to the pictorial diagram or "circles and arrows" approach defined as a *sociogram*. Understandably, this form of analysis discourages use of sociometry because it is so unwieldy when used with classroom-sized groups. The sociometric matrix, which establishes a choice grid, and the sociometric index, which uses a ratio format, are far more manageable procedures for classroom use. As an added bonus, the index procedure offers opportunity to compare individuals and groups in different classrooms.

To construct a sociometric matrix, the examiner simply lists all students' names in both horizontal and vertical margins of the matrix. The choices made by an individual are entered along his or her row in the columns assigned to the chosen classmates. By totaling columns, one can tell at a glance how many times each person was chosen.

Sociometric indices can yield information about a variety of social attributes, such as one's choice status in the group (number of persons choosing the subject, divided by one less than the total number of persons in the group); or one's positive expansiveness (number of choices the subject makes divided by one less than the total number of people). Indices can be used to compare groups, or the same group at two points in time, on characteristics such as group cohesion, group integration, or group expansiveness. Group indices may be particularly useful as pre-post assessments of a classroom where handicapped students have been mainstreamed. Further information regarding sociometric procedures is provided by Moreno (1960); Kerlinger (1973); and Evans (1966).

The Family and Teacher as Information Sources

As previously mentioned, information obtained from parents regarding the handicapped individual's adaptive behaviors is indispensable in designing remedial programs. Counselors must determine the degree to which the handicapped person's behavior is environmentally determined. If discrepancies exist between the child's home and school behaviors, it is reasonable to assume that environmental variables are influential in causing the discrepancy. Consequently, remedial strategies should necessarily consider these environmental factors.

A second advantage in considering teachers and families as information sources lies in cross-time documentation of behaviors. Whereas psychometric tests and classroom observations are limited to short-duration assessments, interviews or rating scale data from parents and teachers yield longer-range verification of specific behavior traits as well as evidence pertaining to rate of developmental progress. However, it must be recognized that these data sources may suffer from subjectivity or bias as contrasted to the more objective standardized assessments.

Teacher interviews should be designed to obtain information regarding the child's independent functioning, personal and social responsibility, and academic competence. An illustration of a teacher rating-scale assessment of young children is the Kohn Competence Rating Scale (Kohn & Rosman, 1972), which evaluates the child's competencies in interaction with the teacher and peers, in addition to performance in classroom activities.

Matey (1975) provides an outline of questions designed to be used in interviewing parents of handicapped children. Each question stimulates a parental monologue, which extends beyond the expected scope of the question. His questionnaire deals with the handicapped child's daily activities, such as dressing, eating, promptness, responsibilities, and social competencies.

Combining parent interview data with information gained from teachers and school records allows the counselor to formulate a more comprehensive description of the child, one that depicts the child's functioning across time and environments.

Integrated Assessments

The foregoing descriptions of data sources for multifactored assessment illustrate their utility in broadening the range of evaluation variables and generating more valid conclusions. However, these separate data sources contribute even more meaningfully when integrated into comprehensive, conceptual frameworks that yield related prescriptions for interventions in major life-adjustment areas. Three examples of assessment approaches that represent movements in this direction are the combination of norm-referenced and criterion-referenced tests, the assessment of work potential, and the Barclay Classroom Climate Inventory (BCCI) (Barclay, 1976).

In practice, it is often useful to employ both norm- and criterion-referenced tests in assessing handicapped populations. It is important to determine through criterion-referenced assessment not only the specific skills of the individual but also how that person compares with the norm. The use of both types of assessment results in a more complete understanding of the individual's strengths and weaknesses, allowing for a more effective intervention program. For example, in older handicapped populations, norm-referenced tests assessing IQ and achievement along with criterion-referenced tests assessing specific work-related skills allow a rather complete survey of the individual's competencies and potential for successful adaptation.

The Barclay Classroom Climate Inventory (BCCI) (Barclay, 1967, 1974a, 1974b, 1976) is a computer-scored instrument that incorporates teacher, peer, and individual input to describe the individual child's behavior within the social context of the elementary classroom setting. The BCCI is an empirically based, diagnostic-prescriptive instrument that integrates teacher, peer, and self-expectations. If one assumes that the description and assessment of social, behavioral, and cognitive skills of an individual are pragmatically based on how others perceive these skills within the parameters of a specific environmental setting, the BCCI may describe the individual child more comprehensively than any other instrument currently available. The BCCI has been used in some studies to examine the degree of social integration of mentally handicapped children in normal educational settings

(Barclay & Kehle, 1979; Kehle & Guidubaldi, 1978, 1979). The diagnostic information obtained from the BCCI significantly enhances the development of the handicapped individual's educational plan.

Several tests measuring work potential are appealing because they incorporate some of the advantages of both norm- and criterion-referenced tests. Perhaps one of the most readily agreed-upon curriculum goals for the handicapped person is the preparation and training for satisfactory occupational adjustment. Finding out precisely what the handicapped person can accomplish in a work-oriented area may be far more productive in enhancing individualized education and rehabilitation plans than just directing the plans toward school-related achievement. A basic assumption of work-potential assessment is to determine the relative strengths that have work-related value, and to design consequent programs to enhance these strengths.

One obvious problem in work-potential assessment is that the person's interests may not be in concert with work-related strengths or skills. Merachnik (1970) suggests that it is not unusual for handicapped individuals to have limited or unrealistic interests, because of restrictions that have hindered exploratory experiences. Consequently, it is imperative in the assessment milieu to adopt an orientation that seeks out potential interest that may be further developed as a consequence of the assessed skills.

The selection of tests to determine the work potential of handicapped individuals should be based on traditional criteria of the test's reliability and predictive validity. The Singer Vocational Evaluation System (SINGER), the Wide Range Employment Sample Test (WREST), the Valpar Component Work Sample System (VALPAR), and the Testing, Orientation, and Work Evaluation in Rehabilitation (TOWER) are examples of work-sample assessment instruments. Although each of these systems represents a significant technological breakthrough in vocational evaluation and adds a relevant dimension in programming for the handicapped, each system has relative strengths and weaknesses. For example, the SINGER, which employs 17 work stations, has a definite relative strength in its audio-visual format for instruction, but has a relative weakness in its lack of research evidence to support its validity. The WREST provides normative data for estimating readiness of a person to enter competitive work situations, but relies on a series of relatively uncomplicated performance samples. The VALPAR employs samples that incorporate motivation levels. This aspect of the VALPAR is quite desirable and is often overlooked in other work-sample assessment systems. The TOWER appears to be a well-researched system that employs 110 work-sample tasks grouped in 14 occupational areas. The qualitative and quantitative standards for each sample task have clear relevance to industrial requirements.

After assessment, exploratory work experiences are mandatory to more fully determine ability, interest, and social adaptability. With the normative nature of these instruments and the specific assessment of relevant work-related skills along with the consequent validity check gained from the exploratory work experience, the rehabilitation or school counselor has a valuable assessment sequence, which will undoubtedly enhance programming for the handicapped.

SUMMARY

The above descriptions of assessment domains and evaluation strategies are intended to provide counselors with assessment perspectives as well as specific suggestions. A truly comprehensive list of domains and strategies is beyond the scope of this article and is more effectively presented in such references as Anastasi (1976), Buros (1972), Coulter and Morrow (1978), McReynolds (1975), Wallace and Larson (1978), and Wisland (1974). In addition, it is not the purpose of this paper to present detailed analyses of major controversies in testing, such as the limitations of projective techniques or the predictive utility of "estimated learning potential" indices for culturally different students. For a well-balanced presentation of this latter issue, the reader is referred to an excellent recent issue of *The School Psychology Digest* (January, 1979), which is devoted to examination of Mercer's SOMPA system (Mercer, 1979). It should also be obvious that evaluations of handicapped persons must include diagnostic information from a variety of specialists, such as physicians, speech and hearing therapists, nurses, remedial reading teachers, home visitors, special education teachers, school psychologists, and counselors.

The counselor's role as a member of the diagnostic team is both unique and essential. Although counselors would not ordinarily administer some of the tests mentioned here, they are specially qualified to perform parent and teacher interviews, sociometric analyses, observations in the classroom, and work-potential assessments. As mainstreaming into regular classrooms increases, counselors' rapport with teachers and students, their detailed knowledge of the teacher and peer group differences within their schools, and their orientation to social adjustment and career preparation will provide increasingly critical contributions to the diagnostic team effort. The counselor's intensive participation in assessment and treatment of handicapped students is clearly needed and long overdue.

REFERENCES

Anastasi, A. *Psychological testing* (4th ed.). New York: Macmillan, 1976.

Anderson, S., & Messick, S. Social competence in young children. *Developmental Psychology*, 1974, 10, 282–293.

Arthur, G. *The Arthur adaptation of the Leiter International Performance Scale.* Chicago: C. H. Stoelting, 1950.

Barclay, J. R. Effecting behavior change in the elementary classroom: An exploratory study. *Journal of Counseling Psychology*, 1967, *14*, 240–247.

Barclay, J. R. Needs assessment in the elementary school. In H. J. Walberg (Ed.), *Evaluating educational performance: A sourcebook of instruments and procedures*. Berkeley, Calif.: John McCuthan, 1974.(a)

Barclay, J. R. System-wide analysis of social interaction and affective problems in schools. Chapter in Proceedings of the Fifth International Conference on Behavior Modification, P. O. Davidson, F. W. Clark, & L. A. Hamerlynck (Eds.), *Evaluation of behavioral programs in community, residential and school settings*, pp. 329–386. Champaign, Ill.: Research Press, 1974.(b)

Barclay, J. R. *Manual for the Barclay Classroom Climate Inventory*. Lexington, Ky.: Educational Skills Development, 1976.

Barclay, J. R., & Kehle, T. J. The impact of handicapped students on other students in the classroom. *Journal of Research and Development in Education*, 1979.

Barker, R. G. *Ecological psychology: Concepts and methods in studying the environment of human behavior*. Stanford, Calif.: Stanford University Press, 1968.

Burgemeister, B. B.; Blum, L. H.; & Lorge, I. *Columbia Mental Maturity Scale* (3rd ed.). New York: Harper & Row, 1962.

Buros, O. K. (Ed.). *Seventh mental measurements yearbook*. Highland Park, N.J.: Gryphon Press, 1972.

Clarizio, H. F. In defense of the IQ test. *School Psychology Digest*, 1979, *8*, 79–88.

Connolly, A.; Nachtman, W.; & Pritchett, E. *Manual for the Key Math Diagnostic Arithmetic Test*. Circle Pines, Minn.: American Guidance Service, 1971.

Coulter, W. A., & Morrow, H. W. *Adaptive behavior: Concepts and measurements*. New York: Grune & Stratton, 1978.

Doll, E. A. *Vineland Social Maturity Scale*. Circle Pines, Minn.: American Guidance Service, 1965.

Doll, E. A. *Preschool Attainment Record*. Circle Pines, Minn.: American Guidance Service, 1966.

Dunn, L. M., & Markwardt, F. C. *Peabody Individual Achievement Test*. Circle Pines, Minn.: American Guidance Service, 1970.

Evans, K. M. *Sociometry and education*. New York: Humanities Press, 1966.

Flaugher, R. The many definitions of test bias. *American Psychologist*, 1978, *33*, 671–679.

Frostig, M.; Lefever, W.; & Whittlesey, J. R. *The Marianne Frostig Developmental Test of Visual Perception: 1963 standardization*. Palo Alto, Calif.: Consulting Psychologists Press, 1964.

Graham, R., & Kendall, B. S. Memory for Designs Test: Revised general manual. *Perceptual and Motor Skills*, 1960, *11*, 147–188.

Guidubaldi, J. *Social competence of preschool children as a predictor of social and academic competence two years later*. Unpublished doctoral dissertation, Harvard University, 1969.

Harper, G. F.; Guidubaldi, J.; & Kehle, T. J. Is academic achievement related to classroom behavior? *Elementary School Journal*, 1978, *78*, 202–207.

Hatch, E. J.; Murphy, J.; & Bagnato, S. J. The comprehensive evaluation for handicapped children. *Elementary School Guidance and Counseling*, 1979, *13*, 170–187.

Hiskey, M. *Hiskey-Nebraska Test of Learning Aptitude*. Lincoln, Neb.: Union College Press, 1966.

Jastak, J. F., & Jastak, S. R. *Manual: The Wide Range Achievement Test*. Wilmington, Del.: Guidance Associates, 1965.

Jensen, A. *Test bias and construct validity*. Revised version of an address to the American Psychological Association Annual Meeting, Chicago, September 1975.

Kamin, L. G. *The science and politics of IQ*. New York: Halsted, 1975.

Kaufman, A. S. WISC-R research: Implications for interpretation. *School Psychology Digest*, 1979, 8, 5–27.

Kehle, T. J., & Barclay, J. R. Social and behavioral characteristics of mentally handicapped students. *Journal of Research and Development in Education*, 1979.

Kehle, T. J., & Guidubaldi, J. Effect of EMR placement models on affective and social development. *Psychology in the Schools*, 1978, 15, 175–182.

Kehle, T. J., & Guidubaldi, J. *Evaluation of the selective re-entry management system in identifying and integrating special education children into normal class settings*. Paper presented at the Annual Convention of the National Association of School Psychologists, San Diego, California, 1979.

Kerlinger, F. N. *Foundations of behavioral research*. New York: Holt, Rinehart & Winston, 1973.

Kohlberg, L., & Zigler, E. The impact of cognitive maturity on the development of sex-role attitudes in the years 4 to 8. *Genetic Psychology Monographs*, 1967, 75, 89–165.

Kohn, M., & Rosman, B. I. Social-emotional, cognitive, and demographic determinants of poor school achievement: Implications for instrument generality and longitudinal persistence. *Developmental Psychology*, 1972, 6, 430–444.

Kohn, M., & Rosman, B. I. Social-emotional, cognitive, and demographic determinants of poor school achievement: Implications for a strategy of intervention. *Journal of Educational Psychology*, 1974, 66, 267–276.

Koppitz, E. M. *Human Figures Drawing Test*. New York: Grune & Stratton, 1968.

Koppitz, E. M. *The Bender-Gestalt Test for Young Children: Vol. II: Research and application, 1963–1973*. New York: Grune & Stratton, 1975.

Koppitz, E. M. *The Visual-Aural Digit Span Test*. New York: Grune & Stratton, 1977.

Lambert, N. Exhibit C: I.Q. trail. *APA Monitor*, 1978, 9, 8–9.

Matey, C. *Guidelines for assessment of handicapped children*. Dayton, Ohio: Miami Valley Regional Center for Handicapped Children, 1975.

McClelland, D. C. Testing for competence rather than for "intelligence." *American Psychologist*, 1973, 28, 1–14.

McReynolds, P. *Advances in psychological assessment* (Vol. 3). San Francisco: Jossey-Bass, 1975.

Medinnus, G. R. *Child study and observation guide*. New York: Wiley, 1976.

Merachnik, D. Assessing work potential of the handicapped in public school. *Vocational Guidance Quarterly*, 1970, 18, 225–229.

Mercer, J. R. In defense of racially and culturally nondiscriminatory assessment. *School Psychology Digest*, 1979, 8, 89–115.

Mischel, W. *Personality and assessment*. New York: Wiley, 1968.

Moreno, J. L. *The sociometry reader*. Glencoe, Ill.: The Free Press, 1960.

Murray, H. *Thematic Apperception Test.* Cambridge, Mass.: Harvard University Press, 1943.

Newland, T. E. *Manual for the Blind Learning Aptitude Test: Experimental edition.* Urbana, Ill.: T. E. Newland, 1969.

Nihira, K.; Foster, R.; Shellhaas, M.; & Leland, H. *American Association on Mental Deficiency Adaptive Behavior Scale* (1975 revision). Washington, D.C.: American Association on Mental Deficiency, 1975.

Perry, J. D.; Guidubaldi, J.; & Kehle, T. J. Kindergarten competencies as predictors of third grade classroom behavior and achievement. *Journal of Educational Psychology,* 1979, 71, 443–450.

Piers, E., & Harris, D. *The Piers-Harris Children's Self-Concept Scale.* Nashville, Tenn.: Counselor Recordings and Tests, 1969.

Roach, E. F., & Kephart, N. C. *The Purdue Perceptual-Motor Survey.* Columbus, Ohio: Charles E. Merrill, 1966.

Sackett, G. P. (Ed.). *Observing behavior: Data collection and analysis methods.* Baltimore, Md.: University Park Press, 1978.

Sanford, A. R. *A manual for use of the Learning Accomplishment Profile.* Winston-Salem, N.C.: Kaplan, 1974.

Sattler, J. M. *Assessment of children's intelligence.* Philadelphia: W. G. Saunders, 1974.

Singer Vocational Evaluation System. Singer Education Division, Career Systems, 80 Commerce Drive, Rochester, New York, 14623.

Stevenson, H. W.; Parker, T.; Wilkinson, A.; Hegion, A.; & Fish, E. Longitudinal study of individual differences in cognitive development. *Journal of Educational Psychology,* 1976, 68, 337–400.

Testing, Orientation, and Work Evaluation in Rehabilitation (TOWER). ICD Rehabilitation and Research Center, 400 First Avenue, New York, New York, 10010.

Thorndike, R., & Hager, E. *Measurement and evaluation in psychology and education* (4th ed.). New York: Wiley, 1977.

Valpar Component Work Sample System. Valpar Corporation, 655 North Alvernon Way, Suite 108, Tucson, Arizona, 85716.

Wallace, G., & Larson, S. C. *Educational assessment of learning problems: Testing for teaching.* Boston: Allyn & Bacon, 1978.

Wide Range Employment Sample Test (WREST). Guidance Associates of Delaware, Inc., 1526 Gilpin Avenue, Wilmington, Delaware, 19806.

Wisland, M. V. *Psychoeducational diagnosis of exceptional children.* Springfield, Ill.: Charles C Thomas, 1974.

Woodcock, R. W. *Woodcock Reading Mastery Tests.* Circle Pines, Minn.: American Guidance Service, 1973.

Wright, H. F. Observational child study. In P. Mussen (Ed.), *Handbook of research methods in child development.* New York: Wiley, 1960.

Zigler, E., & Trickett, P. K. I.Q., social competence and evaluation of early childhood intervention programs. *American Psychologist,* 1978, 33, 789–798.

26

Structured Experiential Training (SET): A Group Rehabilitation Model

Robert G. Lasky
Arthur E. Dell Orto
Robert P. Marinelli

Structured Experiential Training (SET) is a group rehabilitation approach that was developed to respond to the needs of persons with physical disabilities through the implementation of an eclectic and systematic group approach. Disabled persons frequently share common concerns, such as adjustment to the personal impact of disability (Kerr, 1961; Wright, 1964), as well as interpersonal stress and stigma often imposed upon disabled persons by nondisabled persons (English, 1971; Ladieu-Leviton, Adler, & Dembo, 1948). In an effort to help both physically disabled and nondisabled persons to overcome these and related difficulties, the authors felt the need for a group counseling model which went beyond the verbalization of problems.

When disabled persons share their concerns in a group format, they often capitalize on each others' strengths and benefit from the role models in the group. Additionally, they often feel a heightened awareness and sensitivity toward one another that communicates trust and understanding. This awareness highlighted the importance of including a major focus on *mutual concern*, or interpersonal caring, in the SET group model. It was apparent that if group member sharing and caring could be stressed, the constructive impact of the group would be intensified. In addition, uncertainty of future goals often adversely affects the disabled person's ability to meaningfully plan for the future. This realization indicated the need for a second

From *Group Counseling and Physical Disability: A Rehabilitation and Health Care Perspective*, by R. G. Lasky and A. E. Dell Orto. Copyright © 1979 by Wadsworth, Inc. Reprinted by permission of the publisher, Brooks/Cole Publishing Company, Monterey, California.

major focus on *goal involvement,* which could be personalized and developed within the SET model. Action in implementing goals and related behaviors is another important component of SET, which is referred to as *accountability.* This third major factor was emphasized, considering that physically disabled persons often do not become actively involved with rehabilitation planning because of the lack of a system which stresses personal responsibility in the rehabilitation process. These three major emphases are developed more fully later in this chapter.

Structured Experiential Training (SET) attempts to combine the positive aspects of currently utilized group approaches within a systematic framework to benefit persons who are being rehabilitated. A key component in the SET model is the utilization of structured experiential learning and the use of a variety of structured experiences related to group and personal functioning.

In recent years, structured experiences have been used to facilitate many types of goal-oriented group processes (Danish & Zelenski, 1972; Kaplan & Sadock, 1971; Pfeiffer & Jones, 1972; Means & Roessler, 1976; Roessler, 1978; Roessler et al., 1976, 1977). The term "structured experiences" refers to "an intervention in a group's process that involves a set of specific instructions for participants to follow" (Kurtz, 1975, p. 167). Such an intervention then develops through five experiential steps described by Pfeiffer & Jones (1975): (1) *experiencing*—the participant becomes involved in an activity; (2) *publishing*—following the experience, the participant shares or publishes reactions and observations with others; (3) *processing*—the dynamics that emerge in the activity are explored, discussed, and evaluated with other participants; (4) *generalizing*—this involves developing principles or extracting generalization from the experience; and (5) *applying*—using new learnings behaviorally. After reviewing the results of research related to structured experiences in groups, Kurtz (1975) found that such interventions led to (1) more cohesive groups, (2) participants who were more involved in the group activities, (3) participants who perceived their leaders in a more favorable light, and (4) participants who reported that they learned more from the group experiences.

The SET group procedure is viewed as applicable to a wide range of persons having problems with life and living, although its use with persons having disabilities has been a primary thrust. This current model represents the culmination of the developmental changes that have taken place since SET originated as a group treatment approach for rehabilitating substance abusers (Dell Orto, 1975) to its recent application with physically disabled persons (Lasky, Dell Orto, & Marinelli, 1976; Marinelli, Dell Orto, & Lasky, 1976; Pelletier, 1978). SET has also been used with female alcoholics (Trudel, 1977).

Structured Experiential Training (SET) utilizes structured experiential learning, the power of the group process, and an explicit goal orientation. Its focus is on skill acquisition and related therapeutic issues that are significant in the rehabilitation process. It is presented as a model that can provide an alternative group approach that can be applied to a variety of populations and settings.

PRELIMINARY CONSIDERATIONS

Certain factors must be considered to maximize the potential effectiveness of the SET group experience:

1. *Selection of Members.* Potential SET group members are individually screened by the SET group leaders. Group candidates have an opportunity to view a SET group in action on a videotape and are given a written and verbal description of the SET group, in addition to the SET group written contract. Such activities help potential group members obtain a better grasp of their responsibilities in the SET group experience and help to increase their expectations of what they stand to gain from the experience. Prospective group participants are encouraged to ask questions and voice concerns. Rather than automatically screening out potential members on the basis of physical disability or psychodiagnostic labeling, such as brain damage, sociopath, or drug abuser (Yalom, 1975), members are selected on an individual basis, focusing not on apparent deficits, but on potential to benefit from the SET group experience. Primary selection concerns, determined on the basis of the interview, are a member's commitment to become goal-involved and accountable for his or her goal-directed behavior, and his or her agreement with the goals outlined in the SET group contract. Members who express a commitment to these principles and appear able to benefit from the group are invited to become a part of the SET group.

2. *Group Size.* The SET group is usually composed of six to ten participants. This size is consistent with recommended guidelines from a variety of research studies and practical experiences relating group size to time demands, group interaction, and participant satisfaction with the group process (Castore, 1962; Yalom, 1975). However, in certain settings the SET group may be larger or smaller, dependent on how the number of members would affect the optimal potential functioning of the group.

3. *Group Composition.* The SET group has usually been composed of members who are interested in and capable of working toward personally relevant goals. SET groups have been conducted with groups of (1) drug abusers (Dell Orto, 1975); (2) female alcoholics (Trudel, 1977); and (3) physically disabled persons (Marinelli, Dell Orto, & Lasky, 1976). SET groups have also been used with mixed groups of disabled and nondisabled persons.

At this point, SET groups are especially useful when the participants are physically disabled and are grouped on the basis of their unique needs, regardless of homogeneity or heterogeneity concerning disability grouping or related factors. A primary concern is that participants have the potential for a cohesive group experience and the opportunity to observe, model, and learn a wide variety of alternative behaviors and skills.

4. *Frequency of Meetings.* The SET group usually meets once per week for approximately three consecutive hours. This time frame gives each member the opportunity to share his or her personal concerns and/or to report on significant experiences which occurred since the previous meeting. Also, due to the mobility problems of some members, it is more viable to have one longer meeting than two shorter ones. However, meeting times are flexible and may occur more or less frequently, depending on the unique considerations of the setting or group member characteristics.

5. *Written Contract.* A written contract is given to the potential members prior to their inclusion in the SET group process. Subsequently, a mutual agreement is made between the leaders and the prospective group members concerning responsibilities in the SET group. This contract contains information on the goals and general expectations of the SET experience. Contracts have been shown to be highly effective in providing individuals with clearly defined expectations, goals, and interpersonal guidelines, and in enhancing the effectiveness of the therapeutic process (Haimowitz, 1973; Mallucio & Marlow, 1974; Montgomery & Montgomery, 1975; Steiner, 1971). Furthermore, the emphasis on individual and group goals and on mutuality of group members is highlighted as soon as possible, rather than by chance. Participants also have the opportunity to focus on the impact of their signatures on the contract in the initial SET group, and the importance of both personal and interpersonal responsibilities with an agreed-upon framework of interactions.

6. *SET Workbook.* SET group members are expected to record their perceptions of the group process and to keep notes outside the group on influences relating to their goal seeking. In addition, participants are frequently given systematic directions to follow both within and external to the SET group experience. These personal notes, assigned structured experiences, and related SET information develop into a personalized SET Workbook that helps participants to (1) become aware, during the group interaction, of various aspects of themselves and others that may otherwise be only indirectly focused on; (2) determine personally meaningful goals and appropriate group goals; and (3) become a more cohesive group. The workbook provides a uniform direction that facilitates the group process.

7. *Group Leadership.* It is advisable that SET groups be led by persons who have at least (1) obtained their professional entry degree or have related academic experience; (2) had at least two academic group counseling

courses; and (3) had supervised practice and experience in using group approaches (Appendix A). However, when used as a part of a group counseling course, graduate students may conduct the SET group with competent supervision. Rather than an informal structure and limited involvement of the leader, SET stresses using the specialized skills, techniques, and experiences of the leaders, as well as their function as role models and facilitators. Guidance of the leaders develops group cohesiveness and mutual concern. Whenever possible, coleaders share the responsibilities and direction of the SET. Pfeiffer and Jones (1975) have discussed several advantages of using coleaders in groups, including providing alternative models for group members, complementing styles, and increasing ability to deal with heightened affect.

8. *Structured Experiential Techniques.* A key practice in SET is the use of structured experiential techniques to help participants more quickly attain their own goals and the mutually agreed-upon goals of the group contract. Group goals focus upon learning to identify, explore, evaluate, and respond to specific problem areas shared among group members. By providing a guided, relatively nonthreatening here-and-now focus, structured experiences give group participants a unique opportunity to discover the individuality and commonality of group members. Such awarenesses and perceived similarities are usually important factors in achieving group cohesiveness and personal and interpersonal growth. SET groups make frequent use of structured experiences designed to enhance personal and group goal acquisition.

THE SET MODEL

The SET group model is multidimensional and has identifiable phases and stages.

SET Phase Development

SET groups have three sequential phases, which develop from a personal to a more broadly defined life perspective. These three SET phases are shown in Figure 3.

The phases in Figure 3 indicate SET participant involvement, beginning with a focus on individual concerns, strengths, and problems brought by members to the SET group (Personal Perspective), continuing through a focus on the functioning of the group itself as a goal-directed unit (Group Phase), and ultimately, concluding with an emphasis on developing group resources to help SET participants use the newly acquired skills in their everyday lives (Life and Living Phase).

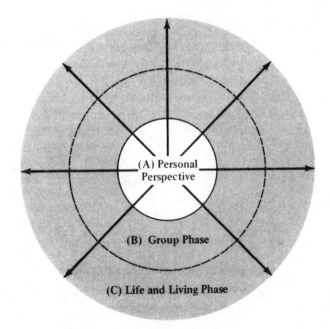

Figure 3. The phases of the SET model.

Phase A—Personal

Phase A focuses on the early development of a SET group and the encouragement of personal responsibility in the group. Structured experiences are used to help individuals to (1) identify personal goals; (2) clarify these goals, using descriptive behavioral language; (3) take responsibility for the excessive or deficient maladaptive behavioral difficulties which have led to problems in living; (4) develop a strategy to attain goals and become accountable for goal-directed behavior; and (5) develop the resources of the group to help group members succeed in reaching their goals.

Phase B—Group

In Phase B, the focus of the SET group is on helping the group to work together in a cohesive manner toward some relevant group-determined goals. Group leaders place increasing emphasis on demonstrated mutual concern and interpersonal sharing. Specific goals for Phase B include (1) encouraging group members to work together toward some mutually determined purpose; (2) helping participants experience the constructive power the group has on all group members; (3) experiencing the effects of facilitative sharing of a common goal; (4) experiencing how to contribute to and benefit from teamwork; and (5) internalizing the values related to goal-directed activities.

Phase C—Life and Living

Phase C of the SET group is oriented toward helping group members internalize the knowledge, skills, and experiences that were attained in Phases A and B. Participants are given the opportunity to develop, work toward, and receive feedback on individual and/or social concerns related to functioning outside of the group. One specific emphasis in Phase C for persons who are physically disabled is to begin active involvement in self-help groups related to physical disability that are designed to (1) provide a supportive outlet for group members following the termination of the SET group; (2) develop community action plans to serve the needs of persons with physical disabilities; and (3) become active providers of rehabilitation services, using various strategies inherent in or consistent with the concept of self-help (Anthony, 1972; Anthony & Cannon, 1969; English & Oberle, 1971; Jaques & Patterson, 1974; Merlin & Kauppi, 1973; Siller & Chipman, 1965). If documented prejudice and negative attitudes by nondisabled toward disabled persons are to be overcome, active and organized consumer involvement is essential. Gartner and Riessman (1977, p. 107) suggest that "the essence of the human services depends on the involvement and motivation of the consumer." There is a need for a self-help consumer organization composed of persons who have a variety of physical disabilities who are working together to enhance service delivery systems and overcome prejudicial attitudes by nondisabled persons. Individual SET group members present and discuss long- or short-term personal concerns which may adversely affect their adaptation to life and living. The group focus is then channeled toward helping each person continue to progress through the SET stages toward a purposeful transition to the world beyond the group. Representative Phase C goals for all SET group members include (1) demonstrating a transfer of the learned goal involvement to long-range real-world concerns; (2) skillfully applying significant experiences from the group activities to everyday living; (3) challenging participants to demonstrate consistent behaviors, affect, and cognitions, i.e., being congruent; and (4) evaluating the gains experienced by the SET group experience relative to the everyday process of life and living.

SET Stage Development

Within the SET phases there are twelve progressive stages, which are shown in Figure 4.

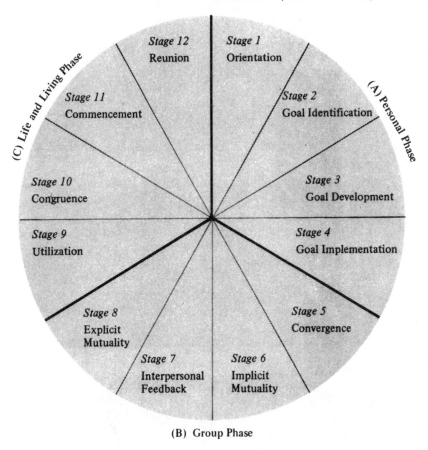

Figure 4. The stages in the SET model.

These twelve SET stages are directly related to the three previously de-scribed SET phases. This relationship is shown by Figure 5.

As shown in Figure 5, in Phase A (Personal) there are four stages, be-ginning with Orientation (Stage 1) and ending with Goal Implementation (Stage 4). A major emphasis in Phase A is personal learning concerning goal planning and involvement. In Phase B (Group) there are also four stages, beginning with Convergence (Stage 5) and concluding with Explicit Mutual-ity (Stage 8). A primary focus in this phase is the development of construc-tive group involvement and demonstrated mutual concern between group members. In the last phase, Life and Living (Phase C), there are also four stages, the first of which is Utilization (Stage 9) and the final stage, Reunion (Stage 12). Phase C stresses the utilization of significant learnings from the

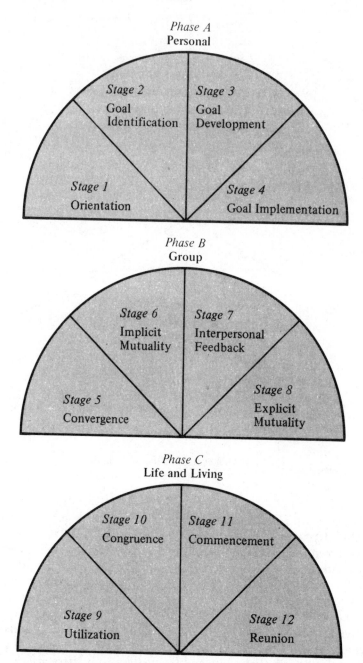

Figure 5. *The phases and stages in the SET model.*

SET group experience to generalized concerns in ever-expanding areas of life and living. Each of the twelve SET stages is more fully described in Table 6.

The SET Group Process

There are three primary emphases in the SET group model: (1) goal involvement; (2) mutual concern; and (3) accountability. These three emphases are augmented throughout the SET group process by the SET group contract, the SET workbook, leadership influence, and structured experiential interventions.

Goal Involvement

SET stresses the importance of group members' working on two levels of goal-directed behavior. On the most obvious level, each group participant works toward self-determined goals that are personally relevant, understandable, behavioral, measurable, attainable, and time-limited. A second level of goal-directed involvement pertains to the developmental process of the SET group, which progresses through three general phases and twelve distinctive stages. Ultimately, the SET group is concerned with goals related to increased intra- and interpersonal awareness, and acquisition of both enhanced interpersonal skills and values that are behaviorally, cognitively, and affectively congruent and that allow the individual increased functional capabilities.

Mutual Concern

Another emphasis in the SET group is on mutual concern, demonstrated respect, and interpersonal responsibility. Much of this focus is based on valuing principles accentuated in experiential and existential therapeutic practices (Barrett-Leonard, 1974; Gibb, 1971). Members are encouraged to become increasingly aware of their contractual obligation to extend themselves by demonstrating explicit concern for one another. While most group models do not encourage participants to be in contact with each other outside of the group, SET reserves the right to prompt external contact and involvement among members whenever there is potential for personal and interpersonal growth. Only by such structured and reinforced external group contact can members begin to transfer skills, behaviors, and values to real-world situations. The emphasis on group support and guided external involvement helps to facilitate the seemingly difficult transitions necessary for the generalization of growth experiences.

Table 6. Description of the SET Stages

Stage	Focus	Description
PHASE A – Personal		
1. Orientation	Clarifying the purpose of the SET group and becoming acquainted.	Group members become acquainted with each other and share their feelings about beginning a group experience. Group participants are introduced to the SET group contract, which describes the SET group, responsibilities of group members and leaders, and ground rules.
2. Goal Identification	Selecting and exploring a personally relevant goal.	Group members become better acquainted by sharing their self-selected goals. By sharing their goals, participants have the opportunity to know each other in a nonthreatening and facilitative manner. Group members also have the opportunity to explore significant aspects of selected goals.
3. Goal Development	Operationalizing and developing a plan to reach the goal.	A sequential plan of action is developed with a step-by-step process toward the goal. Each step in the process must be operationalized (i.e., behavioral, attainable, understandable, relevant, measurable, time-limited). The goal cannot be meaningfully implemented until each step toward the goal is operationalized, with the last step in the process being the ultimate goal itself.
4. Goal Implementation	Actively pursuing the goal.	With the help and consent of the group, the participant is ready for active involvement with the goal, in accordance with Stage 3 guidelines. Additionally, group members provide feedback on goal seeking, citing strengths and limitations in the process. Group members are encouraged to share comments and concerns to facilitate each others' goal involvement.
PHASE B – Group		
5. Convergence	The group works together to formulate a goal which requires total group effort to accomplish.	The Convergence stage emphasizes the SET group coming together to work on a goal which is relevant for all group members. Structured experiences are designed to encourage maximum participation of group members and to apply goal development strategies, learned previously, to the group goal.
6. Implicit Mutuality	Assessing interpersonal relationships and implications of various relationships.	As the group begins to work together, there are varying degrees of involvement in the goal-seeking process. Implications of divergent involvement are explored, with a specific focus on acquainting group members with the concept of mutuality in relation to successful group goal involvement.

Table 6. Description of the SET Stages (continued)

Stage	Focus	Description
7. Interpersonal Feedback	Providing open, honest, and direct feedback concerning group member involvement in the group task.	Continuing involvement related to the goal-seeking behaviors and attitudes of group members often brings some members together while alienating others. Interpersonal relationships and goal involvement are explored, with continued emphasis on the importance of mutual concern among group members.
8. Explicit Mutuality	Demonstrating genuine interpersonal concern among group members.	Explicit mutuality refers to demonstrated concern, respect, and caring among group members. Participants share their thoughts and feelings concerning their giving and receiving mutual concern and how such actions have influenced their beliefs and values.

PHASE C—Life and Living

Stage	Focus	Description
9. Utilization	Expanding significant learnings from the SET group experience to everyday living.	Group members are encouraged to apply significant SET group experiences (e.g., goal development, mutual concern) to their daily lives. This includes establishment of short- and long-term goals, involvement with other people, and movement away from group dependence to independence in coping with real-world concerns.
10. Congruence	Demonstration of consistent thoughts, feelings, and actions.	Congruence in the SET model refers to a consistent integration of participants' thoughts, feelings, and actions with a special emphasis on constructively channeling these focal points toward growth-enhancing involvements. Group members share perceptions about each others' congruence, giving feedback concerning how congruence might be enhanced.
11. Commencement	Sharing SET group experiences and projected perspectives on future accomplishments.	The group discusses their SET experience, focusing on significant group experiences that have had impact on their lives. An important emphasis is on the solidarity of the group, continued goal-directed activities, and demonstrated mutual concern in ongoing life and living situations.
12. Reunion	Coming together to share personal growth experiences and exploring further needs for helping SET members.	The Reunion is held to reinforce significant learnings from the SET group experience and to determine if any members could benefit from further group or other forms of therapeutic involvement. It provides an opportunity to share success as well as to re-evaluate disappointments.

Accountability

A major focus in the SET group process is on personal and interpersonal responsibility. This includes involvement in constructive activities within and external to SET group experiences. Group members are perceived as being responsible for their behavior, rather than attributing behavioral difficulties to external forces beyond their control. This concept of internalizing rather than externalizing personal responsibility has been viewed as a primary factor related to emotional stability and constructive interpersonal relationships (Ellis, 1962; Rotter, Chance, & Phares, 1972). While some problems may be related to forces beyond the control of the individual (e.g., prejudice and negative attitudes by nondisabled toward disabled persons), it is important that group members take appropriate action on such problems

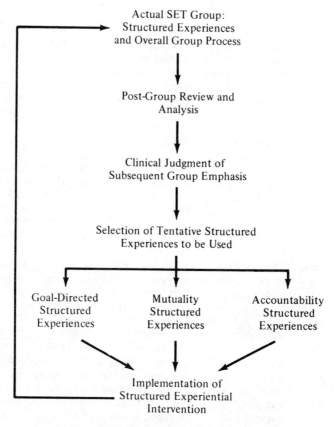

Figure 6. The process of the SET group.

rather than passively accept aversive situations, such as those that violate human rights.

Any one of the three primary factors of goal involvement, mutual concern, and accountability may be emphasized in a particular SET group. The determination of which aspect to emphasize is made by a close evaluation of the previous SET group and clinical judgment concerning the logical focus of the subsequent SET group. For example, the last SET group meeting may have been highly oriented toward goal involvement, with little or no emphasis on mutual concern or accountability. If these omissions adversely affected the functioning of the group, the group leaders might decide to emphasize mutual concern or accountability and deemphasize goal involvement. The process of determining tentative structured experiences is illustrated in Figure 6.

In order to facilitate the development of the SET group and to maximize its potential effectiveness, structured experiential tasks are included in the SET model. Structured experiences are viewed as important to help group members integrate, internalize, and relate to the SET model. Such experiences place greater emphasis on the experiential process and dynamics of the group, together with the cognitive aspects of goal involvement. Too often the latter are overemphasized, with the effect of reducing attractiveness of the group to group members. Conversely, groups emphasizing the processing of group dynamics often lack the structure needed to keep group activities focused.

To help the reader obtain a better appreciation for structured experiential interventions, representative structured experiences are described in Table 7. The primary criterion for whether a structured experience should be used is the potential effectiveness of the experience to facilitate group or personal growth and development.

SUMMARY

SET is an eclectic group rehabilitation model which is especially designed to meet the needs of persons with physical disabilities and emphasizes group members' goal involvement, mutual concern, and accountability. These emphases are incorporated throughout the SET model, which is composed of three sequential phases and twelve developmental stages. Structured experiential tasks are frequently used in SET to help group members to (1) achieve their self-selected goals, (2) become more concerned with the welfare of other persons, and (3) take personal responsibility for their lives. While the SET model is systematic and developmental, flexibility is stressed by encouraging personal goal development, the implementation of many different kinds of structured experiential interventions, and the frequent use of the resources of group members. Most importantly, the SET group is de-

Table 7. Representative Structured Experiential Interventions Used in SET

Stage	Focus	Title and Description
PHASE A — Personal		
1. Orientation	a. Goal Involvement	*Why Am I Here?* In this structured experience, group members are asked to write down their reason(s) for choosing to participate in the SET group. These reasons are read to the group and discussed as necessary.
	b. Mutual Concern	*The Gift.* This structured experience directs participants to pause and reflect on two questions: (1) How can I help others in this group? (2) How can the group help me? Reactions to these questions are shared with the group.
	c. Accountability	*The Signature.* Group members receive a copy of the SET group contract, which describes the group, states group member and leader responsibilities, and gives a listing of ground rules. After a discussion of issues related to the contract, members are asked to sign their contract. Implications of their signature are explored and discussed.
2. Goal Identification	a. Goal Involvement	*Pick a Goal.* Group members individually list three personal goals they would like to work on in the SET group. Participants then rank-order these goals from most to least meaningful. Dyads are formed, with directions to take turns interviewing each other about their goal choices. Dyads are instructed to identify at least one way their goals are similar and dissimilar. Partners share this information with the group; the group's task is to determine relevant similarities and dissimilarities of selected goals.
	b. Mutual Concern	*Spotlight.* This structured experience is designed to help group members select a personally meaningful goal. Group member(s) who have difficulty determining a goal are asked to sit in the center of the group. Remaining group members are asked to list questions which will help the member in the center explore potentially meaningful goals. Each member then asks his or her question in turn, with the person in the "spotlight" giving a response. After each

Table 7. *Representative Structured Experiential Interventions Used in SET (continued)*

Stage	Focus	Title and Description
		round, the spotlighted person summarizes any goal-directed learnings obtained from the questioning.
	c. Accountability	*Be Real.* Occasionally, group members may not take the group process seriously and/or identify irrelevant or inane goals. It is important that selected goals are personally meaningful if participants are expected to grow from the group experience. In this structured experience, group members are asked to reflect on each person's goal. Group members are then asked to (1) select the one goal that was most "real" or relevant to be worked on, (2) give reasons for this selection, and (3) compare the choice with their stated goal. The same process takes place for the least "real" goal. For the latter, group members are challenged to help the person selected to modify the goal in a more personally relevant direction.
3. Goal Development	a. Goal Involvement	*RUMBAT.* This structured experience is designed to operationalize each SET member's selected goal. The group leaders describe RUMBAT, an acronym relating to a goal which is Relevant, Understandable, Measurable, Behaviorable, Attainable, and Time-limited. Examples of how a goal is operationalized are given, followed by one member stating his or her goal and the SET group helping the member to operationalize the goal using RUMBAT criteria. Other SET group members are given a homework assignment to operationalize their goal prior to the subsequent SET group meeting.
	b. Mutual Concern	*Pairs.* Goal development may be difficult for some group members and may require time and effort between group meetings. In this structured experience, the group is broken into dyads, with least known partners being paired. Each dyad is given approximately 30 minutes to help each other operationalize their goals. Subsequently, the large group reconvenes and discusses their task and how working in pairs was experienced. Any un-

(continued)

Table 7.   Representative Structured Experiential Interventions
Used in SET (continued)

Stage	Focus	Title and Description
		finished task or personal business is given to be completed as a homework assignment.
	c. Accounta-bility	*Responsibility Pie.* In order to move the group members toward goal-directed activities, each member in the group must take some personal responsibility. Each group participant is given a sheet of paper with a circle drawn on it (all the same size). Members are instructed to individually draw a slice within the circle, to demonstrate how much responsibility they plan to take in working toward the group goal. All drawings are collected and pinned on a wall for all to see. A discussion of the drawings and related personal responsibility follows.
4. Goal Implementation	a. Goal Involvement	*Winners/Losers.* Group members are asked to name the two members who are perceived to be making the most progress toward their goals. Each choice is given on a 3×5 index card. These "votes" are then tallied. The winner(s) and loser(s) are discussed in terms of how each is different from the other in relation to their goal-seeking and/or group behavior.
	b. Mutual Concern	*Helping Hand.* The focus of this structured experience is to encourage group members who are succeeding at accomplishing their goals to actively help others who are having difficulty. Group members are asked to rate their success in accomplishing their goal on a 100-point scale (0 = totally unsuccessful to 100 = extremely successful). After each has made his or her rating, group members are asked to rate all other group members on the same questions. Often, members will have difficulty doing this, which presents the opportunity to challenge the group to involve themselves with others in their goal implementation, outside of the group. Reports of such involvement may be given in subsequent groups.
	c. Accounta-bility	*The Payoff.* SET group members are given envelopes containing identical and progressive denominations of money (i.e., penny

Table 7.   Representative Structured Experiential Interventions
Used in SET (continued)

Stage	Focus	Title and Description
		through dollar). Then each member is directed to consider who in the group is most productive, and so on to least productive in working on the group goal, and pay each person accordingly (i.e., dollar for most productive, etc.). This symbolic feedback is then discussed with a focus on perceptions of who gave what to whom.

PHASE B — Group

Stage	Focus	Title and Description
5. Convergence	a. Goal Involvement	*The Team.* Group members are instructed to pause and reflect on their SET group, and consider in what way the group might best work together. Participants individually select two goals external to the group, which the SET group could meaningfully attain. All goals are recorded on a poster board, group members discuss each goal, and a consensus is reached as to the group's selected goal.
	b. Mutual Concern	*The Project.* This structured experience is designed to assess how group members will work together on their group project. A box of materials, such as Tinkertoys, is placed in the middle of the group. The group is challenged to construct something worthwhile. (This is the only direction given.) After 30 minutes or more, The Project is discussed, with a focus on who were the doers and the do-nothings. Implications for working as a group are explored, as are suggestions to overcome any problems experienced by participating in The Project.
	c. Accountability	*The Crew.* Usually the more the group works together as a unit, the faster and better their goal will be accomplished. Group members are directed to set their chairs in a straight line, to imagine the chairs are seats in a boat, and then to select the seat, from No. 1 rower to the last rower, which symbolizes how much each perceives he or she has contributed to the group goal. After this has been done and discussed, chairs are reversed. A second discussion takes place con-

(continued)

Table 7. Representative Structured Experiential Interventions
Used in SET *(continued)*

Stage	Focus	Title and Description
		cerning how participants feel about their new responsibility, or lack of it.
6. Implicit Mutuality	a. Goal Involvement	*Partners.* The SET group is randomly divided into dyads, with partners selecting stages of the selected group goal for which they would like to take responsibility. Partners are given twenty minutes to meet and draw up a contract pertaining to their involvement. Each contract should state stage involvement according to RUMBAT criteria or be operationalized in some similar fashion.
	b. Mutual Concern	*Helping Hand.* In this structured experience, a survey is taken to explore who in the group went above and beyond their personal responsibility in working on the group goal. The rationale behind such action is processed in the group. Focus is also shifted to contractual obligations that were not met and reasons behind such lack of involvement.
	c. Accountability	*My Contribution.* After group members have developed their goal in a sequential fashion as in step-by-step, each member is asked to select the three subgoals which he or she would like to take personal responsibility for, and to briefly give a rationale for each. This information is shared with the group, discussed and agreed upon by all.
7. Interpersonal Feedback	a. Goal Involvement	*The Unforeseen.* Group members are asked to reflect on their goal involvement related to the group goal. Each is then asked to write down any problems being experienced in accomplishing the group goal. These problems are then expressed, discussed, and written down on a poster board. The group then determines, by consensus, the three most significant problems, and how each might be overcome, with an emphasis on determining who will have responsibility for implementing selected solutions.
	b. Mutual Concern	*Thanks, I Needed That.* Group members are asked to reflect on who in the group has been the most helpful, regarding the goal-

Table 7.   Representative Structured Experiential Interventions
Used in SET (continued)

Stage	Focus	Title and Description
		seeking process. Each is then asked to bring an inexpensive (less than $5) gift for this person to the subsequent group meeting (a poem may be substituted). Gifts are exchanged, and group members asked to focus on the feelings behind getting and giving tangible feedback.
	c. Accountability	*Guilty as Charged.* Occasionally, one or more group members are deficient in carrying out their designated responsibilities. Group members are asked to select the one member who is seen as least responsible in working toward the group goal. These selections are written on 3 × 5 index cards and placed in a hat. Prior to examining the results, open-ended discussion takes place with a focus on who the group contributors are, and specifically what they have done to be considered contributors. The vote is then tallied and the least contributing member focused on only in terms of what might be helpful to motivate this person to be more contributing.
8. Explicit Mutuality	a. Goal Involvement	*The Call of Caring.* By the time the SET group reaches this stage, increasingly explicit mutual concern is usually being demonstrated. In this structured experience the focus is on how members can help each other attain their group goals. Each member is asked to repeat his or her group subgoal. After everyone has done this, each member lists two people in the group whom he or she can help in some way to reach their subgoal. For each person chosen, the group member also indicates in *what* way help is planned, *where* the help will be given, and *when* the chosen member will be helped.
	b. Mutual Concern	*Beyond.* If mutual concern is being realized by group members, there will be indications of this beyond the group experience. In this structured experience, group members are challenged to develop a plan of action whereby they will have the opportunity to facilitate the growth of others outside of the SET group. Plans are first shared and dis-

(continued)

Table 7. *Representative Structured Experiential Interventions*
Used in SET (continued)

Stage	Focus	Title and Description
		cussed in triads, then shared within the larger group. Important components of this experience include a followup feedback session and similar unplanned feedback sessions.
	c. Accountability	*The Guest.* This structured experience is an extension of "Beyond," previously described. SET group members are asked to bring into the group persons who were directly affected by the planned or unplanned demonstration of explicit mutuality. Guests may be asked to form a separate group to discuss their experiences as recipients of explicit mutuality before sharing these with SET group members.
PHASE C—Life and Living		
9. Utilization	a. Goal Involvement	*Living Goal.* In this structured experience triads are formed. Triads are directed to select one goal which will help the participants to function more effectively in their everyday lives. Group members are then asked to present a role-play depicting important aspects of the goal. After each triad has performed a role-play, in the large group, group members explore relevant aspects of the goal which may not be clear. The goal may be changed to better represent the participants' more relevant concerns.
	b. Mutual Concern	*The Volunteer.* This structured experience is designed to give SET group members the opportunity to share their learnings from the group with friends, or family. From these categories group members are to select one person and try to help that person to become goal-directed. Results of attempts are discussed in subsequent groups.
	c. Accountability	*Lights, Camera, Action.* In this structured experience, group members give a verbal report of how they are utilizing their SET group experiences. Following this, a group member is selected to stage a role-play of the described situation. Group members are encouraged to provide feedback concerning the SET group member's performance, with op-

Table 7. Representative Structured Experiential Interventions
Used in SET (continued)

Stage	Focus	Title and Description
		portunities to replay the situation to improve members' skills in the selected situation.
10. Congruence	a. Goal Involvement	*Leaders.* This structured experience is designed to explore the extent to which group members are actively involved with goal-seeking behaviors. Group members are given the task of directing the group themselves for the next sessions (the actual group leaders may choose not to be present). The group continues in this way, followed by a report with group leaders facilitating the discussion on how the group was experienced without intervention by the group leaders. A special focus is whether or not goal-directed group involvement was continued and reasons for such inclusion or exclusion.
	b. Mutual Concern	*Production.* In this structured experience, group members are given written tasks which they are expected to perform outside of the group before the next group meeting. These tasks will be straightforward, such as developing a plan to help a group member most in need. How these tasks were experienced is the focus of the subsequent group. This is a good test to see if group members have actually owned their avowed commitment to mutual concern. Emphasis should be placed on the creativity and quality of the help.
	c. Accountability	*Evidence.* Group members are given the homework assignment of examining their SET logs closely for signs of progress. A handout, with columns headed (1) Thoughts, (2) Feelings, and (3) Actions, may be used to help give group members a method of organizing the evidence of self-perceived change. Then, group members are asked to cite the most significant thought, feeling, and action which affected their SET experience. Members are asked to predict how each other would respond to these questions.
11. Commencement	a. Goal Involvement	*I've Only Just Begun.* As in the song, SET group members have often only recently started to apply their SET experiences in

(continued)

Table 7. *Representative Structured Experiential Interventions*
Used in SET (continued)

Stage	Focus	Title and Description
		their everyday lives. Group members are asked *how* they are using their SET group experiences, *with whom, where, how often,* etc. This helps provide specific interpersonal feedback on the effectiveness of the group experiences.
	b. Mutual Concern	*The Letter.* Group members are asked to write a farewell letter to the group, keeping in mind that this group is ending. No specific structure is necessary; group members who have difficulty expressing themselves may request help from another group member. Letters are read aloud in the final group meeting and explored for future implications.
	c. Accountability	*Commandments.* Group members are asked make a list of how they might hold themselves accountable for future constructive activities. Contingency contracts, aversive procedures, positive reinforcers, etc., are shared among group members to give all members insight concerning how to keep straight and involved in purposeful goal activities. Individual lists are revised following the sharing of ways to help members continue their goal seeking.
12. Reunion	a. Goal Involvement	*Time Tunnel.* The group is asked to visualize the entire group going on a train ride through a time tunnel. Their task is to select a time when they would like the train to stop so the group could step into the future and examine where they are and what they've been doing; this will be their reunion. Members individually choose a time period from one month to five years. Reactions are discussed with a group focus on selecting a future time for the next SET group meeting.
	b. Mutual Concern	*Impact.* Group members are directed to pause and reflect on what they have experienced in and outside of the SET group since the group began. Members are asked to select one person, either within or external to the SET group, who had the most

Table 7. Representative Structured Experiential Interventions
Used in SET (continued)

Stage	Focus	Title and Description
		impact on them. This experience is shared with group members with a focus on how each member might have as much impact on other persons.
	c. Accountability	*Action Speaks.* This structured experience highlights the accomplishments of group members since leaving the group. Each member is asked to list his accomplishments since the previous group. This information is shared with the group, with a subsequent focus on how group members can be of further help to one another. Interpersonal helping contracts (implicit or explicit) may be designed in dyads or triads and shared with the entire group.

signed to help participants experience and acquire generalizable skills (e.g., goal development, genuine concern for others, responsible social action) which can be utilized throughout their lives.

SET groups are applicable to rehabilitating persons who are interested in and capable of working toward meaningful personal and interpersonal goals. While goal involvement is stressed in SET groups, it is the importance of people working together for common concerns which is most strongly emphasized. The unique aspect of goal involvement highlighted in the SET model is that the process of working toward a goal is in the context of interpersonal sharing and caring. This has been shown by the planning and development of a self-help organization for people having various disabilities by a group of SET group graduates.

Within a SET format, people have the opportunity to be themselves, to explore their functional freedom, to develop skills, to receive feedback from others, to express their aspirations, and to share their joy, sorrow, elation, and pain. Through involvement with others, their peers and allies, the sense of isolation and loneliness is alleviated. These concerns during the process of rehabilitation can intensify the smallest discomfort and distort the most relevant aspiration. Seen as a means to transcend the barrenness of despair, powerlessness, and hopelessness, the SET procedures introduce a shared experience that may not make the long journey of rehabilitation shorter, but frequently makes it more bearable.

REFERENCES

Anthony, W. A. Societal rehabilitation: Changing society's attitudes toward the physically and mentally disabled. *Rehabilitation Psychology*, 1972, 19:117–126.

Anthony, W. A. and Cannon, J. A. A pilot study on the effects of involuntary integration on children's attitudes. *Rehabilitation Counseling Bulletin*, 1969, 12: 239–240.

Barrett-Leonard, G. T. Experiential learning groups. *Psychotherapy: Theory, Research and Practice*, 1974, 11(1):71–75.

Castore, G. F. Number of verbal inter-relationships as a determinant of group size. *Journal of Abnormal Social Psychology*, 1962, 64:456–457.

Danish, S. J. and Zelenski, J. R. Structured group interaction. *Journal of College Student Personnel*, 1972, 13(1):53–56.

Dell Orto, A. E. Goal group therapy. A structured group experience applied to drug treatment and rehabilitation. *Journal of Psychedelic Drugs*, 1975, 7:363–371.

Ellis, A. *Reason and emotion in psychotherapy*. New York: Lyle Stuart, 1962.

English, R. W. Correlates of stigma toward physically disabled persons. *Rehabilitation Research and Practice Review*, 1971, 2:1–17.

English, R. W. and Oberle, J. B. Toward the development of new methodology for examining attitudes toward disabled persons. *Rehabilitation Counseling Bulletin*, 1971, 15(2):88–96.

Gartner, A. and Riessman, R. *Self-help in the human services*. San Francisco: Jossey-Bass, 1977.

Gibb, J. R. The effects of human relations training. In *Handbook of psychotherapy and behavior change*, eds., A. E. Bergin and S. L. Garfield, pp. 839–862. New York: Wiley, 1971.

Haimowitz, M. Short-term contracts. *Transactional Analysis Journal*, 1973, 3(2):34.

Jaques, M. E. and Patterson, K. M. The self-help group model: A review. *Rehabilitation Counseling Bulletin*, 1974, 18:48–58.

Kaplan, H. J. and Sadock, B. J. Structured interactions: A new technique in group psychotherapy. *American Journal of Psychotherapy*, 1971, 25(3):418–427.

Kerr, N. Understanding the process of adjustment to disability. *Journal of Rehabilitation*, 1961, 27(6):16–18.

Kurtz, R. R. Structured experience in groups: A theoretical and research discussion. In *The 1975 annual handbook for group facilitators*, eds., J. E. Jones and J. W. Pfeiffer, pp. 167–172. La Jolla, California: University Assoc., 1975.

Ladieu-Leviton, G.; Adler, D. and Dembo, T. Studies in adjustment to visible injuries: Social acceptance of the injured. *Journal of Social Issues*, 1948, 4(14):55–61.

Lasky, R. G.; Dell Orto, A. E. and Marinelli, R. P. *Structured experiential therapy (SET-R): A group approach to rehabilitation*. Paper presented at the Northeast Regional Conference of the National Rehabilitation Association, Cherry Hill, New Jersey, 1976.

Mallucio, A. N. and Marlow, W. D. The case for the contract. *Social Work*, 1974, 19: 28–36.

Marinelli, R. P. and Dell Orto, A. E. *The psychological and social impact of physical disability.* New York: Springer, 1977.

Marinelli, R. P.; Dell Orto, A. E. and Lasky, R. G. *Integrating rehabilitation consumers and providers: A structured experiential approach.* Unpublished presentation at the New Hampshire Division of Vocational Rehabilitation, Manchester, New Hampshire, May, 1976.

Means, B. L. and Roessler, R. T. *Personal achievement skills leader's manual and participant's workbook.* Fayetteville, Ark.: Arkansas Rehabilitation Research and Training Center, 1976.

Merlin, J. S. and Kauppi, D. R. Occupational application and attitudes toward the physically disabled. *Rehabilitation Counseling Bulletin,* 1973, 16(3):173–179.

Montgomery, A. G. and Montgomery, D. J. Contractual psychotherapy: Guidelines and strategies for change. *Psychotherapy: Theory, Research and Practice,* 1975, 12(4):348–352.

Pelletier, J. *Group work in Quincy: A program update.* Unpublished paper, Massachusetts Rehabilitation Commission, 1978.

Pfeiffer, J. W. and Jones, J. E. *The annual yearbook for group facilitators* (5 vols.) La Jolla, California: University Associates, 1972–1976.

Roessler, R. An evaluation of Personal Achievement Skills training with the visually handicapped. *Rehabilitation Counseling Bulletin,* 1978, 21:300–305.

Roessler, R.; Cook, D. and Lillard, D. The effects of systematic group counseling with work adjustment clients. *Journal of Counseling Psychology,* 1977, 24:313–317.

Roessler, R.; Milligan, T. and Ohlson, A. Personal Achievement Training for the spinal cord injured. *Rehabilitation Counseling Bulletin,* 1976, 19:544–550.

Rotter, J.; Chance, J. and Phares, J. *Applications of a social learning theory of personality.* New York: Holt, Rinehart & Winston, 1972.

Siller, J. and Chipman, A. *Personality determinants of reaction to the physically handicapped. II. Projective techniques.* Unpublished manuscript, Human Resources Library, 1965.

Steiner, C. Contractual problem-solving groups. *Radical Therapist,* 1971, 6:54–71.

Trudel, R. *Structured experiential therapy for alcoholics (SET-A) versus assertive training: A comparison of two structured group formats for helping female alcoholics.* Unpublished doctoral dissertation, Boston University, 1977.

Wright, B. Spread in adjustment to disability. *Bulletin of the Menninger Clinic,* 1964, 28:198–208.

Yalom, I. D. *The theory and practice of group psychotherapy,* 2nd Ed. New York: Basic Books, 1975.

APPENDIX A: PERSONAL AWARENESS EXERCISES USED IN GROUP TRAINING OF REHABILITATION WORKERS

1. How are goals important in your life? Have you set immediate and long-term goals for yourself? If so, write them down and process them, using the RUMBAT format described in this chapter. If you became disabled, how would they change?

2. Assume you are planning to be the group leader with a group of disabled persons. What would be the most difficult issues for you to deal with? Develop an approach which would help you deal with these issues more effectively.

3. Imagine that you are disabled (if you are, select another disability). List those elements you would like to see included in a group counseling model which would be part of your rehabilitation program.

4. If you were a member of a group which included both physically disabled and nondisabled persons, what would be the most difficult issues for you to share with the group?

5. Imagine you are contacted by a local chapter of an organization of disabled consumers and asked if you would like to be a member of a group counseling experience designed to explore prejudice between disabled and nondisabled persons. What would you do and why?

27

Milieu Therapy

Bernard Kutner

The disabled adult must thread his way through the immediate problems of survival and then must regain essential physical skills before attempting to reach the larger goal of resuming a role in life. These are formidable tasks. Not only are there overwhelming personal problems to be managed, but since roles depend upon the needs of society as well as the individual, there may be external blockades to readjustment. For instance, after treatment and retraining, the disabled individual may be denied employment (for which he is now once more suited) because of social rejection, ignorance, or prejudice on the part of prospective employers. Acquiring new roles, readapting old ones, and developing the social skills necessary to enter and manage them are tasks for which milieu therapy may offer one major solution. While exposure of a disabled person to a program of milieu therapy may never cause an employer to feel comfortable with a partially paralyzed person, an epileptic, or an amputee in his presence, the afflicted person, on the other hand, may be better prepared to deal with the prospective employer.

ROLE DISORDERS

Disability, among other things, impairs or otherwise seriously modifies previously existing roles to varying degrees: from minor change (i.e., full- to part-time student or worker) to complete obliteration (i.e., bedbound patient, retired, recluse). These role damages may be directly attributable to an illness or injury resulting in disability (i.e., brain tumor, spinal cord injury, hemiplegia, etc.) or may be the consequences of changes to the person and to his life circumstances occasioned by lengthy hospitalization, aging, and extended treatment programs. Hence, following a personal health catastrophe,

From *Journal of Rehabilitation*, 34(2) (1968), 14–17. Copyright © 1968 by the National Rehabilitation Association. Reprinted by permission of the author and Editor.

the individual may stabilize finally in the role of invalid, or he may be semi-retired or become a permanent resident of an institution.

In the diagnostic work-up and medical treatment plan of the recently disabled patient, it is rather rare to include a listing of the "role disorders" accompanying the illness or injury.[1] One almost never hears of social disarticulations, severed relationships, or fractured associations, but these may, in fact, be concomitants of the physical insult. They require not the cursory attention typically accorded them, but specific and purposeful therapy. In a typical treatment milieu, the patient is "motivated" to become more active, he and his family are consulted about the problems of returning home, and he may also be counseled about possible employment. These approaches to the psychological and social aspects of rehabilitation usually involve individual conferences with social workers, vocational counselors, and psychologists. Occasionally, group therapy is employed as a central or secondary technique. Milieu therapy is relatively a newcomer to this field.

DEFINITION

Since the meaning of milieu therapy has taken on such a variety of nuances,[2,3] we should like to make explicit our understanding of it. It is a theory of treatment and a body of associated methods in which the environmental or residential setting is utilized as a training ground for patients to exercise social and interpersonal skills and to test their ability to deal with both simple and complex problems commonly experienced in open society. The treatment program attempts to engage the patient in various social encounters with other patients, staff members, and administrative personnel. These encounters may be group or individual in nature and expose the patient to increasingly challenging problems, provoke him into personal involvement with the issues at hand, and encourage him to struggle actively toward specified objectives. These experiences provide tests of judgment, of social competence, of problem-solving ability, and of social responsibility. They are calculated to deal with a wide range of conditions aimed at significant, positive accomplishments. The therapy involved in this process consists both of the mobilization of the patient's efforts to become involved in the work of the milieu program and of engagement in the specific projects themselves. Hence, to help in presenting a list of grievances to an institution's administrators, a patient must first be up and about, dressed and fed, and prepared to act as a spokesman or committee member, etc. The management of the grievance procedure, its prior preparation, the follow-up of meetings, and so forth, constitute aspects of the work of patients in a milieu program.

To understand how milieu therapy may play a role in the overall therapeutic process, it might be helpful to conceive of the hospitalized, physically disabled patient in psychosocial terms. Looked at solely from a behavioral viewpoint, the patient may appear to the outside observer as a bedridden, indolent, dependent, incompetent, socially isolated individual living among strangers, eating unaccustomed food, sleeping and rising and retiring by a schedule not of his own choosing, often dressed in bedclothes, and submitting voluntarily to acts that may involve indecent exposure, inflicted pain, and even dangerous weapons. If his medical condition were of a comparatively minor nature, time-limited and rapidly healing, the individual would not ordinarily establish and retain new habits learned as a patient. When, however, the disabling condition involves a lengthy period of institutional care, the medical problem is serious, and residual malfunctions are involved, there is a greater likelihood that some patients will develop and continue hospital habits of living into their posthospital life. It is for those patients who will tend to adopt the role of chronic invalid — who will become socially isolated, indolent, unnecessarily unemployed or retired, and less than competent to deal with the everyday problems of living — that milieu therapy is most clearly intended.

One of the most deceptive aspects of hospital rehabilitation is the condition of the patient at the time of discharge. For the most part, professional staffs may be satisfied that the patient has attained maximum hospital benefits, i.e., that further treatment would yield little or no medical gain. But, following a strenuous effort to get him to the discharge plateau, there is strong likelihood that the patient may have "peaked out" prior to discharge. It is not surprising to find patients backsliding within a few months following discharge without benefit of supporting staff and hospital. Milieu therapy is also designed to help deter or avoid this common regressive change.

WEAPONS OF LIFE

To accomplish its major therapeutic objective — helping to retain the benefits of rehabilitative care — milieu therapy must attempt to provide the patient with an arsenal of social skills to overcome frustration with enlightened self-interest and high morale. These "weapons of life" are necessary ingredients to prevent a tendency to capitulate easily in the face of rebuff or rejection, to avoid new and potentially risky social experiences, to become overdependent, and to reduce the utilization of skills learned in the hospital.

To restore the integrity of a set of adult roles following a massive physical insult which leaves serious or severe functional handicaps, specific role-retaining methods are indicated. There are such concrete role difficulties as finding and holding employment, assuming normal household responsibilities, and resuming old friendships. Severe disability can, in fact, profoundly modify the individual's life to such an extent that a modified or an entirely new set of roles may emerge. A number of studies have been reported pointing to changes in self-image, negative attitudes toward disability, hypersensitivity, and social self-segregation following a personal disaster.[4,5,6] The traditional approach to this complex of problems has been to concentrate most therapeutic efforts on the restoration of physical functioning, in the anticipation that personal and social readjustments will flow more readily once physical integrity is restored. When difficulties of adjustment occur, social, psychological, and psychiatric services are invoked to help smooth over the rough periods. Milieu therapy, on the other hand, attacks the problem of adjustment to new roles by inducing the patient to adopt and test them as part of the treatment process.

Milieu therapy can be conducted either in the form of a therapeutic community, that is, in the social system within the institution, in which the patient participates as part of a democratically structured social order; or he may take part in a specially designed program within a conventional rehabilitation structure (sheltered workshop, halfway house, day hospital, clinic, or rehabilitation center). Fundamentally, the patient is given the opportunity to engage in activity that is functionally useful and to adopt a variety of testable social roles. These could include some of the following: patient government member and/or officer, committee member and/or officer, work associate, volunteer, nonprofessional assistant, housekeeper-homemaker, as well as such conventional roles as friend, neighbor, colleague, acquaintance, or roommate. The key factor in the role-retaining process is the exercise of the role with some degree of professional supervision. The patient's performance is monitored by staff members, and his activities and progress are discussed both within group meetings as well as within patient-staff conferences. To create the opportunities for the conduct of such roles within a hospital, clinic, or other rehabilitation setting, it goes without saying that the organization itself must be geared to permit their free exercise. We cannot here go into the development of a milieu therapy program which others have well described.[2,3] However, some observations about such a program are in order.

FACILITATING ENVIRONMENT

The attainment of new roles through the process of milieu therapy requires from several weeks to several months, depending upon the patient and the organizational structure. Patients with little or no experience in group activities, such as work in a voluntary organization or service on a committee, will require a considerable period of time to warm up and learn what is expected of them. Some patients require a period of time to allow themselves to be drawn into the core of a milieu therapy group. They may participate in only a peripheral manner. Some patients are so threatened by group meetings that they take part in the program only in carrying out group decisions rather than in their formulation. Still other patients need experience in overcoming the embarrassment of speaking in a group. A further difficulty is encountered in dealing man-to-man, on an equal-status basis, with staff members who may come from different social, educational, or cultural backgrounds. It may be necessary to hold instructional classes in public speaking to desensitize the individual by slow stages.

As to the contribution of the environment in the facilitation of developing new roles, one major factor is the provision of a wide latitude of permissiveness. The rehabilitation setting may have either the characteristics of the "total institution" or some degree of relaxation of typical institutional controls. The optimal setting for a milieu therapy program is one in which the senior management and staff members are fully cognizant of the need for achieving increasingly greater patient involvement in the group life of the organization. This may eventually lead to a role for patients in management itself. A rigidly structured hierarchy will make this type of involvement quite impossible. Our experience has pointed to the need for a professional interloper who assists patients to achieve status, gain intended goals, and experience the feeling of success, mediating between patient and administration.[7,8] Group social workers have filled this role, and they have helped promote a considerable measure of patient movement. Whether this would have been possible without the willing cooperation of unit directors and clinical chiefs is highly doubtful. The role of the group social worker in rehabilitation medicine is of prime importance, since the patient sees this person as a guide and model in his effort to affect his environment in some noticeable fashion. A repeated sense of achievement, despite the handicap, is a vital element in the social rehabilitation of the disabled person.

OVERTRAINING

The conduct of a milieu therapy program probably has little chance of significant and lasting effect unless it is carried on with determination. In this respect, an important concept in such a program is that of *overtraining*, since both physical and social regression often occur following the completion of a source of conventional therapy.[9] The training of social skills in milieu therapy should lead to an *exaggeration* of role involvement within the institutional framework. Toward this end, the patient should be induced into activities that are *above and beyond* those he would normally enter in community and family life. It is hardly likely, for example, that a worker will soon find himself in face-to-face relationships with supervisory and managerial personnel after he leaves the program. Yet such confrontations can aid him in meeting and dealing with bureaucracies with the degree of firmness and tolerance necessary to secure needed services.

Since he is almost certain to find himself in situations which require verbal skill, negotiating ability, and monumental patience, the milieu therapy program can increase his threshhold of frustration tolerance, reduce his sense of resignation, and reinforce an enlightened self-interest. While there is certainly no intention to match the individual's experiences in therapy with those he will most likely face in open society, the former contain myriad situations and conditions that would permit the individual to meet and joust with obstacles, barriers, impediments, and frustrations. Success and failure can be examined under the eyes of experienced professional observers, and the individual may thus gain from each such exposure.

There are some clinicians in the psychological, social work, and medical fields who believe that the listless and apathetic patients so frequently seen in rehabilitation settings, especially those with some degree of brain damage, cannot be expected to participate to any high level in environmental therapy. Listlessness, apathy, indifference, and resignation may all be characteristics of individuals who have suffered overwhelming personal reversals. Their social presentation and psychological distance may superficially lead one to the conclusion that little may be expected of them. One may conceive of these psychosocial reactions, however, as concomitants of the illness-disability syndrome, not necessarily intrinsic to the individual, but caused by a multiplicity of interacting personality and environmental factors. A second view of this problem is that the vigorous exercise of new role activities may be self-stimulating and have a cumulative effect. The adoption of one new role may lead to a second and to others in turn, setting off a return flow of other vital social and psychological functions.

The implication of the approach suggested here is that if milieu therapy is offered as part of a treatment plan, that it be a *mandatory* aspect of therapy. If the institution is tooled up to set such a program in operation, patients should be given no opportunity to back away. In the search for a new plateau on which life may be comfortably led, the patient may, with all due tender loving care, sink into abject dependency and chronic invalidism. Moreover, even the seemingly optimistic and enthusiastic patient may, upon repeated rebuffs in the posthospital world, throw in the sponge and regress into a narrow, circumscribed, custodial existence. It is for this reason that milieu therapy should be thought of as an attempt to provide the means for overcompensation on the part of the patient for the noxious circumstances of life that he almost certainly will meet.

CHALLENGE TO ADMINISTRATION

The therapeutic milieu in a rehabilitation unit will call for extremes of forbearance and fortitude on the part of both administration and staff. The activation of patients may touch off demands for the satisfaction of material wants and reforms of administrative practices. Patients may seek to shake off the conventional, administratively sound controls that ordinarily keep a large organization in efficient running condition. When they are encouraged to think out and then act upon decisions affecting their lives as patients, almost invariably the impact involves administrative change. The intrusion of patients into the area of administration is often looked upon as an invasion of territorial rights that are the exclusive domain of the caretakers. To encourage patients in such endeavors would, on the surface, be only asking for trouble.

The poverty programs which require the representation of the poor on the boards of local organizations managing and dispensing federal funds have faced this same issue. Yet, it is absolutely essential that such participation be part of the program. While many patients will never again be involved in the inner operations of an institution nor sit with professionals and administrators in joint problem-solving meetings, such opportunities are offered in the process of milieu therapy so that significant and relevant involvement in meaningful issues is experienced. Here, the patient can take part, without cognizance of his handicap, in the planning and exercise of useful practices appropriate to institutional programs. This involvement of this patently less competent group in hospital affairs may lead to a degree of inefficiency, and even occasionally to a breakdown, in normal practices. In this case, however, the end would appear to justify the means, since the objective is to help the patient to test the *outside limits* of his capacity to deal effectively with his social environment. The patient as well as the hospital must bend strenuous efforts to maintain a high level of patient interest in the program. The failure of milieu therapy to produce significant effects may be attributed, at least to some extent, to the natural desire of hospital officials to "keep the lid on" and to prevent a patient take-over of what is conceived to be hospital responsibility.

Consider the situation of the patient who has been through such a test of endurance and strength as just described and now must face by himself the exigencies of life. Would he not be better prepared, in fact, to meet and deal with the obviously severe tests to which he will be subjected? The sobering experiences of coping with life problems in the hospital, in our view, will be at least comparable, if not in excess, of those likely to be encountered in the community. A tender, cautious hospital program of milieu therapy will provide little challenge. A tough, unrelenting program, on the other hand, should raise the individual's morale, strengthen his determination, and provide him with an additional measure of resourcefulness and those characteristics of socialization necessary to meet head-on the obligations of normal life. The inclusion of a vigorous program of milieu therapy could be a significant addition to the more conventional therapies available in rehabilitation services.

REFERENCES

1. Weissman, R. and Kutner, B. "Role disorders in extended hospitalization." *Hospital Administration*, vol. 12, no. 1, Winter 1967.
2. Cumming, J. and Cumming, E. *Ego and Milieu.* New York: Atherton Press, 1962.
3. Stanton, A. and Schwartz, M. *The Mental Hospital.* New York: Basic Books, 1954.

4. Dembo, T., Leviton, G., and Wright, B. "Adjustment to misfortune: A problem of social psychological rehabilitation." *Artif. Limbs,* vol. 3, 1956.
5. Yuker, H. and Block, J. R. *A Scale to Measure Attitudes toward Disabled Persons.* Human Resources Study No. 5, 1960. Human Resources Foundation, Division of Abilities, Inc., Albertson, New York.
6. Cogswell, B. "Self-socialization: Readjustment of paraplegics to home and community." Paper presented at the National Rehabilitation Association national conference, Cleveland, Ohio, Oct. 3, 1967.
7. Lipton, H. and Malter, S. "The social worker as systems mediator on a paraplegic ward." Paper presented at the 94th annual forum, National Conference on Social Welfare, May, 1967.
8. Weinger, H. J. "The hospital, the ward, and the patient as clients: Use of the group method." *Social Work,* vol. 4, no. 4, Oct. 1959.
9. Abramson, A. "The human community in the rehabilitation process." The Seventeenth John Stanley Coulter Memorial Lecture, presented at the annual meeting, American Congress of Rehabilitation Medicine, Miami Beach, Aug. 29, 1967.

28

Stress Management for Rehabilitation Clients

Lloyd R. Goodwin, Jr.

Stress plays an important role in the life of the person with a disability. The disabled person's need for adjustment and adaptation in most areas of life is fairly well understood and has been described extensively in the literature (Garrett, 1953; McDaniel, 1976; Roessler & Bolton, 1978; Stubbins, 1977; Wright, 1960). What is less well understood is that each demand for adaptation and adjustment is associated with varying degrees of stress (Holmes & Rahe, 1967; Pelletier, 1977; Selye, 1975).

Stress is a factor in the onset, development, and recovery of almost every disease and illness resulting in disability. Once people become disabled, they are confronted with many additional stressful situations that require adjustment and adaptation. Stress is experienced in the rehabilitation process whenever the disabled person is confronted with the need for adaptation and change. Researchers on stress (Pelletier, 1977; Selye, 1975) point out that not all stress is bad, and a certain amount is necessary for successful adaptation to the demands of life. They further point out, however, that too much stress, or "distress," is potentially harmful to health. Helping disabled persons cope with the stress associated with the many demands for physical, social, family, psychological, sexual, and environmental adjustment is an important task for the rehabilitation practitioner. Stress management is necessary to help prevent the onset of new illnesses, to help the client better cope with and adjust to existing disabilities, to help the client cope with life's uncertainties, and to improve the general quality of the client's life. Rehabilitation practitioners have many therapeutic tools to help disabled clients manage stress throughout the rehabilitation process. One tool is educational intervention, which includes teaching self-help skills to clients. Stress man-

From *Rehabilitation Counseling Bulletin*, March 1980, pp. 193–201. Copyright ©1980 by the American Personnel and Guidance Association. Reprinted with permission.

agement or relaxation skill training is an important skill to be learned by clients and rehabilitation practitioners.

STRESS-RELATED DISORDERS

The predominate threats to life and health in the past were the communicable diseases caused by specific pathogens (Todd, 1977). Western society is now largely free of such illnesses as smallpox, typhoid, cholera, and polio (Pelletier, 1977). Today, chronic degenerative diseases and accidents are the major health problems (Todd, 1977). Whether or not we develop an illness or disease depends on many factors, including genetic predisposition, diet, exercise, overall general health, lifestyle, personality characteristics, and stress. According to Anderson (1978), psychological and sociocultural pressures have increased to the point that stress or tension is now the biggest factor in the onset of disability, distress, and death. Stress plays a direct or indirect role in the development of all disease.

> Every disease causes a certain amount of stress, since it imposes demands for adaptation upon the organism. In turn, stress plays some role in the development of every disease: its effects — for better or worse — are added to the specific changes characteristic of the disease in question. (Selye, 1975, p. 35)

Stress is not only related to the onset and development of most of today's diseases but is also related to the recovery or rehabilitation process. As Brown (1977) pointed out, "stress . . . aggravates all illnesses, whether they are infections or injuries, and stress markedly affects recovery from illness" (p.29).

WHAT IS STRESS?

Stress is defined as "the nonspecific [that is, stereotyped] response of the body to any demand upon it . . . it is immaterial whether the agent or situation we face is pleasant or unpleasant; all that counts is the intensity of the demand for readjustment or adaptation" (Selye, 1975, pp. 14–15). Pelletier (1977) delineated two basic kinds of stress: acute stress, in which threat is immediate and the need to respond instantaneous, and chronic stress, which is prolonged and unabated. People with disabilities are confronted with many potentially stressful situations, of either an acute or chronic nature, that require adjustment and adaptation.

STRESSORS

We are all under varying degrees of stress, many of us to the point of distress. "General environmental and social stressors which affect all people to some degree include living and working conditions, increased mobility, and the constant influx of information from mass communications" (Pelletier, 1977, p. 82). Two common sources that are particularly stressful are related to the constant change requiring adaptation in our lives (Holmes & Rahe, 1967; Toffler, 1970) and to our work situations (Friedman, Rosenman, & Carroll, 1958; Russek, 1965; Sales & House, 1971). As Pelletier (1977) pointed out, "Stress is not simply the result of factors that cause you worry, anxiety, or strain. Actually, you are under stress every time you are required to adapt or adjust to personal, social, and environmental influences, positive or negative. Adaptation is necessary all the time, to varying degrees" (p. 83).

STRESS AND DISABILITY

Besides the common sources of stress that affect almost everybody, people with disabilities are often confronted with additional demands for adaptation related to their personal, family, social, environmental, and work adjustment. These increased demands require adaptive behaviors from the disabled person above and beyond the level of adaptation needed by the nondisabled population. The initial shock, anxiety, and emotional distress associated with the onset of illness and disability is a major source of situational stress for the disabled person. Barker, Wright, and Gonick (1946) pointed out that from the very beginning of illness, the person is in a state of conflict. The vacillation between seeking and avoiding treatment is accompanied by emotional stress, which in turn affects treatment. Although each individual may react differently to disability, there seems to be a typical pattern of reaction. This common restorative process was described by Roessler and Bolton (1978):

1. Denial—defending against the trauma by denying its existence.
2. Mourning—grieving for the loss.
3. Depression—characterized by questions such as "why me?" and realizations such as "I will never be the same."
4. Anger—hostility directed at one's world for its injustices and toward others for their inability to understand.
5. Positive coping—a review of the major tasks that remain to be completed. (p. 14)

The stress associated with adjustment to disability also affects the family of the disabled person. In a study by Marra and Novis (1959), disabled husbands and fathers perceived the principal changes in their family relationships to be, in order of importance, (a) their wives had to assume greater responsibility for home management, (b) social and recreational activities were reduced, (c) children assumed more household duties, (d) going into debt, (e) changed plans for a larger family, (f) necessity of wife's employment, (g) increased marital discord, (h) changed plans for the children's education, and (i) changed living accommodations.

This considerable disruption of family functioning is likely to create a very stressful situation for other family members as well. In a study by Ezra (1961) of married men with myocardial infarction, the most frequently mentioned problem from their wives was the stress and tension resulting from their husband's illness. Medsger and Robinson (1972) also pointed out that females with rheumatoid arthritis have a higher divorce rate and significantly fewer remarriages than the nondisabled population. Not all disabled persons learn to cope and adjust successfully to the stress associated with their disabilities. There seems to be an increased incidence of suicide and self-destructive behaviors for some disability groups, compared with the nondisabled population (Farberow, Darbonne, Stein, & Hirsch, 1970; Hopkins, 1971).

STRESS AND THE REHABILITATION PROCESS

The disabled person is also confronted with stressful situations throughout the treatment and rehabilitation process. There is anxiety and stress associated with hospitalization (DeWolfe, Barrell, & Cummings, 1966), surgery (Andrew, 1970), and the transitions of entering and leaving a rehabilitation center (Krause, 1964). When a rehabilitation center provides complete care and assumes total responsibility for all aspects of the person's life, it is not surprising that entry and termination becomes a stressful experience for many clients (Krause, 1964). In studies of patients with spinal cord injury, all indicators of stress—affective and hormonal—increased dramatically just before they were discharged from the rehabilitation center (McDaniel & Sexton, 1970, 1971).

Additional stressful situations can occur when the disabled person seeks assistance from any of the rehabilitation agencies. Filling out agency forms, undergoing evaluation procedures, and generally adjusting to the demands of an agency's procedures can provide numerous stress-provoking situations for disabled persons. Societal barriers, such as prejudiced attitudes of the nondisabled and employers and the restriction of mobility caused by architectural barriers, can cause stress for the most "adjusted" disabled person. Because stress is associated with any life event requiring an adaptive response, clearly the disabled person is constantly confronted with many additional demands for adjustment and adaptation that the nondisabled population usually does not confront.

It is important to point out that stress cannot be avoided and a certain amount of tension is essential for survival, learning, personal development, and progress in society (Anderson, 1978). Stress is not something to be avoided. In fact, it cannot be avoided. "In common parlance, when we say someone is 'under stress,' we actually mean under excessive stress or distress, just as the statement 'he is running a temperature' refers to an abnormally high temperature, that is, fever. Some heat production is essential to life . . . complete freedom from stress is death" (Selye, 1975, p. 19). What happens physio-logically when the disabled and nondisabled are confronted with many acute and chronic stressors that require adaptive responses is sometimes referred to as the stress response.

THE STRESS RESPONSE

When confronted with acute and chronic stressful situations, an innate re-sponse is triggered. This response is popularly referred to as the fight-or flight response and results in increases in blood pressure, heart rate, breathing rate, blood flow to the muscles, and metabolism. These physiological responses prepare humans for conflict or escape (Benson & Klipper, 1976). Because of our society's code of acceptable behavior, much stress becomes internalized because it cannot be dealt with by fighting or running away. Thus, instead of the neurophysiological stress response subsiding and the body rebounding into deep relaxation and then into homeostasis, a negative psychological state persists, resulting in a prolonged physiological stress response (Pelletier, 1977).

What happens during a prolonged and unabated stress response is de-scribed in the three phases of the general adaptation syndrome (Selye, 1975):

A. Alarm reaction. The body shows the changes characteristic of the first exposure to a stressor. At the same time, its resistance is dimin-ished and, if the stressor is sufficiently strong (severe burns, extremes of temperature), death may result.

B. Stage of resistance. Resistance ensues if continued exposure to the stressor is compatible with adaptation. The bodily signs character-istic of the alarm reaction have virtually disappeared, and resistance rises above normal.

C. Stage of exhaustion. Following the long-continued exposure to the same stressor, to which the body had become adjusted, eventually adaptation energy is exhausted. The signs of the alarm reaction reap-pear, but now they are irreversible, and the individual dies. (p. 27)

Many counselors can identify with the prolonged activation of the general adaptation syndrome, which is popularly referred to as professional "burnout." When a car is run constantly at full speed it eventually "burns out," with the weakest part breaking down first. The same process can occur in the human body: "The weakest link in the chain of vital physiological pro-cesses will succumb first. Such factors as heredity, environment, general health habits, behavioral variables, and past illnesses may all play a role in determining whether illness will occur as a result of prolonged stress" (Pelle-tier, 1977, p. 76). Personality plays a part in how a person handles stress. There is also evidence suggesting that different personality characteristics are associated with specific stress-related illnesses, such as cardiovascular disorders (Friedman & Rosenman, 1974), cancer (LeShan & Worthington, 1956), rheumatoid arthritis (Moos & Solomon, 1965), and migraines (Pelletier, 1977).

A comprehensive description of the psychophysiological mechanism of stress on our bodies is beyond this article's scope and is clearly explained in the works of Selye (1956, 1975, 1976), Cannon (1932), Simeons (1961), Pelletier (1977), Benson and Klipper (1976), and Bloomfield, Cain, Jaffe, and Kory (1975).

THE RELAXATION RESPONSE

Just as there is an innate fight-or-flight response, there is also an innate physiologic response that is diametrically different and is referred to as the relaxation response (Benson, Beary, & Carol, 1974; Benson & Klipper, 1976). Benson and Klipper describe the relaxation response as a

> natural and innate protective mechanism against "overstress," which allows us to turn off harmful bodily effects, to counter the effects of the fight-or-flight response. This response against "overstress" brings on bodily changes that decrease heart rate, lower metabolism, decrease the rate of breathing, and bring the body back into what is probably a healthier balance. (pp. 25–26)

Because our stress response is triggered daily, many times to the point of distress, we need to take the time to consciously trigger our relaxation response daily to counteract the potentially damaging effects of the stress response. Learning how to trigger the relaxation response is a skill, and like any other skill, it requires practice, time, and effort. The relaxation response is a relatively easy skill to learn and mainly involves taking time out from stressful schedules to include a daily routine devoted to triggering the innate relaxation response, which will counteract the potentially damaging effects of the stress response and promote healing, health, and psychosocial adjustment throughout the rehabilitation process. The deep relaxation associated with the relaxation response induces psychological and physiological changes that distinctly reduce stress. The relaxation response is not something that just happens, especially when we are daily enmeshed in stress-producing activities. The relaxation response should be consciously triggered, preferably on a daily basis, for it to be preventive, restorative, and curative.

TRIGGERING THE RELAXATION RESPONSE

There is evidence to suggest that many methods elicit the physiological changes of the relaxation response, including meditation (Bloomfield et al., 1975), yoga (Funderburk, 1977), autogenic training, visualization, biofeedback (Pelletier, 1977), progressive relaxation, hypnosis with suggested deep relaxation, and sentic cycles (Benson et al., 1974).

RELAXATION TRAINING IN REHABILITATION COUNSELING

Educational resources for learning the various relaxation skills are available in almost every community for the interested rehabilitation counselor and the general public. Courses in meditation and hatha yoga are available from many universities' continuing education programs, YMCAs, private organizations and groups, and on television (e.g., Lilias's yoga class on educational television). Training for human service professionals in clinical biofeedback, autogenic training, progressive relaxation, hypnosis (especially self-hypnosis), and most of the other stress-management techniques is available through short-term training programs and workshops throughout the country.

Teaching Relaxation Skills to Clients

After rehabilitation workers learn one or more of the stress-management skills and integrate them into their daily schedule, the next step is to share these skills with clients.

There are several ways to integrate relaxation skill training into rehabilitation programs. A counselor in a state-federal vocational rehabilitation agency setting can teach stress-management techniques to clients, individually or in groups. The setting may be the vocational rehabilitation office or community facilities. Counselors located in residential treatment programs for drug and alcohol abuse, the public offender, mental illness, and other specific disability areas are in an excellent position to teach relaxation skills to clients and help them integrate the skills into their daily routines through group activities. Counselors in workshops and other rehabilitation facilities can teach clients how to integrate relaxation skills as a necessary activity of daily living. It is necessary to help clients find an effective relaxation skill that is personally suitable to them so that they are motivated to pursue and integrate the skill into their daily schedule. Also, as Pelletier (1977) pointed out, "These methods cannot be ones which require the individual to drop out. They must be incorporated into the existing social and vocational structures as well as into the basic framework of contemporary life styles" (p. 10).

REFERENCES

Anderson, R. A. *Stress power!* New York: Human Sciences Press, 1978.

Andrew, J. Recovery from surgery, with and without preparatory instruction, for three coping styles. *Journal of Personal and Social Psychology,* 1970, 15, 223–226.

Barker, R.; Wright, B.; & Gonick, M. *Adjustment to physical handicap and illness: A survey of the social psychology of physique and disability.* New York: Social Science Research Council, 1946.

Benson, H.; Beary, J. F.; & Carol, M. P. The relaxation response. *Psychiatry*, 1974, 37, 37–46.

Benson, H., & Klipper, M. Z. *The relaxation response.* New York: Avon, 1976.

Bloomfield, H. H.; Cain, M. P.; Jaffe, D. T.; & Kory, R. B. *TM: Discovering inner energy and overcoming stress.* New York: Dell, 1975.

Brown, B. Biofeedback. *Journal of Holistic Health*, 1977, 2, 29–32.

Cannon, W. B. *The wisdom of the body.* New York: W. W. Norton, 1932.

DeWolfe, A.; Barrell, R.; & Cummings, J. Patient variables in emotional response to hospitalization for physical illness. *Journal of Consulting Psychology*, 1966, 30, 68–72.

Ezra, J. *Social and economic effects on families of patients with myocardial infarctions.* Denver: University of Denver, 1961.

Farberow, N.; Darbonne, A.; Stein, K.; & Hirsch, S. Self-destructive behavior of uncooperative diabetics. *Psychological Reports*, 1970, 27, 935–946.

Friedman, M., & Rosenman, R. H. *Type A behavior and your heart.* New York: Alfred A. Knopf, 1974.

Friedman, M.; Rosenman, R. H.; & Carroll, V. Changes in the serum cholesterol and blood clotting time in men subjected to cyclic variation of occupational stress. *Circulation*, 1958, 18, 852–861.

Funderburk, J. *Science studies yoga: A review of physiological data.* Honesdale, Penn.: Himalayan International Institute, 1977.

Garrett, J. F. (Ed.). *Psychological aspects of physical disability* (U.S. Department of Health, Education and Welfare. Office of Vocational Rehabilitation). Washington, D.C.: U. S. Government Printing Office, 1953.

Holmes, T. H., & Rahe, R. H. The Social Readjustment Rating Scale. *Journal of Psychosomatic Research*, 1967, 2, 213–218.

Hopkins, M. Patterns of self-destruction among the orthopedically disabled. *Rehabilitation Research and Practice Review*, 1971, 3, 5–16.

Krause, E. *On the time and place of crisis.* Boston: New England Rehabilitation Center, 1964. (Mimeograph)

LeShan, L., & Worthington, R. E. Personality as a factor in the pathogenesis of cancer: A review of the literature. *British Journal of Medical Psychology*, 1956, 124, 460–465.

Marra, J., & Novis, F. Family problems in rehabilitation counseling. *Personnel and Guidance Journal*, 1959, 38, 40–42.

Medsger, A., & Robinson, H. A. Comparative study of divorce in rheumatoid arthritis and other rheumatic disease. *Journal of Chronic Diseases*, 1972, 25, 269–275.

McDaniel, J. W. *Physical disability and human behavior* (2nd ed.). New York: Pergamon Press, 1976.

McDaniel, J., & Sexton, A. Psychoendocrine studies of patients with spinal cord lesions. *Journal of Abnormal Psychology*, 1970, 76, 117–122.

McDaniel, J., & Sexton, A. Psychoendocrine functions in relation to level of spinal cord transection. *Hormones and Behavior*, 1971, 2, 59–69.

Moos, R., & Solomon, G. Personality correlates to the degree of functional incapacity of patients with physical disease. *Journal of Chronic Diseases*, 1965, 18, 1019–1038.

Pelletier, K. R. *Mind as healer, mind as slayer: A holistic approach to preventing stress disorders.* New York: Dell/Delta Books, 1977.

Roessler, R., & Bolton, B. *Psychosocial adjustment to disability.* Baltimore: University Park Press, 1978.

Russek, H. I. Stress, tobacco, and coronary heart disease in North American professional groups. *Journal of the American Medical Association*, 1965, 192, 189–194.

Sales, S. M., & House, J. Job dissatisfaction as a possible risk factor in coronary heart disease. *Journal of Chronic Diseases*, 1971, 23, 867–873.

Selye, H. *The stress of life.* New York: McGraw-Hill, 1956.

Selye, H. *Stress without distress.* New York: New American Library/Signet, 1975.

Selye, H. *The stress of life* (Rev. ed.). New York: McGraw-Hill, 1976.

Simeons, A. T. W. *Man's presumptuous brain: An evolutionary interpretation of psychosomatic disease.* New York: E. P. Dutton, 1961.

Stubbins, J. (Ed.). *Social and psychological aspects of disability.* Baltimore: University Park Press, 1977.

Todd, M. C. The need for a holistic approach in medicine. *Journal of Holistic Health*, 1977, 2, 7–10.

Toffler, A. *Future shock.* New York: Random House, 1970.

Wright, B. *Physical disability: A psychological approach.* New York: Harper & Row, 1960.

29

Covert Conditioning and Self-Management in Rehabilitation Counseling

Roger H. Livingston
Richard G. Johnson

Behavior modification strategies have long been used in a variety of rehabilitation settings. These strategies have generally been attempts to exert environmental control of overt behavior. More recently a new behavioral technology is shifting the responsibility for behavior change from the counselor and environmental stimuli to the client and internal or covert stimuli. This new self-management technology is directed toward developing the capacity in clients to regulate their own behavior.

Counseling efforts have traditionally involved the thoughts, feelings, and self-images of clients. But until recently, research psychologists have been reluctant to deal with these covert responses and have provided few techniques helpful to counselors. In the past, behaviorists have generally ignored internal influences and have focused on external stimuli to explain human behavior. This restricted view of behavioral determinants has recently been expanded by cognitive psychologists, who are exploring the influences on behavior of thoughts, expectations, internal symbolic representations, and self-regulating processes. Having overcome their initial reluctance to deal with internal responses, behaviorists are currently demonstrating considerable interest in covert processes and their influence on overt behavior (Goldfried & Goldfried, 1975; Mahoney, 1971; Meichenbaum, 1974). Attention has been focused on two kinds of covert responses. First are the annoying or debilitating thoughts or feelings that are themselves target be-

From *Rehabilitation Counseling Bulletin*, April 1979, pp. 330–337. Copyright © 1979 by the American Personnel and Guidance Association. Reprinted with permission.

haviors to be modified in counseling. Second are the covert responses that may be used to modify overt behaviors.

THOUGHTS AS TARGET BEHAVIORS

Behaviors modified in counseling are usually overt responses, but sometimes the behavior may be a thought or feeling that is annoying the client and is the target for change in the counseling process. Persistent worries, feelings of helplessness, and negative self-images are covert responses that may be problems in their own right or that may interfere with progress in counseling. A direct attack can be made on these negative covert responses. Thought and feeling patterns are learned and can be modified. Clients can be taught to increase the frequency of their positive self-thoughts, for example, by a self-management program using the following steps: (a) identify desirable self-thoughts, (b) monitor and record the frequency of these positive self-statements, (c) use an environmental cue to elicit the desired coverts, and (d) self-reinforce the positive thoughts.

Depression and negative self-evaluation are frequently encountered in clients, and these negative thoughts and feelings greatly interfere with the rehabilitation process. Many case studies have reported the successful treatment of depressive and self-deprecative thoughts by reinforcing positive self-statements. Johnson (1972); Mahoney (1971), and Todd (1972) reported the use of this method in the treatment of depression. Each therapist attempted to increase a client's positive self-evaluations by having the client read positive self-statements printed on 3 x 5 cards before engaging in a high-probability behavior. An interesting innovation suggested by Mahoney was the use of a blank 3 x 5 card that, each time it came up in the pack of cards, served as the cue for a client's original positive self-statement. In addition, Mahoney employed an attention distraction (counting backwards) and a tactile aversion (self-punishment by snapping a rubber band against the wrist) to decrease obsessive negative thoughts. The results were successful in all three studies.

Wolpe (1958) developed a technique called thought-stopping to aid clients in eliminating negative thoughts or images. In using this technique, the client is instructed to engage in the undesirable thought and to signal to the counselor when it is occurring. The counselor then shouts "Stop!", which disrupts the thought. Clients rehearse this procedure, first by saying "Stop!" aloud and then to themselves to terminate the unpleasant images and thoughts. Meichenbaum (1974) further developed this thought-stopping procedure and reported its efficacy.

The rehabilitation client recovering from a disabling illness or injury may be severely troubled by general depression and by almost obsessive thoughts of the loss suffered. These negative thoughts and feelings interfere with rehabilitation. Deliberately practicing and self-rewarding more positive thoughts have been shown to reduce the number of negative covert responses and enable the client to make positive steps in rehabilitation sooner than would otherwise be possible. Thought-stopping techniques have the potential to interrupt these powerful but destructive covert responses so that positive alternative responses to existing physical limitations may be developed and implemented.

COVERT PROCESSES FOR MODIFYING OVERT BEHAVIORS

Thoughts and feelings are not only important covert responses, but they are also important because they can influence overt behavior. The process of deliberately using these mental responses to effect overt behavior change has been called covert conditioning (Cautela, 1972a) or covert behavior modification (Mahoney, Thoresen, & Danaher, 1972). Both of these terms refer to processes for changing overt behavior through mental responses. Four specific procedures will be described briefly: covert modeling, covert rehearsal, covert reinforcement, and covert sensitization. Although discussed separately in this article, the procedures are frequently combined in practice.

Covert Modeling

Vividly imagining how one would like to respond in a situation can provide a model for action. The covert model may be based on previous observations of others or remembered previous experiences in which one's own responses were effective. Covert modeling can be used to enact in the imagination a model originally presented verbally, perhaps by the counselor. The object of covert modeling is for clients to gain a clear picture of the responses they want to exhibit. The ability to generate and vividly imagine such a model can be acquired and improved through practice in counseling.

An example of the use of this technique might be for the counselor to role-play a client participating in a job interview. The client is asked to reenact the role-play in his or her imagination as a way of making the model vivid. The client describes the imagined scene so that the counselor can check the accuracy of the client's perception of the model. The client may be asked to vary the model in imagination to generate and evaluate alternative ways to deal with the job-interview situation. The model would then be redesigned and tried out in imagination until it developed into a model or plan of action that the client perceived well and agreed to try. Once the model is clear, it may be effective to role-play the interview so that the client can try out the modeled behavior.

Kazdin (1973b) demonstrated the effectiveness of covert modeling to help clients increase their assertiveness. Flannery (1972) used covert modeling in successfully treating drug dependency. In these and other cases that reported using covert modeling, the technique was used along with other approaches rather than as the sole treatment. Covert modeling increased the effectiveness of the treatments in which it was used.

Covert Rehearsal

Covert rehearsal differs only slightly from covert modeling. In modeling, a number of different responses may be tried out in the imagination and discarded until the most suitable one to use as a model is discovered. Once the model is identified, further imagined enactments are covert rehearsals that allow the responses to be practiced. This technique allows the client to practice responses mentally that would require special settings, equipment, or personnel if the rehearsal were overt. Covert rehearsal can be performed by the client without the help of anyone. It permits safe rehearsal of potentially threatening responses and has been shown to reduce the client's anxiety associated with problem situations. Overt rehearsals or actual tryouts of new responses may be necessary for the client to gain skill. Covert rehearsals can prepare clients for these actual rehearsals or tryouts.

In the job interview example, once the model was clear, the client could practice in imagination the modeled responses in a variety of interview situations. When the client reports some comfort with the covert rehearsals, a role-played job interview may be the next step before an actual interview with a prospective employer.

Case studies by Susskind (1970) and Yarnell (1972) reported success with this technique, and more controlled experimental studies by Kazdin (1973a, 1973b) and Donaldson (1972) provide additional evidence of the efficacy of covert rehearsal.

Covert Reinforcement

Work by Cautela (1972a) and others suggests that responses that are covertly rehearsed or actually performed can be covertly reinforced. A step toward rehabilitation or the performance of a goal-oriented response can be covertly rewarded with a positive self-statement, a positive mental image, or a feeling of well-being. Many efforts are thought to be self-sustained because an individual has learned to feel good about accomplishing tasks. There are people who have seldom experienced success or had occasion to reward themselves or think positively about themselves. These individuals can learn this kind of self-reinforcement and perhaps influence their own behaviors by deliberately thinking positive self-thoughts when small successes have been achieved.

Many case studies have reported the success of covert reinforcement in altering internal states, such as moods, self-concepts, and feelings (Johnson, 1972; Mahoney, 1971; Todd, 1972). The research investigating the effect of covert reinforcement on overt behavior is not conclusive. Wish, Cautela, and Steffen (1970) reported an experimental test of covert reinforcement that supports the hypothesis that positive mental images can reinforce overt behavior. An attempt by Johnson and Scheurer (1975) to replicate these findings was unsuccessful. Covert reinforcement seems to be an approach worthy of experimentation, but it does not have strong support from research.

Covert Sensitization

Cautela (1966) first used the term *covert sensitization* to describe a procedure particularly appropriate for maladaptive approach responses (e.g., excessive eating, drinking, smoking). In this procedure, the maladaptive behavior is imagined by the client, who then imagines an extremely aversive consequence. For example, an alcoholic would be taught to relax and then be instructed to visualize reaching for a drink in a typical drinking situation. As the drink is about to be consumed, the individual is told to imagine feeling more and more nauseous and finally to imagine vomiting. The vomiting scene is graphically described in detail by the counselor to enhance the aversiveness of the client's image. This sequence is repeated several times during each counseling interview. Also, the client is instructed to practice the scene at home several times each day. The association of the unpleasant stimulus with drinking is expected to reduce the likelihood of drinking.

Support for the effectiveness of covert sensitization comes from anecdotal reports rather than from controlled experimental studies. Cautela (1972b) and Manno (1971) used covert sensitization with overeating. The technique has been used successfully with heroin addiction (Wisocki, 1973) and with alcoholism (Ashem & Donner, 1968). This promising approach to very difficult behavior change problems certainly warrants further study.

SELF-MANAGEMENT

Counseling psychologists have been interested in covert processes as part of a more general interest in self-management; that is, helping clients exercise more control over their own lives (Stewart, Winborn, Johnson, Burks, & Engelkes, 1978). Self-management refers to the ability of an individual to engage in goal-directed activities, even though they are difficult and the rewards are long delayed. Self-management also refers to the ability to eliminate those habitual behaviors that are undesired but are immediately rewarding. Persistently following up job leads to obtain employment, saving money for some special purpose, jogging to increase life expectancy, and giving up desserts all winter and spring to be able to comfortably wear a swim suit in the summer are examples of self-management. Most individuals have self-management skills, but some are better self-managers than others. There are those who manage some aspects of their lives well but have difficulties with other aspects. For a few, the lack of self-management skills presents severe problems.

There are a number of tested procedures for increasing an individual's ability to control self-behavior. These usually involve self-monitoring, learning alternate responses, and rewarding performance of the new response (Krumboltz & Thoresen, 1976; Mahoney and Thoresen, 1974; Thoresen & Mahoney, 1974). These procedures can be taught to clients and used by them to attain the goals they seek in counseling.

ADVANTAGES OF TEACHING SELF-MANAGEMENT

An obstacle confronting counselors who wish to use behavior change techniques is that counselors have limited opportunities to observe the client, monitor behavior, and reward goal-directed responses. The counselor can often enlist a client's family member, a friend, or a fellow worker to assist in monitoring client responses and administering reinforcement. Enlisting such aid presents problems, however. Confidentiality cannot be maintained if others are called on to help. Others may not be committed enough to consistently assist the client, and not all behaviors are performed publicly where they can be monitored by others. Covert responses can be attended to only by the client.

Self-management places the observation and recording of behavior, the management of environmental variables, and the administration of reinforcers in the clients' hands. It places a great deal of responsibility on the client, but the client is often the best person to monitor his or her own responses. No one will be more motivated to attend to those behaviors than the client. Self-management strategies give clients ways to control their own behavior and offer the following advantages over other behavior modification approaches:

1. Clients are motivated to persist toward their goals because they see themselves as controlling their own behavior.
2. Constant monitoring and reinforcement is possible even when the client is alone.

3. Thoughts and feelings, as well as some overt behaviors, can only be monitored by the clients themselves.
4. Clients learn a strategy that they can use on their own with future problems.
5. Self-management can be taught to individuals and groups as a preventive strategy before problems arise.

DISCUSSION

The numerous recent studies that deal with covert behavior and self-management reflect the great interest in this relatively new area of investigation. As is often the case in such pioneering efforts, there have been overenthusiastic claims made for covert conditioning procedures based on clinical observations or inadequately controlled experiments, and later there have been disappointments when clinical "discoveries" were subjected to rigorous experimental tests. Research results support the notion that covert responses can be altered by reinforcement and punishment and that covert processes do exert an influence on overt behavior. Covert modeling and covert rehearsal seem to have merit in helping individuals acquire new behaviors. Less support seems to be available for the effectiveness of covert reinforcement. Research in the area of self-management continues to show promise.

The development of a technology for modifying covert responses to assist individuals in developing behavioral self-control is perhaps possible. Considerable research and experience, however, are needed to better understand the relationship between overt and covert responses and to develop such a technology. Research on covert processes is especially difficult because covert responses can be observed only by the person experiencing them. The reliability and validity of self-reports can be seriously questioned and is of special concern in these investigations of mental activity. In spite of the difficulties, this area of investigation provides rich opportunities for research.

Counselors in training should be aware of the recent contributions of cognitive psychology and examine the view that thoughts, feelings, and mental images can be modified by deliberate change efforts and are important determiners of human behavior. Counselors have been taught to identify and accept feelings and thoughts expressed by clients, but they generally have not been shown how to help clients modify their feelings and thoughts to accomplish their goals more effectively. Cognitive psychology and self-management approaches are not proposed as replacing present counseling theories or methods, but as supplementary views, skills, and techniques that can be used by counselors to understand and help clients better.

REFERENCES

Ashem, B., & Donner, L. Covert sensitization with alcoholics: A controlled replication. *Behaviour Research and Therapy*, 1968, 6, 7-12.

Cautela, J. R. Treatment of compulsive behavior by covert sensitization. *Psychological Record*, 1966, 16, 33-41.

Cautela, J. R. Rationale and procedures for covert conditioning. In R. D. Rubin: H. Fensterheim: J. D. Henderson; & L. P. Ullman (Eds.), *Advances in behavior therapy* (Vol. 4). New York: Academic Press, 1972. (a)

Cautela, J. R. The treatment of overeating by covert conditioning. *Psychotherapy: Theory, Research and Practice*, 1972, 9, 211-216. (b)

Donaldson, D. N. *Positive imagery technique and implosive therapy*. Unpublished doctoral dissertation. Fuller Theological Seminary, 1972.

Flannery, R. B. Use of covert conditioning in the behavioral treatment of a drug-dependent college drop-out. *Journal of Counseling Psychology*, 1972, 19, 547-550.

Goldfried, M. R., & Goldfried, A. P. Cognitive change methods. In F. H. Kanfer & A. P. Goldstein (Eds.), *Helping people change*. New York: Pergamon Press, 1975.

Johnson, R. G., & Scheurer, W. E. *Covert reinforcement: A replication of an experimental test by Wish, Cautela, and Steffen*. A paper presented at the annual meeting of the American Educational Research Association, Washington, D.C., 1975.

Johnson, W. G. Some applications of Homme's coverant control therapy: Two case reports. *Behavior Therapy*, 1972, 2, 240-248.

Kazdin, A. E. Covert modeling and the reduction of avoidance behavior. *Journal of Abnormal Psychology*, 1973, 81, 87-95. (a)

Kazdin, A. E. Effects of covert modeling and reinforcement on assertive behavior. *Proceedings of the 81st Annual Convention of the American Psychological Association*, 1973, 8, 537-538. (b)

Krumboltz, J. D. & Thoresen, C. E. (Eds.). *Counseling methods*. New York: Holt, Rinehart & Winston, 1976.

Mahoney, M. J. The self-management of covert behavior: A case study. *Behavior Therapy*, 1971, 2, 275-278.

Mahoney, M. J., & Thoresen, C. E. *Self-control: Power to the person*. Monterey, Calif.: Brooks-Cole, 1974.

Mahoney, M. J.; Thoresen, C. E.; & Danaher, B. G. Covert behavior modification: An experimental analogue. *Journal of Behavior and Experimental Psychiatry*, 1972, 3, 7-14.

Manno, B. I. *Weight reduction as a function of the timing of reinforcement in a covert aversive conditioning*. Unpublished doctoral dissertation, University of Southern California, 1971.

Meichenbaum, D. H. *Cognitive behavior modification*. Morristown, N. J.: General Learning Press, 1974.

Stewart, N. E.; Winborn, B. B.; Johnson, R. G.; Burks, H. M.; & Engelkes, J. R. *Systematic counseling*. Englewood Cliffs, N.J.: Prentice-Hall, 1978.

Susskind, D. J. The idealized self-image (ISI): A new technique in confidence training. *Behavior Therapy*, 1970, 1, 538-541.

Thoresen, C. E., & Mahoney, M. J. *Behavioral self-control.* New York: Holt, Rinehart & Winston, 1974.

Todd, F. J. Coverant control of self-evaluative responses in the treatment of depression: A new use for an old principle. *Behavior Therapy,* 1972, *3,* 91–94.

Wish, P.; Cautela, J.; & Steffen, J. *Covert reinforcement: An experimental test.* A paper presented at the 78th Annual Convention of the American Psychological Association, 1970.

Wisocki, P. The successful treatment of a heroin addict by covert conditioning techniques. *Journal of Behavior Therapy and Experimental Psychiatry,* 1973, *4,* 55–61.

Wolpe, J. *Psychotherapy by reciprocal inhibition.* Stanford, Calif.: Stanford University Press, 1958.

Yarnell, T. Symbolic assertive training through guided imagery in hypnosis. *American Journal of Clinical Hypnosis,* 1972, *14,* 194–196.

Appendixes

APPENDIX A

Significant Books Related to the Psychological and Social Impact of Physical Disability

The following books are significant contributions to the understanding of the psychological and social impact of physical disability. The organization of this listing is based on date of publication, with newer books listed first.

Physical Disability—A Psychosocial Approach (second edition), by Beatrice Wright, published by Harper & Row, New York, in 1983.
Relating physical disability to psychology, this book provides the reader with conceptual understanding and practical information regarding the impact of disability. The wealth of concrete examples and nontechnical language make this book of great value to a wide range of readers, both professional and nonprofessional.

Missing Pieces: A Chronicle of Living with a Disability, by Irving Kenneth Zola, published by Temple University Press, Philadelphia, in 1982.
The personal odyssey of a handicapped man, who presents what it is like to have a disability in a world that values vigor and health. This book offers a rare insight into the human condition shared by 30 million Americans. A must for those working with the disabled.

Ordinary Lives: Voices of Disability and Disease, edited by Irving Kenneth Zola, published by Apple-wood Books, Cambridge, Massachusetts, in 1982.
A collection of engaging stories by men and women who have experienced first hand a chronic disease or disability. The presentations are not about overcoming extraordinary odds but instead about living a full life.

Adjustment to Severe Disability: A Metamorphosis, by Charlene DeLoach and Bobby Greer, published by McGraw-Hill, New York, in 1981.
Designed for professionals-in-training, practicing professionals, and parents or families of disabled persons, this book focuses on (1) the societal misconceptions that impede the adjustment of disabled persons; (2) the

effects that those misconceptions have on the attitudes and effectiveness of rehabilitation workers; and (3) existing services, laws, environmental changes, and technological advances that affect disabled persons.

The Psychology of Disability, by Carolyn Vash, published by Springer, New York, in 1981.

Based upon the author's experiences as a disabled person and as a rehabilitation psychologist, this book has two primary purposes. The first is to describe the disability experience; the second is to focus on the types of therapeutic strategies used in coping with disabilities. This book is useful for rehabilitation workers, disabled clients, and clients' families.

Annual Review of Rehabilitation, edited by Elizabeth Pan, Thomas Backer, and Carolyn Vash, with the initial publication by Springer, New York, in 1980. Subsequent publications are to follow annually.

Intended to provide an annual review of the advances in rehabilitation, this publication will regularly present a thorough and critical analysis of the literature in the following areas: administration, rehabilitation process, human resource development, service development, total rehabilitation, demographic groups, disability types, and settings.

The Role of the Family in the Rehabilitation of the Physically Disabled, edited by Paul W. Power and Arthur E. Dell Orto, published by University Park Press, Baltimore, in 1980.

This comprehensive collection of original material, selected readings, and personal statements thoroughly describes the knowledge and skills necessary to work effectively with the families of physically disabled persons. It describes the manner in which the family influences the adjustment of the physically disabled family member, and the role of the family in the rehabilitation process.

The Source Book for the Disabled, edited by Glorya Hale, published by Imprint Books, London, in 1979 and Bantam Books, New York, in 1981.

This paperback book is an illustrated guide to easier, more independent living for physically disabled people, their families, and their friends. It explores the attitudes, available options, and illustrates the aids that can make life fuller, more comfortable, and more independent for persons who are disabled.

Access: The Guide to Better Life for Disabled Americans, by Lilly Bruck, published by Random House, New York, in 1978.

This paperback book is intended to assist disabled consumers to overcome architectural, attitudinal, communication, and transportation barriers by providing them with current information regarding the rights and services available to them.

Disability and Rehabilitation Handbook, by Robert Goldenson, published by McGraw-Hill, New York, in 1978.
This book provides comprehensive coverage on various types of disabilities, as well as sections on rehabilitation services, programs, and the role of the family.

Psychosocial Adjustment to Disability, by Richard Roessler and Brian Bolton, published by University Park Press, Baltimore, in 1978.
Planned for the rehabilitation counseling student and the rehabilitation practitioner. This book provides theoretically sound and professionally useful information on the adjustment to disability.

Social and Psychological Aspects of Disability, edited by Joseph Stubbins, published by University Park Press, Baltimore, in 1977.
An excellent handbook for practitioners, which presents a comprehensive overview of disability and disabled persons from a sociological and a psychological perspective.

The Sociology of Physical Disability and Rehabilitation, edited by Gary Albrecht, published by University of Pittsburgh Press, Pittsburgh, in 1976.
In contributions written specifically for this book, the authors bring current behavioral science thinking to the field of physical disability and rehabilitation. Numerous topics, such as the effect of labeling, the patient involvement, and the sociological complexities of disability are presented.

The Psychological Aspects of Physical Illness and Disability, by Franklin C. Shontz, published by Macmillan, New York, in 1975.
This book touches upon a variety of psychological problems related to sickness and disability. When is a person sick? How do people adapt to illness and disability and the accompanying stress? What role do the treatment facilities play in the psychological adjustment of their patients and clients? The emphasis throughout the book is upon the treatment of the patient as a personal entity worthy of individual attention and respect.

Rehabilitation Practices with the Physically Disabled, edited by James Garrett and Edna Leving, published by Columbia University Press, New York, in 1973.

This book is divided into three sections: "The Rehabilitation Scene," "The Disabilities," and "The International Scene." Of a total of 16 originally written articles, 13 focus upon individual disabling conditions and their implications for medical and rehabilitation practice. Two articles introduce the reader to rehabilitation as it is practiced in the United States and to consumer issues. One article is devoted to international rehabilitation. This book is an excellent source of practical information about specific disabling conditions.

The Social Psychology and Sociology of Disability and Rehabilitation, by Constantina Safilios-Rothschild, published by Random House, New York, in 1970.

A provocative, thorough description of the organizational and behavioral manifestations of physical disability and the challenges that they pose to sociological and psychological inquiry. This book represents a complete survey of the theoretical and empirical implications of disability and rehabilitation for sociology and social psychology.

Loss and Grief: Psychological Management in Medical Practice, edited by Bernard Schoenberg and associates, published by Columbia University Press, New York, in 1970.

This book defines concepts and practices for professionals who handle matters related to loss and grief. It deals with the psychological aspects of loss as a result of physical illness and disability as well as a result of death. It consists of 26 originally written chapters, grouped into five sections: "Psychological Concepts Central to Loss and Grief," "Loss and Grief in Childhood," "Reaction to the Management of Partial Loss," "The Dying Patient," and "Humanistic and Biologic Concepts Regarding Loss and Grief."

A Man's Stature, by Henry Viscardi, published by John Day, New York, in 1952.

Probably the best of the books discussing personal accounts of disability, *A Man's Stature* is the story of Henry Viscardi, who, although born with underdeveloped legs, overcame his disability and succeeded in helping people with disabilities and opening society's eyes to others who have suffered disabilities. Essential reading for those who plan to work with disabled people.

APPENDIX B

Significant Journals Related to the Psychological and Social Impact of Physical Disability

Accent on Living is published quarterly by Cheever Publishing Company, P.O. Box 700, Gillum Road and High Drive, Bloomington, Illinois 61701.
Covering a wide variety of topical areas, *Accent* addresses accident prevention, vacation ideas, congressional information, and new products. Its goal is to present a lifestyle for disabled persons that is aware, exciting, and improving constantly.

Disabled U.S.A. is published quarterly by the President's Committee on Employment of the Handicapped, Washington, D.C. 20210.
Provides readers with general information concerning developments in rehabilitation and placement of people with disabilities.

The Exceptional Parent is published bimonthly at P.O. Box 4944, Manchester, New Hampshire 03108.
Provides practical information to families of children with disabilities. Emphasis is on relevant programs, approaches, and resources that are useful to a variety of family situations.

Journal of Applied Rehabilitation Counseling is a quarterly journal published by the National Rehabilitation Counseling Association, Carey Building, Suite A-305, 8136 Old Keene Mill Road, Springfield, Virginia 22152.
Concerned with issues of importance to the practicing rehabilitation worker, particularly the rehabilitation counselor. The focus is upon implications for practice, with less emphasis on technical and research issues.

Journal of Chronic Diseases is published monthly by Pergamon Press, Maxwell House, Fairview Park, Elmsford, New York 10523.
Explores various aspects of chronic illness for all age groups, including long-term medical and nursing care, the impact of the chronically ill on the community, and rehabilitation needs.

Journal of Physical Medicine and Rehabilitation is a monthly professional journal published by the American Congress of Rehabilitation Medicine and the American Academy of Physical Medicine and Rehabilitation, 30 N. Michigan Avenue, Chicago, Illinois 60602.

Focuses upon the field of physical medicine and rehabilitation. Articles include medical, psychological, and social issues as they relate to physical medicine and rehabilitation.

Journal of Rehabilitation is a quarterly professional publication by the National Rehabilitation Association, 633 South Washington Street, Alexandria, Virginia 22314.

The journal is concerned with the rehabilitation field in general. Articles cover a broad expanse of interests and are usually nontechnical and nonresearch in nature.

Mainstream is published monthly by Able-Disabled Advocacy, Inc., 861 Sixth Avenue, Suite 610, San Diego, California 92101.

Primarily a magazine designed to present practical information for the Able-Disabled. Timely articles, editorials, and relevant advertising make this an excellent resource.

Paraplegia News is published by the Paralyzed Veterans of America, 5201 North 19th Avenue, Suite 111, Phoenix, Arizona 85015.

The focus is upon the interests of and for the benefit of paraplegics, civilians, and veterans all over the world.

Psychosocial Rehabilitation Journal is a quarterly professional journal published by the International Association of Psychosocial Rehabilitation Services and the Department of Rehabilitation Counseling, Sargent College of Allied Health Professions, Boston University, Boston, Massachusetts 02215.

Addressing the comprehensive needs of the psychiatrically disabled, this journal is a state-of-the-art publication that focuses on theory, programmatic models, and skills relative to this population.

Psychosomatics is a quarterly international journal published by the Academy of Psychosomatic Medicine, 922 Springfield Avenue, Irvington, New Jersey 07111.

Explores the role of emotional factors in the daily practice of comprehensive medicine.

Psychosomatic Medicine is a semimonthly journal published by the American Psychosomatic Society, 265 Nassau Road, Roosevelt, New York 11575.

This journal is concerned with fostering knowledge concerning psychosomatic problems.

Rehabilitation Counseling Bulletin is a quarterly journal published by the American Rehabilitation Counseling Association, Two Skyline Place, Suite 400, 5203 Leesburg Pike, Falls Church, Virginia 22041.

This journal focuses upon articles illuminating theory and practice and exploring innovations in the field of rehabilitation counseling. It contains a substantial proportion of articles related to psychological issues in disability.

Rehabilitation Gazette is published annually by the Rehabilitation Gazette, 4502 Maryland Avenue, St. Louis, Missouri 63108.

The international journal for independent living by disabled people. Presented are theoretical as well as practical articles dealing with living an enjoyable, rewarding, and productive life. There are also overviews of conferences, book reviews, and practical suggestions for equipment purchase and use.

Rehabilitation Literature is a monthly journal published by the National Easter Seal Society of Crippled Children and Adults, 2023 W. Ogden Avenue, Chicago, Illinois 60612.

This bimonthly journal is intended for use by professional personnel in all disciplines concerned with rehabilitation of the handicapped. The "Article of the Month" in each issue provides an in-depth analysis of a selected rehabilitation topic, while reviews of books and articles allow readers to keep up with current publications in the field of rehabilitation.

Rehabilitation Psychology is the journal of the Rehabilitation Psychology Division of the American Psychological Association, 1200 Seventeenth Street, N.W., Washington, D.C. 20036. Published by Springer Publishing Company, 200 Park Ave., New York, New York 10003.

This journal publishes original investigations, theoretical papers, and evaluative reviews relating to the psychological aspects of illness, disability, retardation, and deprivation.

Sexuality and Disability is published quarterly by Human Sciences Press, 72 Fifth Avenue, New York, New York 10011.

The purpose of this journal is to provide a forum for clinical and research progress in the area of sexuality as it relates to a wide range of physical and mental illnesses and disabling conditions.

APPENDIX C

Organizations Serving Physically Handicapped Persons

American Association on Mental Deficiency (AAMD)
5201 Connecticut Avenue, N.W.
Washington, DC 20015
(202) 685-5400

The AAMD is a national organization (founded 1876) of over 10,000 professionals representing a variety of interests and disciplines and dealing with many types of developmental disabilities. The objectives of the AAMD are to effect the highest standards of programming for the mentally retarded; to facilitate cooperation among those working with the mentally retarded; and to educate the public to understand, accept, and respect the mentally retarded.

Alexander Graham Bell Association for the Deaf
3417 Volta Place, N.W.
Washington, DC 20007
(202) 337-5220

The Alexander Graham Bell Association for the Deaf is an international organization, founded in 1890, whose goal is to foster supportive environments and programs directed to the preparation of hearing-impaired children and adults to participate independently in the lives of their families, communities, and countries. The Association provides information services for parents, educators, libraries, hospitals, clinics, physicians, nurses, students, and others interested in the hearing-impaired. It also maintains a specialized library on hearing and speech, containing over 20,000 volumes and extensive clipping and pamphlet files.

American Cancer Society, Inc.
777 Third Avenue
New York, NY 10017
(212) 679-5700

Founded in 1913, the American Cancer Society's major purpose is to organize and wage a continuing campaign against cancer and its crippling effects, through medical research, professional and public education, and service and rehabilitation programs. The Society conducts programs of public and professional education, along with service and rehabilitation programs at the national and local levels.

American Coalition of Citizens with Disabilities
1200 15th Street, N.W.
Suite 201
Washington, DC 20005
(202) 785-4265

The purpose of ACCD is to promote the human and constitutional rights of citizens with disabilities.

American Congress of Rehabilitation Medicine
20 N. Michigan Avenue
Chicago, IL 60602
(312) 236-9512

The American Congress of Rehabilitation Medicine exists for the purpose of providing a scientific forum for communication among the many disciplines concerned with rehabilitation medicine. It has a membership of more than 2,000 practicing professionals, educators, and scientists who are working actively for the advancement of rehabilitation medicine. The organization focuses its programs and meetings on research findings and new practices, knowledge, and techniques of interest to all professionals in the rehabilitation field.

American Foundation for the Blind, Inc. (AFB)
15 West 16th Street
New York, NY 10011
(212) 924-0420

The AFB is a private, national organization whose objective is to help those handicapped by blindness to achieve the fullest possible development and utilization of their capacities and integration into the social, cultural, and economic life of the community. The AFB serves as a clearinghouse on all pertinent information about blindness and services to those who are blind.

American Occupational Therapy Association (AOTA)
6000 Executive Blvd.
Rockville, MD 20852
(301) 770-2200

The AOTA, founded in 1917, is the national membership, standard-setting, accrediting, and credentialing organization for the profession. Its stated purpose is to act as an advocate for occupational therapy in order to enhance the health of the public in its medical, community, and educational environments.

American Physical Therapy Association
1156 15th Street, N.W.
Washington, DC 20005
(202) 466-2070

The American Physical Therapy Association, founded in 1921, is a membership organization whose purpose is to meet the physical therapy needs of people through the development and improvement of physical therapy education, practice, and research. It also meets the needs of its members through problem identification, coordinated action, communication, and fellowship.

American Rehabilitation Counseling Association (ARCA)
5203 Leesburg Place
Falls Church, VA 22041
(703) 820-4700

The ARCA, a division of the American Personnel and Guidance Association, is a national professional association dedicated to the advancement of the theory and practice of rehabilitation counseling.

American Speech and Hearing Association
9030 Old Georgetown Road
Washington, DC 20014
(301) 530-3400

The purposes of the American Speech and Hearing Association are to encourage basic scientific study of the processes of individual human communication with special reference to speech, hearing, and language; to promote investigation of disorders of human communication, and to foster improvement of clinical procedures with such disorders; to stimulate the exchange of information among persons and organizations so engaged; and to disseminate such information.

The Arthritis Foundation
3400 Peachtree Road, N.E.
Suite 1101
Atlanta, GA 30326
(404) 266-0795

The Arthritis Foundation is a voluntary health agency seeking the total answer—cause, prevention, cure—to the nation's foremost crippling disease.

Bureau of Education for the Handicapped
U.S. Department of Education
400 Maryland Avenue, S.W.
Washington, DC 20202
(202) 245-9416

The Bureau of Education for the Handicapped was established in 1967 for the purpose of coordinating and administering all Office of Education programs for the handicapped.

Council of Organizations Serving the Deaf (COSD)
P.O. Box 894
Columbia, MD 21044

The COSD is a central clearinghouse and contact point for information and combined action by member organizations. Since 1967, the COSD has worked to eliminate social and economic barriers that handicap deaf persons.

Council of State Administrators of Vocational Rehabilitation
1522 K Street, N.W.
Suite 836
Washington, DC 20005
(202) 659-9383

The Council of State Administrators of Vocational Rehabilitation is composed of the chief administrators of the public vocational rehabilitation agencies for physically and mentally handicapped persons in the states, the District of Columbia, and the four territories. These agencies constitute the state partners in the state-federal program of vocational rehabilitation services provided under the Rehabilitation Act of 1973. The organization provides a forum to enable administrators of state vocational rehabilitation agencies to study and discuss matters relating to vocational rehabilitation and its administration.

Disabled American Veterans (DAV)
3725 Alexandria Pike
Cold Spring, KY 41076
(606) 441-7300

The DAV's paramount objectives are to promote the welfare of disabled veterans injured while in the armed services, as well as that of their dependents; and to provide a service program to assist such disabled veterans and their dependents in their claims before the Veterans Administration and other government agencies.

Epilepsy Foundation of America
815 15th Street, N.W.
Suite 528
Washington, DC 20005
(202) 638-5229

Founded in 1967 after a series of mergers, the Epilepsy Foundation of America is a national voluntary health agency leading the fight against epilepsy in the United States.

Goodwill Industries of America
9200 Wisconsin Avenue
Washington, DC 20014
(301) 530-6500

Founded in 1902, Goodwill Industries of America and its member local Goodwill Industries provide vocational rehabilitation services, training, employment, and opportunities for personal growth as an interim step in the rehabilitation process for the handicapped, disabled, and disadvantaged.

International Association of Rehabilitation Facilities, Inc.
5530 Wisconsin Avenue, No. 955
Washington, DC 20015
(301) 654-5882

In 1969, the Association of Rehabilitation Centers and the National Association of Sheltered Workshops and Homebound Programs merged to form the International Association of Rehabilitation Facilities, Inc., with the purpose of assisting in the development and improvement of services of member facilities in providing services to the handicapped.

Muscular Dystrophy Associations of America, Inc.
810 Seventh Avenue
New York, NY 10019
(212) 586-0808

Muscular Dystrophy Associations of America, Inc., a nonsectarian voluntary health organization, was founded and incorporated in 1950 to foster research seeking cures or effective treatments for muscular dystrophy and related neuromuscular diseases.

National Association of the Deaf
814 Thayer Avenue
Silver Spring, MD 20910
(301) 587-1788

The National Association of the Deaf is a private organization founded in 1880 for the purpose of promoting the social, educational, and economic well-being of the deaf citizens of the United States.

The National Association for Mental Health, Inc.
1800 Kent Street
Roslyn, VA 22209
(703) 528-6405

The National Association for Mental Health is a private organization with 1,000 local affiliate chapters whose aims are to improve attitudes toward mental illness and the mentally ill; to improve services for the mentally ill; to work for the prevention of mental illness; and to promote mental health.

National Association of the Physically Handicapped, Inc.
5473 Grandville Avenue
Detroit, MI 48228
(313) 271-0160

The National Association of the Physically Handicapped seeks to promote the economic, physical, and social welfare of all physically handicapped persons.

National Association for Retarded Citizens
2709 Avenue E East
P.O. Box 6109
Arlington, TX 76011
(817) 261-4961

The National Association for Retarded Citizens is a membership organization whose purposes are to further the advancement of all ameliorative and preventive study, research, and therapy in the field of mental retardation; to develop a better understanding of the problems of mental retardation by the public; to further the training and education of personnel for work in the field; and to promote the general welfare of the mentally retarded of all ages.

National Congress of Organizations of the Physically Handicapped, Inc.
6106 N. 30th Street
Arlington, VA 22207

The National Congress of Organizations of the Physically Handicapped is a national coalition of the physically handicapped and their organizations. The organization serves as an advisory, coordinating, and representative body in promoting employment opportunities, legislation, equal rights, social activity, and rehabilitation.

National Easter Seal Society for Crippled Children and Adults
2023 W. Ogden Avenue
Chicago, IL 60612
(312) 243-8400

The National Easter Seal Society conducts a three-point program in service, education, and research at the national, state, and local levels; programs serve all types of physically handicapped children and adults.

National Federation of the Blind (NFB)
1346 Connecticut Avenue, N.W.
Suite 212
Washington, DC 20036
(202) 785-2974

The purpose of the NFB is the complete integration of blind people into society as equal members. This objective involves the removal of legal, economic, and social discrimination and the education of the public to new concepts concerning blindness.

The National Foundation/March of Dimes
1275 Mamaroneck Avenue
White Plains, NY 10605
(914) 428-7100

The National Foundation/March of Dimes (founded in 1938) has as its goal the prevention of birth defects.

National Multiple Sclerosis Society
205 E. 42nd Street
New York, NY 10010
(212) 532-3060

The National Multiple Sclerosis Society was founded in 1946. Its major objectives are to support research, to conduct lay and professional education programs concerning the disease, to administer patient services, and to carry out worldwide programs of information and idea exchange regarding multiple sclerosis.

National Head Injury Foundation
18A Vernon Street
Framingham, MA 01701
(617) 879-7473

The National Head Injury Foundation responds to the comprehensive and complex needs of head-injured persons and their families. The foundation emphasizes support, research, education, and program development. The national headquarters also serves as a clearinghouse for information related to national issues and local state chapters.

National Paraplegia Foundation
333 N. Michigan Avenue
Chicago, IL 60601
(312) 346-4779

The National Paraplegia Foundation was founded in 1948 with the objectives of (1) improved and expanded rehabilitation and treatment of those suffering spinal cord injuries; (2) expanded research on a cure for paraplegia and quadriplegia; (3) removal of architectural barriers to the handicapped; (4) increased employment opportunities for the handicapped; (5) accessible housing and transportation.

National Rehabilitation Association
633 South Washington Street
Alexandria, VA 22314
(703) 836-0850

The National Rehabilitation Association is an organization of professional and lay persons dedicated to the rehabilitation of all physically and mentally handicapped persons.

National Rehabilitation Counseling Association
8136 Old Keene Mill Road
Springfield, VA 22152
(703) 451-7981

The National Rehabilitation Counseling Association is a private organization founded in 1958 with the objectives of (1) developing professional standards for rehabilitation counseling; (2) promoting professional training for rehabilitation counseling; (3) supporting rehabilitation counseling as it contributes to the interdisciplinary approach to the solution of problems.

National Spinal Cord Injury Association
369 Eliot Street
Newton Upper Falls, MA 02164
(617) 964-0521

Focusing on basic research and community services, this association also provides educational resources related to spinal cord injury.

Office for Handicapped Individuals
Department of Education
400 Maryland Avenue, S.W.
Room 3106, Switzer Building
Washington, DC 20202
(202) 245-0080

In 1974, through the authorization of the Rehabilitation Act of 1973, the Secretary of Health, Education and Welfare announced the formation of this office. Its primary focus is the review, coordination, reformation, and planning of policies, programs, procedures, and activities within all federal agencies relevant to the physically and mentally handicapped. The intended result is maximum effectiveness, sensitivity, and continuity in the provision of services for handicapped individuals by all programs.

Paralyzed Veterans of America
7315 Wisconsin Avenue
Suite 300W
Bethesda, MD 20014
(301) 652-2135

The principal aim of efforts by the Paralyzed Veterans of America is to improve programs of medicine and rehabilitation not only for veterans, but for all those with spinal cord injuries.

Partners of the Americas
Rehabilitation Education Program (PREP)
2001 S Street, N.W.
Washington, DC 20009
(202) 332-7332

The Partners of the Americas is currently the largest people-to-people program between the United States and Latin America, and is committed to fostering a closer relationship and understanding among our peoples.

PREP, the rehabilitation and special education program, has been one the largest areas of activity since 1966. The purpose of PREP is to increase opportunities and improve programs for persons with handicaps in the Americas.

The President's Committee on Employment of the Handicapped
111 20th Street, N.W.
Vanguard Building, Room 660
Washington, DC 20036
(202) 653-5044

The President's Committee on Employment of the Handicapped was established by the President of the United States in 1947. Since then, every President has given his personal and active support to full employment opportunities for the physically and mentally handicapped. The objective of the Committee is to help the handicapped help themselves.

Rehabilitation International USA (RIUSA)
20 W. 40th Street
New York, NY 10018
(212) 620-4040

RIUSA was founded in 1971 to offer international services to the U.S. rehabilitation community, as well as to draw upon the expertise of the U.S. rehabilitation community for the benefit of the handicapped worldwide. It is also the U.S. affiliate of Rehabilitation International, a network of national agencies and persons in more than 60 countries dedicated to helping all the disabled.

Rehabilitation Services Administration
Department of Education
330 C Street, S.W.
Washington, DC 20201
(202) 245-6726

The Office of Special Education and Rehabilitation administers programs of the U.S. Department of Education that deal with the handicapped and their dependent families and children. The Rehabilitation Services Administration is principally concerned with the rehabilitation of the handicapped.

United Cerebral Palsy Associations, Inc.
66 East 34th Street
New York, NY 10016
(212) 889-6655

United Cerebral Palsy Associations is a national voluntary health organization dedicated to a continuing overall attack on cerebral palsy. Its primary function is to seek solutions to the multiple problems of cerebral palsy, with affiliates providing direct services to the cerebral-palsied in states and communities.

The Veterans Administration
810 Vermont Avenue, N.W.
Washington, DC 20420
(202) 389-2044

The Veterans Administration, established in 1930, administers a broad range of programs providing medical care, rehabilitation, education and training, income support, and other benefits for eligible disabled veterans and their dependents.

World Rehabilitation Fund, Inc.
400 East 34th Street
New York, NY 10016
(212) 679-3200

The World Rehabilitation Fund has as its objective to assist governmental and voluntary agencies throughout the world in expanding and improving rehabilitation services for the physically handicapped.

APPENDIX D

Significant Films Related to the Psychological and Social Impact of Physical Disability

The following films are useful in developing a more complete understanding of the psychological and social impact of physical disability. The films are presented in alphabetical order; a source for rental and further information is provided for each film. Unless noted, all films are in color and are 16 mm. The list is based in part on the Human Services Development Institute's *Disability Attitudes: A Film Index* (Portland: University of Southern Maine, 1978), and on 1982 and 1983 issues of the *Rehabilitation Film Newsletter* (a Division of Rehabilitation International, 1123 Broadway, Suite 704, New York, New York 10010).

A Different Approach. 21 mins., 1978. Demonstrates a humorous and effective approach to overcome attitudinal problems and assist in the employment of handicapped persons. Features well-known Hollywood stars.

>   Distributed by Modern Talking Pictures, 4705-F Bakers Ferry Road, Atlanta, Georgia 30336.

Am I Being Unrealistic? 24 mins., 1975. Describes the frustrations and fears of a young man disabled with cerebral palsy, as he carries out his university work and seeks employment.

>   International Rehabilitation Film Library, 1123 Broadway, Suite 704, New York, New York 10001.

Attitudes toward Disabled: "On Location." 3 hours. A discussion of life in a wheelchair by a group of physically handicapped persons provides new insights as to attitudes toward disabled persons.

>   University of Wisconsin, Media Resource Center, Milwaukee, Wisconsin 53226.

Being. 20 mins., 1973. Portrays the everyday difficulties faced by a young man who walks with the aid of braces and crutches because of paralysis. Difficulties with relationships and independent living are discussed.

Kent State University, Audio-Visual Services, Kent, Ohio 44242.

Blindness. 28 mins., black and white. Probes a young man's reaction to sudden blindness and describes his efforts to lead an ordinary life in his home, family, and job.

Kent State University, Audio-Visual Services, Kent, Ohio 44242.

Challenge of Blindness. 25 mins., Focuses on four blind persons going through daily life routines and discusses ways to approach a blind person, attitudes of the public, and helping blind persons manage their environment.

The Seeing Eye, Inc., Morristown, New Jersey, 07081.

Choices in Sexuality with Physical Disability. 56 mins., 1982. This film is a welcome addition to the growing number of audiovisuals being produced that address issues of sexuality and disability. It is a particularly useful tool, in that the two-part format (with the first part being nonexplicit and the second explicit) can be shown to a broad cross-section of individuals who are at varying places on the continuum of exposure and understanding of the sensitive issues under discussion.

Produced by New York University Medical Center, Institute of Rehabilitation Medicine. Distributed by Mercury Productions, 17 W. 45th Street, New York, New York 10036.

Continuation of Life. 45 mins. Presents issues related to the psychosocial adjustment to spinal cord injury. Several spinal-cord-injured persons discuss their problems, goals, and feelings.

Sister Kenny Institute, Publications/Audiovisuals, Chicago Avenue at 27th Street, Minneapolis, Minnesota 55407.

Day in the Life of Bonnie Consolo. 16½ mins., 1975. A young housewife, born without arms, goes about her daily activities. She demonstrates and discusses her means of coping with the environment, including the reactions of others.

Barr Films, P.O. Box 5667, Pasadena, California 91107.

Dystonia. 30 mins., 1982. Narrated by Gregory Peck, this is a brief but comprehensive overview of a relatively unknown neurological disease called dystonia. The Grand Prize winner at the International Rehabilitation Film Festival, this film produced by UCLA is very moving without being maudlin. Facts are straightforward and clear.

Produced by Barnett Addis, Ph.D., and distributed by the Behavioral Sciences Media Laboratory, University of California at Los Angeles, 760 Westwood Plaza, Los Angeles, California 90024.

Face Value. 30 mins. A stirring documentary about three facially disfigured individuals and how they cope in a world that honors beauty over almost everything else.

Perennial Education, Inc., 477 Roger Williams, Highland Park, Illinois 60035.

First Encounters. 24 mins. Focuses on the interaction strain between able-bodied and disabled persons from two perspectives: a discussion between able-bodied and disabled persons, and an encounter between a factory manager and a disabled efficiency consultant.

Disability Information Center, University of Southern Maine, 246 Deering Avenue, Portland, Maine 04102.

Fitting In. 27 mins., 1976. Three persons, each with different disabilities, illustrate how handicaps can be surmounted.

University of Wisconsin Extension, Bureau of Audio-Visual Instruction, 1327 University Avenue, Madison, Wisconsin 53706.

Get It Together. 20 mins., 1977. Presents the story of an athletic young man, prior to and following an automobile accident that resulted in paraplegia. Depicts his successful adjustment to disability.

Pyramid Films, Box 1048, Santa Monica, California 90406.

Het Dorp. 26 mins., 1972. Documentary from "World in Action" TV series on the famous village for the handicapped in Arnheim, Holland. Film covers apartments, gadgets, and social and employment facilities that help residents lead productive lives, but the emphasis is on the psychological impact of the residence on those who live there.

International Rehabilitation Film Review Library, 1123 Broadway, Suite 704, New York, New York 10010.

I Am Not What You See. 28 mins., 1975. A frank interview with Sondra Diamond, a psychologist disabled by cerebral palsy; the discussion focuses on her childhood, incidents of prejudice, and her fight for social and professional acceptance.

International Rehabilitation Film Review Library, 1123 Broadway, Suite 704, New York, New York 10010.

I Had a Stroke. 28 mins. Focuses upon the emotional factors of a 36-year-old professional woman's recovery from stroke, including the stress placed on her marriage.

> Filmakers Library, Inc., 133 East 58th Street, New York, New York 10022.

I'm the Same as Everyone Else. 26 mins., 1976. Designed to educate people on the emotional and intellectual level about the impact of epilepsy, this film attempts to supplant ignorance with facts.

> International Rehabilitation Film Library, 1123 Broadway, Suite 704, New York, New York 10010.

Life Another Way. 52 mins., 1982. This film centers around Beryl Potter, a courageous triple amputee who runs a club for disabled people. It shows many aspects of the process of integrating disabled people, many of who were previously completely isolated.

> Hamilton Brown Film Productions, 43 Britain Street, Toronto M5A 1R7 Canada.

Like Other People. 37 mins., 1973. Focuses on the relationship between a couple with cerebral palsy. Attention is given to several issues important to them — their rights to marry, to work, and to live unencumbered by prejudice.

> Perennial Education, Inc., 1825 Willow Road, P.O. Box 236, Northfield, Illinois 60093.

Nicky: One of My Best Friends. 15 mins., 1975. Describes the typical school day for a 10-year-old boy who is blind and cerebral-palsied. Presents the successful mainstreaming of Nicky into the regular classroom.

> Togg Films, Inc., 630 Ninth Avenue, Room 900, New York, New York 10036.

No More Special Me. 53 mins., 1981. This exciting, award-winning film made in Australia features the internationally acclaimed American puppet troupe, "The Kids on the Block." Meet the puppets who have been applauded and enjoyed around the world as they increase awareness and appreciation of disabled people. Parents, children, professionals, and the general community will share the wonderful experience of friendship between disabled and non-disabled people.

> The Kids on the Block, Inc., 822 N. Fairfax Street, Alexandria, Virginia 22314.

Open Boating. 30 mins., 1982. This film constitutes a report of a recreational boating program designed for physically handicapped persons. This adapted boating program, held in Oakland, California, is covered in its entirety by the film. Beginning with water familiarity activities, individuals with a wide range of physical disabilities are shown progressing through various states in their acquisition of boating skills. Boating activities include sailing, rowing, and canoeing. The film not only covers the problems of entering and leaving boats, but—most importantly—shows how these problems are solved.

City of Oakland, Office of Parks and Recreation, 1520 Lakeside Drive, Oakland, California 94612.

People You'd Like to Know. 10 short films. Captures moments in the lives of 10 handicapped children aged 11 to 14. Focuses on the similarities among all children.

Encyclopedia Britannica Educational Corp., 425 North Michigan Avenue, Chicago, Illinois 60611.

Pins and Needles. 37 mins. Explores major issues—self-esteem, sexuality, dependency, denial, access—when multiple sclerosis strikes a young married woman.

Filmakers Library, Inc., 133 East 58th Street, New York, New York 10022.

Some Other Time. 27 mins., 1974. Describes the adjustment process of a young man from the time he discovered that he has multiple sclerosis.

International Rehabilitation Film Library, 1123 Broadway, Suite 704, New York, New York 10010.

Synthesis. 28 mins., 1977. Depicts disabled and able-bodied people in a variety of everyday situations. Emphasizes the importance of integration of disabled persons in our society.

Barrier Free Environment, Inc., P.O. Box 53446, Fayetteville, North Carolina 28305.

The Boy Who Turned Off. 28 mins., 1982. Deals with the plight of the adult with autism and of that person's family. The virtual abandonment of the disabled adult is just as true in this country as in Canada, where the film was made. This film fills a need and does it well.

Carousel Film and Video, 241 E. 34th Street, New York, New York 10016.

To Climb a Mountain. 15 mins., 1975. Follows a young visually handicapped couple as they join sighted friends to climb a mountain.

University of California, Extension Media Center, Berkeley, California 94720.

Touching. 17 mins. Describes the sexual activities between a quadriplegic male and his wife.

Multi Media Resource Center, 340 Jones Street #439F, San Francisco, California 94102.

What Do You Do When You See a Blind Person? 13 mins., 1971. Depicts, in a humorous manner, the interaction between a sighted and a blind person. Presents appropriate ways in which sighted people can deal with and help blind people.

American Foundation for the Blind, 15 West 16th Street, New York, New York 10011.

Index

Index